DEALER TO HEALER

*A Modern tale of a F*cked up Male*

LIAM BROWNE

Magical Vibrations
Full Power Blessings

Liam Browne
xx

Some names have been changed to protect the privacy of family and friends.

Copyright © Liam Browne 2019
All rights reserved
This book or any portion thereof may not be reproduced or used in any manner whatsoever without the express written permission of the author except for the use of brief quotations in line with copyright law.

Cover Art by Matt Crump
Photography by Lucy Reynolds
Cover Design by Paulo Kevin Duelli
Edited by Johanna Craven
Proofread & Formatted by Evelyn Kristen Hills

Atlantis Rising- The Struggle of Darkness & Light by Patricia Cori, published by North Atlantic Books, © 2008 by Patricia Jo Cori. Reprinted by permission of North Atlantic books.

A Memoir
by
Liam Browne
2019

www.liambrowne.com

Table of Contents

Chapter 1 A Stone's Throw, Life, 1987 1
Belize, The Journey, November 2012 3
Chapter 2 Early Days, Life, 1987 16
Alone At Last, The Journey, November 2012 22
Chapter 3 A Stone's Throw 2, Life, 1987 31
Guatemala, The Journey, November 2012... 33
Chapter 4 Sex Times, Life, 1989-2001 52
Tikal, The Journey, December 2012 58
Chapter 5 Sex Times 2, Life, 2001-2007 68
Copan, The Journey, December 2012... 75
Chapter 6 Sex Times 3, Life, 2007-2010 83
12.12.12, The Journey, December 2012 92
Chapter 7 Where Will I Rest My Head? Life, 2011................................ 97
Back To Reality (Of Sorts), The Journey, December 2012................... 99
Chapter 8 Where Will I Rest My Head? 2 Life, 2011 106
21.12.12, The Journey, December 2012 109
Chapter 9 Where Will I Rest My Head? 3 Life, March 2011............. 114
I Joined A Cult, The Journey, December 2012 122
Chapter 10 Where Will I Rest My Head? 4 Life, November 2011... 130
Goodbye, The Journey, December/January 2012-2013 132
Chapter 11 Sex Times 4, Life, 2011 144
Ananda, The Journey, January 2013... 151
Chapter 12 Sex Times 5, Life, May 2012 159
Long Way Home, The Journey, January 2013 165
Chapter 13 Dealer With It, Life, 2008 181
Ananda's 2, The Journey, February 2013 186
Chapter 14 Dealer With It 2, Life, 2008 196
Rainbow, The Journey, February 2013... 202
Chapter 15 Rock Bottom, Life, 2011 214
Mexico City, The Journey, February 2013 218
Chapter 16 Rock Bottom 2, Life, 2011... 228
Taos, The Journey, March 2013 233
Chapter 17 Rock Bottom 3, Life, 2011 248
Arizona, The Journey, May 2013... 261
Chapter 18 Mum, Life 2007 271

Lima, Peru, The Journey, May 2013 278
Chapter 19 Mum 2, Life, 2007 283
Machu Picchu, The Journey, May 2013 292
Chapter 20 Mum 3, Life, 2007 304
Iquitos, The Journey, May 2013 314
Chapter 21 India At Last, Life, November 2011 321
Ayahuasca, The Journey, May 2013 326
Chapter 22 India At Last 2, Life, November 2011 341
Ayahuasca 2, The Journey, May 2013 359
Chapter 23 Awakening, Life, December 2011 382
Ayahuasca 3, The Journey, May 2013 403
Epilogue 424
Acknowledgements And Gratitude 435
Claim Your Free Book! 437

CLAIM YOUR FREE BOOK!

As a massive thank you for buying me book I would like to give you a little present. This is only for you, the people who have bought the book and supported it. It's your exclusive free gift. Whoop!!

If you were wondering what happened to me when I got back to the UK this will give you a peek into the weeks after we left my journey. I wanted to try out hitchhiking after enjoying its so much on me travels. See how I try and bring this dying art back to life.

Join me on a hitchhiking tour of England and Scotland. See how it all works out when I put myself totally at the mercy of the Universe and put my faith in the kindness of humanity to whisk in me around. You will meet some more than colourful characters along the way and be able to implement my self-designed hitchhiking techniques into your own life.

Thumbs out, I'm looking!

You can download 'Hitchhiking- Feel the good Vibrations' by clicking on the link in the eBook or sending me and email at liam@liambrowne.com.

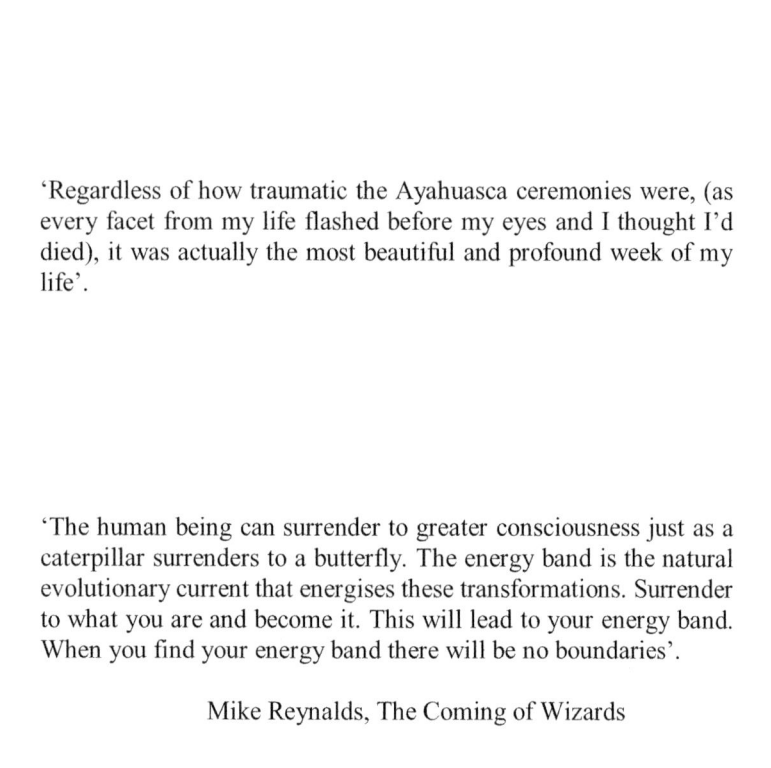

'Regardless of how traumatic the Ayahuasca ceremonies were, (as every facet from my life flashed before my eyes and I thought I'd died), it was actually the most beautiful and profound week of my life'.

'The human being can surrender to greater consciousness just as a caterpillar surrenders to a butterfly. The energy band is the natural evolutionary current that energises these transformations. Surrender to what you are and become it. This will lead to your energy band. When you find your energy band there will be no boundaries'.

Mike Reynalds, The Coming of Wizards

Always for you, Mum

PREFACE

You could say I was forced to write this book.

Compelled by forces, I had no idea existed until I spiralled into submission. The story follows my journey from being a football-mad, lager-drinking, drug-taking, drug-dealing atheist in 2011 to, twelve months later, being in Guatemala for the end of the Mayan calendar.

I was completely rebirthed as a spiritualist, energy healer, and yoga-practising hippy.

This book documents my battles with depression and coming to terms with my mother's death. Added to this is the domestic abuse I witnessed as a child and later in life becoming a drug dealer. Then there was my constant tunnel vision, disrespect and dishonesty when it came to women and sex.

I was going through a massive change. I was constantly having my mind blown by this new mystical world; I was becoming aware of, where the fabric of everything I had ever believed in was being questioned. The book interweaves my spiritual travels in the Americas for the end of the Mayan calendar, and pivotal life events which I hadn't dealt with that had driven me to suicidal depression.

For some reason, I was compelled to start writing a travel journal, which led to an overwhelming passion for writing. Everyone I met and told stories to about my adventures told me I had to write a book, so I did.

The result is a gritty, true and honest account of a lost young man battling with the stresses of modern life and expectation.

There were many obstacles I had to overcome to find inner peace. I had to get over what society and friends expected of me in order to find the stillness that would allow the inner voice within to guide me to become the greatest version of myself.

Through this book, I hope to encourage people to have the inner willpower and strength to change the fabric of who they are. I want the book to help people to be brave and fearless enough to break free from the role society has given them and step into their own power.

My story shows it is possible to step away from the lives we have created and completely reinvent ourselves. I hope it gives people the strength to be able to deal with the ridicule that often comes from friends and family for wanting something different.

Change is possible. You just have to be big enough and bold enough to listen to your inner guide, be at the forefront of human evolution and step into a life that best serves you and those around you.

INTRODUCTION

Imagine waking every morning for five years and feeling like you wanted to kill yourself. Can you imagine how uncomfortable and toxic it would feel to exist inside that body? You'd become aware you were living in a body you thought was the real you. But if this is the case, then what is this entity that has the desire to leave that body?

I'd never identified the body and this entity as separate before. I felt like I was going insane, and this realisation of separateness only intensified the feeling. My toxic thoughts made my body want to escape my mind, and my mind wanted to escape my toxic body. There seemed only one solution to this conundrum.

I battled with the when, where and how. I thought drugs would be the best option, taking a large overdose of something. I didn't want to jump in front of a train or a car and ruin peoples commute and make disruption, and I didn't want to make a mess of it and end up a cabbage.

I gave myself a deadline. I said to my body and my mind, 'I'm gonna give you three years to sort this out and try everything to get better. If you both still feel like this after that, we can commit suicide together.'

With my mind trapped inside my body, I started to become aware of what I thought could be my soul. This also seemed to be trapped in my body and affected by my mind. I knew there would have to be a compromise to keep all parties happy. I was determined to bring some kind of union to my mind, body and soul. I made a commitment to try and eliminate the toxicity that surrounded what I thought was me as a whole; mind, body and soul. I wanted my mind to be quiet and to stop making me feel sick. I wanted to scratch off all my itchy and sore skin. Most of all, I wanted the something that was trying to escape from my body and mind (which I felt could be my soul) to stop tearing me apart.

If I couldn't, then I was out of here.

The decision had been made. I would put my all into getting better and hopefully sane and seeing where it took me. By the end of three years, I'd have either happiness or death. If that meant becoming a monk I'd do it; if it meant getting a sex change, I'd do it. I needed a path and direction. I needed something to live for. If I couldn't harmonise the living conditions of my mind, body and soul I would try death. I wasn't going to fanny about. If I really wanted to die, I had to prove it to myself, and I had three years to do it.

Here we go...

CHAPTER 1
A STONE'S THROW,
LIFE, 1987

I am standing in the middle of a big, dark, empty, entrance room that we had never got around to decorating. I'm crying hysterically. I am holding a rock in my right hand, and I want to throw it at my dad, but I'm finding it difficult to do so. After all, I'm only four. To throw a rock at the man I hold on such a high pedestal seems an arduous task.

The two people in the world I love more than anyone else, are to my left and my right. I'm stuck in the middle of the ever-presents of my life so far. My love for them is unconditional.

I'm trying my hardest to throw this stone at my dad, screaming 'Stop, Daddy' at the top of my voice, through spluttered sobs. Tears and gloopy snot are spread all over my face, dripping onto my jumper beneath my unbuttoned coat.

My mummy sits slumped on the floor to my right, also crying hysterically. Her legs are stretched out in front of her, her back is against the wall, and her head is slumped forward. I can tell all she wants is to let her head fall fully, but she can't let herself. She has to be alert. Has to keep her concentration sharp. She is unable to take her eyes off my daddy.

He stands to my left just inside the open front door. For what seems like an eternity, he stands there casting a huge menacing shadow into the room.

My father seems like something from a nightmare, yet somehow he is still my hero.

The front door shuts, and the little light that had filtered in from outside disappears.

The menacing shadow vanishes, but at the same time, so does our connection to the outside world and any chance of an escape from this building we once called home.

A desperate sob trembles out of her when the last shred of outside light disappears.

She now knows there is now little chance of her being saved by a passing neighbour or someone who may alert the police.

Continually she says, 'That's enough Bernie! Please Bernie, no!

I'm sorry, I'm sorry!'

Panicky, repetitive blasts of 'Please, God, no! Please, God, no!', burst from her lips.

I'm trembling, holding my rock, shouting 'Stop it, Daddy', shouting 'it's okay, Mummy, he won't do it again', then asking Mummy if she's okay, as her hysterical sobbing continues.

I feel like I have to act, but, confused with emotion, I can't bring myself to throw the rock at my daddy. I'm stood to the side of what now feels like a Mexican stand-off in which my two true loves crossfire. I am slightly tilted to my left, subconsciously guarding my mother.

Daddy doesn't even acknowledge me. It's like he's possessed. He's looking directly at my mummy with this menacing stare I have never seen before (or maybe I have, but my mind has deleted such files as they now lie buried deep in the place that allows children to move forward, forgetting the atrocities that have gone before them).

My mother seems stuck in a place of wanting to comfort me but also needing to protect herself. Looking from parent to parent, I become confused at who I should be throwing this rock at. I want to throw it at them both. I want them both to stop. I pull back my arm, ready to release the rock. It seems to take an eternity. It's like I'm in a dream-like state, unable to throw, as this invisible force takes hold of my limbs and slows everything down.

BELIZE, THE JOURNEY, NOVEMBER 2012

We arrived at Belize City airport after a long journey. We got through passport control to be greeted by a local band called Belizean Beats who were playing Caribbean-style Jonny Cash.

Why didn't all airports employ local bands to give arrivals a feel of the local vibe? I wondered what England's honest portrayal would be. A punk band with urine being thrown about, orange makeup covered girls trying to walk in 8-inch heels, people vomiting all over the street and rudimentary fights between highly sexed drunken youths, whilst bankers pickpocketed them all? The whirlwind of thoughts raced through my mind. These particular thoughts I interacted with and didn't use my new-found meditation technique to move them on. I just let them sit and have a good time.

It had taken almost twenty-four hours to get here. The previous day I'd been to collect some Belizean money, which I didn't know had the Queen's head on. It was a younger, better-looking Queen than what I was used to seeing. Maybe it was easier to control the empire with this perception.

After collecting my money, I went to visit the crystal skull at the British Museum. It had been found in Belize at the Mayan ruins of Lubaantun that I would be visiting. I thought it deserved my attention considering I didn't think I would ever be coming back to England.

The skull was tucked away in the corner of a huge room dedicated to Central and South American artefacts. It was radiantly glowing inside its glass case. Cast from clear quartz crystal and about the same size of a human head, it mesmerised me. I couldn't take my eyes off its beauty, how smooth, pure and other-worldly it looked.

I wanted to look at it deeply, and the only place I could do so was from a bench that was facing the side of the skull. It's said that if people look into the eyes of the skull for long enough, they can go into a trance, or even be cursed. Maybe the British Museum had thought about this when arranging their seating plan.

I looked at it and started to meditate.

I had been feeling so lost lately. My life seemed such a mess. I couldn't see anything positive in my past, present, or future. I was hoping this journey to Belize would give me a sense of purpose. I wanted a bright, happy future. I wanted to find inner peace and direction in my life. And I was looking for anything that would help me out of this inner turmoil.

So I felt inclined, even pushed by some cosmic force, to sit and listen for guidance from this mystical crystal skull.

I asked the skull to help me heal the wounds I had been carrying since losing the unconditional love of my mother. I imagined my mates from football taking the piss out of me and thinking I'd lost the plot.

I sensed people coming and going, chattering and taking pictures. I didn't care. I was trying to connect deeply with this skull, the quartz of which could power thousands of computers and watches. Surly that much power could give me some sort of a boost for my travels.

I felt tingles all over my body. I felt this searing heat and sweat began to drip from me. It was so intense. Finally, I pulled myself out, composed myself and headed off to meet my girlfriend, Fhian, who would be with me for the first two weeks of my Belizean adventure.

After I was done imagining what the greeting band would be like at a British airport, we walked outside. The tropical air was infused with coconut, salt and fried chicken.

It was a relief to be out of airports. Filling in stupid forms to describe the purpose of my visit, putting my 100ml liquids in a plastic jiffy bag to prevent them from blowing up and having to present a passport to confirm I belong to a specific piece of land had felt like torture.

Smile and nod, smile and nod, I had thought. Internally I was writhing, but part of my process was not to let that spill out of me anymore. I had even been told it would eventually disappear from my mind completely.

We'd left London for New York, where we'd had a six-hour wait for our next flight to Miami. After getting past a very angry immigration officer, we had six hours of blissful sleep on the luxuriously comfortable marble arrivals floor. We then bounced to Miami, and jumped on our final plane to Belize, praying for a bed soon.

We were hoping that bed would be in Caye Caulker, a paradise island Fhian had read about. As we drove through Belize City, we passed colourful and colourless wooden buildings, most of which looked as if they could fall down at any moment. Scantily clad Garifuna women sauntered across balconies, whilst kids and men swung in hammocks. People were everywhere, and there seemed a very chilled, disorganised pace to life. Most of the faces were Creole — black Caribbeans — but there was also a mishmash of different races; Mexican, Mayan and Spanish. All the cars looked on their last legs. Our taxi's windscreen had a big crack down the middle, but it seemed in good condition compared with the rest of the cars bouncing about the pot-hole-filled streets.

To get to Caye Caulker, you take a forty-five-minute water taxi from the dock. There we were offered weed for the first time, which took longer than I thought, considering we were in Rasta territory. I declined. That stuff sends me loopy, I remembered.

The water taxi cut through the most breath-taking turquoise ocean I'd ever seen. All you can see are palm trees packed with coconuts, mangroves, ramshackle huts on stilts and little jetties leading from the land to the sea.

We discovered the pace on Caye Caulker was ultra-slow; no fuel vehicles are allowed, so the only disruptions are push bikes and golf buggies. All the different races and cultures communicate with each other in Creole, the national language, which is basically broken English. I can't understand more than the odd word, but I love the rhythm and its lyrical delivery.

We were forever saying hello to people as we wandered about. One night I was having a good grope of Fhian's arse, and two ladies approached. One said with a massive ghetto chuckle, 'You can't leave her drum alone man, ha stop smacking her drum.' They just floated off laughing, and I looked back to flash them a cheeky grin.

All the signs on the island are hand-painted, so everyone's business has its own creative feel. One bar's reads:
'No shoes, no problem
No shirt, no problem
No money, big problem'
We spent our time on the island walking around
the streets, lazing in hammocks and soaking up the sun. Although I was enjoying it, I felt like I was in this part of the world for spiritual business and I wasn't finding it here. The local men got pretty drunk

in the evening. After a couple of days, I realised they were drunk in the morning too.

On our last day, we took a snorkelling trip out to the coral reef with a Mayan guy called Frodo. He had the widest smile and good-hearted eyes. He told us the reef operates as a barrier to the incoming waves and without it, Caye Caulker wouldn't exist.

Six hours before we were due to go snorkelling, a Canadian guy called Sean offered me a joint as I swung in my hammock. It seemed sacrilegious in the setting to not have a few puffs. He said it was really mellow stuff and all I had to do for the next six hours was chill in my hammock, so surely I'd be fine.

On the way to the water taxi the other day, I'd remembered not to take the stuff, but today I forgot. The next six hours consisted of me not being able to communicate, unable to read my book, feeling a bit sick, craving chocolate, wanting to cool off in the water, and wanting to have sex like a rabid dog. However, everything seemed like too much hard work. I needed everything I craved to be within hand's reach.

When we got to the snorkelling office, I was still spaced out, thinking everyone was staring at me and unable to remember where the office was. I was freaking out, I couldn't talk, and I needed snacks. Snacks didn't arrive, but the other snorkellers did. I just looked at my feet, feeling unable to communicate.

It reminded me I don't like smoking weed, something I always seemed to forget when it's presented to me in tranquil surroundings.

When we got in the water, Frodo started doing crazy dives, blowing water rings and dancing with the stingrays and sharks. I watched on in my stoned haze. My eyes were fixed on him, and the waters around us were empty. Then, underneath me, swam a shark twice the size of any of the others. I shit myself not literally but metaphorically. I made a bit of a girly sound, but I don't reckon anyone heard it as we were underwater.

Later that evening, we were on the west side of the island and bumped into a couple, called Mr and Mrs Brown, who were from Taos in New Mexico, the place that had been the catalyst for this whole adventure. I been into these off-grid sustainable buildings called 'Earthships' for a few years and always dreamed of building and living in one. I'd had a reading with this psychic who told me via a message from my dead grandma that I needed to get going and do something with my life. Straight after the reading, I went home and booked my place on the Earthship course. All my other travelling plans fell into place from that moment. I knew what my dead grandma was getting at, and I was heading to Taos to work with the Earthship crew in February 2012. It seemed like a bit of synchronicity meeting Mr and Mrs Brown and a spiritual slant I could get my teeth into. I was sure it was the universe bringing me a sign. However, Ron Brown turned out to be your typical larger-than-life American who talked and talked. Every time his wife chatted, he either leaned forward or back so we couldn't see her, and she couldn't really contribute to the conversation.

After a few days in Caye Caulker, we headed for the mainland, cruising on the top deck of a water taxi with a local man called Ellsworth. He told me a bit about how the British won Belize in the battle of St George, off the coast of the island we were passing. There were some sneaky pirates who had tried to surprise the British, by hiding behind the island. The British knew they were there and were prepared. The pirates realised and scarpered. He then told me about the engines on the boat and their capacity and horsepower. I just smile and nod.

Later I found out his brother was called Egbert, and all I could think about was having afternoon tea with Ellsworth and Egbert in the town they were from called Lady Ville. I would have painted my nails and wear a pretty dress, I thought.

The next step of the Belizean trip was to go to the Mayan ruins of Lubaantun where the crystal skulls I'd seen at the British Museum had been discovered. I'd been reading a lot about this place in 'The Mystery of the Crystal Skulls' by Ceri Louise Thomas and Chris Morton. It's one of thirteen skulls on earth apparently left here by extra-terrestrials. Our scientists can't figure out how they could have been made on earth, so this has become the widely accepted point of view of the alternative community.

Lubaantun was a six-hour bus ride from Belize City, so I went to grab some fruit and snacks for the trip. I stumbled across a school fair with reggae music blaring and realised I had ended upright in the middle of this dangerous city. The colours all around me were so vibrant and vivid and most of the mums' bums voluptuous. After surpassing the urge to slap one of the bottoms really hard and possibly get shot for the offence, I arrived back at the bus station.

Fhian had been getting to know an American lady called Rdhian (whose name I had to ask for four times before I could actually pronounce it, and as quickly forgot it again). Luckily Fhian had already introduced herself so we didn't get the customary confused look and giggle when saying our names together. Rdhian told us to get the chicken bus, which is the locals' no-frills option, and as we sat waiting, we got offered a drink called 'seaweed' by a Rasta bloke.

Rdhian bought some and said it was amazing. As I looked at it inquisitively, he said, "It's great for your balls man, fills dam up, and it makes the lady's head relax.'

Perfect, I thought. I wasn't sure if I was being offered a hybrid mix of Viagra and Rohypnol, but thought what the hell, when in Rome...

The guy told me he would go out to sea to get it, pick these little seaweed leaves, take them home, soak them in water until they go white, then boil them up with milk until he got a thick drinkable consistency. He then added peanut butter, chocolate or banana and it sort of looked like gloopy semen. I went for peanut butter.

Instantly, I was addicted. It was amazing. Fhian and I were both hooked, and from that day forth, we hunted out seaweed Viagra wherever we went.

Liam, Fhian and Rdhian with our mouths full of rhyming names and gloopy semen seaweed jumped onto the chicken bus. We discovered Rdhian was from New York but lived in the state countryside now in a sort of commune where indigenous African and indigenous Native American practices were kept alive. I was intrigued and somehow felt it tied in with my Earthship building here in Central America, which would start in January and be my first experience building sustainable houses.

A Belizean called Harry joined us on the bus and became a wealth of local knowledge. As the bus cut through the jungle, he pointed out plants and trees (the names of which desert me) and told us their uses as both medicine and food. We passed orange, banana and grapefruit plantations, and it seemed every plant had its purpose.

He pointed to one and said it was for toothache. He also pointed out the Mennonites, who are like the Amish in their attire. The men (who you mainly see) wear dark coloured denim overalls with a white or light blue shirt and a straw hat and the women, little bonnets with the whole family packed into horse-drawn carts plodding down the side of the road. It's interesting and surreal to see them in the mix of all the other bright, loud and vibrant cultures.

Like two movies from different times have been spliced together.

Harry told us of how he grew up in the bush and now worked on the roads as a motor grader operator, clearing jungle in this huge machine. I briefly contemplated the ecological devastation Harry was causing to this beautiful jungle. Then I think about all the ecological devastation that has been caused all over the west as millions of miles of roads have been laid, ripping apart the skin of our beautiful earth. I then went back to trying to be present and non-judgemental.

After deliberation with Harry, Rdhian and Fhian about where we should stay, I took none of their advice and decided to head for a small village in the jungle called San Pedro Colombia, which is a short walk from the Lubaantun ruins. I was eager to get my adventure started, and this seemed like the first piece in the puzzle. Rdhian pointed out that it would be pitch black when we arrived and asked if we had a reservation at a guest house.

'No,' I said, and she says:

'What do you think they will just have a room waiting for 'YOU' without making a reservation because of course, they'll have a room especially for little old you?'

I had never thought about that before, and her comments made me feel a bit self-important. I shook myself off and assured her we would be fine. Internally I was having doubts about my laissez-faire attitude towards acquiring accommodation. I reminisced on all the times my dad had taken me places without getting accommodation. I was always embarrassed and tense whilst he found somewhere, even though it always worked out. Was I becoming my father?

The next difficulty Rdhian pointed out was that we would need to get a ride from the junction of the aptly named town of Dump, and would have to hitchhike.

I said, 'no problem.'

Fhian looked dubious. It was not a recommended mode of transportation in the dark according to the guide books. However, Harry interjected and said we could jump in the back of his friend's truck.

We said our goodbyes to Rdhian and jumped off the bus and into the waiting truck. Fhian managed to get in the front, and I jumped into the back of the pickup with Harry and four local Mayans.

A drunk man kept telling me in broken English how his village was better than those we were proposing to visit. I smile and nod.

We jumped out of the truck, and Harry said 'wait here'. We waited outside what seemed to be a construction depot in the pitch black. We were in the middle of nowhere; all that surrounded us was thick jungle.

Harry returned twenty minutes later and drove us to San Pedro. He told us about his numerous women up and down the country, his four kids, ex-wife and the woman he was trying to get to leave her boyfriend. She wouldn't, so for her birthday in three days' he had bought her a piece of chewing gum which had been blessed by a bush doctor. After chewing it, she would apparently want Harry forever!

We drove into San Pedro. The town was unlit; no lights, no place to stay. It seemed like it was the Back-a-Bush guest house in the next town of San Miguel or nothing.

We drove around and couldn't find it.
I remained calm on the exterior so that Fhian remained calm in the car with this Rohypnol-flavoured-chewing-gum-wielding potential axe murder.

We saw a shop. I dived in, and the women pointed us in the right direction. Now we just needed to hope there was a room.

We arrived at these big locked gates as a pack of dogs started going mad, emerging from an uninhabited-looking house. Then a man arrived and said, 'it's the next drive.'

Phew! I jumped over a little wall and arrived at the correct gates as a thin white man approached.
I asked 'do you have a room'.

He said 'yes,' I say, 'amazing', whilst thinking 'in your face, Rdhian'.

After thanking Harry and dropping him some cash he left and our Back-a-Bush adventure began with Naud, a thin white almost ghost-like Dutchman.

He welcomed us into his jungle guesthouse and farm, saying 'the place isn't really ready for guests, but we'll make it work'.

I looked up to the sky and thanked the universe for providing us with what we needed. We sat in a thatched roofed open area, filled with hammocks, books, dogs and cats. We were then shown to our open plan room with spectacular huge wooden high ceilings with floor-to-ceiling windows that only showed the blackness of night. I couldn't wait to wake up to see where we were and how it looked being so deep in the jungle.

We woke to find we were surrounded by thick bush. The floor-to-ceiling windows made it feel like we were part of nature and the lush green jungle seemed to permeate the room. Palm trees spread as far as the eye could see, with their green and yellow booty of coconuts waiting to be devoured. The thick, moist aromatic air slowly breezed past my nostrils, and I felt like a jungle colonial aristocrat observing his surroundings, or a writer getting away from it all to unleash his creativity.

After the most amazing breakfast of fruit, honey, yoghurt, scrambled eggs and coffee, we set off for the Lubaantun ruins. We passed a variation of traditional thatched roof, and concrete tin-roofed houses in the village. Kids and dogs played everywhere, and we were continually mobbed by both as the brightest smiles beamed from the often-toothless children. We passed a river, which was full of women washing clothes and later found out that most of them actually have washing machines now but don't really use them, as the traditional river washing is more of a social chit chat and gossip that allows the kids to swim about and have fun.

I daydreamed about the beauty of simplicity as the heavens opened. A woman came running past, calling out something in Mayan as she raced towards her house. A child emerged and started taking in the washing shortly followed by his mother.

I heard my own mother's voice in my head. I longed to hear her shouting at me one more time. Longed to feel her loving, angry slaps on my back again. I imagined the dialogue my mother would use in this situation, and it seemed to fit the scene perfectly.

'Son, get the bloody washing in. I told you to bring it in if it started to rain. What are you doing sitting on your backside, oblivious to what's going on? I've had to run all the way from the river because I knew you would forget. I don't know why I bother asking, you're bloody bone idle. Now get in that house before you catch a cold.'

Universal unconditional motherly love and oh, how I miss it.

We sauntered down the driveway to the Lubaantun ruins, wet from the sudden shower but drying quickly. We came to two signs. One pointed to 'Lubaantun Ruins' and the other, to my astonishment, pointed into a driveway and said the word 'Earthship'.

I couldn't believe it; I turned to Fhian in awe and wonder. 'This is mental,' I said. 'I don't believe it!'

We walked down the driveway, and there it was, a two-storey Earthship being built to overlook the Lubaantun Ruins. A mix of the old Mayan method of living and construction that is only slightly understood and this new method of Earthship building and living that is only slightly understood.

I wondered whether the visionary Mayans, in their time, were seen as hippies and utopian idealists by the mainstream, just like the Earthship movement?

We walked into the grounds and were greeted by Richard, an ex-army, richly travelled English gent who welcomed us into his thirty-five acre property. It consisted of a few traditional Mayan buildings, a huge kitchen/dining room and a few un-excavated Mayan ruins. He was living in Lubaantun and told us of how Michael Reynolds, the Earthship founder, had been there to design and help start the construction of the Earthship with his team. All I could think was, 'is this really happening? Michael Reynolds has been here? Wow.'

The two parts to my trip seemed more intrinsically interwoven than ever. The synchronicity seemed like a massive confirmation that I was on the right path.

Richard took us for a tour around the Earthship construction and told us that his Mayan construction team thought it was mad that he was making a house out of garbage and tyres, as most of them aspire to live in a western-style house. The top floor of the Earthship had a spectacular view of the Lubaantun ruins and the surrounding jungle.

I needed air! Was this actually happening? I felt lost but found in some weird way.

Two hours later, we emerged back onto the Lubaantun road after our little detour, full of magical emotion and anticipation. Santiago greeted us at the information centre as the only guests at the ruins, and we went off alone to explore.

We had the place all to ourselves. The vast central plaza, the grassy ball courts and the towering temples surrounded us, and I marvelled at the fact this had once been a thriving city. I found a nice spot to meditate and fully take in my surroundings while connecting with the energy of the area. The only bad thing about meditating in a jungle climate while wearing shorts was that the mosquitos descended to feast. Luckily the heavens opened, and swimming pools started to fall from the sky. We ran for sanctuary with Santiago. Two Norwegian boys turned up, and we discussed whether the crystal skulls would ever be returned to the Mayans, to whom they rightfully belong.

When we got back to our guest house, the Norwegian boys were there as they couldn't ride their motorbikes back to where they were staying because of the rain. The next day, we took a trip together with a local called Miguel to Tiger Cave. It was a one-hour hike through dense jungle and over the San Miguel River then, a forty-five-minute pitch-black walk through the slippery Tiger Cave. All Miguel had to protect us from possible jaguar attacks was his trusty machete.

He took us as far as we could go before we reached potential jaguar territory, then we turned off our lights, stood and listened to the faint breathing of the majestic animals. Between me and Fhian, we had one ladybird light, which gave off as much light as a car key. Luckily the Norwegian boys had phone apps that even put Miguel's industrial-strength torch to shame.

That evening we were invited to eat a typical Mayan meal with Miguel's family. The women made fresh tortillas to accompany the Gibnut, (AKA the royal rat as the queen ate it on her visit a few years back) and the Kahoon stew. Dogs, cats and piglets litter the room. I'm asked to name a dog and go for Derek (Fhian's dad's name), but I'm told there are already two Dereks in the village, which astonishes us both. I felt Barry was the only other option and loved the thought of a Mayan shouting 'Barry!' through the village. Although with there being two Dereks in the village already, it didn't make it as funny as it might otherwise have been.

We spent the next few days racing around on the back of the Norwegians' motorbikes, seeing waterfalls, fancy lodges, meeting Harry on his motor grader, getting tanned, getting piss wet through, struggling to stay upright on the unearthed clay roads and having a great time.

As we passed the road workers, I saw the devastation that was being caused to the environment just for economic growth. The jungle was being decimated, the habitats of so many animals being fragmented. It was like someone putting death lasers through your house, making it almost impossible to get to the other side. What if sometimes the only food you had was on the other side and you had to cross the gauntlet of death simply to feed your family? That's what was happening to millions of animals all over the world, and I saw it first-hand.

It was Garifuna day soon, so we left Naud and Back-a-bush. Harry picked us up and drove us an hour south to Punta Gorda where the celebrations had begun with traditional drumming and parades. It wasn't the Rio Carnival. About sixty kids followed a truck playing local punta rock as it passed the capacity crowd of three, me, Fhian and Harry.

One girl pointed at me and said 'Jesus!' Then they all pointed and started shouting 'Jesus, it's Jesus!'

We became the carnival. I gave a Jesus-like prayer bow, Fhian waved like the queen, and Harry kissed his teeth, left us and said goodbye for the night.

We bumped into Harry again, and he asked me for some money for the ride, and I said I hadn't got any on me, which was a bit of a lie. We had bought Harry dinner and lots of beers and thought that was enough to cover the trip.

We weren't digging Punta Gorda, so we took a two-hour bus to Hopkins and then another bus down a dirt track for twenty minutes to the coast.

As we were getting on the bus, Harry pulled up in his car. Dread filled me as I knew he would want more money. Fhian and I had discussed not wanting to be around him anymore as we no longer liked his aggressive vibe.

Why couldn't we get away from this man? We were two hours away from where we had seen him last. Was he following us?

He shouted he would meet us in Hopkins. I decided to ask the universe and God for some help. On the crowded bus, I stood crammed between two very large mothers and started to meditated, calling in my angels for help. I asked for Harry to go away, for him to not meet us when we got off the bus, for me and Fhian never to see him again. I said this over and over, so there was no possibility of my intention being misunderstood. I focused hard on what I wanted and went into a trance before Fhian pulled my arm to drag me off the bus.

As we headed for the recommended Funky Do Do Guest House, I was agitatedly looking over my shoulder hoping to get into our accommodation before Harry could latch onto us again. I hoped the Universe had accepted my request.

The Funky Do Do had characters from all over the world

sprawled over various pieces of furniture and hammocks recovering from the previous evening's events. We soon discovered it was a place where people party hard. I wasn't there for that, and I wanted a nice relaxing time with Fhian for our last couple of days in Belize. I was on this purity pledge before I headed for my pilgrimage in Guatemala and wanted my body as pure as it could possibly be. Since I'd become spiritual and stopped drinking, I was very scared of becoming boring, but I was willing to do anything to find happiness. If that meant never drinking and or doing drugs again, I was prepared to do it. Five years ago, I would have filled my boots and sunk all the beers and banged as many drugs down my neck as I could, but I was here for something different. I was here to deepen my spiritual connection and learn more about myself. For four days straight the Funky Do Do crew hit it hard and without my trusty earplugs sleep would have been unmanageable.

We got invited to a party at a German DJs flash beach house that was kitted out with an amazing sound system. I had no fear that I would be tempted to drink and do drugs. Aude was the proprietor, an ex-Space (Ibiza) DJ and we were joined by the entire guest list of the Funky Do Do and two loveable lady Rottweilers to stroke to your heart's content. Spectacular lasers glittered the garden, all under the most incredible starlit sky. Lying down with Fhian looking at all the constellations had to be my highlight of Belize so far.

Just being in her space and sharing something beautiful was all I needed to get high. As those around us danced wildly, their bloodstreams flooded with amphetamines, I found ultimate contentedness looking at the stars with my girl.

CHAPTER 2
EARLY DAYS,
LIFE, 1987

The first house I lived in was number 84 Stamford Road in Longsight, Manchester. It was a semi-detached house with a driveway, a small front garden and a large typical English back garden of the 1980s. Vegetables grew at the bottom end with rhubarb sticking up through dark, sodden soil. Grass covered the majority of the space and the borders were filled with flowers and fruit bushes. I remember my granddad coming round for Sunday lunch most weekends and him and my Dad falling asleep on the couch not long after we'd finished eating.

Memories of happiness and laughter seem to stick with me from these times. My mum had a friend down the road called Caroline, and I used to play with her two children, Vicky and Chris. Chris was autistic, and I used to think he was special. I remember birthday parties of pass the parcel and jelly and ice cream at their house.

At one party, I became fascinated by babies being breastfeed. I wanted to have some milk. I must have been two. I remember pestering my mum who said, 'there's no milk left in there.' I wasn't having it as they seemed full to me. After days of persistence, I was allowed to have a go and, finding my mother's words to be true, I quickly asked for some juice.

Next door to us was an elderly lady called Aunty Hilder, who I remember dying whilst we lived there. I was told she was 'in Heaven now' which I willingly accepted. My Mother and I looked at the sky, and she pointed out which star Aunty Hilder was living on now.

Living here also brought my first experience of school. I remember crying my eyes out when my mum left me at nursery. All I remember was coming home one day and asking me Mum why some of the black boys had two willies.

She replied, 'It's just that their belly buttons stick out and yours goes in.' Still I was fascinated by these exotic-looking creatures. I wanted to have two willies just like them.

Longsight was a very multi-cultural place just outside the city centre. It had a huge Asian and black population. The market was always busy and more, and more Asians were descending on the area. Growing up I thought all Asians were collectively called 'Pakkies' and this is still assumed today by a large portion of white kids from Manchester. For many years this was the only word I had in my vocabulary for Asian people and even for Turkish, Iranian, and sometimes Spanish people. When some 'Pakkies', as I was told they were called, moved in next door, I remember various family members' constant stream of negativity about them. The obvious one was that they all stank of curry. Another one that sticks in my head was that because they had just come from India they didn't know how to use a toilet, so they all shat on the floor in the kitchen. Someone in my family was sure they had seen it through the window.

At my school, white kids were the minority. All I remember is racing in the playground, learning to tie my shoelaces and having to hold hands with kids when we went anywhere.

It was in this house in Longsight that I experienced terror for the first time. I remember coming downstairs in the middle of the night to find blood smeared and splattered all over the hall stairs and landing. I was crying my eyes out. My mum was also sobbing, carrying me as the police arrived. I was scared my daddy was going to be taken away. It looked like someone had been murdered in our hallway. I was screaming as the police asked my daddy to go to the station.

He was saying, 'No, I'm staying here with my family, I've done nothing wrong. It's my house'.

The police found the man who had broken into our house a few streets away. The man had jumped through our front window, smashing the single pane of glass. This had woken me Dad who, when he arrived downstairs found a stranger in his hallway, proceeded to kick ten tons of shit out of him before throwing him half dead out of the door head first.

I remember being horrified as Mum and I tiptoed downstairs, both in floods of tears. I didn't really know what was happening, but that was to become a theme of life. Whenever me Mum cried, I did.

As a young boy, witnessing this amplified the hero status I gave my father. He was so strong that he could pick me up and twirl me around with one arm. We always played together and, looking back at pictures I now realise we had a very special bond.

The police found the man, who turned out to be a smackhead, in such a bad way, they thought they might have to take Dad into custody. Luckily they didn't, but Mum got really scared of living in the area, and this was the beginning of the end for number 84 Stanford Road, Longsight.

Our next move was into this huge house in Stretford (the 'rock holding' house). It was in a safer, whiter area of Manchester, just next to where my granddad lived in sheltered accommodation for the elderly. As the house needed a lot of work, we lived in the upstairs, which was like a big flat. I had a huge bedroom and so did me Mum and Dad. Their room had an en-suite bathroom with a bidet. The bedrooms and kitchen surrounded a huge living space, and we lived there until me Mum left me Dad. I started a new school just over the busy Chester Road and started to make new friends.

I had this enormous Scalextric racing track and would play it every night with me dad. I was also obsessed with dinosaurs, and I had a sticker book and toy figures. I was a pretty introverted kid I and liked spending time on my own in my room reading about dinosaurs.

When me Mum left me Dad, I remember sitting at the top of the stairs at me Auntie Brenda's house screaming, sobbing my eyes out shouting, 'No you can't, I want Daddy. No, no!'

I was hysterically retching from my throat, lungs and stomach. I was kneeling, pulling my legs into my chest, tucking my head between my legs and kicking out if anyone came near me, screaming at them, shear anguish emitting from my tiny body. This was my first experience of having my heartbroken and I wanted to take it out on me Mum, seeing her as the bad person for taking me away from me Daddy.

Me mum had just told me we were never going back to the house and I wouldn't be seeing Daddy for a while. I'm pretty sure me Mum had a black eye at this point, but she always had lumps and bumps all over her.

I wouldn't have it. I wanted Daddy so bad. I wanted to see him every day. How could she take me away from this man I loved so much? Mum and me auntie tried to comfort me, but I was inconsolable. I went to bed and sobbed all night, not letting anyone near me.

Next thing I knew we were living in a flat in a woman's refuge in a huge building in Hulme, Manchester.

The flat was within this huge Gothic-style building. We had a kitchen with a dining table and one-bedroom we shared upstairs. As you entered the building there was a huge entrance hall with a reception and security. At the front of the building were massive security gates and we had to press a buzzer, (that I could just about reach) to get in. The complex housed battered wives and was aptly called the 'The Battered Wives Institute'.

I enjoyed aspects of living here. There was lots of trouble to get into and lots of naughty kids. We would race around the corridors, exploring rooms we weren't supposed to be in and we would go out to the back of the institute and smash the windows of the derelict building behind, before being told off by one of the guards and chased away.

Both me and me Mum cried a lot here. I'm not sure if I had built up some resentment towards her, for taking me away from me Dad.

I really missed him. I remember him coming to the gates one time to see me and trying to force me mum into the car. Luckily one of the guards was there, and we weren't kidnapped, but all parts of me wanted to go off with me Dad, not understanding why me Mum didn't want us to go with him.

I don't think I would have ever chosen me Dad over me Mum, but as a child, I guess your perception is very much clouded. What you are being told by people is just a fragment of the truth, as you are always being protected.

I started another school, dominated by black kids. I found it hard to adjust again, and all I really remember was the huge climbing frame in the playground that kids would spend all playtime climbing. There were only two kids who could get to the top and hang upside down. They would wrap their legs around the centre and just dangle there like bats, exposing their sticky-out belly buttons that still fascinated me. I would watch them dangle, a sadistic part of me wondering what would happen if they fell?

I spent my fifth birthday at the 'Battered Wives Institute'. We had a big party with loads of kids and 'battered' mums all together. I don't think the party was specifically for my birthday, but all the tables from the flats were taken to one big room, and a feast was laid out, and it was a big party, so I claimed it as me own. Me and Mum danced lots.

When the tables were returned, we were given someone else's.

They were all exactly the same, but this one was not ours, I wanted ours. This one was slightly uneven, and the top was scratched. I complained about it for a long time. Whenever Mum and I went into someone else's flat, I would check to see if their table was ours. I constantly nagged me Mum to come around all the flats with me and look for ours. She said the one we had was fine, so I refused to eat at the table and would sit on the floor leaning against the kitchen cupboards in protest.

I had weird little traits when I was a kid. Whenever we went to the shops, I would spend the whole time tidying the shelves, making everything neat and tidy and me Mum would have to come looking for me when she finished her shopping. I was also constantly asking me mum to take off her underskirt, which was apparently pretty embarrassing for her in some situations. The underskirt seemed to be the only thing that would soothe me when I was upset. I would rub it on my face, stop crying and go to sleep.

To this day, I am still slightly obsessed with touch and smell. I love the feel on my tongue of the inside of scampi fries when you bite them in half and lick the inside. It feels like this perfect piece of velvet. Skin is towards the top of my list. I love to stroke it and feel it. The different textures and degrees of softness around different areas of the body fascinate me. I love to breathe in the scent of a woman's neck and let it engulf every cell of my own body as if I'm breathing them into me.

Eventually, we were housed not far away from me nana's in Peel Hall, Wythenshawe. Again I started a new school; my fourth. I was five years old when I started lower primary at Crossacers Junior. We moved into a three-bed semi in an avenue called Welburn, where we were thrown fully in the mix of one of the largest council estates in Europe.

The avenue was pretty 'quaint' in many ways. We had gypsies on one side of us and an old lady on the other. Most of the people in the avenue would stay up late chatting at their gates. There was something nice about it, but me Mum didn't take part in it very much as a lot of it was based around drinking and smoking, two things she didn't do.

I soon became friends with all the kids, and the ringleader when it came to finding trouble. There was a raw beauty I now see to living in these conditions. People were very poor, dramas were always taking place, and the close-knit avenue provided so much entertainment that I would be privy to from my bedroom window in the evening.

The head of the gypsy household next door would spend whole days and nights in his car (when he had one) smoking, drinking and listening to his radio. His scruffy, lawless kids would cause mayhem. His wife, June, who always looked like she had just rolled around in mud, would try and control them, constantly screaming her head off so people in the next avenue could hear. They had a goat in the front garden, and this was a complete novelty for me and these other urban kids.

This was the time in my life, I felt closest to me Mum, even though I was constantly in trouble for something or other. It was as if I had become another person after my parents split up; I was always naughty and rebelled against everything. For some reason, I'd created a new persona, and it would take many, many years for me to realise it was not actually me.

ALONE AT LAST, THE JOURNEY, NOVEMBER 2012

One night in Belize, I was stopped by a Rasta man called Elvis. He was pretty smashed and offered me a job for the next day. He said he would pick me up from the Funky Do Do in the morning and pay me 100 Belizean dollars. As I walked off, he shouted, 'I'll see you at eight!'

Elvis never appeared, so I was free to spend the day on the beach with Fhian. She elegantly lay in the sun switching from brightly coloured wooden chair to hammock.

I did some yoga on a sand drive leading to the beach under a canopy of coconut palms. Towards the end of my practice, whilst balancing on one foot with my other leg outstretched and my fingers attached to my big toe, I felt someone approaching. A face appeared over my shoulder and said, "What are you doing man?"

"Yoga" I replied.

Without removing himself from my personal space, he asked, "What's that?"

Between breaths, I said, 'stretching'.

He took half a pace back and just stared at me as if trying to fathom what this crazy man was doing and what on earth yoga could be. After a while, he snapped out of his confusion and got down to his daily task of sweeping the drive free of leaves and slowly swept around me. I think this sweet man was autistic or had some form of learning disability.

Every day I was transfixed, watching his rhythmical sweeping task. It took him about four hours to sweep the drive, which was about ten metres long. He made these beautiful swirly patterns in the sand. His technique consisted of two sweeps, a two-step hobble towards the direction he was heading, and then another two sweeps. He was lovely, and part of me just wanted to cuddle him.

That afternoon I was meditating in the sea, and I felt something grab my leg. I jumped out of my skin thinking I was being savaged by a shark, grabbing my leg in terror and expecting the searing pain. Then I realised it was a local kid playing. We both laughed our heads off and played in the sea, raced underwater and hung out for a few hours.

That night we ate with this crazy American lady. The restaurant was just a table in her kitchen and chaos seemed to be the theme. She was completely nuts and never stopped talking and complaining in this massively hysterical way that had me almost in tears. Her boyfriend was Elvis, who had offered me the job the previous day; he had no idea he had ever seen me before. Watching him wash the pots completely stoned and drunk was mesmerising. I feared for whoever would be eating there next.

We said our goodbyes and departed Hopkins, hitchhiking to the bus junction. We were heading for the Hummingbird Highway and our last night together at Yamwits Lodge, an orange and grapefruit plantation. From there we were picked up to go moonlight cave tubing and spent the evening floating lazily down the cave river with our guide.

It had been daylight when we had entered the cave, and after an hour of floating on rubber doughnuts and seeing underground waterfalls, magical rock formations which looked like anything from a lady breastfeeding, to an eagle, we emerged to a starlit sky. The surrounding jungle had come alive with sound, and we could hear so many howls, tweets and croaks. Fireflies sparkled in the darkness. I held Fhian's hand, looking at the stars whilst we nonchalantly floated down the river. It felt special, but as always, doubt about where this relationship was going spiked in my mind like a sharp pain as the whirlwind of uncertainty again crept in.

In the evening, I finally had my favourite food —broccoli— for the first time in this rice, bean and chicken-obsessed society. We had the restaurant to ourselves and were joined by the owners' son Rupert, who ran the plantation. He told us all about the orange trade and how it had taken a big hit since a parasite disease had descended on the country a few years back. He told me about the intricacies of the big multinationals trying to run them out of business. I was mildly interested in the plight of the independent, but as my body needed sleep, I just smile and nod.

That day, Fhian would be going our back to her corporate job in London. We went back to Belize City where she was flying from and unsuccessfully searched for seaweed like crack fiends. We were then amusingly hassled and told to get a room from a crazy local for kissing in the park. It was then time for our emotional goodbye. We didn't know when we would see each other again, which felt weird.

I hauled on my rucksack, blew a kiss and headed off to start my solo adventure and my spiritual quest. I had a feeling we would never see each other again. The relationship had been pretty difficult since its birth, but there was this intense magnetism between us.

Part of me felt undeserving of this amazing lady who was willing to wait for me whilst I went off trying to find myself and figure things out in my manically depressed and confused mind. There was this intense love, but there also seemed to be these obstacles that prohibited us from taking our relationship to the next stage. I wanted her to open up more, to be more connected with her heart and less distracted by the constant stream of entertainment that takes so much of one's attention when living in London. I knew I never wanted to live in London again, but that's where she wanted to be, so how could we move forward? I also felt like this new spiritual side of me was something I wanted to share and explore with her, but it was something she had difficulty understanding. I just wanted to let the universe figure it out. If we were meant to be, I was sure we would. If not, we would both go on to be happy. As well as the usual fear, doubt and insecurity of being a solo traveller, I had I constant swirl of dialogue in my head telling me we weren't right together and I needed to make this journey alone.

When I first started to travel alone, I got flustered, and the voices in my head started telling me I was a loser and had no friends. I guess it was just that evil alter-ego twin that sits inside, making us question our self-worth and direction. If I listened and fuelled it, it could take me on this downward spiral to suicidal thoughts. All I could do was refuse to listen and tell it to piss off and eventually it would.

My next stop was San Antonio in the north of Belize, close to the Guatemalan border. I had read about a famous healer from there called Don Elijio Panti who had died over a decade ago. His two nieces, called the Garcia sisters, continued his traditions and had a guest house called Chichan Ka where I was hoping I could get a room.

After two chicken busses and being directed by a lovely Mayan lady, I arrived to be greeted by Maria Garcia. She did have a room, and we discussed the upcoming end of the Mayan calendar— my reason for being there. She said the changes that were to come would benefit all of humanity and then she told me a fascinating story which opened my mind to her world. She'd had the opportunity to attend a conference in New York through her work with the UN. When she arrived she found the snow to be black and dead and quickly realised how dirty the place was. It really upset her that the snow was so impure, as she had had dreams of seeing fresh white snow. After two days in New York, she said she couldn't feel life and felt that the whole city was dead. There was no colour, no animal sounds and no clean air. The garbage that lined all the streets disgusted her, and she felt as though she had to leave. She said the sounds of the crickets were what she missed most and, longing for home, and the UN thankfully returned her to her basic sanctuary in the jungle and what many Westerners would class as a third world dirty existence.

We talked about how people needed to start living simpler lives that didn't plunder the Earth's resources. I was immediately reminded of a passage in a book I had recently read called The Reluctant Shaman by Kay Cordell Whitaker: She talks about how these people called the Woosai were up in the trees ready to kill everyone after almost all the people of their world had been destroyed. They knew that if they killed each other, their people would be lost forever. Their world was already destroyed, and they knew there would be no future for their offspring. They had so much hatred and distrust for each other. However, they had to find a way to move together. They would have to find peace and combine their efforts to bring their planet back to life, thus creating a better future for themselves and their grandchildren.

It took them hundreds of years, but they began to work together, using ancient knowledge and always putting the planet first. Through this commitment and common goal they realised they were not as different as they had originally thought. Underneath, they all wanted a better future for their families. They wanted a brighter, cleaner future for their children and the planet they called home. They found a new religion that was centred on sustainability and equally respecting all life.

Maria and I went on to discuss moving into a new age, an age that had been prophesied for eternity by all civilisations all over the world throughout time. 12.12.12 and 21.12.12 are constantly referenced by The Egyptians, Incas, Mayans, and Angkor's (Khmer). These dates had been thrust into my consciousness over the last twelve months, and I felt blessed to be in these lands for these cosmic happenings.

We were moving into a new age, the age of Aquarius, an age of love, light, health and happiness. The world was set to change, and many prophesies say that each person alive today was born at this time because we have a mission to accomplish. For me this meant moving inside and searching for what my life's mission was, asking something higher than myself to show me what I should be doing and removing all the fear and self-doubt that surrounded me.

These prophesies prophesy have been denied by the Catholic Church, Christianity and various other organisations. The Spanish Conquistadors who arrived in Mayan lands tried to eradicate the prophesies and traditions and spent 500 years insisting that any spirituality other than strict state-run religion was to be quashed. They did a pretty good job and many Mayans today have no idea of their traditional spiritual practices. In England, the Pagans were eradicated and burnt again in the name of Christianity. Everything I'd read about ancient civilisations pointed to either the New Age, the Third Millennium, the Age of Aquarius, the Beginning of the Fifth Sun, or the end of old calendars and the commencement of new ones.

Despite the varying terminologies, however, they have a great deal in common, and The Native American Prophecy of the Condor and Eagle states that 'back in the mists of history, human societies divided and took different paths: that of the condor (representing the heart, intuitive and mystical) and that of the eagle (representing the brain, rational and material).' In the 1490s, the prophecy said the two paths
50
would converge and the eagle would drive the condor to the verge of extinction. Then, five hundred years later, in the 1990s a new epoch would begin, one in which the condor and the eagle would have the opportunity to reunite and fly together in the same sky, along the same path. If the condor and eagle accepted this opportunity, they would create a most remarkable offspring, unlike any seen before.

And to me, that's why it's important for everyone to find their calling.

Again, Whitaker, in her incredible book, sums up her personal challenge of trying to break free. After meeting death and destiny in an 'out of body experience', Whitaker talks about death and our individual quest, not allowing ourselves to live by the rules of another. She tells us to step forward into our own power and learn all the things we were put on the planet to learn. This made me think again about not having any emotional ties whilst I was searching for myself.

After coming back to her body, Whitaker contemplates her life, saying how scared she was to step into her power. She knew she had let go of all her dreams and was living as someone else. She wasn't living the life her teenage self had wanted to live. She had forgotten because of societal and family expectations. The more she realised this, the more upset she was with herself and a total dislike for herself was found. She had destroyed her true essence, and all she now felt was worthlessness.

This is exactly how I had felt most of my life; being tied to expectations of what I should have acquired at a certain time, what was expected of me at certain ages, and the job I should be doing with the skills I have. I would stress about what I didn't have, seeing where others were in their lives, with their houses, cars, security and feeling like I had achieved nothing. I was always comparing myself to others and forgetting who I was and what drove me. I didn't feel confident enough to be the real me and I didn't feel like I knew who he was anyway. I wanted to find him to find my essence. I felt trapped in so many ways.

But this journey was my escape.

For years, I'd felt like Sylvia Plath sitting on her fig tree in her book 'The Bell Jar'. I saw my life branching out before me like the green fig tree in the story: She gave the analogy of sitting looking up at the fig tree. Each fig represented a different path she could take in her life. The different offbeat lovers and places they could live, the children she could have, the different exciting careers, the cities and far-out places she could explore, eating different food, smelling exotic smells. There were so many options, and she wanted all of them. She was struggling to make a choice as she thought choosing one would mean she would lose the rest. She couldn't make up her mind. She didn't know what to go for. The longer and longer she mulled it over and procrastinated, the fewer the options there were as the figs started to wither and die and drop from the tree to her feet until she had nothing at all to choose from.

Our thoughts and dreams become polluted by a need to fit in, survive and be seen as normal. Society herds itself like sheep, driving us to act in a certain way. People self-regulate, with little need for the powers that be to step in and make people behave. We get taught that to think anything outside the norm is just a silly dream, an unattainable fantasy that we created in our inexperienced youth.

But it's dreams that drive us. We should never let go of them; anything is achievable at any age. People have to have the confidence, belief and heart to break the shackles of the society they have become a part of. Like Twain says:

"Twenty years from now you will be more disappointed by the things that you didn't do than by the ones you did do. So throw off the bowlines. Sail away from the safe harbour. Catch the trade winds in your sails. Explore, Dream, Discover".

There are a lot of lost people out there struggling to make sense of the world, I didn't realise this until I got depressed myself and started to see the mental misery that exists in the world. It's like a huge section of humanity has no purpose and can see no purpose in anything.

We don't come here with a manual of how to live. Through meditation and spirituality, I have realised that all we can do is look within our hearts and the answers will be presented. We have to be compassionate with all people; those with different views, different ways of being and know that every person we meet— happy or sad— has an internal war going on inside them.

We then realise that what we put out we get back. This realisation really changed my life. Some may think trying to better yourself emotionally is self-absorbed, but it's actually self-observation. It teaches us not to be taken over by obsessive thoughts and feelings and to become more open-minded to the emotional lives of those around us. As human beings, we can truly wake up and evolve into a more conscious species.

I was snapped out of these internal musings when Maria offered me a Mayan blessing by her very old frail mother. I was shown to my room, and I laid down my bags in what would become my home for the next two days.

The Mayan blessing consisted of embers being burnt with different herbs and oils. The frail old lady prepared a sacred space, whilst chickens, dogs, cats and horses fluttered about, and she laughed at me for not being able to speak Spanish and heading for Guatemala.

I sat down on a bench, and the ceremony began. I was cleansed with the scents, and then my wrists were held whilst she jabbered prayers. Suddenly a wave of energy floated over me, and I became entranced in meditation. She went from wrist to wrist saying prayers and calling in the Mayan elders to bless me.

I didn't really know what was going on for the rest of the ceremony, but it felt powerful, and I drifted into deep meditation, taking in all my surroundings; the smells, the sounds, the energies, the vibrations. I was deeply trying to feel where I was, trying to allow my being to merge with those of the Maya. Hoping beyond hope that this immensely complicated, sophisticated, spiritual, astrological, dignified indigenous culture would reveal to me in the coming months some of its divine wisdom. Apparently I came round about 20 minutes after the ceremony had ended. I didn't know where I'd been, but it felt beautiful.

I had been officially baptised into the Mayan world.

The next day, after my bucket wash in the garden, I set off for an hour's walk to the un-excavated ruins of Picbanntun. Halfway along the dirt road, after passing the village of San Antonio, waving and saying hello to kids, families, adults, dogs and pigs, I managed to thumb a lift. I jumped in the back of the pickup with a load of workmen. I asked one of the men, 'Picbanntun?' He pointed to in the opposite direction to where we were going. I banged on the side of the truck and jumped out.

When I finally arrived, I mooched around, absorbing the energies of the place and managing to climb a couple of temples in the vast jungle that had engulfed these once-grand structures. I had the whole place to myself. It felt quite eerie being there alone, but I never felt in danger or scared. My new-found faith made me feel protected. The only things trying to get me were the mosquitos.

I covered up and ascended the largest temple, finding a place to meditate on a plinth in what I imagine would have been the courtyard. It had a tree above it and hanging from it was a large branch that had become tangled in the vines. It was pointing downwards like a sword, ready to sacrifice its deeply privileged Mayan subject. I thought this was another meditation opportunity not to miss, so I lay looking up at this large implement dangling above me. I trusted in the Maya and closed my eyes and drifted off, hoping the engines of this place would give me strength for the future.

I hitchhiked back to San Antonio and headed for the Do Elijio

Panti National Park. I got there, paid my entrance fee, had some tea with the Park Ranger John who told there were no other people in the park so I had it to myself. This seemed to be a theme of the spiritual spots. I got to a sign for caves one way and waterfall the other. I ended up walking through the jungle alone for well over a mile, but I assumed I would be able to see it when I arrived.

Eventually, I ended up at the cave and got a bit scared that I was alone, as the ranger had told me there may be Jaguars about and it was best to take a guide. I was twitching and took a little look in the cave, then ran off in a camp fashion, floundering my arms around like Jim Cary in Ace Ventura.

I headed down another path looking for my waterfall, sure I couldn't have walked past it. After running and walking for another hour I couldn't see it anywhere, then I got back to the sign and realised I had taken the wrong road — what a dick.

It was getting late now, and I knew I had about two and a half hours till it went dark. I ran down the correct road for two miles bouncing down jagged steep rocked paths. I came to another sign, which was unreadable. I went down one path, got to a stream and decided I had gone the wrong way. So back to the other path, over the stream, and down a steep hill until I reached the bottom.

There I saw the most beautiful steep waterfalls. It was so tranquil and pristine and something I longed to share with someone. I drank the crystalline water, jumped in and bathed my aching body.

I approached Maria's just as the sun was setting. Exhausted, I calculated I had covered twenty-two miles, nine of which were unnecessary. I crashed on the bed and didn't want to walk again for a very long time. Next morning my legs were in agony, but I set off again.

CHAPTER 3
A STONE'S THROW 2,
LIFE, 1987

Tears were streaming down my cheeks and I was spluttering panicked pleas of 'Daddy stop'. I weakly threw the rock towards him. I was petrified of my daddy and too scared to actually do any damage.

I have no way of dealing with this beast I am in love with, who is possibly about to end the life of another person I am in love with—my mother.

Daddy strides across the room, and cries of 'no Bernie, no Bernie' intensify. My panicked 'No Daddy no' become more and more dramatic. 'It's ok, Mummy' is coming out of me still, but I'm afraid to be near either of them.

He picks Mummy up by the hair and throat and drags her up the stairs with less dignity and grace than you would an opposing solider you had just captured. He punches and pushes her as she tries to scramble up the stairs. She runs for one of the rooms, but he catches her before she can hide, and forces her onto the couch. He straddles her whilst, her arms are flying about, and when he sees a gap, he punches her in the face. He then manages to get her arms under his knees, so he now has unrestricted access to punch her pretty face.

Her crying is full of pain, full of anguish. There are deep sobs, tears and snot all over the place, mixed with the blood gushing from various openings.

Having managed to unstick my feet and race up the stairs after them, I cry, 'Stop it! Stop hitting her, Daddy!'

I then just fall to the floor and sit holding one of my teddies. Deep tears from the depths of my stomach are surfacing through my eyes, and my body is trembling. I watch my beautiful mummy being destroyed by the beast that my daddy has become.

My father calls her disgusting names whilst he commentates on the reasons for the beating she is being given. All I see is blood pouring from her face, my daddy punching her like she was a punching bag, this animal on top of my mummy.

I tremble, each thudded punch striking me like lightning. I

stand up and try to grab him off her, but am pushed to the side like a piece of paper.

Mummy tells me to go away, and halfway through the sentence, a huge fist crashes down on her, splitting her mouth.

'No. Daddy no, stop it now, Daddy'.

He pins her arms tighter and begins to breathe deeply. Continual insults are thrown at her, but slowly they turn to more rational thoughts as he tells her she can't take away his son, she can't leave him, he needs her and he loves her. Remorse starts to come as he sees what he has done. Gone is the veil of rage and passion.

'Don't hit her again, Daddy, please don't hit Mummy again,' I cry.

He looks at me and starts to cry, looks at her and cries harder. Daddy is now sobbing; we are all sobbing. Mummy's face is a mess.

'Okay Daddy, promise you won't hit her again.' Panicked and terrified, I repeat this over and over.

Between breathless cries, he says he won't.

I'm unsure of how to react or what to do. I tell them I am going to get a cloth for Mummy's face.

'Promise Daddy,' I plead.

He nods.

'I love you, Mummy,' I say. I rush into the ensuite, wet a flannel and sprint back into the living room, wiping Mummy's face as she sobs.

Daddy is still on top of her and cries as he looks at us both. I can't stop saying 'please don't hit her again' and 'I love you, Mummy' over and over and over and over and over. I'm terrified the violence could return at any point, knowing my every word and action could flip the switch inside my daddy again. The panicked tension in the air seems to have disappeared. The man my daddy had become seems to have gone, and a remorseful, pathetic, blubbering one has taken its place.

What happens after this is a blur. Daddy takes us to the hospital and insists my mummy had fallen down the stairs.

It's 1987, and there is little to be done if a husband is beating his wife — even raping one's wife is legal.

My mum's face is a mess for weeks. I don't know what exactly happens to my daddy with the police, but I will not see him for a very long time. It feels like my heart is breaking, and love is being denied me.

GUATEMALA, THE JOURNEY, NOVEMBER 2012

I got up early the next day, saying my goodbyes to the Garcia sisters and excitedly heading towards the Guatemalan border. I felt like I would be truly entering the home of the Mayans now.

I would slowly be making my way to meet the group I would be going on the pilgrimage with, leading up to 12.12.12. I felt that Guatemala would allow me to engulf myself in spirituality and the cosmology this land was so renowned for. It was the reason I was here. I wanted to become more spiritual and more connected to myself and my true purpose. I was eager, excited and slightly nervous about what the next few months had in store for me and how my journey would unfold.

I hitchhiked to the next town, getting a ride with a family on their way to church. Two bible-clasping boys with pristine white shirts sat on a little bench on the back of the pick-up whilst I lay down on the metal bed, without taking off my bag.

We arrived at the church, and I thanked the father and dropped him a couple of notes. He was of Mayan descent and I asked which church he attended.

'Methodist,' he replied.

'What will you be doing for the end of the Mayan calendar?' I asked.

'The 25th of December is the date we celebrate. Nothing for the Mayan dates,' he replied.

I almost cried. What a great job the missionaries had done over here, totally eradicating the traditions of many Mayans and brainwashing and bribing them into whatever crude pompous form of Jesus-slavery they had to offer. I'd heard that in small villages, chickens and washing machines had been used to bribe the locals to attend one Christian church over the other.

At the border, I dodged a load of currency dealers who were like vultures praying on white-skinned people. As soon as I arrived in Guatemala I felt like I was in a bigger, more dangerous country. It was busy everywhere, with people selling stuff, people hustling, money exchanging hands, sweets, fruits, dogs, buses, overwhelming madness...

I quickly realised I had no way of communicating with anyone, it was all Spanish. Luckily Fhian had bought a book with loads of pictures that I could just point at and 'smile and nod'. Some of the pictures were bizarre, like a girl in a bikini lying on a beach. I wondered when I would need to point at that.

I arrived at Lago de Peten Itza, needing a shower. My plan was to stay there one night and take a bus to Lago Atitlan the next day, then head for San Marcos, a spiritual hotspot I'd been reading about.

I checked into a hostel, and at first, they tried to put me in a room which was exposed to the elements, but I was getting bitten so much I insisted on a mosquito-proof abode.

The centre of the hostel felt like a lush jungle with plant life twisting its way around the wood carvings on the walls. There were hammocks everywhere.

I soon got chatting to an American girl and boy, and we went to grab some food.

Rose was from Florida and Cameron was from Portland. They were both laid back and travelled a lot. For some reason Rose thought it was hilarious and posh when I asked whilst looking over at the food vendors, 'does anyone fancy a snack?'

There were treats on display everywhere, so I ended up saying this a lot. She broke down laughing every time.

At the hostel, I bumped into some people from the Funky Do Do and one of the Norwegians from the Lubanntun ruins. That evening everyone persuaded me to go to a place called Semuc Champey with the Americans the next morning. It apparently had amazingly beautiful idyllic pools, an underground river and cave systems.

We left at 6 am for the eight-hour minibus drive there. There were 18 people in a van smaller than a VW transporter. The drive was hard work, and we only had two fifteen-minute breaks and two toilet stops.

We passed the most amazing local markets and busy towns and villages selling delicious food and the freshest looking fruit and veg. Unfortunately, the driver thought it was apt that we stopped at McDonald's.

I ran off with Cameron to look for local food and then watched nearly all our western co-travellers chowing down on those beautiful locally sourced delicacies that were the cause of all that obesity in their motherlands.

The last couple of hours of the journey were spent winding round the bumpiest roads I'd ever seen.

Our heads were smashed against the roof; then on the return to earth, our bottoms got smacked down onto the lightly cushioned metal seats. It was all about endurance, and the thousand-foot drop down the ravine didn't help my state of mind. The landscape was lush and green with jagged, mountainous jungle littering my eyes, as bruises started to litter my body.

The next day we jumped in the back of a pickup with a load of other travellers and stood – holding on for dear life as we made the twenty-minute journey down the ravine.

On the way, I called Rose.

Cameron said, 'Who is Rose?'

I said, 'Rose is Rose.'

He said, 'her name is Grace.'

I said, 'She's called Rose.'

'No, she's called Grace.'

'Oh no,' I said. I had been calling her Rose for two days. Feeling like an idiot, I asked why she hadn't corrected me.

She said she'd thought it was an endearing English term like luv, petal, or darling.

We entered a cave in candlelight. Apparently there were 15 miles worth of caves in the mountain. If it rained, the caves got flooded and if you were in there, bye, bye.

The fifteen of us crawled through tiny holes, climbing up waterfalls and swimming with one arm when the water got too deep.

After this was a mountain trek to the idyllic views of Semuc Champey, the beautiful lush jungle surrounding a waterfall that disappeared into an underground river. Some of the water stayed on the surface and created these perfect turquoise blue pools with little waterfalls leading to more pools. It was like an oil painting dripping into your eyes. None of it seemed real.

Natural slippery slides led down to each set of pools and sticking to her name, Rose gracefully crashed into a wall whilst the onlooking crowd gasped and winced. She wasn't too badly hurt and managed the rest of the pool plunges with grace.

Cameron gives me a couple of guitar lessons that night. I really wanted to get the hang of it. He played so well, finger strumming away. I managed an E, A and something else before my thought drifted to the matrix and being able to have skills downloaded into your brain.

If I could have five downloads, they would be mastering the guitar, speaking French, mastering yoga, memorising Shakespeare's work and knowing all philosophical history.

The next day I arrived in Antigua where I would meet the pilgrimage group in a few days.

First, I want to get to San Marcos. For some reason, the place was calling me. I felt like I was in a rush to get there.

I said goodbye to Grace and Cameron, who were both heading home to the States the next day. I made my way towards my first chicken bus in Guatemala. This was when the term 'chicken bus' hit home. I got on, and they kept letting people in until there was no space anywhere. We were jammed in like battery farm hens, and occasionally boxes of chickens were rammed into the overhead rack to mirror the humans rammed into the bus.

The ticket collector man tried to rip me off, and locals helped me, but not being able to figure out the price or understand Spanish, even with my point and smile book, I still paid too much. It didn't matter. It was only three pounds for a three-hour bus ride.

The next thing I know, something is happening; a kerfuffle as my mum would say. A pickup truck of armed police approached and jumped out to rush to the front door. One of them tried to enter the back door where I was sitting, and I'm thinking, 'is there a shootout about to take place on my bus? Will I be caught in crossfire? Will I be evacuated on to another bus and will I have to pay again?'

I had no idea what was going on. There were lots of raised tense Spanish voices, and I was sure a gun was about to go off. I thought about getting my pointing book out to see if there was a picture for 'shoot out'.

Then the police left, and the bus set off again, kerfuffle over.

I arrived at San Marcos at about 9 pm, after fourteen hours of travelling uncomfortably. The bus had taken three hours longer than I thought it would.

I asked a guy where the place I wanted to stay called La Paz was.

He looked at me funny and said, 'I don't know.'
Then I got another guy. He said, "no La Paz here".
I pointed on the map. He said, 'no.'
I pointed again.

He said, 'no.'

I asked where this was.

He said, 'San Marcos'.

I said 'yes', he said "no" and pointed at a different San Marcos. I had passed the San Marcos on the lake three hours ago. Gutted, what a Ravi.

The guy took me to a place to stay for the evening. I was told the first bus back was at 5 am.

The interesting thing was the observation of myself under those circumstances. A year ago, if that had happened I would have gotten so angry with myself for not realising I had passed a lake with volcanoes. I would have been so angry with my guide book for not stating this mistake could be made. I would have been so angry with the bus driver not realising I wouldn't want to go to that San Marcos.

I would have worked myself into a rage and hated everything and blamed everyone and beat myself up mentally. Anyone around me would have been affected by my mood and would have heard all about it.

It was so refreshing to accept I had made a simple, silly mistake, see the funny side, enjoy my night and look forward to the next day. I was learning to forget about the way I had been taught to react to difficult situations. I was forgetting what I thought were natural impulses and learning that I could react in a calm and serene manner to anything.

The next morning, I was up at 4.30 am to get the 5 am bus.

A few hours later, I arrived at the magnificent Lake Atitlan with its four stunning volcanoes providing a spectacular panoramic view. I then crossed the majestic, breath-taking lake and felt like I had landed somewhere very, very special.

Three local kids escorted me to La Paz. There were no rooms till the next night, but the owner directed me to somewhere there would be.

I had breakfast at La Paz and got chatting to the flamboyant owner, Benjamin, a well-travelled, classy Guatemalan character who was immaculately dressed. He was someone I felt I could listen to all day. La Paz exuded his personality; calm, serene and subtly stylish.

We got on really well, chatting about the places he had lived in Europe and the fact he used to own a vegetarian restaurant in Liverpool, which seem a bit of an oxymoron to me. He was very interested in my pilgrimage and the healing I was doing, and we agreed to exchange therapies.

He sent me to a guest house called Unicorn, where I was given the coolest triangular-shaped hut called Orion. I made a couple of friends and then went and strolled around San Marcos.

I quickly realised that this was the place for me. There were organic juice bars, vegetarian restaurants, massage and holistic therapies everywhere. Everything was eco, sustainable and environmentally sensitive. There were signs for yoga, meditations, retreats and courses everywhere. It seemed like I was back in India, and I loved it.

The view of the lake from the Mayan villages above was breath-taking. I strolled around saying hello to everyone I passed, getting funny looks for being barefoot and then played football with a few kids outside their house, whilst their mum laughed her head off. At what, I will never know.

The locals lived in the villages in the foothills of the mountains, whilst the newcomers and the tourists stayed close to the lake. Some of the houses closest to the water had disappeared in the last few years, as the water had risen over seven metres. The lake is thought to be over five hundred metres deep, and apparently the water level rises and falls every fifty years. Scientist can't explain why which makes this a very mystical place.

That evening, I kept seeing flashes of light in the sky, so I went down to the dock. Was this going to be my first encounter with some sort of extra-terrestrial activity?

It was completely pitch black, and I could see nothing. What I then witnessed was incredible. There was an electrical storm going on behind the volcanoes, and every time the lightning struck, the whole sky behind the volcanoes lit up, revealing the three magnificent natural structures.

I sat in awe, waiting for the next strike. What was incredible was that the weather was perfect on the lake and you couldn't hear any noise from the lightening. People were trying to take pictures, but nothing could do it justice. I was just happy to be having the blessed privilege of witnessing such an event. Feeling an air of serenity pour over me, I truly felt like I had arrived somewhere magical. I knew I would never forget my first night in San Marcos.

The next day I headed back to La Paz and instantly felt at home in the beautiful dormitory Benjamin had built. I started the day with yoga, chatted with

Benjamin's friend Josanna, who was a permaculture expert who had lived in the Findhorn community in Scotland for eight years. She had such a calming presence and looked like a beautiful Atlantian high priestess.

I was talking to people who fascinated me, people who were on their own incredible journey, not just travelling around the world getting drunk and seeing sights. They had actually done important work to better humanity and develop themselves. This was what I desired; to be enriched, to give me purpose, grounding and stability. This was my nectar.

I spent the next two days wandering around chatting to people, having a Mayan sauna, and eating great food in the commodores, which were cheap local eateries. I was captivated by the pace of life in San Marcos. The vast array of conscious people and projects happening blew me away. Everyone you passed said hello. Most of them stopped to talk to you. It felt like a little utopia.

I learnt about energy healing just before I left England. I did my level 1 and 2 courses and was stunned and amazed that it actually worked. I thought it was a load of bollocks until my teacher showed me how to do it.

I had arranged the first healing of my travels on a guy called Connor with MS I had met at the Unicorn. Beforehand, I had arranged to have a massage from Benjamin. The massage was amazing, the best I'd ever had. I'd felt this instant connection with him when we'd first met. He had such great energy. In spite of myself, I could hear my mates' voices in my head calling me a massive gay for thinking about another man like this.

Benjamin told me that the really sore parts of my calves— which I have had problems with all my life— were caused by stored emotions that I hadn't released.

My healing with Connor went great. He told me he hadn't felt such peace for a very long time. It gave me the confidence to start giving more healing whilst on my travels.

The healing was intense. I felt like I had given everything, maybe making a few mistakes in protecting myself. Afterwards, I felt sick and drained. Along with the MS, he'd had a lifetime of substance abuse and addiction attached to him. Although he had been clean for a little while, the demons were still inside him. I later found out that when he'd had had a healing from a master monk in

Tibet, it knocked the monk out for two days. I took it easy and decided on a forced fast in preparation for meeting the meditation group.

I knew for sure that I would return to spend more time in San Marcos after my pilgrimage. Already it was pulling me back.

I arrived in Antigua, and Ladan Radcliffe was there to greet me with a massive hug. It was great to be with her and share her excitement for the ten days that were to come.

When I arrived at the hotel, I bumped into Rob, who I knew from my meditation group back home. Rob was a massive Mancunian guy, ex-boxer, ex-bouncer and basically the last person you would expect to see on a spiritual pilgrimage. He was a healer and medium and a beautiful person with a wicked sense of humour.

Someone then told me Rob, and I were sharing a room. Disaster, I thought. He always snored loudly in the meditations, and I wanted to get some sleep. Fortunately, Rob had asked for his own room not to ruin my trip.

Antigua was one of the most beautiful cities I had ever visited. It had a very colonial feel to it, beautiful single storey buildings all differing in colour as if a paint bomb had been thrown through the streets. The place just oozed class and sophistication. Everywhere just looked cool, with its grid-patterned roads and cobbled streets.

I met lots of people in the group. There was Joyce; a brilliant Jamaican energy healer who spoke in tongues and the language of light I had just started to learn about. She was sharing a room with Kerry, a beautiful shamanic specialist from Liverpool. There was Lilly from Russia who was an artist and soul retrieval expert, and Melinda Cooper, the clairvoyant from London who I took an instant shine to. Then there was Laden's daughter, Vanessa, and her friend Donna, the whispering youngsters of the group. There was the crazy Brazilian, Sandra, Phil 'The Hat' from Bristol, Sandra the medium and her husband Wayne the businessman, the lovely Marylyn and Linda the Reiki practitioner. Then there was Debra, the life coach and her partner, Paul from Burnley, Dan 'The Knowledge' and his partner Dee the energy worker, again from meditation group back home.

When everyone had met up, there seemed to be a lingering unsolved problem. Ladan had been guided spiritually to bring 21 souls to Guatemala for 12.12.12, but there were only twenty of us. I think she was a little pre-occupied with not having 21. In a way, she thought she was failing to fulfil her guide's wishes. I told her to chill and that everything would work itself out.

We went onto the roof of the hotel and started our first meditation together. After we had meditated and connected to the energy of the Maya and Guatemala, we all hugged heart on heart, (so heads to the right people and it only counts as a hug if it lasts for 20 seconds).

They were massive hugs. They were the kind you give your mum or partner when you haven't seen them for a while. It was deep, really deep, and felt like we'd all become connected. I felt like I was starting to get some of what I craved from my spiritual community; a sense of love and the roots that were missing from my life.

It was a beautiful thing to be around this diversely special group of people, and I felt very honoured to be part of it. I was really looking forward to tapping into the collective knowledge of the group over the next ten days and trying to forget this person I had created who I didn't like anymore. I wanted to try and remember my true essence.

That evening we had our welcome meeting in a local restaurant with our newly acquainted guide, Josh, who would be whisking us all over the country on our pilgrimage. He was high-energy. A very charismatic and knowledgeable guy with some amazing tattoos, a mohawk haircut and a black stud in his ear.

As he was telling us about his life, he spoke about San Marcos. I asked if he knew Benjamin.

He said, 'Yes, I've known him since I was two years old'.

'Crazy man,' I said, 'I've just spent the last few days with him!'

That evening a few of us stayed up chatting about our excitement and all the amazing things that were going to happen. Rob told us an array of stories about being a bouncer in Manchester and fighting. It was obviously all in his past, but the vivid way he told the stories fascinated me and the two young girls in the group gawped. Me and my roommate Dom went to bed in a kind of excited haze, trying to figure out what our part was in the midst of all these extremely gifted and special people.

We were up early for the next meditation on the rooftop and began making our fifth-dimensional rainbow bridge, which lost me as I floated off into another world.

I could never remember what happened in the meditations. It

never seemed to stay in my mind. Instead, it just floated through, and I struggled to follow Ladan's instructions, hoping my subconscious would do the work for me.

When we came back to this dimension, we were taken on a little tour of Antigua. The churches and cathedrals were so intricately designed with pastel colours, and they gave me an immediate energetic lift. Boring estates the world over should take heed— paint those grey buildings pastel yellow, blue, green, pink and purple and a lot of social problems would fade away. Colour therapy man, I thought in a haze of 1960s psychedelia.

I spent a lot of time chatting with Melinda and found her fascinating. I had no idea that she was quite a famous clairvoyant in the UK. She was Rob's mate, and he would constantly take the piss out of her for being so ditzy. She said she would like to read me. I said 'ok'. She didn't have her cards but said she would read my palm and give me some messages. I was impatiently looking forward to the experience.

Later that day was our first group bus journey, which was luxurious compared to the shuttle buses I had become accustomed to. We were heading for Lake Atitlan and Josh's home town of Panajachel. We were staying in a hotel called Dos Mundos, and it felt like we had the whole place to ourselves. Smart little cottages surrounded lush decorative jungle and a swimming pool.

Melinda decided now was a good time to read my palm. Straight away, she became this other person; completely focused, the ditziness gone, and a totally professional and compassionate demeanour in its place.

She started off with my Piscean tendencies; very emotional, forgetting things very quickly, not liking confrontation, backing off from arguments, but remembering things from way back. By reading my aura, she sensed I had been in love twice and had two massive heartbreaks around me. She could see the negative times in my life had taken place at the ages of seven and seventeen, and that each new decade would see massive changes in me.

She told me I had changed a lot in my twenties and that I was now a totally different person. She said she saw me in the future in the snow wearing a mask on some kind of expedition. She said I would write two books which would be published, and that I should have already written two (I instantly knew what they should have been). She told me that when I was a child, I had been very introverted and shy and that I had started to wear a mask to make people think I was confident and without any worries. She told me that I wasn't the extrovert and party piece she had taken me for and that I put on an act. Spot on Melinda, I thought.

She told me there was somebody in my past that I had never quite gotten over and I knew it was my ex from University. Immediately she said I had kissed a lot of princesses and then she started laughing her head off. 'Just a couple' I said.

She said I had lost two people close together, and then she said, 'Who died of cancer?'

Bang.

Wow. 'Me mum,' I murmured, as this wave of energy pulsated through my body, and I tried to stop the emotion from spilling out of me.

'She stands around you, you know.' It was very quick, very aggressive, people get years, and she got nothing. 'And Mary is standing with your mum,' she said.

She asked me what the Irish connection was. Me dad, I told her. Then she said, 'Mary is connected with him'.

She then said there was a John or Joe, who was my child guide.

'He died young and keeps you childlike; he is your laughter,' she said.

So that's why I have this laugh, I thought. I said, 'I don't know who it is.'

She then blurted out, 'Your mum's here. She was two totally different characters, very complicated.'

Then she came out with, 'Who had the drinking problem?'

'Me granddad,' I said.

Then the one that hit me hard, 'Why did you call two people "Mum"?'

At first, I felt guilty, as if my mum was upset with me.

Melinda said, 'Who was the other women you called "Mum" and spent a lot of time with?'

I knew instantly and felt even more grief. It was my French mum, Laurence who became like a mother to me after my mum had died. She treated me like a son and was there for me more than anyone else. She became my living guardian angel when my mum passed.

I had drifted away from Laurence in the past year and immediately wanted to get in contact and say 'I love you, French

Mum'.

Melinda said, 'Your mum wants to thank her very, very much for all that she did and wants to tell her that she is extremely grateful to her for getting her little boy through such dark times.'

Then she started going all over the place. It was as if vast amounts of messages were being sent and she was trying to transmit them simultaneously.

'Your mum's telling me you wrote something and put it in her coffin?'

Tears filled me as I remembered.

She said, 'Your Mum got really upset when you did that and that she reads it every day.'

This was the poem I put in her coffin that I had written after I found out she was very ill:

Mum
Trying to get from the other side of the world to see you, Mum
Trying to get on a flight so I can be near you, Mum
The pain I felt today really brought meaning to you, Mum
When I sit back and think of all the times I needed you, Mum
Bring tears to my eyes every time I see you, Mum
A heart-wrenching almost drowning sensation fills me, Mum
Don't know what to do just got to get near you, Mum

'Your mum said she felt you doing this on her arm when she was in the coffin.' Melinda was waving her arm in a stroking motion, and I just couldn't speak. It made me break down, words wouldn't flow, and I was choked. It took me right back to that moment in the Chapel of Rest, thinking of the strength I felt I had to give the rest of the family and not really knowing what the fuck I was going to do without her.

All the moments I wanted to give her in the future flashed before my eyes; being at my children's births, being the best grandma in the world, becoming best friends with the person I planned to spend the rest of my life with, holding me in my sad times, me holding her in hers, and seeing her pride whenever I achieved anything, however big or small. I felt like I had no one at that moment.

My mother was my world, my linchpin. I wondered if I could carry on without her. I truly felt that if I could be one hundred per cent sure we would be reunited after death; I would take my own life immediately.

She said, 'She heard everything you said over the coffin.'

I welled up even more; I remembered talking to this corpse. I knew she was no longer in there, but how could something that was such a big part of me not actually still exist in some form?

Melinda was breaking down at this point as well. 'She said, where's her ring?'

'It's at home.'

'Why didn't you bring it? She really wanted you to bring that ring,' Melinda said. She said, 'She wants to enjoy this journey with you, and that's her portal to you, so get it posted'. She said my mum was quite choked up, and it was making Melinda feel quite upset. How could she be affected like this by something that sceptics say doesn't exist?

I never realised how much that ring meant to my mum.
Melinda said she felt my mum was so full of love. 'She loves you so, so much,' she said.

I welled up and got this tingle down my spine and felt all this love fill me.

The reading had given me the good kick up the arse I often needed to guide me in my life. Hopefully, the same kick that had been the catalyst for this trip.

Melinda said my future relationships were deciphered by two lines on my palm. Two marriage lines stood out, and she said I would have two children; one with one wife and one with the other. She said I would have my first child at 34, and this blew me away. I kind of wanted one sooner, to provide my life with the unconditional love that had been absent since my mother's death. But it really excited me, and I wondered who the mother would be? I knew that the lady I was in love with who provided me with this bundle of unconditional love would become unconditionally loved and worshipped by me for eternity.

She said, 'what's your girlfriend's name now?' I said, 'Fhian.'

She said, 'I can't see her in your future.

I felt really strange after the reading had finished and had a million questions. I thanked Melinda very much for the messages. It's weird, but after me Mum died, I felt for the first time in my life as though I had to start behaving myself. It was as if I was being watched. It was a weird feeling, but it made me start making changes for the better. Maybe my mother's death was the catalyst for my spiritual awakening.

The reading brought up a lot of emotions. I didn't want to hurt people anymore, and I wanted to be honest, but as always I wasn't 100% sure of my feelings and what the right thing to do was. What was my heart, and what was my head? This always seemed to be my problem.

I sat and contemplated this pre-destined life and got massively excited about the prospect of having my first child at the age of 34. Something in me knew this would bring me some kind of inner peace and focus.

The third day of the pilgrimage started with another Rainbow Bridge meditation. I was imagining myself sitting inside this yin and yang cube that Ladan said had six corners, but I was sure a cube had eight corners. By the time I had figured out I was right, I wasn't sure if that's what she had actually said. It seemed the meditation had moved onto the cube being inside your heart, enveloping the earth inside a yin and yang cube.

Breathe!

I had no idea if I was supposed to be imagining myself in the first cube inside another cube that was wrapped around the earth, surrounded by a fifth-dimensional tetrahedron. I was properly lost!

I decided to give up and hope my subconscious would pick it up and process it. I focused on quieting my mind.

After the meditation, I collected my crystals from the altar and couldn't find my piece of labradorite I had bought to gift to the spirits of the lake and the lost city and souls that reside there. I was gutted. I had bought it specifically and had looked at it every day of my trip so far. I resigned myself to the fact that I would have no gift for the lake.

We set off on a boat across the lake to visit Santiago De Atitlan and its evil saint, Maximon, who predicted the lake was going to rise and that the villagers would have to move from where they were living. The people didn't listen and cut his legs and arms off and threw him into the lake.

When his prophecy came true, many were drowned and more displaced. They made him a saint and worshipped him by feeding a model of him liquor and cigarettes every day.

When we got above the point in the lake where the ancient lost city was located, we turned off the engines, and our guide asked for a minute's silence, in respect of the spirits.

We started to meditate.

At the end of the meditation, people started to gift their pieces of labradorite and I was feeling a bit sad that I'd lost mine. Then I decided to gift myself to the lake, taking off my clothes and diving into the 500-metre deep water in my boxer shorts.

It felt amazing to be able to give myself to the lake, and I assumed I was supposed to lose the crystal for this exact reason. Many of the group had vivid visions of a lost society beneath the lake, with its narrow streets and little houses. Rob said he was being enticed around by an elegant Jaguar jumping over the walls.

As we made our way through the winding, scruffy back streets to Maximon's current residence, we saw women breastfeeding, people selling fruit, ladies making clothes and bead bracelets and families building. There were little girls as young as three helping their father fill buckets with cement. Their faces were covered in dirt and the brightest smiles beamed back at us.

Maximon's residence seemed more like a crack den than a place of worship. Cigarettes and booze littered the whole room as Maximon took centre stage, with his two current guardians sitting on either side of him. In a year's time, Maximon would be moved to his next residence.

In his current form, Maximon is a stuffed doll that sits upright on a wooden chair with his legs dangling down, like some kind of warlord in a spaghetti western. We paid our respects to the saint. Josh fed him many cigarettes, and his guardian took the liquor that we had all made a wish on. The guardian blessed it and feeds it to the grateful alcoholic that was Maxi-mon.

That evening we were off to a shamanic ceremony in the mountains overlooking the lake. As we made the treacherous walk along the cliff top, some of the group were a bit scared of the steep drop below and couldn't believe parents would let their kids play next to such danger.

I argued there was no danger. Why would the kid jump off the edge?

I remembered an episode of The Human Planet, where there were infants standing in the doorway of a treehouse with a 200-foot drop below whilst the mums just went about their business. It's as if we create kids that are stupid and prone to accidents because they are so wrapped in cotton wool. In the west, you see parents weighed down with a 20kg baby pack in case of all emergencies and trotting little Peter off to the hospital after an aggressive sneeze.

We arrived at our cave ceremony and were told it wasn't going to take place in a cave and would be on top of a hill. The shaman arrived looking like any local in jeans and a shirt, and I instantly thought they had just got someone off the street to say a few words. The local jeans and shirt wearing 'shaman' got out what I can only describe as burgers and started to build a fire. Lilly took some Polaroids of some local kids, and they all posed to attention. One boy shouted at his brother for having a really dirty T-shirt, which made me piss myself.

The 'shaman' was talking us through the ceremony, and I was half-listening, thinking, this charlatan is having us over. All of a sudden, I couldn't take my eyes off him. He was calling in the ancestors and talking about the importance of the upcoming dates. All the ancestors were focused on these times, he said, and he told us how lucky he felt to be alive at a time that only happens every five thousand, two hundred years and on a larger scale every twenty-six thousand years. He said none of his grandchildren would experience these times and that we were all gatekeepers of these specific dates. Ancient prayers were uttered, and the spirits called to assist in the ceremony.

The first ten of us were called to be blessed and cleansed around the fire. I went pretty dizzy and was sitting in a meditative pose when the next ten were taken into the centre.

Josh was sat down, and the shaman started doing an individual ritual on him. I assumed this was for our entertainment, and the shaman spat sprayed the blessed liquor we had been allowed to bring from Maximon all over and around Josh. As he chanted and prayed, firing liquor in the air, I realised this wasn't for show, but still, I had no idea what was going on. The shaman then got a shaken Josh up and, once he had regained his composure, Josh said, 'As I was entering the circle with the group, the shaman identified an entity or dark spirit on me and said it needed to be cleared before the ceremony could continue.' Josh then told us that a while back he had taken a hit of LSD for eight people and nearly died. Apparently he still had some bad energy attached to him from this experience, and the shaman had to get rid of it.

I felt really moved that Josh was comfortable enough with our group to share such an experience, considering we were only on day three.

The ceremony continued, and the rest of the group, plus Josh, had their clearing and blessing.

When the ceremony finished, the shaman thanked the spirits, and we came back to reality after being utterly transfixed for the past two hours.

We travelled from the lake to Guatemala City to catch a flight back to Flores. On the way, Phil 'The Hat' had arranged for us to have lunch and meditation at his friend's holistic centre. It was called Parialaj and ran and owned by Phil's friend Lydia.

Set in the lush jungle, we were immediately pounced on by a massive mastiff-labrador cross called Paolo. We got a tour around this very spiritual place. There were altars all over the grounds depicting the Indian god Ganesh, the Mayan Kej and the Virgin Mary. We were then transported over the road to a magical place with the most spectacular circular altar with a crystal skull at all its cardinal points.

The skulls were just spectacular, and I was completely blown away. I had never seen such an amazing space. The four colours of corn were represented in the four directions of The Mayan Cross. It was comprised of Day Signs (glyphs) which were oriented towards the four directions. Each direction was a grandfather/mother, a cosmic force that has character and specific qualities which influence the Day Sign. Each direction had a colour, two of which appeared in each Mayan cross. The vertical axis had one colour, the horizontal axis another. These directions/colours contributed to your unique energetic signature and determined your compatibility with other Day Signs. The east was red and represented Father Sun, the way of the visionary, knowledge, the crocodile, the serpent and offerings. The west was blue/black and represented Grandmother, moon/ocean, the way of the teacher, monkey, bird, rainstorm, dawn, and deer. The south was yellow and represented Mother Earth, the way of the healer, the road, wisdom, the sun, the net, and seed. Finally, the north was white and represented Father Sky, the way of the sacred warrior, the jaguar, flint, wind, death and the dog.

The skulls were mesmerising. There was a huge black obsidian skull, one smaller white quartz skull, and a smaller black obsidian skull. I was in some kind of skull orgy. I was being drawn to these skulls time and time again and had no idea why. I wanted the purpose to be revealed!

The skulls are supposed to hold all the information of the universe, of history, of the future, of everything. Quartz crystals are in every bit of technology we have; mobile phones, computers etc., so in the form of an unexplainably sculpted skull, how could they not retain information?

The powerful elite has long attempted to sabotage the ancestral memory by distorting the image of the skull in our minds, like a marketing campaign or clever PR that manipulates people's brain's for their gain. Connotations of pirates, poison, Halloween ghouls and death have all been symbolised by the skull in a negative fashion.

In Mayan culture, death is celebrated, even looked forward to. It was a thing of beauty like birth. Our society has a fear of it, and we don't see it as a transition. It's the one thing that is guaranteed, and we are seen as morbid if we discuss it.

We see it as an end, nothingness and since the death of my mother and feeling her around me all the time this became something I wanted to start to question.

We all gathered around the ceremonial space and had a short meditation, then got the chance to connect with each skull as they were passed around the circle. The sheer weight of the black one was intimidating, but they all had their own individual energy.

Lydia used the skulls to channel information, which was what had brought her to Guatemala in the first place. Parialaj was a vision she'd had, and she made that vision a reality in five years.

I really loved the skulls and felt this very special place was where I would like to spend the 21.12.12 celebrations. There were lots of options bouncing about for that date; going to Chitzen Itza, the main astrology site of the Maya, or to the rainbow gathering in Palenque. Both would be amazing, but crazy busy. Being with the skulls was looking like my preferred option so far.

There were rumblings around the group, and a few of us had started whispering how after the shaman ceremony we felt maybe Josh was number 21.

We were off our tits when we arrived at Flores to meet our local guide, David. I don't think he knew what had hit him when he got on the bus. It was as if we were all really pissed or on drugs. For some reason, that short time in the air had sent everyone loopy, and we were all singing, laughing and having a great time. Josh thought we had gone mad, David thought he was about to encounter the worst two days of his life, and we were all buzzing. Mainly Ttotalling Brits on tour were causing a ruckus.

CHAPTER 4
SEX TIMES, LIFE,
1989-2001

From the age seven until about thirteen, my life was consumed by football. I was obsessed. I lived, breathed and drank it. Every week I religiously bought Match magazine and Shoot, and one called Football Superstars that came out monthly. I played every day. I always had a ball at my feet.

When I got to high school, I started playing for the school team. I was a really ferocious little player, full of energy and passion. I had a reputation for fouling people and doing dirty tackles. I just wanted to kick people as hard as I could. I was a leader, and I ended up being the captain of the team I played for at the weekends.

This is where I ended up playing from the age of 11 until I was 21. This all came about after me mum hooked up with me step-dad. He managed the first team of Wythenshawe Amateurs, so I left the team I was playing for in the depths of Wythenshawe for one on the outskirts. From the moment my mum met me step-dad-to-be, all my time was taken up by football, watching me step-dad's side play on a Saturday, then going to watch the players he wanted to sign on a Sunday.

On Sunday afternoon, I would play in my age group, year after year in all weather conditions, on all types of pitches. There was dog shit all over some of the pitches we played on. There were also pitches covered in rocks and bricks or burn-out marks that destroyed the grass and were leftover from whatever the local youths had been up to the night before.

I also remember dingy change rooms that stank of piss and the syringes scattered all over the place, which we were told to avoid as we tiptoed towards the playing field. There was a lot of aggression on the pitches, lots of young boys with varying degrees of social problems from dysfunctional families living in a place where being a tough man was idolised. We were all thrown together to play a very physical game and attempted to take some of our aggression and frustration out on each other.

The rest of my time would be spent at the football club where me step-dad spent most of his time. This place became like a home away from home for me and all the colourful people who graced it. Lots of the guys who played and helped out with the teams brought their kids, and it became a pivotal part of my life for ten years. Football was all I knew, and all my friends were associated with it.

However, there was a period of a year or so at the age of thirteen or fourteen when I lost interest. At thirteen I discovered girls, and it took me a while to figure out that football and girls could go hand in hand. When I started high school I had a really tough couple of years to start with. I went from being one of the most popular boys at primary school to a not so popular kid in high school.

I used to get the piss taken out of me by my mates for not having kissed a girl yet. At thirteen, that was seen as being frigid, a word that I didn't even know the meaning of when I first heard it. I always had girlfriends at primary school, but I had never kissed any of them properly; I just played football and then maybe punched them when I was walking past.

I did have an attraction for girls, though. I remember going on holidays with me dad or me mum and being obsessed with some of the beautiful topless women around the pools and on the beach. They would always play with me, and I would be really mean and cheeky to the ones that deep inside I liked. I remember being in Tunisia with my dad and a topless woman would always let my lie on top of her. It was completely innocent for her, but I was overly excited. I would manoeuvre my body so her breasts would cover my skin.

As I got older, I would fantasise as I walked down the beach, imagining what all these gorgeous women would be like to hold and kiss and touch. I had no idea really about sex at the time, but something in me was so very drawn to beauty and curves and trying to see what was between their legs. It would make my mind go wild. I would go missing for hours and find my favourite one, usually with the biggest boobs and a lovely slim brown body. I would position myself, so I could sit there and stare without being noticed.

At high school, my hairstyle wasn't doing me any good. Me mum wouldn't let me have it cut like I wanted, but eventually, she gave in, and I started donning curtains. I would wet my hair, comb it back then split it down the middle. Then I would pull it forward again and create an entrance to my face, as opposed to the bouffant I had been hiding behind for so long.

This was a defining moment in my school life and my social status. I went from being a nobody with the ladies to being sought after. I was starting to get noticed, and I was loving it.

The first girl I started going out with was a beautiful brunette from my class called Katie. Like most of the fit girls, she had nice legs and wore her school socks pulled up just over her knees. It was as if opening up my face to the world had allowed people to see me for the first time, and they were starting to like it.

I had only held hands with my now-girlfriend, but with the school disco coming up I realised this would be my chance to kiss her. My mates were putting pressure on me to do it, and I was massively nervous. I had no idea what I was supposed to do, so at home I would practice kissing the inside of my arm, pressing my lips against my skin and then thrusting my tongue in and out and swirling it around. This is what it kind of looked like when I saw it on TV, and I would get a funny tingle that would shoot to my penis and embarrass me in front of me mum.

The disco came, and I kissed her. I kissed her for a very long time, and it was amazing. I became overly giddy and excited. I'm not sure if I'd been drinking, but I couldn't get rid of my erection. There were some very pissed kids there. I remember one thirteen-year-old got taken by ambulance to hospital after drinking a bottle of whiskey.

I started bouncing around the disco. I wanted to kiss all the fit girls. For some of them, there was a queue. Some people would queue for a long time and then get to the girl and be turned away. Like queuing to get in a club and getting to the front and being turned away by the bouncers for wearing on the wrong shoes.

At one point, my friend grabbed me and whipped his finger across my nose. 'Can you smell that?'

I said, 'What is it?'

Then he told me about a girl who would let you finger her, so I went and got in that queue.

It was as if I had become addicted to women. That evening I wanted them all, I wanted to have sex, I wanted to know how it felt. It was like an explosion had taken place inside my head, heart and genitals. Football disappeared from my horizon, and I became infatuated with girls. I started to move further and further up the league table of attractiveness as I became more and more aware of the way I looked, what I wore, and how I did my hair.

My friends, however, were still telling me I was virtually frigid, so I went on a mission to kiss every attractive girl in the school. What did I have to do to shake off this unwanted label? I'd even fingered lots of girls. I'd play under the table with the girls in my class, exploring the wondrous gems that lay between their legs. I was completely addicted.

I then started to go out with a girl from the year below me and fell in love; she was twelve, and I was thirteen. On New Year's day of 1995, I made it my resolution to lose my virginity to her that year, so we went home and did it that day. Then we did it as often as we could. I thought that the quicker you did it, the better you were, and I could do it really quick, so I thought I was amazing.

Everyone at school found out. Maybe I told everyone, and it spread. It was like I had opened the flood gates and all the other boys became desperate to lose theirs. I had gone from being this frigid thirteen-year-old to being the first boy in my year to have sex, and all in less than twelve months.

Football didn't even register anymore. All I wanted to do was have sex with my girlfriend as often as possible and be in love, a feeling I had never felt before, but something I was now addicted to.

Soon other lads were starting to lose their virginity too, and we would compare notes and chat about it in the most immature of ways. We all had no idea what it was about, no idea about contraception and no idea about STDs. We were just horny little kids with parents incapable and unwilling to educate us, and we wanted to shag each other as often as possible.

Just after my fourteenth birthday, disaster struck. The girl I was with got pregnant. The school found out, then her parents, and then mine. She had just turned thirteen, so was taken for an abortion and we were told we could no longer see each other. We were in love, and it felt like our hearts were being ripped apart. Getting rid of the baby didn't really register with me. I didn't want a kid, that was for sure, but I also don't think I even had a say, as the school and my girlfriend's parents dealt with it all.

Knowing that me mum and me stepdad were going to be told by the school, I ran away to me dad's for a few days. I didn't want to face the music. When I finally did my whole world changed. Me mum and me stepdad would no longer let me do anything. I had to be home really early, I wasn't allowed to have girls around and they watched my every move. Inside all I still wanted was sex, sex, sex, but this was the point when my focus allowed football back in.

My life revolved around two things from then on— trying to find the most beautiful girls to have sex with and to play football as much as possible. I went out with nearly all the best-looking girls in the school; in my year, the year above, the year below and once the year below that.

I even got the unattainable beautiful girls who were really posh and played classical violin. I wanted them all. The violin girl had parents who were lecturers and had written books. It was like being taken into a world I didn't know existed. I would go to her house, and she would play Beethoven on the piano, and I would have to tell her to be quiet because Match of the Day was on the TV. Beethoven and anything outside of my reality of sex and football just seemed pointless.

Because I lived really close to school, I had a tactic for getting girls back to my house. I would ask a girl I liked, fancied or just wanted to have sex with if she wanted to wag class and come to my house and watch TV or play computer games. Once they were at my house, which was always empty in the day, I would take then up to my room. Once they were in my room, it was game over.

Everywhere I went, I wondered what girls might be there and who I could potentially have sex with. This lasted for almost sixteen years; every moment of my life was shadowed by these thoughts of potential suitors. I would fantasise about girls who were taken or who were a lot older and fantasise about any girl who took my eye.

At college, the same pattern continued, but for around 18 months I had a relationship with a stunning redhead who I hooked up with as we were leaving high school. She was completely nuts, but I fell in love with her. We were an item until I lost interest. Again she got pregnant and had an abortion. I didn't even think about the consequences at the time, I just thought it was a bit stupid of the girl to not take her pill and put herself through something that was avoidable.

Once this relationship was dead, I was back on the hunt, and again I got this unattainable stunning religious girl at college. She was a virgin and wanted to save herself until marriage. It was getting to the point where it was going to happen between us and for the first time in my life, I did a decent thing and broke it off. Something in me knew it was a massive thing for her and for me it was just sport.

Girls came and went, short relationships, brief moments of love, and as many one night stands as I could have. I got a reputation, and many girls didn't want to go near me. It also seemed that the reputation made girls inquisitive about what it would be like. I was no great lover unless I was drunk and my inhabitations were gone and my confidence high. When I was sober I could never figure out why I could have great sex with one girl and then be awful with another. There didn't seem to be any pattern. It was just really bad or really good.

I was always counting the number of girls I had slept with and typically adding a few to make me look even better in front of the people I was boasting to. It was as if this number 64 my brother had given me (girls he had slept with) was the Holy Grail and I had to get to that as soon as I could; otherwise I was a failure and unsuccessful as a lover and a Browne.

When I was in relationships, I was still after getting as much as I possibly could. It was like I had to live up to this persona I had created for myself whenever I was out with my friends. I would get paralytically drunk and forget my whole evening, but more often than not I would wake up in my bed at home with my clothes neatly hung up in my cupboard and no idea how I'd gotten there. This kept happening until I was into my early twenties and I realised I couldn't do it anymore. I wasn't getting as much sex as I wanted because I was always too drunk.

That's when I restricted my drinking and found ecstasy.

TIKAL,
THE JOURNEY,
DECEMBER 2012

The next day we woke up early to head for the ruins of Yaxha which was situated above a beautiful lake. David told us the lake was full of crocodiles. After most people had sprayed themselves to death with insect repellent, we sat on the bank readying ourselves for meditation, choking from the fumes, some kneeling and some cross-legged looking out to the lake.

Once our eyes were closed in meditation, the thoughts of potential crocodiles that were currently residing within its depths ready for breakfast vaporised. Ladan led the meditation, asking the permission of the gods to allow us access to the lake and Yaxha. The Lady of the Lake was called in, and the masculine and feminine energies were merged.

As always, I disappeared into a dream within a dream. It was intense, and the atmosphere was pure and gentle. The lake was perfectly still, reflecting the surrounding mountains perfectly.

Towards the end of the meditation, a male and female from the group were chosen to make offerings to show gratitude and to ask for guidance. Dan and Rice and Pea Joyce were chosen.

It had got to the stage on the coach that when I screamed 'Rice', Joyce would then say 'and Pea' and then everyone else would echo it the second time I shouted 'Rice'.

Joyce and Dan each said a blessing and threw their respective crystals into the lake. Joyce started speaking in the language of light. I had no idea what she was saying, but it sounded very beautiful, and somehow it really reverberated in my consciousness, as if I had heard it before.

She told us of how the language had just started coming out of her one day. Some call it speaking in tongues, and some say it is a lost language they used to speak in Atlantis. Others say it's a language from another planet. Lots of people say it's bollocks.

I like bollocks in that case.

We all paid our individual respects to the Lady of the Lake, and everyone started discussing the amazing experiences they'd had during the meditation. Some had seen the Lady of the Lake rising from its depths and blessing our journey, giving us permission to be connected to all the energies of the lake.

As we approached the little jetty, the perfectly still lake started to ripple from the other side, tiny little waves making their way towards us. There was absolutely no wind. We stood there in amazement, thanking the lake for such a spectacle.

A very steep wide path led to the ruins of Yaxha. I could imagine all the Mayans carrying goods and building materials up this massive expanse that took us twenty minutes to scale. Carrying only wrist cameras, most of our group were exhausted from the climb and halfway up, we stopped at a small ruin full of hieroglyphs for a rest.

David and Josh took it in turns to dazzle us with their knowledge of all things Mayan. Like McEnroe and Bourg, it was difficult to separate them. They told us how scientists and anthropologists couldn't explain how the stones to build the temples had been transported to their locations.

We made our way to the first temple, and Josh said, 'Do you guys realise you have the wind God Ik (pronounced eeeeek) following you?'

I'd just thought it was the wind. But as we approached each different area and temple, the wind would whip up on cue on this very warm, still day and breeze around us.

We got to the two main temples with the plaza in between and were told to simply find a space and meditate alone. I called in the wind God Ik, and on cue the wind would caress my cross-legged lotus. I tried this a few times, making sure it wasn't just a coincidence. But as I had learnt in the last year, there was no such thing as a coincidence.

We walked to the next set of four temples, and a few of us climbed to the top of the largest one. Josh showed us how the Mayans would climb the steps in a criss-cross fashion with their heads bowed to earn the respect of the gods so they would be allowed to ascend the nine levels of the underworld. The steps were huge, and I couldn't imagine how the tiny Mayans could make their way up these structures, especially with their heads bowed.

It was well worth the climb. Looking out behind the temple, I could see the vast canopy of dense jungle. The sounds of birds and howler monkeys and the aroma of plants and flowers filled the hot midday air.

The last gift Yaxha had to offer us was its largest temple that looked over the lake we had meditated by. It gave stunning views of the nearby Lake Peten and the surrounding jungle.

Marylyn battled up the wooden stairway that had been built to preserve the temple and keep clumsy westerners safe. I was a little bit in awe of Marylyn. As we boarded the bus, she looked like she had just run a marathon.

Jaguar Inn, where we were staying for the night was a plush setting deep in the Jungle of Tikal. We arrived a couple of hours before sunset, grabbed some food and waited for the night time sounds and sights of the jungle to materialise. Once the sun had left for a rest, the stars came out to play, and as I ate, people came in with stories of moving stars and weird movements in the skies. The infinite sky infiltrated my eyes and imagination as always. I loved thinking about what was out there looking at us, the past the present and the future all simultaneously being processed by the connection of sight and mind.

Phil 'the Hat' had a star app on his iPad, so we tried to figure out a few constellations and how the zodiac related to different places in the sky. The easiest ones to spot seemed to be Jupiter, Mars, Orion's belt, and The Pleiades.

There were a few murmurs of going into the park at night. It was illegal, but I was well up for it as I really wanted to see the stars from a Mayan observatory.

As me and Phil 'the Hat' were stargazing, David and Josh asked if we wanted to go.

'Yeah, man!' Josh told us it would cost a two hundred quetzal bribe each.

I said, Amazing, yeah!'

Josh asked the rest of the group, expecting three or four yeses.

He got lots, including Marylyn who had just ran a marathon and now fancied a triathlon.

Like excited school kids, we set off in the pitch black, guided by Josh and David's flash lights. We could see nothing when the lights were off, but we were happily wandering into the unknown.

We had to take it quite slow as people were struggling in the pitch black and with the rugged terrain, though everyone seemed extremely calm and focused. As we approached the entrance to the main Mayan grounds, we each asked the spirit guards of Tikal for permission to enter, which we all seemed to be granted, without the need for the two hundred quetzal bribe.

We got to our first small temple and were blown away by the view of the stars from its summit. We walked into the massive expanse of the main plaza with Temple One built for the Cacao King dominating. Facing it about a hundred metres away was the slightly smaller Temple Two that had been built for his wife. The Temples were massive, cutting through the night sky in an intimidating way. We were told it was unknown how they were built, as scientists say the only way they could have been constructed was from the top down, which made no sense to our rational minds.

The two temples were flanked by the housing quarters of the elite, and we wandered from the centre of the plaza to the main altar. The altar was also a fire pit that had been made especially for the end of the Mayan calendar ceremonies on 21.12.12. Looking at our surroundings and then back at each other, you could see a glint in everyone's eyes, silently knowing what we were all thinking. It seemed like an unmissable opportunity, a once in a lifetime moment. Josh knew the look on our faces, which were being illuminated by the moonlight. He said we'd have to ask permission and it seemed like again we were granted it, as we started to hold hands around the huge main altar.

We stood with our arms fully stretched out, just about managing to keep hold of the person either side. I felt at complete peace, connecting with my guides, the Mayan energies, all kinds of spirits, and what I can only describe as things.

After about twenty minutes of deep meditation, a bird or a bat swept from out of nowhere, flapping its wings right in front of my face. It immediately snapped me out of my meditation, and as I opened my eyes I could see nothing. I then realised how much pain I was in. My arms felt as if they were coming out of their sockets and my knees were aching. I wanted to sit down. I tried to get back into the meditation, but I was too aware of my discomfort now and wanted this to end.

It went on and on and on and on, and I was getting more and more uncomfortable and pissed off. I closed my eyes, opened my eyes saw everyone else had their eyes shut and thought I was letting the team down. I again tried to get back in but I couldn't, so I looked at the stars which were amazing for a nanosecond until my arms and legs wanted to snap. I wanted out, or I wanted to sit down.

I was thinking, *what's the point?*

Why are we all putting up with this?
Am I the only one in pain?
Surely not?
I questioned myself for being impatient. I questioned my body for not being able to put up with this and questioned my mind for all this questioning. Twenty minutes later, Ladan started to talk I was like 'Yes, thank God! I thought I was going to collapse.

Ladan's news was bad. She had been guided that we had to take two steps to the left then two steps to the right to activate something I had no interest in knowing about. I just wanted to get whatever it was over with, so I could just sit down.

In my head, I was like, 'Come on, let's sit down, chill and look at the stars, do some hippy chanting or something'. But no, back and forth, two steps left, two steps right, agonising.

How was Marylyn doing this? She was in her sixties. Was I being a girl?

Regardless I'd had enough. My inner evil self was saying 'Liam just walk away, fuck them you don't need this shit. I stayed. We moved two steps to the left, two steps to the right. I felt like I was in a line dancing competition at a tacky rodeo event.

Then we stopped.

YES, we can sit. I braced myself for the delight of the flat, unstrained bliss the dusty earth below was about to offer me as a reward.

NO YOU DON'T.

Back into meditation, everyone went. I'd had enough. Another five minutes passed, and I began to wonder whether this was an endurance test I hadn't been given the drug to be able to compete in. Had everyone been told something I hadn't? Was everyone around me, including two teenaged girls, a sixty-three-year-old lady, and some middle-aged people all super athletes?

Then Ladan started to groan and stumble, and I'm thinking, 'What the fuck is going on now?' She started to spasm and almost dropped to the ground but was held up by poor Marylyn and David, the guide. She stooped really low, and her whole frame looked distorted.

I'm thinking, 'Come on, Ladan, we don't need a show. I want to sit down and rest.'

She continued to spasm, and instead of asking if she was all right, my evil side was cursing. 'What is she doing? Why is she dragging this out even further? I want to sit down and rest. Is it because the Mayan Gods haven't floated down from space that you have to provide us with some made-up magic?'

Almost half her usual size, Ladan spoke in this deep, low voice, introducing herself as Lord Arcturian. I was thinking, 'This is bollocks! This is bullshit! It's just a show, surely not, Ladan, you don't have to try this hard. It's embarrassing.'

She continued to address the group in this low voice, shaking from side to side.

I was convinced I was with a bunch of nutters and that I was having the wool pulled over my eyes. As I stood there procrastinating about this whole experience, doubting all those around me and labelling them as gullible, naïve idiots, from nowhere, it was as if two bolts of live electrical cable had been thrust into my back.

Bang.

I was on my tiptoes, my whole body was vibrating and tingling, and this massive vibration went through me. It was like nothing I had ever felt before. It was more intense than the time I electrocuted myself and ran around the dining table at my mum's house six times, my step-dad thinking I had gone mad. My whole head had this amazing buzzing all around it. It felt as if I had on one of those hats they use when they electrocute people. Something had hold of me, had control of me, my body had been taken over. Energy had passed through every grain of me, every bit of skin, all my bones, every fibre of me, each and every cell had been cleansed, every organ, every muscle, every tendon, all my blood, all the water inside me. Everything had been touched by this force. I knew something profound and unexplainable had just happened to me.

I was taking notice now and instantly thought, 'Okay, wow this is real! This is real! This is actually happening, I believe, I believe. Ladan is actually channelling something and I one hundred per cent believe it, I know it, I have no doubts. The energy that was now part of me let my heart know that the voice in my head was bullshit. This is real, this is happening'. I instantly apologised for my doubts and surrendered back into meditation and listened diligently to every word Lord Arcturian was uttering through Ladan's body.

It felt like the whole circle had electrical energy running through it. This is why I had come on this trip; to experience something otherworldly. At my most doubtful point, I had realised you don't get this stuff for free. You always have to put in hard work. I was experiencing someone channelling for the first time, which was just nuts. It felt like one of the most poignant moments in my whole life. I hadn't had such an intense feeling since my mum had died.

Everyone was shaking but was fully focused whilst Lord Arcturian spoke. He then bid us farewell, and we all very slowly came back into our bodies and out of meditation. As we opened our eyes, everyone looked mesmerised. We all knew we had just been part of something very special, probably one of the most amazing experiences of our whole lives. It was the kind of experience we had all dreamed this trip would provide.

We all hugged in a very calm not excited way, contentedly reassuring each other how special and important the last hour had been. I went over to Ladan and just rested my head on hers for a few minutes, and she held me whilst others also held her. It was as if we were just all saying thank you for having been the one to give us such a touching treat and bringing us all here together. Ladan looked very drained and still slightly stooped over.

Once everyone had composed themselves, we started to share experiences. A lot of people had experienced similar things during the painful standing meditation. Our two guides Josh and David said they'd heard a jaguar enter the plaza but didn't want to frighten anyone as they knew we were safe in that space. Vanessa heard its deep panting and David saw a spirit jaguar appear in the middle of the altar. Josh said when he opened his eyes, he saw us all around the altar with lights shooting from our heads into the sky, and that in the gap between each person, these huge Mayan gods stood towering over us. Dominic told me that when he opened his eyes we had all disappeared and there were huge figures in the gaps where we should have all been standing. I asked if anyone had heard the bat or bird and everyone said "no", so I have no idea what that was. Did I imagine it or was it just something to knock me out of the meditation, to get me worked up so that I was in complete denial until the very last moment? David mentioned the number 12 was again significant. He was right. There were 12 of us.

As we headed out of the main plaza, a light started coming towards us in the distance. We were the only ones in Tikal, we backed up, a little apprehensive, stepping back towards a tree and turning off our flashlights.

I was thinking, 'Not more trippy shit.'

All we could see was the light, and it was getting closer and closer but, we could see no figures attached to it. All huddling together, with no idea what this could be, everyone's minds were racing, scared anticipation blossoming. Josh realised it was the guard with Debra and Paul from our group. They were both so excited to see us and told us how they had seen strangely moving stars and lights. They were oozing with pleasure and amazement like they had just won the lottery.

None of us had the heart to tell them what we'd experienced. We had left without Paul and Debra, so they had found the guard, and he had come looking for us.

I guessed there were only supposed to be 12, however standing up for that long would have been a lot easier with an extra two people's arm widths in the circle. Maybe then I wouldn't have reverted to the old scared, fearful, angry and moaning Liam Browne. However, without the pain, there may not have been such joy. I would have gone through that pain for another few hours to experience that feeling of being plugged in again.

The guard and Josh were talking, and the guard asked where we had been. Josh told him we had gone to the main altar.

The guard said, 'You can't have been.' They had walked through there looking for us and saw no one.

We headed off to the observatory still in a daze.

The view was spectacular. We could see everything so clearly, The Milky Way, the depth and density of the differing stars and planets. We all lay on our backs looking above, deep in thought. One star was flashing red, blue and green. Others were coming towards us and then backing off, others were making squiggly movements, and then there was an array of shooting stars which filled everyone with excitement and delight every time they shot across the sky.

Sitting there made me think about reading The Book of Destiny: Unlocking the Secrets of The Ancient Mayans and The Prophecy of 2012 by Carlos Barrios, a shaman and member of the Mayan Elders Council. He talks about how interesting it is that we come from the stars and are part of this great cosmos. We are this tiny speck of sand in the Universe and are all linked to creation by God. We all have a role in this world; to find our purpose and live it.

I started thinking about what my role was. Would I find my

path? Would I find happiness? Would they both fit together somehow? I was so calm and serene that for once, I didn't want answers now, as the thoughts were filling me with amazement and excitement instead of fear and dread. I sat and contemplated with no expectation other than that it was going to be such a great adventure.

Suddenly the howler monkeys brought us back to reality. The noises grew intense, and it sounded like a war.

David told us there were eight packs in Tikal, and they were very territorial. We listened for a while hoping the girls below weren't too scared. The noise was deafening and looking over the canopy, you could only imagine what battles were taking place.

The noises got more and more intense, and David said he thought it was time to leave. When we got down the girls told us the noise had been so close it felt like something was going to jump out of the trees at any moment. They had been shouting up for us to come down as they could hear the jaguar again. I felt like we were invincible that evening and nothing would have bothered us if we had just all drifted into the jungle for the rest of the night.

Tikal in the daytime was vastly different. It didn't have the intensity of the evening. It was like all the tourists were trespassing on our sacred place that we all now seemed to know so well. We walked up a few of the temples and took some photographs over the canopy of the jungle. I discovered the observatory we had climbed was off-limits in the daytime (well the night time too) as a few people had died climbing it the previous year, but rules don't really matter when you have already broken them all. Most of us would have been put off from even attempting it at night after seeing it in the day. It was massive and so steep, with many of the huge stone steps either missing or damaged.

As we sauntered around the grounds, Ladan said it was time to do the Medicine Wheel Meditation, for which we needed lots of rocks. We found this perfect little raised platform, in the view of all the passing tourists. A year ago, I would have been majorly anxious and nervous about people seeing me. But I had started to learn it was just my own fear. It's the same feeling I had when I started doing yoga in public places. I was very conscious of people seeing me doing it. I would never think like that about kicking a football about. This made me try and reprogram my brain and forget about my social conditioning. Whenever I wanted to do yoga outside, I just pretended I was playing football.

As I gathered my confidence and took a big breath, we gathered in a circle. Joyce and Rob were chosen to represent each cardinal point, the male and female energies shared. Joyce danced around the circle like an African tribal lady, singing, speaking in tongues and throwing water about, which soaked most people right in the face. I was looking at Rob as she approached him and he had this look on his face as if to say, 'I know this is going to happen I'm not happy about it, but here we go smash, splat, wet, face, smile and nod!'

We all made offerings and thanked the Mayan spirits for giving us this space and providing the rocks for the wheel.

As we opened our eyes, we realised the whole plaza was empty. All the tourists had somehow disappeared, and we had the place to ourselves. I'm not sure if people had left out of respect or if it made them uncomfortable. Maybe the Mayan spirits had escorted the tourists on alternative routes?

Josh had taken it on himself to get more involved with everything we were doing now, and his role was becoming more and more important. Everyone was starting to figure out and welcome him as that realisation hit that he was in fact number 21.

We left an array of gifts and treats for the gods, said our individual thanks and continued the tourist trail.

The Howler Monkeys were hanging around the canopy again, not being as vocal as last night. Josh and David told us to be careful and not to stand under them because they find it funny to position themselves above tourists and aim their piss and shit on the gawping faces below. Josh and David actually admitted to not telling annoying groups, typically Americans, about the treat and often watched just outside the line of fire whilst chaos ensued.

Whilst we were looking up at them, one threw a large nut at Rob, who picked it back up and hurled it back at the monkey shouting, 'Don't throw stuff at me, I'm from Manchester mate!'

David looked horrified for a split second and then relieved as the nut just missed the monkey, saying, 'Wow if that would have hit we would have been in a whole lot of trouble. We would have been attacked.'

Rob said, 'It's ok, I used to be a bouncer.'

CHAPTER 5
SEX TIMES 2,
LIFE, 2001-2007

After college, I went to a drama school called the North Cheshire Theatre School. There were drama girls and twenty female dancers. It was like being in a free sweet shop.

At every party, I would sit in the corner smoking weed and drinking beer and just wait for a girl to come and sit on my knee. That was the girl I took to bed. I was so crude in those days. All I talked about was sex.

I would sit in the common room and talk about my nights out with me mates and the adventures I had been on. All the girls would sit there listening intently, turning their noses up and saying they would never sleep with me. Then as soon as they were slightly drunk at a party, they would want to try it out. It was so easy.

There was little competition. I was the only lad's lad. The rest were real thespians; some were gay, and some were just really young, so it was as if I had the whole cake to myself and I ate as much as I could fit in my mouth. I slept with the younger girls at my house, at their houses, at parties. I slept with the older dancers who had older boyfriends but were still intrigued when they'd had a few drinks. I slept with girls who I couldn't even remember as I would black out from drink so often.

More often than not, when I woke up in the morning, I was unable to recall the evening's events. My drinking at weekends with the football lads was relentless, full of drunken nights out, coke-fuelled nights, acts of violence, everything young, boisterous men did from my area. Life revolved around football, which was filled with xenophobic, homophobic, racist, sexist attitudes that we had all picked up from the older people in the world we were submerged within.

I quit drama school as I wasn't enjoying it. There was too much musical theatre, and all I wanted to do was act. I had also slept with most of the attractive girls who attended, so it seemed pointless.

I started working as a window fitter with a friend and going to acting classes at night with a teacher called David Johnson. I got so much abuse from my football mates for wanting to be an actor. In the world I was from, being an actor instantly meant you were 'gay'. I was called 'Christopher Biggins' for about five years.

When I was 19, I found myself having a free house. I never went on holiday with me mum, step-dad and me sister as I couldn't stand being around me step-dad without an escape. We had tried it a couple of times, and we just wanted to kill each other. Mum would end up really upset, so from the age of twelve I would go and stay with my dad. From the age of sixteen, I would have the house to myself, which meant party time.

One time they were away, and I was preparing a piece for a drama showcase which needed to be rehearsed through the week. I was playing Alfie in a scene from the film where the nurse cups his balls and tells him he has shadows on his lungs. I was doing the piece with an older lady from the group. We arranged for her to come to my house and rehearse as I had the space we needed. So we got down to practising and the scene was going really well. At the end of the scene, the two characters kiss, so we did, but the kiss lingered on for a while, and it was like time stood still. When we stopped kissing we both shrugged it off as if it was just the characters and prepared to go again. We discussed the performance and the good and bad bits and things we needed to improve or do differently. We started the piece again, and it was going really well; the sexual tension between the two characters was very present. She cupped my balls and caressed them, as blood started to move to that part of my body. She then told me I had shadows on my lungs and came in for the kiss.

An hour later we were in my bed.
Our lovemaking taking us from the living room to the dining room, the hallway, up the stairs and into my bedroom. Finally, I said cut, and we discussed the scene.

This became a regular occurrence for the next few months.

I would drive to her flat, and we would do the scene as foreplay. This lady, who was twenty-two years my senior, started to teach me a thing or two, giving me sensations I'd never felt before. When we came to perform the scene for our drama teacher, he looked at us and said, 'Well some of the sexual tension you had before has gone,' and chuckled. Somehow just by seeing our scene, he knew we had indeed been sleeping together.

I had so many sex stories that I would constantly tell. It didn't matter if I was in a relationship; I told everyone about all my conquests, boasting about what I got up to. Having sex in friends' beds, having sex on the floor of friends' family lounges, having sex behind shops, on fields, in toilets, anywhere I could, the more dangerous, the better.

The pinnacle of these escapades was when I made a film in France. The character I was playing was very close to who I was as a person. He was a bit of an idiot and someone who really fancied himself and tried to have sex with everyone that moved.

I got on really well with one of the actresses, and we had been having sex during the shoot. On the ferry on the way back to England, we had been getting drunk and playing 21 in the casino. I lost all my money so, feeling horny, I took the girl onto the deck of the ferry. I pulled down her jeans and put myself inside her standing up against the safety railings. It was pitch black out to sea where my head was facing. We had our heads nestled into each other's shoulder as I trusted deep inside her.

Suddenly we heard this noise. It was people clapping and a horn going off. As I opened my eyes, a massive cruise liner was slowly passing. It was about thirty metres from where we were stood half-naked. All the decks were full of people, and they were all clapping and cheering at us. We realised we were coming into port and this cruise liner was heading out.

We pulled up our jeans, our naked lower halves fully exposed to the passing audience, then headed inside to the stairwell to finish what we had started. Then, as the PA system was announcing the commencement of disembarking the boat, two kids came racing through the fire exit. They stopped, looked at our naked lower halves and ran off. We decided enough was enough and went to find our friends.

These kinds of experiences were what I constantly sought; some kind of seedy, pornographic life-style, full of women, drugs, alcohol and good times. I wasn't actually as good at it as I made out to people. I built myself up as this huge Casanova, but inside I was very insecure and nervous around new people and women I really liked.

The next big love in my life was a girl I met in Cyprus on a lads' holiday. We were doing what lads our age did, going off to the sun for a drink, sex, fun and laughter. I wanted to sleep with as many girls as I could. I wanted it to be a competition, and I wanted to win. Girls were everywhere, and on the first night, I scored. On the third night, I scored, and on the fourth day I crashed a moped into a wall and broke my penis.

Me and me mates had all hired mopeds, and the guy renting them to us made us all have a go to make sure we were okay on them. Everyone was a bit jittery, but when it was my turn, it seemed really easy.

We all sped off down the road, and some of my mates went in a different direction, so I turned around and went to follow them. The next thing I know I lost control and, like a greyhound let out of the traps, I headed straight for a wall. I smashed into it, still within sight of the rental shop.

The rental man came running down the road, screaming and flailing his arms at me. I was shaken up, and when I pulled my shorts open to look at where most of the pain was coming from, I saw that I had a two-inch gash down the front of my penis and blood was pouring down my leg. The rental man was screaming that I would have to pay for the damage to the bike when my rental period was over. I thought 'my sex life might be over mate'.

My mates were all laughing so hard. When I'd ridden off, the rental man had said to them all that I was a natural.

I felt like my holiday was over. 'No more shagging for Browne', was my first thought and I wondered what the point of being away was if I couldn't fuck.

That night I got straight back on the bike and practised on the open road. The same night, I fell in love at first sight with the most beautiful girl I had ever seen in real life.

A Norwegian princess.

I played the gentleman. I pretended to be another person or maybe the person I was deep inside. I was doing what was needed to make this girl fall in love with me. When we spoke, there was a lot of dishonesty about my past. I knew if I'd been honest, I would never have gotten the girl. Frustration brewed inside us both as my penis had an out of order sign dangling from it.

Finally, on the last night we had sex. It was exquisite ecstasy mixed with excruciating pain as she slid up and down my injured shaft. We had fallen in love, and it was to be the start of my first long-distance relationship and the start of my mind seeing other parts of the world and cultures as I had never seen them before.

I'd always been on package holidays, surrounded by other British people with their only intention being to get pissed every night and to go home with a tan. I thought this was what being abroad was. I soon found out that this was a very clouded reality of what the world was truly about. I started to question all the things I'd been told by my peers about England being the greatest country in the world. It all started to break away bit by bit as my eyes became wide open, taking in all that I saw. Trips between Norway and Manchester took place for over a year before my Norwegian princess came to England.

Was I faithful during the long-distance?
No.
Was I faithful when she was living with me? No.
Did I love her?
Yes.

Well, I thought I loved her. My ego loved the attention she got wherever we went, and the way most of my mates' jaws dropped when she walked into a room.

We then moved to London and lived together for six months before the relationship fell apart. I started getting with other girls and finally falling in love with a funny German.

I think part of me had used the Norwegian girl to move to London. I had always wanted to move there, but I had never had the balls to do it as I was so involved with my mates and my football team.

Like everyone where I lived, I was too scared of change. Meeting her and knowing of her desire to study law in London gave me the push I needed to leave.

I thought that I would move to London, become a big star actor and sleep with loads of beautiful models and actresses and do loads of drugs. The big star actor thing didn't happen, but sleeping with lots of beautiful girls did. I was in my element.

I remember the first modelling job I got for K-Swiss. I went for a fitting, and I was in this room trying on clothes when these models came in and started getting undressed next to me. The two most beautiful girls I'd ever seen in real life were next to me naked, and I had to leave the room as the blood in my body was moving to places that would have made the situation awkward. I went outside and rang my friends and told them what was taking place. They all said I was chatting shit, unable to fathom the reality I was momentarily involved in.

The relationship with the East German girl lasted about 18

months. For once I had met my match, and neither of us was particularly faithful, but in many ways, we did have the most amazing relationship.

We could just chat and laugh hour after hour with each other. We were both constantly stoned, and neither of us was ever without weed. We also had the most amazing ecstasy-fuelled sex life. We travelled Europe together, exploring mountains, beaches, lakes and getting into various scrapes and mischief. She was the first relationship I'd had where it wasn't just about looks. Before this, I'd thought girlfriends were just pretty things you had on your arm, and when you turned up at parties, they went and chatted to the girls and you the boys, then at the end of the night, you went home and had sex. For the remainder of the week you would both bitch to your respective friends about the shortcomings of your partner and do the whole thing again on repeat, with no shared interests.

I broke up with The German as I was too interested in other girls and, although I loved her, I was no longer in love with her. I was sleeping with other girls, who she knew about, and I didn't really want to hurt her anymore.

The week after we split, we were out together with friends, and we all got really drunk and really high, and I had girls all around me. I remember very little of that night other than the fact I could see these massive brown eyes looking up at me. The next day I had a phone number in my phone and a desire to text it. I did, and after the first date I had fallen in love with the most beautiful Greek girl I had ever seen.

She looked like Audrey Hepburn. It was like an eruption of love, and I fell hard. However, I was still seeking suitors whilst I travelled the world alone, and more so when I was with old friends. It was as if I had to keep up the persona of the person they knew me as, and I couldn't just be comfortable in my own skin.

I always thought that this constant desire to sleep with women was a natural thing. I felt that all men had it because it was so strong in me and other men talked about it so much, though they didn't act on it. I thought that most of them were just too scared, to be honest about it, but I was letting the burning desire inside of me out, while other men were suppressing it. I thought that the power of it in me must be hereditary as my dad and my brothers were the same. It was like numbers counted, and I was always after sleeping with more women than they had. I'd grown up hearing them talk about women and their conquests. It was as if it was expected of me to follow. Like going into the family business. It felt like the only way to be a true Browne.

I was doing exactly that, and straight away, I cheated on the girl I was madly in love with. Was it this desire for numbers still? Was it to fill an emptiness inside? Was it to seek recognition from my family and friends? Or was it just a security mechanism that made me feel safer in my relationship knowing, that I'd cheated on her so I held the power, and she couldn't hurt me in the future? I didn't know, but at last I was starting to become aware of it.

The relationship with the Greek girl saved my life. It was in its infancy at the time my mum died, and now, with my expanded multi-dimensional awareness, I know the universe gave me this angel to look after me and be the stable down-to-earth rock I needed to get through the toughest time of my life.

We were so, so, so in love.

I couldn't stop looking at her. She was the most beautiful thing I had ever seen, inside and out. Whoever we were with could feel the love we had for each other blossom out of us. We both felt like we had found the one, the person you will travel through life with, that person you'd had been waiting for in your dreams. We fantasised about our life together, about having children and naming them. I knew she would be the most amazing mother ever, and I could see how beautiful our children would be. We spent so much time in bed with each other, that's all we wanted to do. We just wanted to see each other constantly all the time and hold each other as tightly as possible. It was this intense love I had never felt before, and it was so beautiful.

Still, in many ways, I was dissatisfied. I was still seeking other sexual partners, and part of me was hoping I would meet someone better. I had all that I needed when I look at it now.

But I was constantly seeking the intensity of those first six months of a relationship. I had this mind-set that having sex with someone I didn't love made my relationship fresh and that my focus would then return to the girl I was in love with. I never felt any guilt when returning to her bed after a sexual conquest. To me, at the time it was just an action, and she was my girl, and as long as I wasn't having full-on affairs it was ok. Part of me wanted full-on affairs though.

COPAN, THE JOURNEY, DECEMBER 2012

When we arrived back in Antigua, everyone went straight to bed, so we would be ready for the early start and the seven-hour bus ride to Honduras and the ruins of Copan. We did our daily meditation on the bus, and I didn't want to come round after it, because I seemed to be in such a good space.

There was immense laughter on the bus. 'Laughter is the best medicine', they say, and I think we were about to overdose.

I would cry, 'I need something in me mouth!' and snacks would arrive in abundance.

I'd scream, 'Rice' and everyone would reverberate, 'And Pea'.

I'm not even sure if half the people knew where that line came from, but they laughed anyway.

As me and Melinda were chatting, she gave me her headphones and said, 'Listen to this.' It was 'Bump' by Ed Sheeran. It inspired me, and afterwards, I wrote the first song I had written for eight months. It only took me ten minutes. It went like this:

New Beginnings
21 Souls, all coming together to spread the love
Senders of light, working through the night
All our lives, played out to be here now
All our strife, worthwhile to be here now
And where we go, leaving behind the old
Pastures new, ready to evolve

Ascension to fire
Ascension to water
Boiling together in our blood
Ascend to the earth
Ascend to the sky
Where we will all find love

We are guided, each and every day
By the good, and bad that try to lead us astray
And we give thanks, to each and every soul
Without you, we'd have never found this home

Ascension to fire
Ascension to water
Boiling together in our blood
Ascend to the earth
Ascend to the sky
Where we will all find love

Each soul, healing each other all the way
All this love, I can feel it as we pray
Every day, this bond is stronger, don't go away
But with this gift, we have to lead others all the way

Ascension to fire
Ascension to water
Boiling together in our blood Ascend to the earth
Ascend to the sky
Where we will all find love

Sent from the Heavens
Information download
Stored in our bodies
Ready to off load
To help the people
To help the world
Help everybody to live and learn

Baba Nam Kevalam
Baba Nam Kevalam
Baba Nam Kevalam
Baba Nam Kevalam
Baba Nam Kevalam

Baba Nam Kevalam is a mantra that was given to me by Benjamin, my new friend, who seemed like an old friend. It means 'love is all there is!' I think the Beatles turned it into 'All you need is love'.

I needed to polish it a bit, and find the right time to gift it to the group.

But I couldn't sing, and I was tone-deaf. Maybe it would be more upsetting than a gift, I thought. Maybe I could get someone else to sing it?

We got to the Honduras border in high spirits, getting our

stamps, filling in pointless forms and being held in this depressing room for thirty minutes.

Suddenly something hit me. I'd felt amazing, and then out of the blue I had pain all down my neck and felt sick and faint. I got back in the bus, and everyone could tell I'd taken a turn for the worse.

Everyone said how dark the energy was and how the locals were looking at us strangely, as though we were pilgrims.

Phil 'the Hat' said he thought I could have been hit by a psychic dart.

'A bloody what,' I thought. Was Phil Taylor in there working for the dark side? I didn't know what psychic dart was and didn't want to sound un-spiritual by asking. I felt like I was being possessed, so refrained from further inquiries.

Ladan and Joyce performed some healing on me on the way to the hotel. Then Rob asked if he could work on me to try and pull this energy out. It felt like something was shifting, but not entirely. The pain was in my head and all down my back and made me feel really sick. My head was spinning, and I felt like I could faint at any moment.

We arrived at the hotel, and I was still in a daze. I felt weighed down, and my energy was low. Rob said he needed to get this thing out and we found a quiet spot whilst he worked on my head, neck and shoulders. He could feel the energy not wanting to shift and said, 'It's a powerful little bugger'. Feeling like I was in Harry Potter or something, I laughed to myself about the image of this 18-stone bouncer pulling this invisible (to the untrained eye) intruder from me.

I could feel the energy shifting around inside my body. Moving up and down my spine. Rob talked me through the whole process, and he managed to release the energy via my neck. Whatever it was reluctantly popped out of me and disappeared into the universe. I felt an incredible release. Rob told me I was probably too open and not protecting myself properly, which was imperative with the spiritual work we were doing in this part of the world. He said go and drink plenty of water and rest for a while. I instantly felt black to myself and bounced around the hotel telling everyone I was back.

Fhian was on my mind. We had been chatting regularly over the internet and part of me was missing her. Another part of me also felt held back by this duty to be constantly in touch. I was procrastinating about what the best thing to do was, wondering if she was the girl for me. I needed her to open up more and be more soppy and loving like me. I needed a higher level of love. I knew it was inside her, and that was the most frustrating thing. It was buried under whatever she had covered it with from childhood experiences or social expectations. She always portrayed the stern demeanour of a successful and strong woman, and I wanted her to just melt into my arms.

We embarked on our trip to the hot pools. Josh had taken a turn for the worse, and it was his turn to be healed by the group. As he sat at the side of a large pool we made a circle, holding hands and chanting OM. It sounded so soothing as it bounced off the hot water.

Sandra Brazil swam around, and under us all whilst we were chanting. The light changes of the water's flow and the occasional brush of a flailing limb made it feel as if we were being joined by love-hungry dolphins.

It was beautiful how we all came together whenever anyone was feeling sick or down. Instead of pill-popping, we soothed or healed the person back to life. It was moving and felt like the way people would have looked after each other in more advanced and conscious civilisations.

Next day was the short walk to the ruins of Copan to see the amazing temples. It was also the day of the male healing ceremony. I was hoping any blockages in my being would come out and be healed.

As we entered the ruins, two rainbow-coloured parrots flew over the group and landed by us, confirming the arrival of my rainbow brothers and sisters.

The meditation started, and I fell in deep. The ladies were walking around in a circle whilst Ladan orchestrated events. My body felt like it was spinning in an anti-clockwise motion, some sort of mini-tornado was popping into my head. I could hear people releasing stuff around me, via coughs, burps and massive farts. I could also sense someone letting out really guttural cries. I thought it was Rob, but it turned out to be Josh who was sitting next to me. The women were whispering the words, 'You are in safe hands, and you are loved' into our ears, and instantly it made me cry my eyes out.

The girls went around to each guy, and at times I had two ladies holding me tight as I sobbed in meditation. The intense feeling of safety I felt with these people was incredible. When it was over, everyone was in this hazy loving glow. We all thanked each other with hugs. Rob and Wayne looked at me and Josh and called us both mard arses, returning the tone back to one of down-to-earth laughter, fun and beauty.

That evening we went to another Mayan ceremony, this time with a lady shaman.

We peacefully meandered through the cascading forest and gently sloping hills. An oblong-shaped palapa led to a large rock circle where we sat. As the final touches were made to the ceremonial area, the fire and candles were lit, and a small performance began. Mayan tribal music was played, and the King of Copan approached with his queen by his side and some of his high-ranking officers. It seemed a little theatrical, but apparently this is a big place of interest for American travellers.

The ceremony began. The shaman connected to the gods, reciting a great monologue of prayers to call in the spirits. The ring of people was then called in one by one to be purified by the shaman and to make offerings to the ancestors. Everyone said a little prayer.

For some reason, I couldn't really get into this ceremony. Again my rational mind was asking me what I was doing there and what was the point and blah, blah, blah. I was thinking, I'm not feeling this. Why not am I not connected spiritually? Am I spirited out for the day or am I just not spiritual, or is this not spiritual? Am I forcing this?

Arrrrrrrrghhhhhh shut up, voice in my head!!!!!
It made me think about perception and how I had been critical of the first shaman in his jeans and normal street attire but been completely encapsulated by the energies and impact of his ceremony. Then this shaman looked the part, in full traditional dress, in a perfect setting, with people helping her, gaining our attention straight away. It made me think about the moral of a story in a short film I had written a while back about misjudged preconceptions and how we have an assumption of someone based on the way they
dress.

It was 11.12.12; one day away from one of the big
dates of the Mayan Calendar and the day of the female healing. We took another seven-hour bus ride, this time back to Antigua.

Not long after crossing the border, we took a detour to some beautiful ruins that were situated between the plantations of the

American's United Fruit Company, which basically caused the 30-year civil war.

The Americans bought lots of cheap lands and displaced many indigenous people. Then a new president was elected in Guatemala who wanted land reforms, giving land rights to Guatemalan people. Obviously, the Americans didn't like this, so at the time of the Cold War and American paranoia about communism taking over the world, the fruit company and the CIA presented Guatemala as this massive communist threat. The Americans went to war with the Guatemalan president, assassinating him and replacing him with a far-right puppet president, so the United Fruit Company could continue raping Guatemala's people of what was rightfully theirs.

So next time you buy Chiquita bananas, think of all the bloodshed it has caused and all the evil that company has oozing out of it. Would you buy a banana if the company was run by Hitler?

The ruins we arrived at were about the size of four football pitches with a massive tree of life in the middle of the plaza. I wondered how long it would take my tree surgeon friend Steve to cut it down and how much he would charge? The trees here were hollow, and the Mayans would cut them down with machetes.

We walked up and over the ruins and came to a raised section looking over a smaller plaza below. The women sat in a semi-circle, and the men stood at the base, ready to be the consolers today.

There were tissues at the ready and strict instructions that the men were not to be too touchy-feely. We could only touch the ladies on the shoulders. We began to chant Om. The meditation spoke about all the pain women had been through during this reign of masculine energies throughout the last 5,200 years. They were carrying that pain for all the ladies in their life; all the mothers, all the women they had been in past lives, and all the atrocities suffered every day by women all over the world.

Some of the women were starting to sob, and Josh began to drum, whilst other men played rattles, and the rest of us continued to chant. The crying got more intense and, without realising, it the tone of the music we were producing changed frequency to help heal the ladies.

I was directing my Om's at different areas of the circle. Though my eyes were firmly shut, my voice was very much open, trying to soothe the women's pain.

Someone's sudden sobbing immediately touched and moved

me. Thoughts of my mother came up as they had through a lot of the healings. I felt compelled to see who had moved me in such a way. I slowly opened my eyes to see that it was Sandra's tears that were affecting me.

I worked my way around to Sandra, and we had this deep eye contact as if we knew each other, not in the capacity of the last week, but something a lot deeper that I couldn't figure out. There was a very loving connection, and I wanted to know more.

The only lady I hadn't connected with during the meditation was Linda. She was lying on the floor in a right state with big Rob gently rubbing her forehead saying softly, 'You are in safe hands and you are loved.'

I nestled in and gave my energy to Linda, trying to soothe and heal her and let in the light of the Christ Conscious energy. There seemed a really nice flow, with our energies combined. She eventually came round, and when she was almost back to normal, Rob called her a mard arse. We all laughed and again knew we had all been part of something ridiculously special.

I didn't think adults could have so much fun on a bus. On the way back to Antigua, the whole group was laughing so hard. Rob's big brass tones were either taking the piss out of Melinda or someone else.

The bus had a microphone, via which Josh had informed us about much of Guatemala's dark history and a plethora of facts and stories about Mayan culture. His knowledge for someone of his age overwhelmed me.

Now it was time for the group to grab the microphone. Everyone talked about their experiences on the trip. It got emotional and deep. It had been an intense nine days so far, and it wasn't over, but it was a chance for us to all show our gratitude. Many beautiful words were shared. It was touching to see how close we had all become as a group. We had learnt so much about ourselves and developed friendships and connections that would go past this life.

A lot of thanks were given to Ladan for organising the trip and for everything she had done for us all, meditations, activations and even the channelling. Lots of people spoke of how important Josh had been to the group and how him becoming number 21 was fate. We began to believe that everything we had all done in our lives was in preparation for this; to be in this group and to experience and share these times with these 21 people.

I had started calling Josh, 'Neo', like in the Matrix, though at times in the last nine days— well the last year actually— it was me who had felt like Neo. I had come to realise there was something more to the world and life, my rational mind being unwilling to accept what was going on, questioning it all and being unable to see my part in this crazy world.

Josh had been working with terrible groups for the last four years, most of the time unable to unleash his humble, respectful knowledge of the Mayans. He had been waiting for a group like us to come along. He said he was expecting a load of airy hippies with no real depth and what he got were 20 very real down-to-earth people who he adored and had made him feel part of them from day one.

Josh took the mic and told us what this trip had meant to him and how he felt it was a real catalyst for change in his life. He said he had never felt love like the love we had all given him in the last nine days. His words were very moving, and his inability to control his emotions led other people to lose control of theirs, including me.

After a moment of quiet reflection, the iPods got plugged in, and the microphone became a stage. Wayne belted out a few old classics, Joyce sang a bit of Sir Bob, I shouted "Rice", she shouted, "and Pea".

The bus driver was called Fernando, and fortunately, someone had the Abba classic on their device, so twenty crazy tourists serenaded Fernando at full pelt. It was mad, it was similar to being on a coach with a load of pissed football blokes coming back on the motorway after an away win.

Madness.

After some careful consideration and telling myself this was the moment— 'Don't bottle it Browne, (I call myself Browne when I have to be forceful with this Liam character I play) do not bottle it this is perfect! — I finally grabbed the mic.

Everyone expected me to blast out a bit of Oasis presumably, but I scuffled through the pages of my notebook and blasted out 'New Beginnings', for each and every person on that bus. Although my singing was terrible, it went down well and possibly touched a few of them. They wrote the song really. Then it was back to more random singing as we meandered through the total gridlocked roads on the outskirts of Guatemala City.

CHAPTER 6
SEX TIMES 3, LIFE,
2007-2010

She used to wake up in the night and tell me she'd had bad dreams about me having sex with other girls. I would lie and say, 'I wouldn't do that babe,' but deep inside that was what I sought.

Was she psychic? Were her dreams telling her the truth?

There were girls in bars, girls I met in the street, even the lady who I was signing on with at the job-centre became a conquest. It was as if I forced myself to do it. I knew I wouldn't see them again and I wouldn't particularly enjoy it, but inside I felt it a missed opportunity if I didn't pursue a girl I knew was interested. I never turned down the chance of another notch on the bedpost.

Whenever I saw a pretty girl anywhere, I would fantasise about getting into a sexual situation with her. When I would get on the tube in London, I would scan the whole carriage and decide which women I would sleep with. I would quickly go 'yes, no, no, no, no, maybe,' and if I found one I really liked, I would look at her as much as I could, imagining how she would be as a lover. I never had the balls to talk to them though, even though sometimes they were giving me signs. I was too scared to approach. I never knew what I would say to open up a conversation.

I was terrible at chatting girls up. If I had an 'in' I was great, but without one, fear kept me from saying anything. I would build my ego back up by telling myself I had a beautiful girlfriend anyway; when inside, I just wanted to rip the ladies' clothes off. I thought this was normal behaviour.

I could never get away from women, the bags of joy on their chest and the treat between their legs. Deep inside, I wanted this soul mate, this person I always wanted to be with, this perfect woman who I saw no fault in. But I still couldn't see how I would ever not cheat.

After my girlfriend and I had been together for almost two years, I got the lead part in a film called 'brilliantlove'. It was all about the passion of new young love. The script was very sexually explicit. I loved the love in the script, and I loved the writing and the visual description of the way the characters lived. There was no way

I was going to say no to it. I thought this would be my springboard to becoming a proper film actor.

Obviously, my girlfriend wasn't very happy about all the sex in the film, but she was willing to support me.

I fantasised about all the girls I would get to sleep with during the film and the women who would want to sleep with me after seeing it.

The film 'brilliantlove' was again a reflection of the person I was and the person I wanted to be: a character completely consumed by the love of his girlfriend with no interest in anyone else. He was also on the outskirts of society and lived hidden away making his own rules. His life consisted of art, creativity, love and love-making. This sexual exploration was mixed with exploring different drugs and the way they intensified sex and creativity. This was something I'd had a lot of experience with and something again I constantly sought. I loved making love high on drugs, and I wanted it to always feel like that. It was like I was always trying to hold on to transient sensations.

The relationship with the Greek girl came to a very sloppy end. She slept with the lead singer of a band called 'The Kooks' when we were on a break, so I decided I wanted her back. I felt that if I could find someone as amazing as her or better, then I would be happy.

I was seeking women everywhere. I would meet women and sleep with them straight away. There was a point when I had so many numbers on my phone that I was arranging to meet different girls three or four times a week.

I thought this was what I had always wanted, but I didn't seem any happier. I was actually feeling more and more depressed. I couldn't sleep and was on all different types of pills for anxiety and stress. I felt and looked a mess. Still, I was women-hungry.

One of my friends had been telling me about this dating site called My Single Friend. He wanted to go on it and said he would put me on it too. I deemed it as a pretty sad way of meeting people, but I guess what's sadder is only being able to meet people when you are so wasted that you don't remember.

I thought arranging a civilised date and getting to know someone properly, seemed appealing.

I kept getting emails off the website as my friend had set me up a profile. I kept deleting them as I thought the website was asking for money.

One email came through asking me to view my profile, and when I did I couldn't believe what my friend had put on it. It was beautiful, and I thought women would love it. Then I had a look at the site and saw that there were thousands of really hot girls on there.

I started to clean up. It was so easy, such a good way to arrange dates, and soon these dates were turning into sexual conquests. I was ruthless and almost always succeeded in seducing them.

I was running around dating, sleeping with girls here and there, being the promiscuous man about town, wondering why I had spent so much time procrastinating about women on nights out when this was perfect, and I didn't have to get shit-faced.

I was one to one with the other person and didn't have to worry about other people's opinions or the nervousness of approaching a girl in a bar when she was surrounded by her friends. This way I was pretty much-guaranteed sex; maybe not always on the first date, but on the second it was happening.

But I knew that all I wanted was to be with 'the one', the girl I was going to spend my life with.

One woman, I met lived in Wimbledon and invited me to her flat. I went around, and we drank some tea. She was quite a bit older than me, but she was stunning; half-Burmese, half-English with beautiful light brown skin and these pouty pillow-like lips I wanted to penetrate.

We ended up getting intimate, but there was no sex. I was just given blow jobs which were amazing. She then employed me to paint the windows in her flat. It was a pretty big job and took me nine days. Her landlord paid me a day rate, and it was a nice little earner.

I would paint all day and then she would get home from work at about 4 pm, make me a cup of tea and then give me a blow job. Then I would clean up and go home.

I ended up getting seven blow jobs in nine days, and the only reason it wasn't nine was because I had to leave early on two occasions. I told this story to anyone that would listen.

Internet dating seemed relatively effortless, which was how I liked things. I was sleeping with all different types of girls; younger, older, black, white, tall, small, lawyers, students, artists, office girls. But I had seen one woman on the site who really took my fancy. At first, she wouldn't reply to my email, but after another approach I had my bite and got a date with an American model. We arranged to go out on a Saturday night.

I had been ill for the last few weeks and didn't really want to leave my flat. In preparation for a weekend of going to a screening of 'brilliantlove' on Friday and my date with the beautiful American model on Saturday, I just wanted to bed down and get better.

A girl I had not seen for a while got in touch and wanted to see me, but I wasn't feeling well and wasn't prepared to make any effort for her. We'd had a fling about six months ago, and now for some strange reason she wanted to see me again.

She sent me a text that said, 'nice disappearing act you did on me a while back! Anyway, I hope you're doing well. I was just wondered if you fancied going for a drink sometime? Jane xxx'

This was a tricky decision as it was Thursday, I was on death's door, and I had a date with a 35-year-old, 5'10 ex-catwalk model in two days.

I kept telling Jane that I was sick. I asked her if she fancied coming round to mine?

'No,' she said, 'we have to go for drinks somewhere before I come to your house.' Busted!

I wasn't budging.

I'd had this cold for two weeks now and needed to get rid of it. I had a busy weekend coming up, but now I had Jane on my mind; the body, the taste, her smell, that glossy hair, that bottom. Oh my god, that bottom..., I got shivers down my torso thinking about it.

So now I wanted her at my house.

How do I get her here?

I said the only way she could see me was if she came over to me.

After some persuasion, she eventually agreed.

She had really long, thin, dark hair that caught the wind, revealing her perfectly structured jaw and face, high cheekbones, glossy thin lips and dark brown eyes. She had a distinctive mole on her right cheek.

She arrived wearing a very sexy suit, which could make one think she was an elegant city high flyer. Her legs were toned with the sort of calves that melt in your mouth, her skirt was cut just above the knee, with a small pleat revealing a section of her thigh. Her silk blouse ruffled in the wind and her small pert breasts slid across the soft material. The sexual part of my heart fluttered at just the thought. Her outfit was completed by a fitted jacket. She was slender without looking too skinny, and the way she glided around my flat made me want to take her clothes off before we had even eaten.

After I had made us some food, we got down to having sex.

She had the most amazing body, not one bit of fat on any part of her, and her skin was just loose enough so I could grab her and feel her move. It was amazing to have her physically in my flat, to explore her perfect body, but there was nothing else.

The conversation didn't flow. I would ask a question, and instead of elaborating on her experience, she would just say, 'it were good', in her thick northern accent.

This became a comedy sketch for me and my housemate over the following two years. We would pretend we were an interviewer, interviewing someone who had just done something amazing like sailing around the world, winning the world cup or saving the planet. We would go into heavy detail about the amazing things they had done and then ask, 'how was it', and one of us would reply in a thick northern accent, 'it were good' and then both break down in hysterics.

The next day, I woke with perfect-on-the-outside Jane to my left, her body draped over mine. I had to rush off to London to meet a friend, but I couldn't resist one more exploration of Jane's beautiful body. We got the train together, and I remember her asking me if I was going to call her. I said, 'yes,' but knew I wouldn't. As the train pulled into Waterloo, I kissed her goodbye and told her I had to run to meet my friend, not wanting to be in this awkward situation anymore. When the doors opened, I sprinted away never to be seen again.

I met my friend and then headed to the screening where I had arranged another date. The girl arrived and instantly I wasn't attracted to her, so we just chatted and watched the film. I then went to a club night where my friend was DJ-ing. We all ended up dancing, and a girl latched onto me. She was a young half-German and wanted to come home with me.

We got to my place and got down to things on my couch, kissing and touching and feeling each other. As I was taking off her jeans, she said, 'I have something to tell you'.

'Okay, what?'

She said, 'What the worst thing I could say right now'?

I said, 'We can't have sex'.
'No, worse than that'.
I was thinking, 'has she's got a cock'?
Instead, I laughed and said, 'You're a man'? She said, 'No, I'm definitely a girl. But what could be the worst thing I could say right now?' she said.
I awkwardly I said, 'You're on your period'?
'No,' she said. 'Not that'.
I couldn't think of anything else. I was getting a bit scared, I'd never been in this situation before. I'd had plenty of girls take you to this stage and then go, 'We can't, I'm on my period,' or 'No, we can't, I hardly know you,' as we were on top of each other completely naked, but this felt weird.
What was it she was hiding?
Would I have to kill her?
She said, 'Promise you won't be freaked out?' 'Yeah,'.I lied, 'I promise'.
She said, 'Well, I haven't done this before'.
I said, 'You haven't had a one night stand'?
She said, 'well yes but no, I haven't done this before, I'm a virgin'.
Woah, woah, woah, woah.
I hadn't come across one of those for almost 15 years. I was in shock. She was 19 but had never had sex before. These people didn't exist where I was from.
She told me she really wanted to do it.
She was tired of being a virgin, she said.
I said, 'Are you sure you want to do it with me?'
She said, 'Yes, I do'.
I was in no way a guy who got off on deflowering
girls. If anything, I was thinking, this could make a mess. I realised I had no protection, so I went around the streets of Surbiton at 4 am looking for a late-night shop that sold condoms. Eventually I found them, and when I got back, I laid out towels as I didn't want my bed getting ruined with blood. Then I got on with it.
It was like trying to get a square peg in a round hole. It was really difficult, un-sexy, and painful for us both. But she got what she wanted, and I had another notch on the bedpost.
The next night was the date I was looking forward to. I arrived at Tottenham Court Road to meet Miss America, and as she flew out

of the station I looked at her and melted. I would never have approached her in a club as I would have thought she was out of my league.

We got on really well, and I discovered she was an artist and the lead singer in a band, with all these cool tattoos. She was like the girl I always had imagined myself with. Cool, arty, tall and so, so beautiful, with blue-green eyes that captured my imagination.

We then headed to my friend's bar where I always took the women I was on dates with. I must have taken ten or so women there in the last few months. I did it to show off in this huge egocentric way and to keep up my persona, as this 'I don't give a shit about women and I can have them all, and you wish you could too' guy. It was pathetic, but that's where I was at, and who I had always been.

We couldn't keep our hands off each other in the bars and taxi, and when we got to her place, we just about made it to the bed. We made amazing love all night. I hadn't really ever been with such a tall woman. There were limbs everywhere. I thought, 'this is what it would be like having sex with a gazelle.'

We woke up the next day, and we both knew we were going to see each other again. We had this explorative sex all morning and then I got a text from my friend Kaye. I had forgotten I was having two models round to my house for Sunday lunch.

I was an hour away from home, and they were already there.

All I wanted to do was stay in bed with this woman who I had a feeling I would soon be falling in love with. But I had made plans, so I rustled around the dimly lit room to find my jeans and headed home.

I got my flatmate to meet the two girls. When he saw them, he said his jaw just dropped. They walked around the streets and waited for the wanderer to return.

As we all ate Sunday dinner together, I told them about Miss America and my exploits over the last three days. I then realised I had scored a hat trick; three women in three days. 'I got a Hat trick' became my intro to the story that I told for the next few months.

Miss America did become the next woman in my life.

She had a daughter and, though I never thought I'd fall for a woman with a kid, I was smitten again.

Her daughter was really cool and went to a Steiner School, which I learned was this alternative educational system that nurtured the individual rather than trying to churn out the same person as contemporary schools did.

I felt like I was with a woman now. I was learning so much from her about health and nutrition as her and her daughter were both vegan and lactose-free. She gave me books on philosophy to read and introduced me to some really cool people. At the time I was touring the country with my film, and we were on the phone to each other for hours each day. It was amazing, the connection was intense.

One day I woke up and wasn't really feeling it any more. I loved her, and I'd become close to her daughter, but something had changed for me. Maybe it was the lust which had disguised itself as love being over, maybe it was a derogative comment one of my friends had made about her when I was out?

I told myself it was a scent thing; that our smells didn't match. It sounds mad, but the scent is very important to me. She didn't smell bad, it was just that our scents didn't mix well.

Again I hurt someone really badly. She had let me in and trusted me, and I had gotten carried away and made her feel that we were going to be together for a long time. That's how I'd felt though. I had fallen head over heels in love with this girl from San Diego, who wanted to take me over there for sun, surf and love. We'd discussed all these outlandish plans for our life together. Then I had just abruptly stopped it. What happened to me? Why did I go off in this dream world? Why couldn't I rein it in? Why did I allow my heart to take me floating along on candy floss and then get scared, panic and run away?

At the time, I was still going out with friends and doing drugs and sleeping with girls. I would go out, sleep with a girl and then go back to my girlfriend's house and hang out and have no level of guilt in me at all. I was living this constant lie. It was like I was in a game and was always trying to avoid detection. I was stealing from shops all the time, I was avoiding train fares and always on some kind of fiddle or trying to get something for free. I was so open about my conquests that my friends could never really get close to my girlfriends. If they did, they would feel torn, as they knew what I got up to when we were out.

My female friends would tell me that I was a great friend and one of the best people they knew in terms of many of my values, but when it came to being a boyfriend, I would be the worst person to go out with as I led two different lives. I could see where they were coming from, but I hadn't ever cared about it before. I knew I was so, so affectionate to the women I loved. I did get up to all sorts of unfaithful acts, but for some warped reason I thought this was acceptable because I loved them and made them feel so special when we were together.

My mates could never figure out how I ended up with these amazing women. Most of the time, I felt like they were too good for me and I didn't deserve them. But fundamentally, I always wanted better, never thought they were good enough for me and thought I was above them. I always wanted that soul mate, was always searching for the one, always certain she was out there, and I would eventually   her.

12.12.12,
THE JOURNEY,
DECEMBER 2012

I had been feeling sick all day and not eaten, so I decided to get into bed early. I wanted to be ready for the 5.30 am Cherokee Sundance on the rooftop with Kerri the next morning. While most people went for food, I started to think about what might happen tomorrow. Would there be a significant occurrence as the nine days of countdown to the end of the Mayan calendar began? Would this be the catalyst for a world no longer consumed by greed and material wealth, but committed to love, light, health and happiness?

Would spiritual knowledge and wisdom be unearthed and catapulted back to the forefront of modern society? Would the global powers willingly accept a new direction, and release to the masses the knowledge that had been hidden for so long?

Learning anything beyond what the church believed had long been considered an act of disobedience and disloyalty, and therefore the work of the devil. It had been the basis for the witch hunts, leaving global indigenous traditions almost eradicated. As a result, we had been left without any spiritual direction.

I thought about all the people I was with. In the past, Melinda would have been killed for reading my palm. Yoga would have been banned, and anything that connected us with our true self would have been outlawed.

It made me think about how I had come to this point and how revealing this stuff in a book felt so scary. I felt like I would be judged by society, and all my friends and family. It all felt so far removed from the world I had grown up in, and from the lager drinking, xenophobic, sexist, slightly racist, homophobic, young man I had once been. But I felt so committed to finding inner peace, a purpose and happiness that I was willing to accept ridicule. I wanted to remember my true self and essence.

I'd been in a constant battle with my ego, wondering why I was no longer hanging out with people who partied all weekend. Deep within, I knew this was no longer making me happy. Every time I'd gone on a drink or drugs binge in the last few years, I had found myself thinking there must be more to life than this.

Just telling friends I was doing yoga freaked them out and they started to think I was a massive hippy and had lost the plot. I was unable to share a lot of the stuff I was doing because they would have thought I was insane.

I began to think about the spirituality of my ancestors. I was with the Mayans now, but what were my roots? Were they Celtic, Pagan, Druid maybe? When did my ancestors have to start conforming out of fear of being ostracised and murdered by the church?

A fire was beginning to burn in me, sparking a thirst for knowledge.

I woke to the 5.30 am alarm, showered and prepared myself for the day's proceedings by wearing all white and made my way to the roof terrace to meet those who had decided to start the day with the Cherokee Sundance. As I stood there meditating with Ladan, Joyce, Linda, Kerri, and Lilly, waiting for the others to arrive, Ladan suddenly started to convulse again. She was being held up but kept forcing herself down. Her knees went weak, and her whole body looked heavy and her limbs all loose. She ended up on the floor, screaming in agony, breathing really fast and hard. I was bent over to support her on her left side.

The screaming was intense, and she was in so much pain, you could see the strain on her face, all the veins in her neck pulsating. She gritted her teeth and grabbed my arm so tightly I thought she was going to rip it off. Her breaths were getting really fast, strained and painful as if she was pushing something out.

I was thinking, 'Is Ladan pregnant, or has she been implanted with a new Jesus?'

The screams and the convulsions, or what I now deemed as contractions, were getting faster and more intense, the pain contorting her face and her whole body rising and falling as the pain got stronger and stronger. I stroked her temples and forehead as the searing pain and body spasms continued.

At this point, Sandra and Debra joined us. We were all sitting or kneeling, and although these screams of pain and distress were emanating from Ladan, there was a very soothing calming energy coming from the seven of us, like we had created this veil of impenetrable protection.

Calming songs were being sung, and soothing noises and chants were being made. The contractions gradually got faster and more intense, and the pushes and the forcing something out were getting more and more determined. The strain and concentration on her face were remarkable to watch. Everyone was eagerly awaiting whatever it was that was about to pop out of her. The final pushes came, and the grip she had on my hand was crazy, then all of a sudden the release came. Relief spread across her face, and her tense body started to relax. Sandra was the person at the business end, and as Ladan's breathing started to form a more regular rhythm, she realised whatever it was she had just delivered had not been delivered to her. She became flustered and started screaming, 'Give me my baby, give me my baby, give me my baby.'

Sandra passed Ladan her baby. As soon as she was passed this ethereal ball of energy, Ladan's expression immediately changed to one of peace, joy and love. She was looking at something I couldn't see, and after a while, the channel spoke through her again.

It told us this was the new dawn and the Messiah had just been delivered to help people through this time of transition.

As we leaned Ladan up against the wall, I realised how drained she looked. All the energy and glow she had previously been radiating had completely left her. We'd all witnessed something very special. The feeling was one of a new arrival, that radiance that surrounds the labour ward of a hospital or a house that has just brought home a new baby. We all hugged again and got Ladan into a more comfortable position.

Seeing all the women gathered around Ladan was moving. I then realised I was the only male present; none of the other blokes had made it. What did that mean? What did it all mean? I felt extremely honoured to be there to witness it.

Ladan was shattered, but the rest of us decided to go ahead with the Cherokee Sundance.

It was a bit like Tai Chi. We went around the four cardinal points welcoming in the new day and connecting with Mother Earth and Father Sky. It was really peaceful and calming, and every part of me felt at ease.

When finished, Linda came up to me and said, 'thanks for showing us your bum throughout that.'

To my horror, the white fisherman pants I was wearing had fallen right down at the back, exposing my black boxer shorts. Thank God I hadn't gone commando!

We gathered around the shattered Ladan who thought it was

funny that I had kept so calm during it all. I told her that after Tikal, I didn't think anything could really surprise me anymore.

We then realised that the birth had taken place at 6.12 am, which was 12:12 pm in the UK. So the time of birth was 12:12 on the 12.12.12. Madness, but so, so perfect.

At midday, we reconvened with the whole group on the hotel roof. It was time to connect with the 12:12 energies on the 12.12.12.

It was to be the final time we would all meditate together. Ladan took us deep. I felt as if I was following her, word for word. She asked for us all to be shown the right path in this new age we were entering. I felt utter peace, so happy and joyful. I didn't want to come back to this world I struggled so much with. I wanted to stay in bliss. All my limbs were fully relaxed, and my head was bent over almost touching the floor. I wanted to hang there forever.

What we had all experienced in the past ten days had blown me away. I was so privileged to be with these people. It had been the most amazing experience I'd ever had. We sat there in awe and amazement at the energy we all created together.

Debra beautifully went around each person, blessing them with some sacred water and kissing them on both feet. It felt like the perfect ending to the meditation. Ladan then gave each one of us a beautiful small ball-shaped crystal so we would all stay connected when we went our separate ways.

I decided to buy 21 rainbow friendship bracelets and give them to the 21 souls I had become so accustomed to on so many levels over the last days. I wished that all their hopes dreams and prayers would come true.

We sat in hammocks or lay on the grass as Josh surprised us by being our Mayan speaker for the evening. He gave us the best lecture I have ever witnessed, about how, to the Mayans, science, spirituality and art were all interwoven. All as important as each other.

It was such a concise and passionate account of the importance of these times and the impact they have made on the whole world. It was insightful to think that the Spanish had almost decimated a whole civilisation and its beliefs and had tried to destroy and hide the achievements these advanced people had made over many thousands of years.

As I listened to Josh, I thought about how good he would be at teaching, lecturing in universities to history, anthropology, science and art students.

As we all stood around, it was time for cuddles and goodbyes. I was genuinely upset that this experience was ending. I wondered what I would do without everyone, I was so used to their company and energy now. How would I continue on the right path without them? Could I meditate alone and start making decisions for myself again? I was emotional and scared that Ladan was leaving and I would have no physical contact with her for a while. I'd become reliant on her guidance and energy and was worried I'd crumble without it.

I didn't know what my next move would be. I knew I wanted to go back to San Marcos for a while and then figure out what I was doing for the 21.12.12. Dominic and Debra were hanging around in Guatemala, so we decided to stick together for a while. It had been so nice not having to make any decisions for the last ten days, and now it was going to be back to hoping I made the right choices.

One chapter of my adventure was ending, and the next, I had a feeling, already knew exactly what it had in store for me. I received those all-important last heart-on-heart hugs, and we all went our separate ways.

CHAPTER 7
WHERE WILL I REST MY HEAD?
LIFE, 2011

I stand looking through glass, pondering my options for the evening ahead. There are two very distinct life events that could take place. They are both completely different, there is certainly no choice involved for me, as the outcome of where I will be spending my evening lies completely in the hands of another person.

I'm in London, south London to be precise, in a large 1960s-built building. The room I stand in is adorned with rich mahogany fixtures, high ceilings and people wearing wigs. I stand in a room within that room, but there is only one ceiling. The glass panels that make the walls of my room don't reach the ceiling.

There are chairs behind me, but I'm looking out, nervously fantasising about my potential outfits for the different events that could take place that evening. One outfit will be chosen for me. The other will be vetted by my girlfriend, Fhian.

I can see the reflection of my face in the glass. I play with the depth of my body, manipulating the light and swaying back and forth and side to side, making sure my hair is looking ok. Just outside my separate space behind me, sits my Dad and my friend Mat. We are all eagerly waiting to hear what outfit I'll be wearing that evening.

The first possible outfit will be associated with the film I starred in called Lotus Eaters. The film premieres at the London Film Festival tonight, one of my potential destinations for the evening. Lots of my London friends will be attending, and I'll be taking part in a Q&A with the other cast and crew members and talking to the press.

After the screening, there is a big party planned in the British Film Institute building on the South-bank, and I've told everyone that I'm going. But there is a very distinct chance that I won't be in attendance. Very few people know the other possible destination for my body tonight and my other possible outfit.

For the last six weeks, I have been staying with Fhian. I moved out of my flat, put my various belongings in different storage places and, in a way, left society. I handed over my phone and my wallet to my dad, as there is a possibility I won't be leaving this room-within-a-room the same way I came into it.

BACK TO REALITY (OF SORTS), THE JOURNEY, DECEMBER 2012

I rose early to say goodbye to the group, half asleep, I managed a few cuddles. There was no morning meditation.

I had no idea how to start my day. I had to find a place to stay with Dominic, so busied myself with that. Gone were the days of luxury hotels and back it was to budget dorms in hostels. I'd convinced Debra and Dominic that San Marcos was the place they wanted to be after the pilgrimage and we planned on spending some time there together.

We arrived at the central plaza later that evening to meet Benjamin. He elegantly strode towards us, looking like an old-money French bourgeoisie who would have been more suited to trotting around Cap Ferret in mid-August.

I assumed we were going for a coffee and maybe some food close by.

We jumped into his VW camper van, the likes of which I hadn't seen before in Guatemala, then stopped outside some big gates. I had no idea where we were or what was going on, but I was excited.

We jumped out and were introduced to a wide-grinned American called Tucker, who was wearing a Japanese silk jacket. The others smoked a joint, and we headed to the reception where we are introduced to Isaac, Pamela and David, all from New York. They were over here to shoot a movie about the end of the Mayan calendar.

Isaac was head of the Shamanic Society in New York, Pamela was a renowned Reiki Master and David, a documentary filmmaker.

We all jumped into Benjamin's van and, moments later, arrived at a large drive leading to a Roman-arched entrance. We were greeted by Gabbi, a beautiful, elegant lady wearing a traditional Mayan blouse, and making it look very high fashion with her tight fitting jeans and heels. We also met Derek, the owner, who was a larger-than-life American.

As my eyes swept the kitchen (where a cook was preparing food) and back to where I was being led, they were met with the image of this Roman-themed swimming pool. Stairs led from the path to the pool from all sides. Sitting within tropical overhanging plants was a huge concrete Acropolis-style column and a seating terrace that looked straight out of a James Bond film. I couldn't believe where I was and what I was seeing. I imagined how proud my mum would have been, and how posh she would have thought I had become, hobnobbing in such abodes.

We were taken below ground to see the spa and jacuzzi which were situated next to two massage rooms, with a small passage leading to a sauna and steam room. High-end granite adorned both the walls and floors. There was a huge lounge with French doors that looked symmetrically out over the swimming pool. It was spectacular.

We were then taken to a room in the apex of the building, and Derek told us how he'd had the place built from scratch. The room had bed-sized sofas all around it. It had some smutty undertone, and I was sure I had seen rooms like this in porn films. I lay back and chilled. Luckily no one started taking off their pants.

I was instantly drawn to Isaac, and we spent a lot of time talking. It was fascinating to be with a real shaman after the last few weeks I'd had. He had been taken on a trip to the Amazon in the mid-1990s, had done an Ayahuasca ceremony, and it had changed his life completely. Immediately my ears pricked up.

I had heard quite a bit about this plant medicine over the last few years and had already made my mind up that I wanted to do it in Peru. It was high up on my list of things I wanted to experience on this trip, but I didn't want to do Ayahuasca until I was in the Amazon. Isaac told me about the way he combined his marketing business with his shamanism in New York, I was again blown away by the people I was with.

After much chat and mingling, a musician turned up, and we were led to the lounge. A fire had been lit outside the French doors. The lady sat on the floor and took out this instrument that I can only describe as a spaceship or a wok with the lid on. I later found out it was a hang drum and you can only get them made in Switzerland. She kneeled down with the wok between her legs as we sat on the sofas, facing her.

The swimming pool and magical gardens were out of focus behind her as she began tapping the instrument. The sound it made can only be described as otherworldly, like nothing I had ever heard before. As she got into her groove, she would make these beautiful screams and screeches that took me to another world. It was as if I had drifted into an altered state of consciousness.

She finished, we all came back to reality, and all asked for more, but she had to rush off to her brother's birthday party.

When we were dropped back at our hostel, Dominic turned to me and said, 'What just happened? I thought we were just going for a drink with your mate'.

'I had no idea,' I said,

'When we first arrived, I thought "what is Liam into here? Is it a drugs deal? Is it some hedonistic game? Or am I dreaming?"'

In a spin, we made our way back from the millionaire mansion to our three-pound-a-night budget bunk beds.

Benjamin drove us back to the lake the next day. We discussed vegetarianism, something that was pretty new to me. The night before, Benjamin had told the heavy-set American, Derek, that 'his body was not a cemetery for dead animals'.

He told us that the way people ate meat today was terrible, as we eat our food a long time after it has been killed. The animals people eat have had very unnatural lives, pumped full of antibiotics, and when they are killed, they are full of fear. That fear, terror and anguish that is stored in their cells are taken into our bodies. He said that any goodness that comes from eating meat is secondary to all this. I thought, maybe it's like being person number two in the *Human Centipede* film.

I found it interesting to think that we only eat herbivorous and rarely carnivorous creatures. I learned that animal flesh contains a high portion of toxins and that 80% of food poisoning comes from meat or meat products and that, by eating meat we are compelling our bodies to adapt to a diet for which it was not designed.

I remembered learning at university about and how inefficient and wasteful the meat industry is. I thought that, once people became conscious of where their food comes from and how it affects them, their minds would gradually open and they would come to realise that all creatures are as important and conscious as themselves.

I had been pretty sure I was going to stay a vegetarian after the pilgrimage, but now it was like the penny had finally dropped. It felt weird like I was coming out or something.

When we arrived at the lake, we hired a private boat to take us to San Marcos. We bounded across the choppy lake, and I instantly felt its power. It was comforting and made me feel like I was home.

That evening was my first dancing chant session, and it was to Benjimin's mantra of Baba Nam Kevelam (love is all there is). We danced around in his front room chanting for about half an hour and then sat in deep meditation.

The next few days, I was on a high. There were amazing people everywhere, and I felt so happy and confident, walking around the place, chatting, and just blasting out these big hugs to everyone I get within hugging distance of.

Josanna, the Atlantian Priestess, was there again. Her grace and stature intimidated me, and I began to have sexual fantasies about her. She was nice and friendly and interesting and so attractive, even though she was old enough to be my mother.

I met a guy called Ananda, and it turns out he had helped bring up Josh, our guide on the pilgrimage. It was odd this connection was again happening. Benjamin, then Josh and now Ananda. Ananda hadn't spoken to Josh for a couple of years and was planning on seeing him for the 21.12.12.

I hardly saw Dominic and Debra as they absorbed all the treatments, atonements, activations, kinesiology and chocolate ceremonies. Debra looked like a new woman. She was in awe of San Marcos and grateful to me for convincing her to come.

Dominic was soon draped in local artisan clothing, and everyone was digging San Marco and La Paz. Me, Ananda and two Aussie girls I met formed a family.

One day, we all headed for the rocks to swim and chill and sit, chatting about our lives. I spoke about my dad and how funny and crazy he was, stating his life's interests as tits, karaoke, painting and decorating (now replaced by Sudoku, which he pronounces Sudukki) as he's retired. I told them his favourite joke, for which I needed a volunteer.

I asked Emma, 'Have you ever had a parrot on that shoulder?' pointing to her left.

She said, 'Yes'.

I said, 'That's no good.'

So I asked Ananda, 'Have you ever had a parrot on that shoulder?,' pointing to his left.

He said, 'No'.

I then asked, 'Have you ever had a parrot on that shoulder?' pointing to the right.

He said, 'No'.

I said, 'Open your mouth.' He did, and I said, 'You've had a cockatoo in there'.

The Aussies fell off their respective rocks pissing themselves laughing, whilst Ananda the Krishna devotee fresh from his midday prayers was left jaw-dropped.

Jane couldn't wait to get home and do the joke on her two boys, Emma couldn't stop laughing at the fact that Ananda was the victim and I told them how my dad does that joke to every girlfriend I've ever brought to meet him. We all became mildly inseparable for the next couple of weeks.

One night we found out a Mayan ceremony was taking place on the top of the hill overlooking the lake. We were told the Mayan shaman had recently completed his training, which had been lost for a generation in his family.

The ceremony was in preparation for 21.12.12. The fire was constantly burning, and we spoke Nawals, which are affirmations you say in your head for loved ones, loved ones in spirit, the people of the world and Mother Earth. During each Nawal, every person was given a candle to offer to the fire, and we were supposed to either ask for something for yourself, a loved one, the Earth or healing. It was powerful, and I tried to think in my head of all my friends and send them all good vibes. When it got to new births, I asked for health for all the babies that had come into my life, all those that we due to come into my life and for amazing souls to be sent to the friends of mine who were trying.

It was, of course, the Nawal about those in spirit that cut me up the most. It was so nice to have support from Ananda, Emma and Jane as if they instantly knew I needed extra love in at that moment. It was also nice to give them my support for their own losses and to be able to feel and help their pain. We had chatted a lot about my mum's passing and how I could now get so many positives from it. I'd also told them about how I had this weird way of communicating with her from time to time.

Everyone held hands in a big circle and said our thanks to the spirits, each other and ourselves for being there. When the ceremony ended, we formed a massive cuddle ball and held on to each other for a long time. It was pretty amazing.

There started to become a little crew of us in the evenings, eating at La Paz, or a little commodore around the corner. Some

German girls, an American and a Guatemalan couple, became part of our evenings. We didn't really venture far, but the love from this group of people was addictive. There was so much laughter and hysterics, it was infectious, and other tables would start laughing because we couldn't stop.

One night I was starving at the commodore I wanted food quick, it was a major emergency. I ordered and sank back into my chair and said, 'I am absolutely ravishing.'

After a second, everyone said 'are you?', and started laughing at me, knowing I had meant another word. I blushed and cursed my vocabulary, citing my dyslexia for this Freudian slip.

After the laughing died down, none of us could think of the word I wanted to say. It was frustrating everyone. It wasn't until the next day when Ananda ran up to us shouting 'ravenous!' that we overcame the frustration. We were mildly annoyed that we hadn't gotten it quicker than the native Guatemalan. We rolled around laughing and then ravishingly trotted off for breakfast.

We all (well, mostly me) became obsessed with the local chocolate, which was the best I had ever tasted. It came in these little cylindrical wrappers with pecan, raisin, coconut, and almond flavours. There was amazing hot chocolate everywhere, and my sweet tooth was throbbing all the time. The local chocolate was sold by the beautiful local Mayan girls in traditional dresses who balanced baskets on their heads and were always telling you they had no change if you didn't have the right money.

I was drinking fresh coconut water every day, which was prepared by a man wielding a machete who would then delicately pop a straw into the hole he'd made.

Even though I had this new family, I was feeling a bit lost after leaving the pilgrimage. Meditation by the lake seemed to pacify some of my negative emotions of overwhelmingness and detachment. Making decisions about where I was going next scared the life out of me. My thoughts, as usual, were a thousand miles an hour and my control of them was limited.

Dominic and I talked about how we were feeling and what our part had been on the pilgrimage. We realised we were like the middlemen that kept everyone happy; we floated from group to group keeping everyone in tune with each other, which we realised was a very important job.

I tried Qigong, which was revitalising and such an amazing

way to start the day. I then bumped into Isaac again and gave him a tour of La Paz.

We sat down for a drink and some breakfast, and I said, 'What are you doing here man?'

'I don't know actually,' he said. 'Maybe I'm here to see you'.

We spent a few hours chatting. The best story he told me was about an apprentice shaman who had been training with a master shaman for a year. One day his teacher told him to meet him outside the church in the plaza at midday. The apprentice arrived at 11:45, waited for his teacher, and as time passed the teacher didn't show. A man in a suit came and sat next to him for a while, but his teacher still didn't arrive. After a while, the man in the suit left, and he waited a further three hours, thinking this was some kind of test. After another hour, he left.

The next day he went to meet his teacher. The teacher asked where he had been the previous day, and the student replied, 'On the bench waiting for you and you did not arrive.'

The teacher said, 'I was sat next to you for 30 minutes, and you didn't greet me, so I left. Why did you not great your master? Do you only recognise me in these gowns? Am I not your master without them?'

The moral of the story for me is that we can learn something from everyone, never rule someone or something out because of their appearance, as you never know what gem they may have for you.

It turned out Isaac's wife was a Qigong master, and I was amazed I'd gone from never hearing of this thing to being told about it twice in a morning. I had to rush off for the chocolate ceremony I had been looking forward to. When I arrived it was already in full swing, so I headed back to La Paz for lunch with Benjamin.

CHAPTER 8
WHERE WILL I REST MY HEAD? 2
LIFE, 2011

My other option for the evening is actually prison. Which prison I have no idea, but prison nonetheless. Meaning I'll be wearing prison clothes. Options on style and design are very limited, I believe.

I imagine I will be spending the evening acquainting myself with new surroundings, possibly getting to know a potential hardened criminal who will become my roommate and sleeping above or below him on a thin mattress, as opposed to styling out some threads and going to a glitzy party with lots of my friends, beautiful models and actors and then making love to my beautiful girlfriend in her big comfy duvet-covered bed.

That conundrum is out of my hands, and firmly in the hands of the judge I am facing. He comes into focus when I decide to bend and sway away from my reflection on the glass wall. He looks like your stereotypical judge, leaning back on his chair, draped in robes and squinting at people over his half-moon spectacles and addressing them in an impatient, superior manner.

My barrister has told me there is very little chance of me not serving time. It will be a minimum of six months, but could be more, she says.

At my first trial, I'd actually thought that if I was found guilty, I would go to prison that day. I'd stood up to face the jury, praying for a not guilty verdict, watching the appointed leader stand up and deliver my fate. As he said 'guilty on all counts', my world sank. I couldn't imagine not touching my girl every day, or not going for big long runs in the beautiful royal parks of Kingston-upon-Thames.

I turned to face me Dad and Mat. Dad smiled and put his thumbs up, mouthing the words 'Well done, son.'

Mat jabbed him in the ribs and whispered something in his ear. His expression immediately changed, and he put his hands on his head and called out, 'Oh my God".

After they finished telling me in more detail that I was guilty, they said that I had to come back for sentencing. To my surprise, I was let out of my room-within-a-room and made my way with me

Dad and Mat to the corridor.

After their condolences, I asked what happened. What made me Dad think it was a good verdict?

He said he'd thought he heard them say 'not guilty' and was over the moon.

'But I didn't have me hearing aid switched on,' he said.

Me and Mat laughed as much as possible under those circumstances.

This was the very reason I had already moved out of my flat and wrapped up my affairs. I hadn't realised you don't go straight to prison.

And now here I am again, hoping my dad has his hearing aid turned on whilst I await my fate. A sadistic part of me really wants to go to prison for a while, to get away from the world and all the pressures that surround my life. I feel it would give me time to have a really good think about what I want to do with my life, but more than anything, it will give me time to write. Writing a book is something that has always been in my thoughts, but something I never seem to have the time for.

I am thinking positively about both options minus the bumming. I have planned things in the outside world as if I was going to prison, and have arranged everything for the film premiere as if I am going to be there. I also have a story for everyone if I do indeed get sent down.

That story is 'Liam's gone to prison'.

Only a few people know about the predicament I'm in. I was embarrassed about the situation more than anything, embarrassed that I had been caught and the circumstances that surrounded it. Embarrassed about the state of my life, embarrassed that I can't see anything positive in my past, present or future.

I have no ethical and moral problems with what I have done. I firmly believe that what I did should not be illegal, but if it has to be, then the only fair thing to do would be to make cigarettes and alcohol illegal too.

What upsets me the most is that I don't want this to be my life anymore. My lifestyle had changed a lot and when I got caught the thought of drug-fuelled parties made my skin crawl. I was still occasionally taking ecstasy, but not as part of two or three-day benders. I enjoy it in moderation and sex whilst high takes me to another world of bliss.

But I am looking for something new now, a new way of living and of being more connected to my soul.

I stand there wondering what people will think if they don't see me for a minimum of six months, wondering what my cellmate will look like, wondering if a miracle might happen and I'll be put in a mixed sex prison.

What is the judge going to say?

21.12.12, THE JOURNEY, DECEMBER 2012

We left early for Lydia's place, the Aussie girls deciding they would join us for the 21.12.12 celebrations. It felt like such a tricky decision as there was the rainbow gathering in Palenque and the big events at Tikal and Chichen Itza I could have visited. I figured a low-key ceremony with little western influence would be more fitting, and the Crystal Skulls were beckoning me.

Most people had told us that this date was a time to go within, meditate, be quiet and feel the new age arrive. I was brought up to think that if I was celebrating something I had to be massively inebriated before the actual event even arrived, and possibly not be able to remember it the next day!

We arrived at Paralajh and via a note and some difficult translations, discovered Lydia had left for Argentina. It turned out we were looking after the place for the next four days. Even with this added responsibility, I immediately felt like I was in the right place, as instant peace showered me.

The 20th consisted of getting things ready for the next day and me and Dom were let loose with machetes, helping the local boys maintain the grounds and thin the trees on the outside road. I was trying to explain using sign language and pronouncing English words in a Spanish accent that me and my mate Steve back home did this with a chainsaw and could have done what we were doing in a day in about 10 minutes. However, it was so much fun whacking things with a machete and made me feel very masculine.

That evening, the Mayan shaman who would be leading the ceremony arrived. We cooked him food and, late in the evening, we held a ceremony to prepare the altar for the next day's events which had been 5,200 years in the waiting.

It was just us five westerners and the shaman. We had no idea what was going on in the ceremony as it was mainly in Spanish and Mayan, but we were all asked to help, with masses of candles, honey and sugar piled into the fire pit in the middle of the altar. It was a pretty long ceremony, and by the end I was struggling to stay awake. We were now into the day of the 21st. The planets had aligned, and the start of the new age and calendar were beginning.

When I awoke the next day, I set my intentions for the day and asked for someone who could translate to be there for the ceremony. After breakfast, Mayans from the surrounding areas started to arrive. The vibe was very special, and everybody was getting various things ready. Ladies picked brightly-coloured petals from flowers with vibrant smiles, men set up instruments, and the shamans got the ceremonial altar in perfect shape.

Chatting outside the altar, I met the translator I had prayed for that morning. Juan was a Guatemalan now living in Canada with almost perfect English.

Thank you, God, I thought, I will have some idea at least of what is happening.

Juan's wife Maria was a nana, which is a bit like a shaman, and she would be playing a big part in the ceremony.

Each person was cleansed by the shaman before they were permitted to enter. Our auras and energies had to be cleaned so no negative vibes would cross over into the new world. Once everyone had been cleansed, and all shoes had been removed, proceedings began. Once again, I sat with my favourite large black obsidian crystal skull. We were all welcomed, told of the importance of the day and how lucky we were to be a part of it. I thought about how European culture only teaches us to live in a material existence of consumerism.

It was interesting to think about how female energies had started to take force in the last 10 years; men caring about their wellbeing, the influx of gyms the decrease of pubs and increased consciousness about diet. Yoga and meditation are in every city, town and sometimes even villages. How would things look in another 10 years? It seemed the yin vibration was starting to glow.

Maybe it's time for us to stop settling for the way things are, to stop turning a blind eye by doing business with crooks and companies that make life hell for people on the other side of the world. Maybe it's time for us to make informed decisions about everything we buy instead of looking at only convenience and price.

Most people are locked into the system; they think they are free, but their cages are just masked to the physical eye.

The movie *Zeitgeist* puts it brilliantly: '*The whole system is evil, the people in it, psychopaths worse for society than anything else*' They are responsible for war mass genocide, famine and mass environmental degradation worse than any murderer or rapist.

The ceremony began, and everyone stood. A few pendulum-wielding Guatemalans vigorously swung them around. Two of them looked as if they had enough Botox to feed the local village for the next three years. The Nawals were introduced, and prayers and teachings were given. Candles were passed around, allowing people to make an offering and fresh honey and sugar were constantly being placed on the fire by the shaman.

I wished all the couples from the eight weddings I'd attended that year a lifetime of happiness together. There were offerings for tolerance and justice and letting go of grudges and moving forward. I remembered how I used to be infested with anger and bitterness towards people and thought about how it was now gone. I forgave everyone and, in most instances, realised it was me that was the problem. I knew I had to take responsibility for every situation, regardless of whether I was right or wrong. I knew doing so would make me feel a lot lighter.

At one point, a queue formed and, being British, I thought it was best to get in it. I discovered it was a healing queue and, when I approached the shaman, I had to ask spirit to heal any particular problems I had, be it physical, mental or spiritual. I asked for good knees, so I could do my yoga teacher training in the near future. He did some wavy thing around my head with his incense-filled lantern goblet, and I was hoping he wouldn't smash it into my face. He said a few prayers and I threw some candles in the fire, concentrating hard to connect with the energies of the day. Many of the Nawals were focused on personal healing, becoming more conscious and spreading the awakened spirit.

After we got through all the Nawals, it was time to dance around the fire. The atmosphere was electrifying. People let go and allowed their bodies to loosen and feel the music pulsating. There were so many smiles and so much laughter as the childlike shaman wove in and out in a clockwise and then anti-clockwise dance. The band joyfully played, and the Mayan glockenspiel, this guitar called a Chirimia, and a funny-looking drum called a Tun were being enthusiastically strummed or pounded.

Afterwards, the shaman noticed that a native Indian face had formed in the embers of the fire. There it was, a large-nosed red Indian, so perfectly formed in the flashing red lights of the dying fire. It was a moment of knowing the indigenous energies wanted to send a message and a gift.

As the final swirls of smoke floated upwards from the fire, people were offered the chance to stoke the fire in each direction, making affirmations for the new Baktun which is the next 5,200-year cycle. I meticulously marked a cross in the ash, at each point praying for a world of peace, love, compassion and understanding and for me to stay on the right path and help spread these values.

Once everyone dispersed, we helped tidy up, then headed for a lie-down. I instantly fell asleep.

Sixteen hours later we all resurfaced. The energy of the ceremony must have knocked every one of us for six, including Marco the Shaman.

On the 22nd was another ceremony. This time it was a smaller event with just three other westerners joining us. The plan was to do the ceremony and get back to Pana (the lake) for Ananda's birthday. Ananda rang, and I told him we had to be here all day as the ceremony wasn't over. He was disappointed. I then rang Josh to tell him of our plans for a surprise and the wheels were in motion.

Paolo, the dog, bid us goodbye, and off we went for a chicken bus adventure. We got on the bus almost standing on top of people, seeing boxes of chickens pass by our faces, people somehow climbing over each other to get on and off, and the conductor scaling the roof of the bus whilst in full flight. He would swing along the back of the bus, swinging outside the front door and comfortably managing to take care of all his duties, stay in one piece and collecting money at the same time.

We managed to lose Dom and Jane at one point as we ran for our final bus. Our bags were flung on the back as it was moving and they didn't make it. We were a bit worried at first, then realised there was another bus behind.

We made our way to Josh's house through very narrow lanes and alleys. I had no idea where to go, so when we passed a guy, I asked: 'Joshua? And pointed around.

He looked at me as if I was daft.

Then I did an impression of Josh's walk and mimicked having a mohawk haircut. This was a winner, and he pointed me in the right direction. In shock, everyone followed.

I shouted Josh's name a few times, and he emerged from around a corner, greeting us gleefully. I introduced the Aussies and we settled in to surprise Ananda, all hidden from view, ready to jump out and sing 'Happy Birthday.'

We heard him arrive with Josh's mum, Gabriella, and then we started singing. He was elated and couldn't believe I'd tricked him all this time.

That evening, Ananda insisted on booking us all into a hotel called the Rancho Grande. It was Grande by name and grande by nature; another level to what I had been used to staying in. But the more I got to know Ananda, the more I was realising, this was how he rolled.

CHAPTER 9
WHERE WILL I REST MY HEAD? 3
LIFE, MARCH 2011

I had arranged a date for Friday night with a beautiful blonde nurse I had met on this site called Mysinglefriend.com. I had been having quite a prolific time for the last few months, and this girl was to be my next conquest.

We meet at Surbiton train station at 10:30pm. As we entered a bar and started to get to know each other, I already knew sex was on the cards. She was beautiful, very sexy and I couldn't wait to have my hands all over her.

She wanted to stay out and have a few more drinks, so the barman told us of a place around the corner, and we made our way there. I'd never been there before. Bouncers were on the door and as we approached the girl and I were having a good laugh. I'd taken half an E, so I was buzzing and so looking forward to sex on ecstasy.

I thought the bouncers would nod us in, with it being a bar. But no. Disaster struck, and the guy started searching me. He found a bag of E's in my coat pocket.

'What are these?' he asked.

I said, 'You know what they are, mate'!

'Are you going to sell these in here?'

I said, 'No, mate, I'm out with a girl. I've never been in here before'.

'I'm gonna have to call the police. I can't have you selling these in here.' He made the other bouncer trap me in the doorway as he called the police. The other bouncer kind of wanted to let me go, but I stood there almost frozen. I could have made a run for it and, looking back, I'm pretty sure I would have got away, but for some reason my body just stood there, frozen.

The blonde girl was sitting outside. I couldn't see her, but I knew the other bouncer was talking to her, asking her questions about me.

I wanted to make a dash for it.

I wanted sex.

I wanted to experience this beautiful woman.

I wanted to lie in bed for the next two days, fucking over and over again. I started to think about the consequences of being found with forty Es in my pocket. I figured it wouldn't put me in too much trouble, but the fact that I had another eight hundred in my flat would put me in a whole world of shit.

Two police officers approached, told me they were going to arrest me, and that's when, for some stupid fight or flight moment, I decided to make a run for it.

The CCTV footage would have been a massive hit on YouTube. I jumped through the policemen, and the officer chased me, whilst still having hold of my coat and T-shirt. I spun out of the garments, and as I did, I got a glimpse of my date in super slow motion. She was sitting on the step of the shop next to the bar looking directly into my blue eyes. I'm not sure if I managed a wink, but I thought if I could get away, I could text her to meet me and we could have this amazing escaped-criminal sex.

The next thing I knew, I was being smashed from the side. I tumbled, just managing to keep my balance. I then felt bodies and arms on me as I wriggled and pushed and kicked and screamed.

Bang, I was eating gravel, my adrenaline was pumping, arms, feet and knees are all sticking into various parts of my body.

I knew I was screwed. There was no way I was going to get myself out of this one. I knew my flat was going to be searched.

Pandemonium was taking place in leafy suburban Surbiton, entertainment for the whole bar and all the passers-by. I was lifted and bundled into one of those caged armoured police vans.

I saw the girl looking at me. I had a little giggle to myself, wondering what she will tell her friends when they ask, 'How did it go?'

Will she have the bottle to re-tell the tale?

Will she find the funny side?

Will she find true love?

I wonder if there has ever been a failed first date
to rival this one.

I arrived at the police station, still semi-naked
with the handcuffs so tight that blood was running down my fingers. Eventually, they loosened them and allowed me to put my t-shirt back on. I gave the sergeant an old address, telling them I didn't live in this area and was just visiting from Manchester.

I realised I had acquired a few injuries from the fracas. I had a cut on my face and a massive gash down my right arm, which to this day is still scarred. They put me in a cell and I was still pretty high from the E, so sleep was not happening.

I was trying to get my story right in my cloudy head, wondering how I could get out of this situation, who I should ring, wanting to get hold of my flatmate to destroy or hide what was in my bedside table. I was kicking myself, banging my head and fists against the walls.

How had I been so stupid as to walk into a pub with all those pills in my pocket? All I had to do was put them down my pants, or leave them at home when I'd dropped off my bike. I had been in clubs thousands of times with twice as many pills and never been caught. My massive ball sack would engulf them to avoid detection by the wandering hands of many a doorman. I had crossed borders all over Europe and even been on flights with a ball sack full of drugs.

All I had been thinking about since I got the pills was that this was not my life anymore. I was done with raving and the culture surrounding it, and I was going to give the drugs back the next time I was in Manchester. I was also thinking about how, over the last few weeks, I had been meaning to move them to my allotment where they would be safer and untraceable if I was to ever get into a situation like this.

I assured myself they would not find my address. Possession of 40 ecstasy tablets would mean I would be let go and I could then go back to my flat and get rid of the drugs. I could then try and get back in touch with the hot blonde nurse.

There was also over a thousand pounds in cash in my room. It wasn't from the sale of drugs, but rather from the gardening, painting and decorating, and artist's assistant work I had been doing.

I hadn't sold any drugs in the couple of years since my mum had died, but had been searching for ways to make myself happy again. I had thought about trying to sell them again, so had some in my pocket in case I saw anyone I knew. For the first time since Mum had died, I wondered if maybe she could see what I was up to.

When she was alive in Manchester, and I was in London she had no idea what I was up to but now (even with me being a complete atheist at the time) I felt like she could see me and I needed to sort it out. When my mum was alive, I had felt this cocky air of invincibility, knowing I could always count on her to stick by me and help me out of a hole. But with her gone, I felt like I had no one.

But because I felt so low I was willing to try anything to rekindle my happiness.

Contemplating my situation and life in the cell made me feel so, so low. I had never felt like this before in my life. I was single for the first time 12 years; maybe this was the reason I was feeling so down, or maybe being single had led to the realisation that I had not dealt with the death of my mother. With so many parts of my life in disarray and this dissatisfaction, I felt with myself and everything around me, my anger with the world and the people in it had turned into a deep depression.

Depression as an illness was something I had ridiculed since I became aware of it in the late 90s when the footballer Stan Collymore had brought it to public attention for the first time. I remembered thinking, 'How can you be depressed when you have the world at your feet? You're rich, you can have any woman you want and happen to be amazing at the one thing most boys would give their right arm to be amazing at.'

I could never understand it.

Even when friends of mine were suffering from it, I felt they could just change their state of mind, start doing things that made them happy and stop feeling sorry for themselves. Now I was in it, and nothing I did seemed to shift my mood. I was questioning everything about myself. Loss and loneliness filled every cell of my body every second of every day. But I was determined to get happy again. At times I could see no way out, but I tried to recreate the things I thought used to make me happy, like having lots of money, being at parties and having different women draped all over me constantly. But after buying the drugs, I realised I didn't want to be in that world anymore. I wanted the women but not the drug-fuelled party nights that turned into days. More than anything, I wanted love and to be happy and to have some sense of belonging— something I never remember having.

It was as if the unconditional love I had from my mother and that I'd had for her, had vanished. Now I had no one to give this unconditional love to and no one to give it to me. It was like this lack of love was eating at me. I felt completely isolated.

As I sat in the cell, I decided, 'I have to change my life. I have to start being a good person and doing the right thing.' I didn't want to hurt people all the time, I wanted my life to become simple, settled and sorted. My instant thought was to get back together with my ex,

'The Greek', who had been my rock when my mother had died.

I would get back together with her and surround myself with safe people, people with simple values and stop living in this fantasy world full of dreams and wild ambition. When I was out of this cell, I would get her back, stay with her forever and have babies with her. It would be me and her for the rest of time. She would be my love, and the babies we had would provide me with that unconditional love I so craved. I would do all I could to get a normal job, work hard at something, get a trade and have reliable people around me.

My mind drifted back to the last time I had been arrested. It was when I was in Ireland on a university trip. I had taken a load of pills over there with me. We had been in the Temple Bar area of Dublin for the evening, and as we came out of a club, some of my uni mates wanted to buy weed off some Arabic boys. They were getting ripped off, so playing the big man, I went over and got the weed at a good price, gave it to my mates and off we went to get a kebab. As I was leaving the shop, two police officers approached me and asked to search me. I told them I didn't have anything. The found 18 ecstasy tablets and two Viagra.

They said they would have to arrest me, and as I got in the van, I was petrified. At the time, I thought it would be a massive punishment for possession of such a substance, and I was convinced I was going to be put in prison for a long time. I got in the van devastated and started to cry, mainly for the pain I would cause my mother after all the hard work she had put into me and all the unconditional love she had given.

The police officers had seen me on CCTV buying something from two guys on the street and then giving it to my friends. The female police officer who was dealing with me was pretty attractive, and I was having all these fantasies about her.

I was high, having taken a few pills, so my libido was now in overdrive. I put the tears on heavy and went on about never having done anything like this before. I said I had just bought the ecstasy and Viagra for my friends who were all posh and didn't know how it worked. I told them my dad was from Dublin, and funnily they seemed interested in this and warmed to me from this point on. I told them stories about my dad and the street he was from, and I began to bond with the officers. I think I had gone from idiot English boy to one of their own who'd made a mistake.

I spent a long time in the cell, and I was anxious about what was going to happen. Every time the cute police lady came to check on me I had fantasies of her commanding me to make love to her in the cell. I wanted to feel her body against mine under those thick, itchy prison blankets that were keeping me warm. Instead I had a wank so my mind could rest a little.

I was interviewed and then eventually released on bail. I wasn't actually sure what was going on and why they were letting me go, but if someone offers you freedom you instinctively take it.

It was now light outside, and the police officers pointed me in the direction of the hostel I was staying in. I remember running down the side of the River Liffey, the strong wind almost standing me up as I tumbled forward into the torrential rain that was soaking me to the bone. I arrived back at my hostel as the coaches were leaving for the day's trip. Everyone knew what had happened, but luckily the teachers thought it was only weed I had been caught with so no harsh words were actually spoken.

The mood changed two nights later when we got back to the hostel. The police turned up. They wanted to interview me again back at the station.

I had to bring my wallet and all the cash I had.

The hostel was not happy, and the university ended up getting banned from using it in the future. I was kept in a cell for a long time. I was interviewed and had my fingerprints taken by the attractive policewoman. I was alone with her in the fingerprint room, and again my imagination created all these erotic images of what we could be doing to each other covered in criminal ink.

The male police officers told me they would have let it go, but she had a bee in her bonnet about it. My ego told me she wanted to see me again and feel her hand on mine as she pressed my fingers into the ink. After another interview they released me, and the police officer said I had to attend court on Monday. However, he said "as you're leaving the country on Sunday, just forget all about it".

My wallet was given back to me, and I noticed the money had been moved into a different compartment. I was served a bail receipt for 280 euros which coincidently left me with ten euros in my wallet. Very kind and precise of them I thought. Had I paid a bribe or was this the actual price for my freedom? Either way, I was a happy man, and my mother would be none the wiser. Thank God!

Back to my current predicament. Morning came, and a CID officer was assigned to me. He was a really nice Irish guy who asked me about the address I had given.

I stuck to my guns, and he left.

He came back again and was still pushing for a local address.

He came back for the third time, and I told him my real address! For what reason I will never know. It was so unlike me. It was as if my body, mind and soul had enough and wanted me to be in this situation.

They searched my flat, found the pills and the cash and assumed it was from the sale of drugs. My defence had now become that I was a drug addict, I had a massive problem with drugs and had bought these pills to serve my habit over a period of time and save money in the long run. They didn't buy it, but my brief did. I was charged with possession of a Class A drug on two counts and with intent to supply a Class A drug on one count.

I was going to prison for a very long time.

I started to build up my case.

I went to see drugs workers and counsellors in a fraudulent manor, Narcotics Anonymous, Alcoholics Anonymous, and Cocaine Anonymous meetings. I was trying to prove drug dependency and to show that I was rehabilitating and contributing to society whilst awaiting trial.

My depression deepened. I couldn't stand myself and couldn't sleep. I couldn't even look at myself.

I despised everything about me and wanted to disappear. Suicidal thoughts raced around inside me, and
at times I just wanted it to end. I had difficulties even speaking. At some points, it was as if my voice had disappeared. My whole chest was consumed with fear, and it had spread to my throat. I was scared to communicate, and social situations petrified me. Even around friends I felt like an outcast. I felt like I was infected internally in some way and I felt so uncomfortable in my body. London seemed to amplify the situation. I felt trapped inside the M25 but had no idea where else to go.

The next contact I had with the police provided me with a miracle.

The sergeant handed me the charge sheet and said, 'Oh those pills you had only came back as a Class C after they were tested, so we are only going to charge you with that. You can go now'.

I was speechless. How could this be? I had referred to them as Ecstasy the whole time I was in custody.

I knew someone had to be looking out for me.

The amount of time I would be spending in prison had been drastically reduced. But even with such amazing news, my mood was still so, so low.

All my friends told me I would be better once this was behind me. I hoped they were right, but I knew deep inside something was going on with me that I had no understanding of and very little control of.

The counselling was helping a little, but as I had been referred to her as an addict, I felt like a major fraud. Even at the Anonymous meetings, I was attending, I felt like a fraud. It was strange though; I soon started to feel like I was gaining something from them, I found myself learning stuff about my anger. As I progressed through the 12 steps I felt like a form of cognitive restructuring was taking place within my brain.

It was also the first time I was being confronted with the idea of God. Many people at the meetings placed their faith in whatever power they thought was out there which was greater than themselves. At my first meeting, I got this very uncomfortable feeling flow over me during the serenity prayer. As they mentioned God, I looked at everyone as if they were mad.

A proper London geezer took me aside after the meeting and said, "I saw how freaked you got at the mention of God, I did the same at my first meeting". He said, 'God can mean whatever you want it to mean; something out there you believe in or someone you have lost, or something like the universe that is bigger and greater than you'.

I hadn't really even thought about the universe before. It occurred to me that all these guys were pretty normal. They all drove big cars, and all seemed like proper lads from similar backgrounds to mine. They were similar to a lot of the gangster types I knew from back home. I could see they all had colourful histories, and I was finding it interesting being part of this world I hadn't even known existed a few weeks ago.

I JOINED A CULT, THE JOURNEY, DECEMBER 2012

The sun was just about to rise, so I decided to go for a walk to the lake. Already there was a street vendor serving freshly squeezed orange juice.

The lake was perfectly still and the view of the volcanoes spectacular. I had never seen the lake so quiet, it was simply breathtaking. Very few people were about and, sitting on the dock, I fell into meditation as the sun rose over the mountain behind me.

I was still stuck in this space of not knowing if I should be with Fhian. The girls told me that if I was having doubts, I should end it as it was not fair on anyone. Sometimes I wanted Fhian to be here to enjoy all these amazing experiences I was having. But I knew she wasn't on this path and didn't accept the awareness I was now filling my life with. I wanted to be free and being with someone submerged in the system was difficult. There was also the fact her heart always seemed closed and guarded, and I wanted it to open and blossom and allow me full access. I procrastinated with the girls, and their advice was solid and mature. I knew I had to talk to Fhian as soon as I could.

Jane and Emma were from Sydney and knew they had to be in Guatemala for these special times. Jane owned a quirky café, and Emma was this little rocket of a character who worked as a counsellor/social worker. She used to be a crazy activist, full of anger at the wrongs that were taking place in the world. We both discussed how in the last few years we had realised being angry and fighting something only makes you unhappy and stressed, resulting in more of the problem you're fighting against. Mother Teresa's famous quote was that she would never attend an anti-war protest as that means people are angry with something and that gets you nowhere in a situation. But she would attend a peace march or rally as it concentrates on the things you want, not what you don't want. The rule of the universe is that it will always bring you what you focus on.

Therefore, I discovered it's best to ask for what you do want and concentrate on that, rather than letting your thoughts flow to negative vibes. As Dr Emoto discusses in his book about water molecule experiments, water can hold thoughts and emotions, and as the body is 80% water this demonstrates how our bodies also hold onto thoughts which can be extremely detrimental to our health. Having bad thoughts is held onto by the water within us, so we become what we think.

We left Pana for San Marcos, first stopping to say goodbye to Josh and Gabriella. Walking from his place to the lake, we wandered through small alleys. Music was always playing, and at one point a man and woman in traditional Mayan dress sat playing a guitar and harmonica. It was the perfect accompaniment to a magical walk, their smiling faces showing many gold-coated teeth radiantly reflecting the afternoon sun.

As we stepped off the boat, I saw the familiar face of an old Polish guy called Almik, or Santa as some people knew him, because he was old and had grey hair and a big grey beard. He was a friend of Connor, who I had done some healing on a few weeks ago. I asked him where Connor was he said, "He's gone home back to Belfast, but he broke his walking stick man, he's walking on his own now."

This wave of tingles blew over me. My ego was telling me it was all down to my healing, but another part of me was saying 'rein it in, you can't have had anything to do with that.'

I walked off in a kind of daze, as Almik shouted, 'He broke the stick, man! Can you believe it? It's great!'

We saw in Christmas at the local church which was teeming with converted Mayans. Music gracefully sauntered by our ears, while the tree lights outside the church well and truly defeated on them. It was as if the lights had the devil within and the screeching sound coming from them terrorised all in the holy courtyard. It was like this religion could only give you joy with equal amounts of suffering.

The 28th of December 2012 was my first encounter with the Chocolate Shaman. Keith was a tall, wiry man living in a modest little house with one bedroom and outside space that he used for the ceremonies. We gathered in the ceremonial space, and as the place started to fill, Josh, Emma, Jane and Ananda arrived. The chocolate-hungry explorers sat on cushions or crossed-legged on the floor, striking their best meditation poses as the cups of chocolate were passed around.

Keith entered with a big warm Cheshire cat smile across his face and proceeded to tell us his experience of becoming the Chocolate Shaman. Before we drank, we were told we couldn't drink this if we were a dog, horse or parrot as it would kill us. I was thankful I wasn't a dog, horse or parrot.

He told us he was part of the first wave of people who had been born with spiritual healing gifts and had been given the task of teaching the second wave of people (us), who would surpass the first wave. They, in turn, would be given the task of teaching the third wave, who would become adults in the next ten years and would need our guidance. Again they would surpass us in anything we taught them and so the process would continue.

Gopi Krishna sums it up really well in his book 'Kundalini for the New Age'. He talks about the wealth of knowledge future generations are going to bring and that it will far exceed our expectations. The spiritual connection will be powerful, and our understanding of the capabilities of the brain will deepen and bring great awareness.

Keith explained that cacao is a lost ceremonial medicine with similar properties and uses to ayahuasca, peyote and mushrooms. He told us about the difficulty he had had in finding out its origins, history and uses. Unlike those other medicines, cacao wouldn't take you on a forced journey on which you had little control— you had to be ready and relaxed for the chocolate and willing to take yourself on that journey. Like he said, 'Cacao will take you to the door, but unlike ayahuasca, which will bust down the door for you, you have to open the door yourself'.

I downed the glory liquid, sat back and listened to the rest of Keith's story, starting to feel very mellow and chilled.

After half an hour of Keith's introduction, he asked us to close our eyes, look inside, find the smile in our hearts and bring it to our mouths. It felt like my whole face was starting to glow. There was a sassy Spanish-looking girl sitting against a wall opposite me, and I couldn't take my eyes off her. She had a real sexual energy about her, and I could feel my sexual energy mixing with hers. I asked for it to stop, for me to be able to focus on the inner work I was there to do. Sexual thought after sexual thought kept coming into my head, and then finally, I settled.

People around me were in tears as each person went through their own process. I learnt about blocking— when we tell someone it's okay, not to cry and in turn remove them from their process when actually the best thing we can do is hold space for that person. If we block, the emotion gets pushed down and can be stored in various parts of the body and lead to sickness and disease. It made me think about how we rely on drugs to suppress symptoms, but they have all types of possible side effects that are on that little sheet of paper that comes in the box we never read.

We need to be still and listen. That's what I had been trying to do for the past few years, after realising I couldn't drink, do drugs or eat wheat anymore because it made my body feel so bad. I asked questions and listened, and eventually the answers came.

In the ceremony, I watched people process. Keith spent time with the people who needed to get into a certain space or were struggling with emotion. He either helped the person himself, or put them with someone to hold their space, and in some cases, people gave others energy healing. I was still trying not to look at the hot Spanish girl, but she had this magnetism, and my resistance was waning. I wished there was not such a distraction when I was supposed to be working on myself.

After four hours, people started to disperse. Then this guy, Thomas, who had these beautiful electric blue eyes that lit the room with their glow, started to sob painfully. Keith talked him through it and his apprentice, Angela held his space and gave him energy. It was so interesting to observe someone being in a different world with their eyes shut and you being in a room with people holding their hands up like little satellite dishes, directing energy as if it was the most normal thing in the world.

Thomas cried, laughed, and looked terrified. The whole time, ten of us were holding his space, and Keith was allowing the process to flow. Thomas then journeyed to meet his goddess, and it seemed like he had a good time with her and it got a bit raunchy at one point. Inter-dimensional sex looked very interesting.

That evening I had booked a treatment room in La Paz and had a healing session with Ananda. With him being a Krishna devotee, he wasn't in need of massive healing. When I was working on his aura, I was getting directed to go out of the room. I was being told there was a small tear in the aura that was trying to take me through the window to outside. There was none of this in the manual—everyone else's aura I'd worked on was no more than a foot or two away from their body. I refused to go out the door, so I just moved on to his chakras. I started thinking about why this had happened. Had I done something wrong, or did some people have bigger auras than others?

I then remembered reading that the Dalai Lama's aura covered the whole town he lived in, in northern India. I deciphered that Ananda must have a massive one, being a Krishna devotee. Ananda, you have a massive one was a running joke for the next few days.

There was a little jetty just out of town, the water crystal clear. It was quiet and became a kind of sanctuary for me for the rest of my stay in San Marco. One day, me and Ananda arrive, and there was a tanned girl lying down at the front of the jetty with two boys. She had the most amazing body; dark brown skin with a perfect slightly curvy hips. The glisten of the sun made her shimmer.

It got me thinking about the Spanish girl at the ceremony and how my mind wanted to devour her. I wondered if I would bump into her again. The beautiful girl suddenly stood up I realised it was the Spanish girl. She sexily strutted over to us to say hello. I nervously gave answers to her words, having no idea what was coming out of my mouth. I deciphered she was called Maia. Why I was so attracted to her? Part of me hoped I wouldn't see her again, and part of me wanted to see her again, immediately.

I wondered what I was going to do when my little family left. I would be alone for New Year's Eve. As soon as I thought this, I was asked by Benjamin if I would work at La Paz while I was there, and help set everything up on New Year's Eve. I would work four or five hours in the evening and, in return, would get a free room and free food.

I didn't have to think about it; I snapped his hand off. I loved being in La Paz, I loved the tranquil surrounding, the soft, slow vibe and the fascinating people from all over the world who came and went. I was excited to be part of the place.

I had two weeks before leaving for the Earthship build. There was so much I wanted to do in San Marcos before I left; there were yoga courses, healing courses, stained glass making courses, raw food cooking courses, silent meditation and a dark box retreat where you sat in a pitch-black box for three to five days. A crazy Tibetan yoga guy, Yos, had broken the record recently and done 49 days. When he told me, I said in a thick Mancunian accent, 'Gutted you dint make your half-century mate', which went straight over his head!

As my family left, I dashed off for a Spanish lesson, some Hatha Yoga and then it was back for cacao ceremony number two. Today was different; I knew faces, but not people. The sassy Spanish lady was there again, and we sat back and let the cacao flow into our bloodstream. Keith went around the room working on people. The Spanish girl, Maia was sitting to my right, and we were separated by four people. I was finding it a lot easier to focus my energy today and thoughts of her were few. I was thinking, 'Wow I've got over this.' To each person Keith was working on, I tried to send healing Christ Conscious energy of love and health. Amazing things took place during the ceremony.

A French family of two adult sons and their father had many emotions coming up; there was a lot of tension between one of the sons and his father. Keith worked through this with them for about an hour, trying to get to the crux of the problem and allowing emotions and pain to surface as and when. What resulted was the father and son embracing, which they had never done before. It was powerful and the type of thing that would otherwise have festered on for the rest of their lives. It was the way I'd felt after ecstasy hit me the first time; thinking the world's problems would be solved if you could get all the leaders high on E when they met.

I had set an intention for this ceremony. I wanted direction and wanted to know where I was going to end up as a result of this journey. As I sat in meditation, I had this vision of being at home in Gatley, working on getting the local Cinema back up and running. There was an image of me meditating on top of me van outside the doors of the cinema, and then there was the complete makeover, and it became the focal point of my village. It was a creative hub where kids could screen their movies, and it was also a yoga and meditation centre. It wasn't turned into a supermarket to provide the best economic solution which had been suggested throughout the 11 years it had lazily and scruffily laid dormant but was instead owned and run by locals. The whole place was lit up. There was a central plaza at the front with seating and space for a little market and for people to gather and chat. There were no cars adorning the front of the cinema, scruffily parked half on the curb, the bus stop had gone, and it was this beautiful, open, fresh space for people to enjoy and take pride in.

In this space I was constructing in my mind there was also small educational centre that was teaching local colleges and universities the benefits of sustainable development. The building became home to creative freelancers, and there were no cars, which was a necessary requirement of anyone wanting to live there. Everyone became part of the community, spent their money locally and added some ambience to a once decrepit-looking space. Bikes were being cycled all around the village, and people smiled as they passed each other. The building next to the cinema had been turned into a community café, and the top of the building was being used to project films onto the side of the Tatton Cinema. People nestled on cushions to watch a classic, and 'brilliantlove' was to be the first film screened in the mini cinema.

I came round, and Maia was sitting next to me. I had no idea how she'd got there.

Keith then looked deep into me he said, 'Do you know what you have been doing here today?'

I said, 'Sort of,' as I still didn't fully understand. 'Sending my love around the room to different situations.'

He said, 'You're a very powerful man with great healing abilities.'

In shock, I sat back and continued to listen.

'You are of the Christ Conscious Energy, you know that?"

How did he know this?

'And you are very important for the future. There are around a million or so people with your energy on the planet at this time, most of whom are still infants.'

This made me take notice. Keith was the fourth person who had randomly told me this.

The first time I'd been like, 'yeah ok', the second I was thinking, 'this is just a coincidence', and the third time made the hairs on the back of my neck stand up and I'd thought, 'Why are these unrelated people telling me the same thing?'

Now I thought maybe it was something I should take notice of. I had no idea what I was to do with it or what it meant, but it was nice to have it confirmed again.

I wanted to be shown a path; a path to a good honest life and ultimately happiness. I wanted to know what the bloody hell I was supposed to be doing on this planet.

Keith made me turn to face Maia and told us to look deep into each other's eyes. We did, and I could see a lot of pain and confusion in there— or was that just my reflection? Then he said, 'You two have some stuff to work through together. I don't know what, but you need to spend some time talking, hanging out, go for a meal after the ceremony, talk. I'm not saying it's sexual, but my guides are telling me you can help each other.'

We did as Keith said. I wasn't thinking about having sex with Maia now, that energy had gone. She really needed someone with her after receiving quite brutal revelations which centered around her sexual vibe. But she agreed she really needed to hear them. Many of the issues she had, I'd experienced in the last few years that I'd had been working on myself, so it was easy to offer support. It was like he'd put us together because I was a year ahead of Maia in my development of controlling and becoming more respectful of my sex. It was fascinating; she told me about all the sexual adventures she'd had, and it made me seem like a prude. She said people got the wrong idea when she looked at them. Most of the time she was looking and sending love, not sex, but felt her energy was really confusing.

Maia was actually Basque, not Spanish. She was from San Sebastian and had been working in an orphanage in Costa Rica before she had come to the lake. After our food, we made our way back to Keith's place to help package the next batch of cacao to be sold. It was like a little drug factory. People were filling clear plastic bags with hot liquid cacao and weighing it on digital scales. Another guy would then put the plastic bag of cacao across this small guillotine and seal it. Finally, Keith laid the bags down on the floor of both the bathroom and ceremonial space to harden.

Our work ended, and Maia and I made our way back towards La Paz as she was staying in a bakery next door. She had been locked out of the bakery and had nowhere to sleep. Maia ended up sleeping in my room. We chatted for a while and went to sleep.

CHAPTER 10
WHERE WILL I REST MY HEAD? 4 LIFE, NOVEMBER 2011

In my room within a room, I start to hear words flowing towards me from the big man. He says he'd thought the verdict would go the other way based on the evidence provided.

Good start, I think. Maybe I will get to the film premiere.

He says he couldn't believe the police hadn't stuck with the initial charge of Ecstasy, the class A drug, as everyone had been sure that's what I'd been caught with. Even with the lab results, it shouldn't have been dropped to Class C.

'The police have made a big mistake,' he says. 'Very fortunate for you, Mr Browne'.

My head is all over the place. Part of me wants to go to prison, and part of me wants to stay in the free world; the world I have so many issues with and which makes me feel like I want to kill myself on a daily basis. The programming of my brain tells me to avoid prison at all costs, but a major part of me is really drawn to the possibility of solitude for a sustained period of time. No social events, no constant striving and living up to expectations, no phone calls and texts, no Facebook, no remembering birthdays and no pressures of buying gifts at Christmas. However, I am still favouring what I know, as the unknown has always scared me a bit.

He reads out his sentence.

I tentatively bring him into focus through the glass. The room goes silent. I think about the state my mother would be in if she was alive. I contemplate whether or not I would have told her. I think I would have avoided it at all cost to protect her fragile emotions.

The judge speaks.

The words 'one hundred and fifty hours' community service and no suspended sentence' register in my brain. As these thoughts flash through my mind, I'm sure I've missed something.

'No,' he repeats, 'one hundred and fifty hours' community service and no suspended sentence.'

I am going to the premiere!

I'm getting one hundred and fifty hours' community service and no suspended sentence.

This was never on the cards. My barrister had told me I would do a minimum of six months. Part of me feels numb, knowing I have to go back out into the world and start achieving things. It scares me more than anything. I don't know if I'm ready. Part of me wants to be taken into the holding chamber and to prison, where I can write my book.

The judge addresses me directly and acknowledges that I seem to be doing everything to get my life back on track and that with the references (from seven amazing friends) he has received and the circumstances that ensued my situation, he is satisfied that I am of good character and will pose no threat to society.

I think, 'I only pose a threat to myself, Sir.'

They keep the thousand pounds they found in my flat as costs, and I have six months to carry out the one hundred and fifty hours community service.

Me dad is over the moon, hoping he'd heard right this time. My barrister is gob-smacked.

I am a free man, without this big cloud looming over me any longer. But I felt like that cloud has lifted and the hurricane it had been hiding might now gather some momentum and smash me even further into oblivion.

I am free. It's time to celebrate, go to the film premiere, to be uncomfortable in my skin and want what everyone else has. I felt like I was still in prison though, a prison within me from which I cannot escape.

At the premiere, me Dad enjoys the free buffet as usual. He is completely unaware of what is going on in the film but enjoys being in new surroundings as models and actors swan around with their pretend confidence. I'm not sure if it is to celebrate his son's freedom, but he smashes a pint of Guinness all over the floor. Maybe it's an Irish tradition I've never heard of.

The few friends who had known about my predicament can't believe it, they are more overjoyed than I am. It is amazing to hold Fhian, knowing I can do it for as long as I want now. We make sweet love in her big duvet-covered bed. All seems sorted now, but inside I am still in the midst of war.

GOODBYE, THE JOURNEY, DECEMBER/JANUARY 2012-2013

New Year's Eve 2013, Fhian wanted to talk. I hooked onto a Skype connection, and she was at a friend's party. I really wanted to have 'the chat' with her. I really needed to now. But it was New Year's Eve, and it would ruin her night. But when was the right time? She was always rushed, or we were squeezing each other in, and she only ever wanted to talk about happy stuff.

She knew from our few exchanges that something wasn't right. She'd pushed me for answers on certain topics, like her flying to Mexico and me not knowing where I'd be and whether I wanted her there. Why did I feel like that? Surely if she was the love of my life, I would have wanted her there in a flash? I was trying to figure my true feelings out. Did I want to marry and have children with her? What was the point if we were not going to end up doing that?

She wanted to know what was wrong, what was going on. So I told her. She pushed for it, so I was honest about how I felt, that I didn't know if we should be together, that I was unsure about the relationship, that ultimately, I couldn't see it working out. I had been wanting to have this talk for a couple of weeks. I loved this girl so much, but something was telling me I had to end it. Something wasn't right, and it was heart-wrenching to hurt someone you loved so much and on a night that is deemed so important. She pushed, and I opened up.

Being pushed together with Maia had made me realise I couldn't go on with Fhian. It had been the final straw that had pushed me into action. Fhian had been the first girl I had made this concerted effort to be faithful to, and I couldn't be cheating on her and acting as if nothing was going on. I knew that was what would happen, and I didn't want to be that person. That person was in my past, and I didn't want him coming back.

But it had happened, and I felt bad. Maia and I had woken in the morning and had sex. Straight away, I knew this was why Keith had put us together. Temptation had been too much for me, and I had taken the fruit. I knew I had to speak to Fhian so she could move on.

I wish I had spoken to her before this had happened with Maia. I felt awful and felt like I'd let myself down massively. As I looked at her through the screen, it was as if another lesson was being brought to me. I had to be honest, I had to be truthful about my thoughts, I had to work on my brain and this internal torture of wanting to sleep with every beautiful woman I saw. This plague, this curse. I admire the men who can cope with it. I wanted this aspect of me to change. I didn't want to lie and deceive anymore and, although I had changed massively in the last 18 months with regards to monogamy, I knew I still had an awful lot of work to do.

I told Fhian I loved her very much— which I did— but I needed to do this trip alone, without her as my distant partner. It was the end of another beautiful relationship, with another amazingly beautiful women. It had been fraught with battles between two strong, stubborn characters and it was now over. I felt a huge relief at having gotten it off my chest. I didn't tell her about Maia because I didn't feel it was right. Maia had been the rocket up my arse I needed to make me act and do what I had been fretting about for the last few months. It had catapulted me into action, and I really wish I had been able to tell her before the sex.

I wanted someone who was on this path with me. I was so eager to have children and to bring them up in a holistic and spiritual way. Fhian wasn't the girl for that. She was still entrenched in the dogma of the masses, and I felt restricted in that world.

I helped set up La Paz for New Year's Eve, did some yoga, met a guy called Gavin and a couple of Finnish people, and tried to get my head straight. I was going insane and felt like I could be sick at any moment. I was getting ready to bid the most fascinating, weird, surreal, unbelievable year of my life goodbye. The year in which I had changed my outlook on the world and my life more than any other. I had no idea what it all meant, but I was on this path now, and I hoped it would get a little easier. I was so busy working and meeting new people that I had little time to think about the monumental part of my life that I had just let go of.

It was my first night working, and I floated about the restaurant, unsure of what I was supposed to be doing.

Finnish people arrived. Iiro was very tall, with pale blond skin and long blond hair halfway down his back, with these piercing blue eyes. He could have walked straight into a Lord of the Rings film with no makeup and no costume change. He had this really powerful assured presence about him, and it was like he was from another planet or age.

Marianne was the sweetest little Finnish elf princess, with Deirdre Rasheed glasses, a constant smile and giggle. They wanted to use the kitchen so we could all do a chocolate ceremony together.

'Is it Keith's chocolate?' I asked.

'No,' they said. They had picked various cacao up on their travels so far and had done ceremonies in Finland, so they knew all about its powers.

We brewed the chocolate and sat in the restaurant and began the ceremony, calling in the cacao spirits, sitting back and letting the magic happen.

I was in a weird place for the next few hours, similar to when I smoked weed. I felt pretty alone and paranoid, so I snuck off and lay down on my bed to ready myself for seeing in the new year.

The atmosphere in La Paz was magical. People swirled around the dance floor, and I kept everyone fuelled. This Guatemalan Hip-Hop Mayan Cosmos band came on at 11:30 and apparently sang about consciousness and the political struggles Guatemala had gone through over the last 500 years.

I saw in the new year, kissed a lot of men and women, danced lots and at 3 am sauntered off to bed, alone. It was interesting that the Gregorian new year seemed a lot less important than the 12.12.12 and the 21.12.12 dates to all the people I was with.

It was my first sober New Year's Eve as an adult. I was looking forward to not having to struggle to retrace the evening's events when I woke.

The first day of 2013 was spent having breakfast with Gavin. I discovered he was this 26-year-old from New Orleans with too many talents to mention. He was a Neurological Science PhD student who had already completed his Sivananda Yoga teacher training. He was massively intelligent, spiritual, great at yoga and extremely good looking. I was a little bit in awe of him and wondered why it had taken me so long to get on the right path. Gavin intimidated me a bit and being in his presence made me feel like a bit of a waster. It wasn't all the things he had done, it was my lack of talents that kept running through my mind and my not knowing what I wanted to do with my life.

We ordered vegetarian and ended up getting a plate of sausages. We gave them to a neighbouring family.

After wanting to make no more friends and focus on writing, I had come across a new amazing person I wanted to spend all my time with. We went for a swim by the dock, headed back to La Paz and chilled out with the Finnish people until I started work again.

It was difficult working with the Mayan ladies in the kitchen at first. They only spoke Spanish or Kechi, both of which I was less than competent at. A couple of them were very territorial when it came to the kitchen, and I actually don't think some of them knew I was working there. After a couple of days though, I'd won most of them over by making them laugh. We laughed a lot in that kitchen. Most of the time I had no idea what we were laughing at, but we laughed hard, and my laugh seemed to make them laugh. The ladies I was working with— Elizabeth, Flora, Sebastianna, and another Flora— all dressed immaculately in traditional Mayan attire; long colourful skirts and beautiful intricately-made blouses which were sometimes very floral or depicted Mayan cosmology. They cooked good clean food, and La Paz was renowned as having the best vegetarian food about. My role was to keep the guests happy with a smile and some good chat and make sure they got their food.

La Paz and San Marcos started to fill up with people over the next few days. The lake was apparently the busiest it had ever been. We were letting people camp in the gardens and all the rooms and dorms were full. I was showing people to their rooms, or section of grass, taking food orders and trying to start the tamescal (sauna).

During a busy time, someone paid me for two camping spots, and I went into the kitchen after just ordering two hot chocolates for another couple.

'Dos campinya,' I said, waving a fifty *quetzal* note about and putting it in the money box.

Sebastianna then said, *'Con leche?'*

'Si,' I said, for the hot chocolates.

I then went back to entertaining people. On my return to the kitchen, Sebastianna was making two pineapple smoothies with milk. We then discovered she thought I had said two pineapple smoothies (pina pronounced 'pinya'). She had then asked me with milk, and I had said yes, thus two pineapple smoothies had been made.

The girls fell about laughing. We all shared the smoothies and continued to laugh about it for the rest of the night.

The La Paz gardens were so beautiful and fragrant, and now

they were filled with campers. Part of me wished I had a tent so I could stay there. The whole place smelt like Spain does in the evening when the night flowering jasmine let off their scent as you go out for dinner. The whole of San Marcos smelled like that and memories of childhood Mediterranean holidays with my dad filled my mind.

I loved the evenings I spent with the Mayan ladies and, although communicating with them was difficult, they were a complete joy. I had this real special bond with Elizabeth and I wanted to take her home with me in a purely platonic way. It took a while, but eventually we were all hugging. It was difficult for them as their culture doesn't promote contact with men who are not family or husbands.

One night we decided that to help my Spanish, my name would be *Sanaoria* (Carrot), Elizabeth's *Tomate* (Tomato) and Flora was *Pappas* (Potatoes), so I could add some words to my Spanish vocabulary. The Spanish lessons weren't really doing any good the majority of the time; I would just say *'bon provechio'*, in different tones to mean different things. It actually means 'enjoy your food', but I liked to use it in most situations.

In the evenings, the Finns plus Gavin, another American Flora and Maia and Aida, who were both from the Basque Country, (which Gavin thought was called 'the Best Country') would all hang out at La Paz. Somehow I had formed another family within three days of my last one leaving. It was such a special atmosphere, and I just wanted to soak up the energy and knowledge of all these amazing people.

One day I took a *tamescal* with the Finns. I got in wearing me skimpy little shorts, thinking I was pushing boundaries. They bowled in stark naked. A slightly conservative American in the corner couldn't speak properly for the duration, and I felt overdressed.

Apparently taking a sauna in Finland is like an Italian making a hand gesture— they're pros. They told me how everyone in Finland had a sauna, and every block of flats had a communal sauna for the residents. I wondered how less uptight British people would be if we incorporated this practice into our culture.

Imagine having seen every person in your area naked. It would obviously make us less prudish, and the fantasies about seeing people naked would disappear.

A couple of nights later, I decided I would always take saunas naked from now on. It was slightly dangerous whilst lighting the fire, but very liberating when inside. I was in there with the three Finns and Maia. A couple from the States came to get in, they saw us lot naked, felt overdressed, stepped out, took off their swimsuits and got back in. The American lady was amazing, and it was a pleasure to be able to see her naked, although my glances towards her were staggered so as to not seem like a pervert. Inside, however, perverted thoughts were all that were whirling around my mind, imagining the two of us left alone in the sauna, locked in for my internal fantasies to become a reality.

We lathered each other's skin with salt to exfoliate and then with honey to moisturise. It was then washed off in a very cold shower and then back into the sauna. We laughed and told stories. It was amazing to hang out. Again I drifted off, wondering why this couldn't be something I regularly did at home with friends. Dissatisfaction with my culture festered inside me. Why was this something we only did on holiday? Surely this could be our relaxation. Surely everyone could have one of these in their garden. Surely this could replace our need for TV as our entertainment and relaxation. Surely then we would get to know the people we lived close to in a more authentic fashion.

Everyone left the tamescal; all but me and Maia.

Immediately we were on each other. The sexual tension had built, and built whist everyone else was there. We came together, our bodies slipping and sliding across each other's skin. We made love on the floor, on the seated area, almost standing up against the door. It was hot, it was sweaty, and it was incredibly passionate. She was beautiful and sassy, with this stereotypical Latino body and attitude. Her golden-brown skin glistened with sweat, and the flicker of candlelight illuminated different parts of her as I pushed her hard against the concrete. She spoke to me in this deep husky tone, telling me what she wanted and how she wanted it. Sweat was dripping everywhere, pools were being created on the floor. The temperature rose and rose. The way she said my name in her thick Basque accent drove my senses wild. We writhed about trying to grip each other's lubricated bodies. It was like trying to hold something you could never capture. Ecstasy filled the tamescal as we lay there in each other's arms, naked on the cobbled stone floor.

With our bodies satisfied and relaxed, I hoped none of the

kitchen girls would walk in. As soon as I was content and satisfied, an air of guilt and dissatisfaction flooded my mind. Why could I not enjoy this fully? Why was I now beating myself up? Was sex meaningless without love? Was it Fhian I wanted to experience this with? Would being in love have made it all that more satisfying? I felt guilty for having these thoughts, but these thoughts I had.

Everybody in the new little family was due to leave in the next couple of days, and there was a final supper cooked by Iiro. We all did a cacao ceremony and sat around laughing all night. The most incredible heart-on-heart hugs signalled everyone's departures.

Still high, Maia and I made our way to my little shack, which was like a little sanctuary away from the main buildings and rooms of La Paz. The bed was against the left wall, and on the right, three lines of shelves were filled with my possessions, clothes, crystals and stuff. Next to the door was a window and outside was a sink and place to wash up. To the left of my shack was a free-standing shower and toilet that I had all to myself. Out there, I would watch Maia walk out past me naked to take a shower as I was cleaning my teeth. I would say something funny, and she would say, 'vale' in this casual I-don't-give-a-fuck kind of way. (She told me 'vale' means 'ok' or 'alright' after she had said it about a 100 times) She would glide past me, her perfectly tanned deep brown body with its womanly hips swinging from side to side. I would watch her ass fluidly move, taking in its amazingness.

I knew most men would kill to have this woman in their space, and although I was appreciative of her beauty and what a funny and incredible person she was, something left me dissatisfied. I longed for Fhian and the love we'd had. Something in me needed to feel pure love, soul mate love. Something I had been searching for since it had become obvious I couldn't have it with my mother forever. I needed to find a sexual version of it. Someone to adventure with and create a family with. Where was she? Was she Fhian in the future? Why was I so messed up about all this?

The next day, Gavin and Flora left. I had to be at the Chocolate Shaman's at 9am. I'd said I would pop into Gavin's room to say goodbye before I left. As I opened his door sleepy-eyed, the vision of Flora making love to him greeted me. I walked in and without either of them moving, kissed and hugged them both, said, 'Goodbye, beautiful people,' turned around and left.

I later found a note from Gavin that read:

'Liam. It has been such an amazing time connecting with you. Each and every time we hang out, I am so inspired. I really do feel like we were brothers in another life-time. But now I love you like a brother and can't wait to see all the amazing things you will accomplish. You have such a beautiful way with people and can do anything you put your heart to. Keep in touch, my man. I would be happy to help with any project in the future. I could never forget that laugh and I hope we will reunite again. I will hug you like a brother.
With lots of love,
Gavin.'

I welled up. This was such a moving note from someone I was so in awe of. He was a bloody genius and had the world at his feet and women at his... It was this brotherly love we had, and I truly hoped we would meet again.

In the past, it had been so rare to connect with people on this level, and now it was becoming an almost daily event. Maia and Flora left for Shamuc Champey, and I was left, well, with whoever was to come next.

When Maia left, I felt some relief to have my space back to myself and to try and process how my life had changed over the last couple of weeks. Things had been strange with Maia. I showed her no affection in front of our friends and was even a little off with her from time to time. I felt that public affection was only for the love of my life.

Maia kept telling me that she felt that I had given her so much, teaching her about how to try and control the sexual energy and appetite and the meditations and breath control I had taught her. She wondered what she had given me. She had been upset because she felt like she had just taken from me; taken my sex and my emotional counselling and given me nothing. Finally, I'd told her about Fhian and how she had been the catalyst for allowing me to make that decision. I told her that I hadn't split up with Fhian for her, but meeting her had made me realise that I couldn't do this travelling with Fhian as my girlfriend, waiting for me on the other side of the world and me having to be there for her as I travelled.

This revelation made Maia feel better. She was able to see the part she had played in my changes and why Keith had put us together.

During my time in San Marcos, I had become a familiar face around La Paz, and other faces had become familiar to me. There were regulars for the evening food, and I would sit and chat with everyone.

People from all over the world came into that little space. It was fascinating to hear how the universe had brought them all to San Marcos. There were young people starting their adventures, and there were old people who'd had lots of adventures and been brought back to San Marcos over and over again.

There was one lady called Jamie who seemed to pop in quite a lot. She was stunningly beautiful, with this toothy smile that lit up the space around her like a glow-worm. She would come in and use the tamescal, pop in for lunch and spend the evening with friends. There was a real connection between us, and I couldn't put my finger on what it was. She was stunning, and I really did have a sexual attraction to her. I really wanted a private tamescal session with her. We had arranged it a few times, but it never seemed to work out.

I attended another couple of cacao ceremonies and then decided to have a private ceremony as I knew there was stuff in me that needed to come out or be healed.

The one-on-one ceremony consisted of me sitting in front of Keith and drinking cacao with him.

'So what do you want from this?' he asked.

I said, 'To see if there is anything inside me that needs releasing and to possibly give me some more direction and a calmer mind.'

We started with the smile in your heart meditation and Barbara, Keith's partner asked if she could join us.

'Of course,' I said. I sat back fell into the meditation, and we seemed to very calmly work through some stuff. It was like my whole body was being worked on in some way, various parts of me would vibrate intensely, and it was like I had a glow all over my body. I looked within, and I felt pretty clear, my body felt free from poison and pain.

Keith then noticed something and asked me to bring it to the surface and work with it. It was like this ball of light tingling the top of my head. It was like energy was moving to different parts of my body, and invisible hands were touching me. I felt amazing, happiness was glowing within me. My mum drifted in, and it was like I was a baby again. I sank in my chair as if I was being cradled and snuggled into her motherly body.

I started to sob softly, allowing it to process.

The next thing I remember was being sat upright. All my chakras started to be worked on (by whom I have no idea), from top to bottom, then my head was pushed forward, and my higher chakras felt like they were getting a lot of attention. The force at which my head was being pushed down was pretty powerful. This amazing otherworldly glow seemed to be vibrating in a soft thud all around my body. I didn't want to come back; I was in another world being looked after by something. I wanted to stay there, not return to the stuff I had to sort out in this world.

Keith brought me back around two hours later. My eyes had been closed the whole time. He said, 'That is the quietest one on one I think we have ever done.' He told me everything seemed exactly how it should be, and he felt I was on a path I just needed to have faith in. I wondered why I hadn't had these profound experiences of dragging up locked-in emotions like most people had.

I went for a swim in the lake to gather my thoughts.

I had been to the ceremony that morning, but I hadn't stayed long as it was really busy. San Marco had become inundated with hippies from the Chichen Itza's 21 celebrations and the Cosmic Convergence gathering on the other side of the lake. There were more and more beautiful girls around San Marcos now, and I was being more and more distracted. All these conscious, beautiful creatures floated past me with their pearly white smiles and colourful flowing dresses. The vibe of San Marcos had changed, and it wasn't the place it had been when I'd arrived.

I went to see Keith the next evening.

He said, 'You had a lot of work done on you by forces that most people know little about.' He said he didn't know exactly what they had done, but it would become clear to me. 'Maybe not for a month, or six months, maybe a year or two, so just be patient, and follow your path.'

The next morning, I was getting a shuttle to Guatemala City. It was time for emotional goodbyes with the Mayan ladies. We had a little dance in the kitchen, and they had a little drink, and I found out Elizabeth, my favourite, was a little bit in love with me, so I paid her extra attention. It was then goodbye to Dom and a few others I'd bumped into.

I sat on a wall watching the odd person pass me, contemplating this amazing place; all the love I had felt here and all the amazing people I'd met.

I wanted to see Jamie. I wanted to connect with her before I left, I wanted my energy to be close to hers again. Then she walked around the corner; I had manifested her within a minute. We got lost in chatter. This intense connection was there, and I was kind of gutted I wouldn't get to hang out with her again. There was something between us I wanted to explore. I wasn't sure what it was. Was it another amazing friendship? Was it a sexual experience we were supposed to share? Or was she the girl, the one? I didn't know, and I was leaving the next day.

We said our goodbyes and, as we parted, a massive part of me wanted to kiss her. I bottled it, and we had a heart-on-heart hug, and I went back to my shack.

Would I see this place again? I was intoxicated by it. I had never been anywhere like it before. Life seemed perfect and utopian, but I was sad and still lost, so I had to keep moving.

I woke early, ran down to the little jetty and started to meditate. Today was all about my mum. I had her ashes and wanted to offer them to the lake. A perfect stillness glistened across the water. A few Mayan men in tiny wooden boats sat peacefully in the distance. I asked the lake if it was okay to leave part of my physical mum in this special place. In the distance, I saw this sparkling object. It was pretty far out, but I decided this was a sign of where my mum wanted to be.

Diving in I swam towards it realising it was afloat being used by one of the fishermen. I was out far, and I focused on doing a little ceremony for my mum, telling her this was one of the most special places I had visited on Earth and I wanted her to be here forever. I knew she'd love it here, with all these enlightened souls. I circled the float twelve times whilst releasing her ashes into the lake. I was filled with beautiful emotions of release and love and pride. I could feel me Mum's approval, I could feel her there with me. I was in this magical moment, tear-filled love entwined with my mother's energy. I was tingly, it was intense, as tears dribbled down my face and mixed with the great mystical waters of Lake Atitlan and my mother's ashes.

It was such spectacular scenery; a vast lake surrounded by mountains and overlooked by the two great volcanoes. It was stunning and perfect early in the morning, the sun rising over the tops of the volcanoes, the calmness, the quiet, the cold water so still, enveloping me. I headed back to the dock.

I thanked every part of my life for bringing me here. It was magical, spectacular, otherworldly. I stood and felt everything around me, looking at the lake and volcanoes and then looking at an internal peace I was feeling. I put my trainers back on and happily sprinted back to La Paz to collect my things and say goodbye to Benjamin. As I was leaving, he approached my room, and we had this massive embrace. I thanked him for what I had learnt from; his compassion, his love and his way.

He told me in his flamboyant manner, flailing his arms around dramatically, 'Thank you for bringing so much love to La Paz. It's so refreshing for someone to have your energy without the need for drink and drugs'. I left the most amazing place I had ever been, for one of the world's most dangerous cities.

CHAPTER 11
SEX TIMES 4,
LIFE, 2011

I had a brief moment of being back together with, Renie, the Greek girl after the arrest. Deep down, I'd thought she'd be the girl I would end up with. I thought we would have this beautiful life living together living in Corfu, growing vegetables, drinking coffee and making babies.

We'd been seeing each other again for a few weeks, but something didn't feel right. She went to Corfu for a couple of weeks and, as usual, I was back on the hunt for women.

There was a new girl in my friendship group called Sarah, who I was interested in sleeping with, and it was on the cards to happen at a barbecue for a friend's birthday in New Cross. I didn't want a girlfriend who lived in East London as it was so far from Kingston, but she was hot, and I wanted to try her out.

I'd stopped drinking. The arrest had been the catalyst for this, and in some way, I wanted to be congruent with the stories I was telling at my counselling sessions and the various anonymous meetings I was attending. It was pure sexual desire without intoxicants.

At the barbecue, I got talking to a girl called Fhian, who blew my mind apart. There was something about her that wasn't like the other girls in our friendship group. She was super smart and had this air of maturity and sophistication about her.

I had known of her for quite a few years, as she was friends with some girls, I had gone to university with. I'd always known she was my type aesthetically, but I'd always had this impression that she was stuck up and loved herself. I'd never actually had a proper conversation with her, and when I did, she blew my mind.

My theory was torn apart. I spent the whole night chatting to her, and when I wasn't, I had this desire to be near her. I wanted to be in her space, to feel her presence, to hear the words come out of her mouth and to be made giddy by her mischievous laugh.

Sarah was still bouncing around, but I had nothing to say to her. All I wanted to do was be near Fhian. Her amazing cackling laugh made me fantasise about being naked with her. She was so interesting and intelligent, and one of the most beautiful women I'd ever seen in real life. I couldn't get her out of my head.

I thought she had a boyfriend, but after some Facebook investigatory work, I discovered she was single. I cut to the chase, added her and asked her out. No flirting, I asked her straight out, and she said yes.

Boom. I was in.

At the time I was auditioning for a role in a film where I would have to play a tango dancer. I was trying to learn to tango, so for the first date, I thought I would kill two birds with one stone and take her to a tango lesson.

I was so nervous about meeting her because I really liked her. I was nervous about dancing as well. The fact I was so nervous showed me something deep within me: I was never nervous on dates so this woman was special.

I didn't realise it at the time, but the tango lesson meant I got to touch her body straight away. When I did, this electricity flew up and down me. It felt perfect, and I could already feel how amazing she was going to be naked. Wild fantasies were running through my head over and over.

Neither of us were that good at the tango, but she definitely picked it up quicker than I did.

We did some kissing in the bar afterwards, and I knew this was going to be more than a few dates some sex and bye-bye.

I left her at the station as we were going in opposite directions. We stood and kissed for almost an hour, neither of us wanting to leave, a part of both of us wanting to take it further.

I headed home absolutely buzzing. I was in a dream world again. I knew she was going to be my girlfriend. We went on a couple more dates and were soon madly in love.

She was being warned off me from all quarters. We had so many mutual friends, and my exploits were not exactly private. However, I had captured her imagination, and she said she liked that I thought about things differently. All the people who knew the way I was didn't want her getting hurt. I promised her that I'd changed and that I really didn't want to be that person any more. I wanted to be free from lies. I knew something was changing in me; the twelve-step meetings I was attending were making me try my best to be honest.

It wasn't because of her; she wasn't the girl I met who made me change, I had just gotten to a point in my life where I really didn't like myself. I wanted more honesty in everything I did. I didn't want to be the cheating person I'd always been. I was at a point in my life where I wanted to stop hurting people. I think the added pressure of her being warned off me by everyone spurred me on to change and to change people's perceptions of me. I didn't want the tag I had created anymore.

I made a vow to become a better person.

I made a promise to myself, and I made a promise to her and everyone I met. I told everyone that I was going to be a new Liam and I wanted to do everything I could to avoid messing this up.

I was completely mesmerised by her. She was amazing, intelligent and wanted to change her lifestyle and live a different life in the future like I did. We couldn't get enough of each other, and it was the most amazing sex I'd ever had. It would go on for hours and hours, and we couldn't put each other down. Hours would sometimes turn into days, and we would have to lie the mattress flat on the floor so the bottom of the bed wouldn't fly around the room making noise and keeping all her housemates and the street awake. We had this electrifying connection. I wanted every part of her on and in me. Our scents mixed together was like the most wondrous concoction ever created. It was all I wanted to breathe in for the rest of time. I wanted to crawl inside her and become her, I wanted to eat and devour her. In the morning I would breathe her in, and her beautiful scent would stay with me for the whole day and spur me on, knowing I would get another hit that evening. I'd never had a sexual connection like this with anyone before. I wanted her every minute of every day.

In my head, I was still battling every day; battling to change, battling not to compare her to my ex, who was constantly on my mind. I was always comparing them. Although it was amazing with Fhian, there were things The Greek did better, things she thought about differently and concepts about life that we had that Fhian didn't agree with. The sexual chemistry with Fhian, however, was like a formula science had been looking for since its inception.

Opportunities presented themselves with other women, but I kept to my word and kept saying, 'no, I'm with Fhian, and I won't mess it up'. I had this constant head chatter telling me I should be with other girls and she wasn't enough for me. It was like I was being tortured; this mental madness continually went around in my head.

I was in constant peril.

I refused to go out and put myself in situations where I might be tempted by women. I only wanted to go out if it was with her. Other than that, I would stay in. I was fighting these constant urges to be with other women. I fought and fought them, I knew I was getting all I needed and more. But at times when love wasn't being shown as much as I thought I needed it, the voices would start up again.

For the early part of our relationship, I was tortured by the pain I had caused Renie. I was unsure if she was still the one. I was asking myself if either Fhian or Renie was the one or if actually, it was someone else. All I wanted was the one, the one I would have my family with. I needed family to give me that unconditional love I had so desired since my mother's death.

I was madly in love with Fhian, but I didn't want a life in London. I hated the place and all the constant social commitments.

Renie was a real family girl. She didn't have all the social commitments Fhian had. I felt like she had given me more attention as she didn't have as many friends as Fhian, and I always felt like I came first to her. Whereas with Fhian, I often felt second best.

I had felt as though I had from Fhian what I hadn't had with Renie, but now I wanted some kind of happy medium. This internal torture was at times too much, and I wanted it out. I wished I could just enjoy what I had.

Fhian and I were having a beautiful time together and were so loved up. But I had to break away from London. I was going insane and wanted to kill myself. I knew that something there was killing me, and almost every day I felt like I wanted to die.

I hadn't told Fhian about the court case I had coming up, because I didn't really feel it was an impressive story to bring up on the first few dates.

But I wanted to be honest with her and give her the option of breaking it off before we got too involved. I got the bottle up to do it, telling her there was a good chance I would go to prison for about a year. She wasn't over the moon, but she said she too was in love, and we should cross that bridge when we came to it. Although she didn't want anything to do with the court case, she still wanted to be my girlfriend.

My friends were starting to see a change in me. The way I talked about women had changed, my vocabulary had changed, and my need for constant sexual attention was fading away. It was like time was disconnecting me from my old self.

I didn't get sent to prison, but I still ended up leaving Fhian and moving back to Manchester.

I had to get out of London. It was killing me, and I felt that doing my one hundred and fifty hours' community service in Manchester would allow me to reconnect with the area and see if there was anything for me there. I knew London wasn't for me and I couldn't stand the place and its madness. I felt lost and lonely and like I didn't belong there, even though I had lots of friends. The girl I was in love with was there, but the depression was making me search for answers. One of the first answers I was internally told was to get away from London before I died.

Fhian was gutted. We missed each other a lot, and we really wanted to test our relationship, to see if it could work far into the future because the love was so intense. With her being committed to London, we had a long-distance relationship, meaning lots of trips back and forth. When we were together it was intense, we fought and argued a lot but, man, we loved each other so much.

There were tests to my fidelity, and one of them was going away with my old lad mates from Manchester on a stag party. I was dreading the event because I was going to have to drink for three days straight and get involved in activities I didn't think I was into any more.

I hadn't really been part of this group of friends for eight years, and I was a completely different person to the person who had left their world so long ago. I was also a little scared of the temptation of women who would be everywhere we went.

I ended up having an amazing weekend and great banter, bonding with people I'd felt I would have nothing in common with anymore. There were no girls involved, and I was about to return from Benidorm with my first faithful relationship still intact, a year after its inception.

We were all at the airport, and everyone was massively horny, and all the boys were looking forward to getting home and getting it on with their ladies. I knew I wouldn't be seeing mine for a week or two. We were all ogling every girl that went past, with three days of drinking in us and no release.

Three girls approached us.

They sat around me.

They told us about the dirty week they'd had with some guys they knew.

They saw them every few months.

They were all married and said that these weekends away kept their marriages going.

We all looked at each other with these frustrated stares.

One of them came and sat close to me.

She had really big tits and was pretty.

She started flirting and telling me I looked like the lead singer from Kings of Leon, which I found very flattering. My ego inflated even more.

I told her I had a girlfriend and that this weekend we had been together a year. I told her how I had changed and, for the first time in my life, I had been completely faithful.

I hoped this would be enough to remove her interest, but part of me wanted to take her there and then on the cold marble floor of the airport lounge.

She looked at me in a way I knew meant she wanted to fuck me.

I couldn't believe it!

I was in a huge airport lounge and had a woman coming onto me. Not just interested, but giving me all the signs for sex.

Our flight got called, and we walked towards our gate.

The girls followed us, and we said our goodbyes.

I hugged the other two girls and say bye, then the girl I had been talking with gave me a hug and held me for quite a while. She whispered in my ear, 'It's a shame you have a girl. If you're ever down south and single, you should look me up'.

My penis tingled.

Inside I was like, wow, this is horny.

I said bye and walked off to catch up with my mates. As I did, I saw a disabled toilet door open and imagined taking the women in there and having sex with her before my flight.

My mates all start telling me about how much the woman was on me. The three women slowly walked past us, giggling and hovering as if they wanted something.

They finally walked off, and my urge to go grab the woman's hand and take her into the disabled toilet subsided.

I felt like I had been poisoned.

I couldn't think straight, the hangover horn was in overdrive, and a moment ago I was standing next to someone willing to relieve this tension.

Part of my ego kicked myself for not taking advantage of such an opportunity.

Then the girls walked past again and glanced over.

I considered it.

This queue I was in wasn't going anywhere. I bottled my urges, trying to stay strong.

I stood laughing with the boys about these relentless women, but as I did, my mind drifted in and out of sexual fantasy. I even considered taking all the women into the toilet, my appetite now so filled with desire and debauchery.

We all started talking about sex and how we would have loved to get into these women if we didn't have girlfriends and wives.

I was actually considering it, though.

They walked off again, and at last I was sure that was the end of it.

Part of me was frustrated, and part of me was relieved that the moment of temptation had passed.

I was still having sweats like some smack-head watching his dealer walk past with the drugs, knowing the disabled toilet would be the perfect place to shoot up.

I turned around. We were only a few people away from having our passports scanned and getting on the plane. It looked like I'd be going home unscathed.

I kept looking straight ahead.

Then one of me mates said, 'They're back.'

I looked, and they were hovering again, looking over at us.

The girl who was all over me smiled.

ANANDA, THE JOURNEY, JANUARY 2013

I had been told not to go to Guatemala City. All the guide books and people had I met had told me about muggers, murderers and kidnappings. None of these people had actually witnessed any of these but they talked about them as if they were real. Guatemala City is widely regarded as one of the most dangerous cities in the world with supposedly over twenty murders a day. However, being from Manchester, I guessed it didn't have as many fights as us per day (most of ours being on Friday and Saturday nights for looking at someone in a way they deem as offensive or for supporting the wrong football team).

I was due to meet my host for the next few days at The Pan American Hotel.

I was expecting it to be quite a swanky place after deciphering the level of Ananda's wealth and style. Even so, considering I was in what is now classed as a fourth world country, I wasn't expecting this!

The small front doors had a security guard adorning them who happily let me in. I was typically dishevelled, carrying a dirty rucksack and a huge cracked plastic bottle of water. I walked through the gold bar handled doors and through a short mahogany clad corridor into what I can only describe as a large bourgeois hotel's dining hall, more fitting to waddling women with Louis Vuitton bags hanging from their forearms. I briefly took in my surroundings, imagining I was in an elegant suit or uniform, about to have an important meeting about the future of the country or the exportation of three hundred million dollars' worth of cocaine.

I was greeted with a huge hug by the grinning, warmly welcoming Ananda, who I learnt was known as the Prince of Panajachel. Desperately needing a wee, I had to close my gawping mouth and head for the bathroom. I returned to find Ananda sitting at a brilliantly white-clothed table. I sat. Ananda had already ordered, and all I had to do was sit back and chill.

I surveyed my surroundings; a huge square room with a balcony peering over at us and people sauntering about. It was stunning in a classic, old money way. It wasn't bling, it was cultured, rich subtlety at its best. Traditional Mayan-dressed waitresses served, and stern-looking waiters whose chins never dropped below ninety degrees took care of other matters.

We sat and drank tea, and it was like seeing an old friend, not someone I'd only met a few weeks ago. It was a pleasure to be in the presence of this massive aura-possessing Krishna devotee again. I automatically crossed my legs to mould into my new persona of a bohemian poet, sipping my tea with my pinkie stuck out and laughing outrageously to everything Ananda said in an exaggerated you're-the-funniest man-in-the-world fashion.

Shortly afterwards, we jumped into Ananda's Mercedes SUV to race around one of the most dangerous cities in the world. The people seemed a lot more polite and less angry than the people back home, but a lot of guns were still being flashed about.

We headed for Ananda's palace in downtown Guatemala. We were ushered through a barrier by the guard and garage doors magically opened, leading to a small courtyard. Big colonial-style double wooden doors provided an entrance into the Magical world of Ananda, The Prince of Panajachel.

The décor in the house was sublime; Indian meets Roman meets a hint of Spanish. Inside met outside with atriums towering the three floors of the building. The first floor consisted of a huge open fire, lounge, Krishna kitchen, Krishna altar, dining table and regular kitchen. The centrepiece was a beautiful stone staircase that led to the first floor. Ganesh, Shiva and other deities accompanied Krishna throughout. A huge Ganesh filled an alcove at the top of the stairs.

My room was Indian and dark wood themed, with Buddhas welcoming me to the left and right of the comfiest looking bed. The next room was Ananda's altar room, with an array of deities, including Shiva Dha'Krsna, Narasimha, and the Six Gosvamis of Vrindavan.

He introduced me and asked them for permission for me to be there, and they welcomed me with open arms.

Outside Ananda's bedroom was a semi-spiral metal staircase that led to the study, music, breakfast, reading and chillout room, with big, bed-sized comfy sofas. This led to the roof terrace with views of the surrounding areas, including the mountains in the east.

I settled into the big sofa and instantly fell into meditation. I felt so comfortable and at home and it was like Krishna wanted to say hello. I sat there and drifted off with Krishna for the first time, whilst Ananda prepared some much-needed chai.

I had the honour of making Puja (offerings) to Krishna in Ananda's Temple. Ananda purified me with mantras and water, then I offered incense to Krishna and his many guests on the altar. I did two circuits of the ten or so deities present on the altar and then a circuit of Ganesh to the rear, and in the corridor, and to some of the family and friends I had pictures of in my room. Each time, I would wave the incense in a clockwise motion four times around the feet, three times around the head and seven times around the whole body. An air of calm surrounded my body as I carried out the practice.

The next day we had arranged to go and have our Mayan calendar reading with Maria, the Nana who I had met on the 21.12.12 journey. Maria lived in a heavily guarded part of town. We had to go through a roadblock to get in, but once inside, it felt like any normal residential area.

Maria couldn't have been much more than five feet tall, but her presence was overwhelming. She gave us a thirty-minute Powerpoint lecture about Cosmo vision, and the Popol Vul, which is the sacred book of the Mayan people. It states that the Mayans descended from a mother civilisation called Tula which gave rise to most of the ancient civilisations. Many books state that they all came from a continent now gone that was in the middle of the Atlantic Ocean called Atlantis.

It is said that the Mayans fled Atlantis and that the Mayan ruins of Tulum (the only ruins out of the many thousands that are on the coast) look over the Bimini Islands, which are thought to have been the highest mountains in Atlantis. I'd been reading a lot about Atlantis over the last year, and its many strange unexplainable elements had permeated my brain.

It sounds like a wonderful place that had existed on Earth hundreds of thousands of years ago. It was a continent in the middle of the Atlantic with a civilisaion far more advanced than the one we live in now. If you move all the world's landmasses back together as we are certain it once was, there is a rather large gap between Africa and America. This made me think about the story I had heard about a boy at school in the thirties before we knew the landmasses of the word were once joined. The boy asked his geography teacher if South America was once attached to Africa.

'Don't be so stupid,' replied the teacher.

What we think of as fact is always changeable. Science seems to always think it's got it right but is often proved wrong in the future. It typically seems that what the mystics say is eventually proved by science and physics to be correct. They say that the civilisation on Atlantis did not have idols, and everyone spoke the same language. When Atlantis fell, its survivors spread across the globe and their tongues were changed so people could not understand each other anymore. Plato actually wrote a lot about Atlantis and was convinced of its existence.

Apparently, it was not too dissimilar to where civilisation is now. Those in power started to bombard their people with subliminal sounds, codes and images, electromagnetic frequencies and other mind-controlling methodologies. In Brave New World, Huxley warns us of the future, and many other authors have been warning us for centuries.

It is said Atlantis' downfall came as a result of a time of darkness and flagrant abuse of wisdom and sophisticated technologies being utilised against humanity and Gaia. I took a lot from reading Patricia Cori's channelled book. The issues facing the planet now are startlingly similar to her description of what led to the destruction of Atlantis.

She shows how the focus has shifted from a deeply spiritual awareness to the pursuit of materialism as the main hobby, drive and addiction of our society.

Gaia is calling us all to action. All of us who hear this call are moving into position. I heard this call about seven years ago. I was travelling in Prague and stumbled across an exhibition called Earth from Above by the photographer Yan Arnes Butrand. It took my breath away. I was awakened to what humanity was truly doing to the planet. I had to be torn away from the images. The written messages accompanying them explained the atrocities that were taking place regarding the environment and shattered what I had always been taught and felt. It was like a veil had been lifted, and I could now see the truth.

It resonated with me like nothing had before in my whole life.

I now know that this was part of my spiritual awakening. It was my awakening to expanded consciousness and my first awareness of being on a different plane of consciousness to the masses around me. It was the start of my anger towards the powers that be and my anger towards people for not being awake to what was going on and not wanting to take individual action. It seemed to me that we have so much beauty we seem set on destroying.

I returned to university in 2007 and started a module on sustainability. My first awakening was gathering momentum. I became obsessed with climate change, sustainability and other environmental issues. I was very angry about it all. I couldn't believe it. I was awake to this, and very few people even cared. It was like I had just witnessed a massive explosion in a room or a lightning strike or a robbery, or a rape, or shooting star, or a man naked a few yards away from me and as I turned round to say, 'Did you just see that?' everyone stared at me blankly and said, 'See what?'

I would get so angry that people weren't recycling and that certain things were even allowed to be made. Why was the world set up in such a way that made it difficult for me to be green? My mind exploded, and I had no idea why it grabbed me like it did.

I think she's right when she says civilisation is stripping us of our natural intelligence, our desire and will, and undermining our energetic interaction and personal exchanges.

I find it strange that civilisation looks to technology as a way out of the dilemma. For example, when I heard about carbon capture and storage, I just thought it was mad.

Why not just stop making the pollution, or the car scrappage scheme? Surely maintaining old cars is less damaging for the environment than making new? To me it's about stepping back about living more simply like the Mayans I have met, being more at one with nature and regaining our close bond, relationship and knowledge of plants and the Earth's systems.

We need not lose the ability to see and sense the world around us forever. What if we could accept the possibility that evolved cultures pre-date our established records by tens of thousands of years? Would we be quite humbled if we could reach into the great libraries and retrieve the real story of our ancestral accomplishments? If we could all read the ancient texts, and the Akashic Records, then would we believe.

We have seen war and peace, death and renaissance, famine and abundance occur over and over again as life-cycles of the earth. Why can we not see that for there to be an end to it, we must change? All systems, all governments, everything must be changed.

Where was I? Back to Maria's slides, which explained how the oppressors burned the manuscripts of knowledge, silenced the speakers of mystical truths and rearranged the pictures of the past to ensure their hold over us while setting the vibratory tenor of life on Earth.

Those of us in democratic nations who have been the power for so long in recent history believe we are free men and women, proud of governmental decrees and our sacred rights and liberties. The majority of people in these countries believe in patriotism, which is an idea that places their country above all others. We need to start seeing we are all one.

Politicians tell us we need to make this the best country in the world. What does that mean? Can we not settle for being a good country, one that is non-aggressive? Surely striving to be the best will only cause problems for everyone else?

Awakening has made my life a lot more difficult in terms of wanting to know what goes into making stuff and not wanting to be part of something associated with murder or famine or environmental degradation or the exploitation of people and less powerful countries. Many people just don't take any notice of these things.

Maria figured out I was the Mayan sign of Kan 7 by taking my date, time and place of birth. My element was air, and my key was energy and inner fire. My growth was revealing inside information and handling energy and power.

Kan is the serpent of fire, the energy of the inner fire that begins in the base chakra, known as the Kundalini. This fire activates sexual energy as both reflections of that energy and the force of life. Kan is human evolution and spiritual development, it also knows truth justice, intelligence and peace and symbolises the cycles of time and change. Maria said that people with this sign are great athletes, physically strong and have great mental ability. They are very active as children and young adults they need to channel their energy more than any other sign.

My mum, school teachers and girlfriends would all agree with that analysis of me. They had to subdue my energy, I had a strict diet, and I had to see a child physiologist for being overactive at primary school. They tried to relax me with plasticine and under no circumstances was I allowed fizzy drinks!

Maria said that Kan's greatest obstacles are ego and overthinking. They must also learn to manage their strength and energy, partially their sexual power. Many will be drawn to them because of this power, which can cause them to lose their way. My life seemed to fall into this bracket. The Kan characteristics resonated with me; I'd had this mad sexual energy since the first time I kissed a girl.

It was like another awakening.

Looking back at my adolescent days, I went from being happy with my football magazines to wowing girls in one kiss.

I realised now that, yes, most of my thoughts had been women-based up until the previous year. I'd been obsessed, and it had distracted my every movement, my every thought and my every decision.

There and then I decided on an outright sex ban for six months to learn to control my sexual energy. I had to try and get past my sex addiction and the need to always have someone by my side. I had to find myself and become comfortable with who I truly was before I embarked on family and lifetime commitments. I wanted to focus my energy on building myself up to be a person who would succeed in this world and not cause pain and suffering to his friends and family.

Maria said Kan people are quick to adapt and are welcome everywhere, even though deep down they do not know their own intentions. The seven signifies the middle of the number thirteen. Seven can't commit to any one group but is able to communicate with all.

This can lead to issues in belonging. This was exactly how I had felt my whole life. It had destroyed me in many ways and still does. But she also said seven has the ability to bring people together who are poles apart. I had felt this my whole life. I had been stuck in the middle of fighting and arguments but had managed to get on with everyone and deal with adult-made issues from an early age.

Maria finished with a passage that said Kan people believe the greatest truths; that the simplest and loveliest things are free. They understand all the money in the world cannot buy the enchantment of the mist-shrouded trees, the sun setting in the distance and the varied hues reflecting on the soft, rippling waters of a magical lake. They see the world through the magnificence of creation and thousands of such majestic realities exist, from the smile on a child's face to a butterfly on a stalk of grass.

When we take time to feel and absorb, this is when we start

down the path of self-discovery, exploring our inner space in harmony with all existence. This is where we become one with the immensity of creation.

I felt a little uneasy being away from Ananda's place for so long. It had this magical quality, and I could understand why Ananda had become a bit of a hermit for the last few years.

I had my first Skype with Fhian since we split. I felt like it was the right thing to do. It was really hard chatting to her as I was really missing her.

I floated off thinking about the woman I would end up with, wondering where she was now and what she was doing, not knowing she was going to fall in love with me and have my babies. I said to my friend Tie, 'imagine who is waiting somewhere for me to spend the rest of time with me. Wow, she is going to be more amazing and compatible than all of them.'

She agreed! I was opening up to the universe to truly find my soul mate.

CHAPTER 12
SEX TIMES 5, LIFE,
MAY 2012

I turn to my mates and say, 'I'll see you on the plane, I've gotta go'.

Taken over.

I walk towards the girls, and the one who likes me steps forward.

I say, 'Come with me' and grab her hand.

She says, 'Okay' and follows me.

I know exactly where I'm going.

I take her into the disabled toilet and lock the door behind us.

For some reason, there is a chair in the middle of the room.

We start to kiss, and I take out her huge left breast. Then I sit on the chair and lift up her skirt.

We then realise I am only half-hard, so she takes me in her mouth.

A little life flutters and I'm ready to go.

I pull her onto me again.

I pull her knickers to one side and pop myself in.

I take her breast into my mouth, remove the other and start playing with it. She is bouncing on top of me, and I am trying to cum as quickly as possible, so I don't miss my flight.

In some way, I'm still conscious of the financial ramifications and ball ache of missing it. I cum whilst my head is nuzzled in-between these huge breasts and remove myself. I politely and, almost as if programmed, say, 'That was nice.'

I extract my head from her breasts and pull up my pants, say goodbye and run for my flight. As I am approaching the flight, sheer horror dawns on me. I can't believe what I've just done. I've destroyed the sanctity and sacredness of my relationship.

I'm completely gutted.

For what purpose? Well three minutes of lust and fun, so I could get rid of my alcohol-fuelled horny hangover and cum.

As I stepped onto the flight, all my mates' eyes were on me. I couldn't really see what their expressions were, as I was hanging my head in shame.

I was destroyed, and so disappointed with myself.

They asked what happened and I just shook my head and said, 'I can't believe I just did that.'

They all laughed and said, 'Only you, Browne' and, 'Don't beat yourself up,' but that's all I could do. I had destroyed something which I had promised myself I wouldn't do. I had let myself down, I had let Fhian down, and I had let down all the people I'd told that I had changed. I'd also proven all the people right who had warned Fhian that I would fuck her over.

Now I had.

I rested my head on the tray table all the way home. I was disgusted with myself. In the minibus home, I covered my head with a blanket and blocked the world out. Inside that blanket, there was a war and a disgruntled man torturing himself.

For weeks, I couldn't believe what I had done.

I decided not to tell Fhian. My mates said, 'What good would it do? You're sorry about it, and she won't find out, so just leave it'.

I was in two minds but eventually decided against it. The only thing that allowed me to stop beating myself up was the assessment of my reaction to what had happened.

At any other point in my life, I wouldn't have even allowed my conscience to be affected. I would have had sex with the girl, bounced onto the plane like the big man, high-fived all my mates and been buzzing about what had happened. I would have told the sex story over and over again, and people would have sat there in amazement and said, 'Only you Browne, only you,' and I would have felt like a hero.

I could see some change in me, and that was a positive. I didn't tell anyone about the woman at the airport, and I was very wary around the boys that knew. I never once bigged it up, and when it was mentioned, I instantly showed remorse and said, 'Yes I know I'm an idiot'. I had this amazing girl who was a goddess. She was tall and had stature, and we looked great a couple. I'd jeopardised that for a moment of madness with a woman with big tits in an airport who meant absolutely nothing to me.

The old Liam within saw the comical side of it and wondered if it was out of the area of any jurisdiction if Fhian did ever find out. Airports were classed as international territory once you'd passed through passport control. Therefore, how could I be found guilty of any offence? It was like a better version of the different area codes rule, but this was just the monkey inside me creating things for me to laugh at that I would usually share with the world. I was keeping this safely inside, hoping one day these thoughts wouldn't ever-present themselves in my mind.

I pondered this as I thought about everything in life. All this head chatter made me so tired, and I wished I would be able to let go of it all one day soon. Would that day be when I killed myself, I wondered? Most days that felt like the only way I would be able to turn it off.

I still wasn't sure about Fhian. I had so many doubts. I wanted to be one hundred per cent faithful to the women I would have my babies with, I wanted to have no secrets from the woman I would partner with through life and would worship on a daily basis.

The fact we were on completely different paths seemed to become more and more prominent as my spiritual evolution continued. All I wanted to do was yoga and spiritual learning, whereas Fhian wanted to socialise, party and do 'regular people' stuff.

I was bored of regular people stuff. I'd found something that was magical and questioned the very fabric of existence. My spirituality was the only thing that had ever consumed me.

I was leaving Fhian again, this time I was heading off travelling to Guatemala for the end of the Mayan Calendar for a minimum of eight months. She wasn't that happy about it, but I think she saw it was something I needed to do.

The months leading up to my departure were strained. I felt that she wasn't going to be the girl I was going to spend the rest of my life with, and the reasons for that started to be more and more prominent as my spiritual change continued to intensify.

I was on this path of discovery, and she was very happy with her life and her job in the city. We both wanted change, but I was willing to make moves for a different life, and she wasn't. I was happy to still have her in my life as I loved her company and loved the connection we had, but without change, I could see no future.

My trip of self-discovery became my focus, and although we had some great times leading up to my departure, part of me knew we wouldn't stay together. Part of me felt I would find what I was looking for on my trip and wouldn't return to England. I wanted to find a home, and I had a feeling that would be shown to me on my travels. I told people I had this feeling I wouldn't come back.

I didn't like being in London at all anymore, and trips there made me anxious and uneasy. However, I did have to go there for work. I was doing these promotions jobs, which meant I would stay with Fhian whilst in London. On one of these jobs, I was working at a half-marathon event in Richmond giving out coconut water. I had a promo girl working with me who was a very pretty blonde. On Sunday we finished really early, and after we had been to Fhian's to drop off some stock, we headed for the lock-up. On the way, the girl wanted to stop by one of her friends'.

We found a place to park, and as we did, the heavens opened. We decided to sit in the van. We were chatting and then she started talking about sex and situations she had been in where she could feel sexual energy. She was a dancer and was telling me that when she got injured, she went to this physiotherapist. She really fancied him, and every time she went to him the sexual energy built and built.

She started talking about the places he had touched her, and she described how it made her feel out of breath, tense, and that she could feel between her legs had moistened. As she described this, she leant over me and touched my legs the way he had touched hers.

Before this point, I'd had no sexual fantasies about this girl. I'd just thought she was nice and attractive. As she stroked my legs, things changed. The saliva in my mouth became thicker and stickier like it always did when I was in an erotic situation. I was trying to figure out if the girl was actually coming onto me or if it was in my head. I still wasn't one hundred per cent sure, but I was quite hard. I tried to manoeuvre my penis, so it wasn't on show.

She continued to tell her story which I was half taking in, the other half of me trying to decipher what was actually occurring. She leaned over me again and again, often holding eye contact as she did. The air in the cab of the van had changed. It was steamy, moist and hot, and I was overheating. In my head, I was now taking the girl into the back of the van and having sex with her on the plywood floor between boxes of coconut water.

I asked her if she was coming onto me.

She said, 'Yes, I fancied you as soon as I saw you and I've found it very distracting being around you these last two days'.

I was thinking, 'Now I'm finding it very difficult being around you, leaning over me in such a provocative way. My penis is hard, I'm sweating, my saliva has changed, and all I want to do is throw you in the back of the van and fuck your brains out.'

She tells me that she was telling her friends about me last night, that she hadn't met anyone like me before who was spiritual, but also still normal and funny.

She said she had wanted to kiss me from the start.

I was flattered, my ego was buzzing.

I wanted her in the back of the van.

I said it.

I said, 'Do you want to go in the back of the van and have crazy sex?

The sexual tension in the front cab was thick; you could almost taste the pheromones.

She said she really wanted to, but she had just met my girlfriend, and that made it weird.

I was thinking, you just met my girlfriend, but you just put on this show?

I was overrun with sexual desire. I wanted her.

I wanted to taste this beautiful blonde dancer who could probably do the splits across me.

I asked her if she could do the splits. She said, 'Yes'. I said, 'Wow'!

I tried to persuade her that we should just jump on each other as this energy was intense right now. I could see she wanted to, but something was holding her back. I wondered why I was open to this. I knew Fhian, and I wouldn't be together that much longer. So I thought, why not, let's just go for it.

I asked her to kiss me. She did, and it got pretty heated, but still she wouldn't come into the back of the van. We kissed and kissed, and the passion grew and grew, and the windows got steamier and steamier, but it wasn't going any further. She felt amazing; she had these beautiful curves, and every part of her felt so supple. I grabbed and grabbed at her fleshy parts, imaging pulling myself into her.

I knew that vocalising what was going on in the van had been the wrong move. If we had just kissed without words, the actions and the energy would have led to sex, and none of it would have been discussed. I had made a mistake by speaking and needing conformation of what was truly happing. Every other sense and emotion was telling me that she wanted me, every one of her actions, body language and energy was telling me she wanted me, but for some reason I had needed to hear it. It had been a fatal error that had made her vocalise and rationalise what was going on. Without this, girlfriends and other doubts that had been far away from her thoughts when she was telling her story and leaning across to touch me would have remained far away, and we would have been in the back fucking.

We kissed again and went to her friend's, the moment gone. Maybe this was the only time in our lives we would be thrown together in such a situation, and we had both let it slip. Maybe my vows and spiritual work had created blocks and stopped me from falling back into my old ways. Regardless, I'd kissed a girl and had been more than willing to take it further.

I dropped the girl off in Farringdon and never saw her again.

There were lots of times when I was with Fhian that I had wanted other girls. There were times that I had wanted to feel someone else when I'd wanted to experience a different size, shape, smell, colour or feel. Somehow it had never happened, other than the airport slip up. I had tried to keep myself away from any possible situations, but sometimes they just came to me. Most of the time, I let it pass me by, but this one seemed to have ignited something within.

When I returned to Fhian, I didn't feel guilty. Something with us had changed, and my belief and faith in the relationship had disappeared. I felt like I could never breathe or properly assess the relationship as she always had stuff booked in for us.

Maybe this was what happened with most relationships? We fall in love, and then we just have a sequence of events that never stop and make it seem almost impossible to leave or even take stock.

Was this what had happened to me for the last eighteen months? Had I just gone along with the moments?

LONG WAY HOME, THE JOURNEY, JANUARY 2013

After ten hours of blissful sleep, we got up to make the two-hour drive to Comalapa. We arrived to meet Genevieve, the coordinator of the Rameo Earthship house-build.

I instantly felt like I was on a new part of my trip. Gone were the long hugs I had become accustomed to. It was handshakes and construction now.

Genevieve showed us the beautiful U-Model Earthship they had built last year above the site that had been prepared for the Rameo build. We were then taken to the Long Way Home Comalapa HQ and their current project, which was a school build. It was the first day of school, and all these bright toddler grins greeted me.

Firm handshakes were exchanged with the boys and on-site locals (including Rameo who doesn't even know he's famous) and westerners alike. It felt strange to not be blasting out the love to everyone I meet, but I didn't want to come across as a weirdo. I remembered eating hummus and carrots on building site in England; they had never heard of it and instantly thought I was gay.

There were glass bottles, plastic bottles, tin cans and car tyres everywhere, making parts of the place look more like a recycling centre. Here, however, it was being recycled into buildings.

Ananda left and I was given the task of clearing out one of the rooms where classes would be taking place. I worked with a German volunteer named Marvin.

Within minutes I was covered from head to toe in dust, my beautiful locks matted. I was taken up to the Earthship site by Long Way Home's founder and CEO, Mat, to help with the prep. We were shown how to make the glass bottle bricks, which were both a structural and decorative feature of these houses. The bottles were cut about three inches long and were gaffer taped to a matching bottle, creating a brick.

Making my first contribution to the house felt like a special moment, and I enjoyed getting to pick Mat's brain about how and why he set up Long Way Home and his connection with the Earthship people. He had volunteered for The Peace Corps about ten years ago in Guatemala and went back to the States thinking about jobs and the future. He decided the western life was not for him, so he set up Long Way Home as a non-profit organisation and has never looked back.

I asked how he chose the family that would live in the first Earthship they built.

He said he was looking for a single mum, as they were at the bottom of everything in Guatemalan society and were really looked down upon, especially Mayan single mums. His mum was a single mum, so this was his homage to her. The family he chose was Maria and her three children who now all lived in the beautiful Earthship we were sitting outside.

Maria's daughters helped as much as they could; cleaning bottles, making snacks, washing the pots or washing clothes. Always with a massive smile, and none of them were over fourteen. I thought of my sister. It took her a minimum of nine days to take some (now gone mouldy) washing from the kitchen to be sorted out, after being asked around fourteen times to move it.

These kids were inspiring, and they were always immaculately dressed in traditional attire; gorgeous multi-coloured long skirts and the most stunning flowery blouses.

For the duration of the three-week build, I would be living in a cool little hut with lovely surrounding gardens. It was not quite Ananda's place; it was rustic and eco.

We spent the evening sitting around a log fire and meeting the rest of the volunteers. One of them, Rosa, is an Earthship pro and was currently setting Michael Reynolds up with a load of seminars in her home town of Christchurch, New Zealand.

Comalapa has more artists than any other place in Guatemala. There is a vibrant pastel-coloured tomb cemetery and a massive mural spreading about one hundred metres up the street, depicting the history of Comalapa and its 98% Kechi-Kel Mayan population. It shows all the killings that have taken place at the hands of the Spanish, and all the struggles that have infested their culture over the past five hundred years, and the civil war that was started by the America Fruit Company. Men stopped wearing their traditional dress in fear of persecution and being forced to enrol in a war they had nothing to do with.

While we were making brick bottles, a crazy English guy, Shane, arrived. He had a wealth of knowledge on pretty much everything and was one hundred miles an hour. Every time he got up to do something, Marvin would lean across and ask me what he had just said.

One of the days before the volunteers, arrived me and Melvin went off to collect the tyres that would be used for the house walls.

We picked up a wagon at 6am and got to ride on the rickety wooden back loader which would definitely be illegal in both our home countries. The sights we passed were incredible; different coloured pastures and volcanoes in the background as we raced around the mountain roads.

We spent the day stopping at garages asking for tyres, ticking off our list the exact sizes. Each time we got lucky, we got down from the van and threw the tyres onto the loader and jumped back on. The sun was so hot, and there was no escape from it on the back of the truck. After a while, we both fell asleep amongst the rubber tyres in a huge traffic jam.

Going through these towns, I started to daydream. What it would be like on these industrial mechanical garage clad streets if the feminine energy that we were supposed to be moving into had already taken place in the last Mayan cycle? Would these dirty places be replaced with wool shops, pretty fabric shops and book clubs? Would there even be roads? How would the world look if women had dominated for as long as men?

That evening, a girl called Leah arrived from Pittsburgh. Like me, she had awakened, becoming tired of the way life was and questioning what she had been brought up to believe in. We'd had a lot of similar experiences, and instantly I felt like I had a bit of what I needed back, plus crazy Shane, with his militant vegetarianism and guerilla warfare against everything.

That Saturday was me mum's birthday and a day I like to do something nice on. My initial plan was to be alone for the whole day and go for a big walk. As it turned out, I woke up, did a full session of yoga, had some nice tea and a lovely breakfast, tidied the place and washed the pots, chilled a little bit then headed to the market to buy food to cook everyone a meal that evening.

The colours and smells were mesmerising. Women chattered and went about their business whilst a child suckled away at their breast. Avocados and exotic fruits and vegetables lay scattered across the floor and on tables. I found the coconut stand, and I was in heaven. I drank one and took one for later. I found large bags of roasted fried broad beans and munched away at them for the rest of my stay in Comolapa.

I walked to the park via the lovely rolling hills of the countryside to a waterfall I had been told about. I thought of the poem I had written on my way back to my mother's house when I was on the train from London:

Always
Sad times, miss you mother
In distress, miss you mother
Got great news, miss you mother
Times of joy, miss you mother
Homeward bound, miss you mother
Empty home, miss you mother
My long embrace, miss you mother

I thought about the trippy event that had taken place on the anniversary of my mum's death, the 17th of September 2012. Fhian and I were sleeping in my campervan in the countryside, and I woke early thinking about my mum and the five-year anniversary of her passing. I was writing a poem in my head and was trying to muster the energy to get up and get a pen from the glovebox. I eventually made myself rise, and as I opened the curtain, three female peacocks were walking towards me in the field facing the van. I was transfixed. Tears started streaming from my eye sockets, and tingles shot up and down my spine, my mother's energy was on me, in me and I started to scribble down the words of the poem that was floating about my head and now had a new twist to incorporate.

5 Years On
Among the morning due
My thoughts rushed to you
As I lay still my heart beats true
My new lady beside me
The countryside surrounds us
Waking in the van
She sleeps perfectly still
My mind though is nothing but you
I listen to the feelings within
Words, poems and sonnets
Flash by
I must find the strength to rise from the warmth

Something to scribble on
With a tap and a flutter, a jab and judder
Pure love makes me rise
I pull back my curtain
To face the uncertain
We arrived at night
Nothing was in sight
Instantly my spine tingles with delight
Before my eyes recognise
Three peacocks sent from you
From Heaven
Three females
As they walk towards me no fear is present
Eyes fixed on your son
Lids fill with tears
Your feeling engulfs me
Energy sent from Mum
Beautiful feelings surround me
Impossible to describe consciously
Maybe like being held as a baby
They turn they're gone
Disappear into the early morning sun
Their job, their mission done
As they go I'm there with you
Fully emerged in this gift
Present in my every thought
I stand outside, overjoyed
Spending time with the energy that is you
Magical moods merge
Meandering memories return
So blessed I am to have this mum

As I climbed up the final few stairs revealing the park and all its beauty, I wondered why I hadn't seen how stunning it was when I'd passed through earlier. Rich green grass was surrounded by pretty flowers, boys happily played football whilst a man went all the way across the park on a zip line. I saw something that made my heart pound; calla lilies everywhere, one of my mum's favourite flowers and the one I got tattooed in her honour when she passed. It brought me to tears, and I found a spot on the spongey green grass facing the flowers. They were elegantly pointing to the sun, their regal stems supporting them while bees tirelessly worked away at their rich nectar.

I lay back fell into deep meditation and thought solely about my mum. All the good times, all the laughs, all the cries and that unbreakable connection of mother and child. I heard the little cough she always did and the sniffle she always had, and how it was so amazing to laugh with her in public as her laugh was more distinguished than my own. Combined, it was a force.

I came round thanked the Universe for this gift. I asked the park keeper if I could take a flower, then I went down, picked the most beautiful one and floated back to the volunteer house.

I hugged everyone with tears in my eyes. I couldn't stop smiling, unable to believe what the world had just presented to me.

I asked for a vase for my flowers and then Rosa pointed out the painting of calla lilies on the sink. My mind and heart were about to explode; joy and love were oozing from me.

My final homage to my mother for the day was to prepare a nice meal with Leah for the whole house; guacamole with tostadas for the starter and rice and steamed vegetables for the main. We sat around together I got everyone to hold hands. The food was blessed, thanks were given to my mum and the universe for today's events, and we all tucked in.

The next day, the Earthship crew arrived, along with all the volunteers. Michael Reynolds was going to be there for some of the build which was AMAZING, inspiring and monumental. I was excited to be seeing my friend Jack, who I had met through Fhian. I'd got to know him a little bit over the last couple of years and, being an architect, he was always interested in the Earthships.

On the first day of the build, we made our way to the site through the cornfields, up the steep mountain and down again, the sun shining brightly. As soon as we got on site we were plunged into action. With ninety-five people on a residential site it should have been chaos, but even without a formal briefing and sledgehammers, pick-axes, and large rubber tyres flying all over the place, somehow the whole process seemed to flow. At one point, I stepped back, and it was like watching ants in an emergency situation.

I grabbed a sledgehammer and began to pound earth into a tyre, a moment I had been looking forward to since seeing the Earthship movie, 'The Garbage Warrior' seven years ago.

I was next to Michael Reynolds pounding tyres; it was like an amateur musician standing on stage at Glastonbury about to play with his idol, his inspiration, a person who had helped change the direction of his life, or a bird spotter finding himself sitting in the same twitching box as Bill Oddie.

It was inspiring. The man behind all this was pounding away at a tyre at the age of sixty-seven, not sitting back like any other architect in a shirt and tie assuming himself above the manual workers, but getting into the thick of it. Everybody was pounding away. 'Dirt bitches' (aptly named, regardless of gender) filled up the tyres with dirt as we compressed it with the sledgehammers. When we needed more, we shouted 'Dirt!' and within seconds a bucket was thrown into our tyres and back to pounding we went.

Some groups were helping make the rebar cages that formed the domed roofs, others were digging routes for services and damp-proofing. All the while, a DJ was pumping tunes. Biggie and Tu-Pac blared out. It was like being back in a Vauxhall Nova with blacked-out windows in my youth, thinking we were gangsters cruising the mean streets of Cheshire, pretending to shoot gangs of lads with an A-lock.

I pounded to the beat, blowing up tyre after tyre with dirt, creating these huge building bricks which would form the main walls of the house. The atmosphere was electric. It was like everyone was in party spirits; no steel toe capped boots, hard hats, high visibility jackets or lengthy health and safety introductions.

I started to daydream about an essay question I'd gotten at university: 'Is there a business case for sustainable development in construction'? This question had gotten my back up as, as you may know, you are not allowed to have an opinion at University; in an essay, you can only use references. I passionately felt that there shouldn't have to be a business case (is it economically viable compared to conventional methods?) for sustainable development.

I felt it was more of a responsibility, ethically and morally, to the planet.

It was like saying, if we see the planet as a mother who provides us warmth, food, shelter, water, beauty and a home, it has to be economically viable to stop raping her of her resources.

So when I was faced with this question, I couldn't answer it, as I'd felt there was no way I should have to try and prove an economic advantage for doing the right thing. In the rational world, we have to show evidence of economic viability before we can act. How do we do that when it is such an effort to test sustainable buildings, as they have to meet the same codes as badly-made conventional buildings and there seem only to be expensive alternatives allowed?

Simple economics told me that if every building had to incorporate a full system of sustainable devices then the price would come down as demand grew, but for some reason, this was not valid in an essay. Later, after submitting an angry essay and even angrier presentation, I found Earthships. They live in harmony with the planet by encountering natural resources without depleting them. But because these homes cost nothing to heat and cool all year round, they don't keep water, gas or electrical companies (the biggest rapists) happy. So big businesses try to put a stop to them,

The volunteers were people from all over the world, of all skin colours, genders, sexual orientations and beliefs. All coming together with a common goal. It was inspiring to see what we could do in such a short space of time.

When lunch was called, vegetarians got to eat first, and it was fascinating to see more than half the site put down their tools and get in the food line for the vegetarian option. I couldn't imagine seeing that anywhere else on a building site of western people.

Bonds were growing on-site and after the massively hectic commute each morning— busy trains, gridlocked roads, rushing unhappy people, aggressive cyclists and pollution— oh sorry, London flashback... I meant to say, after sauntering across hilltops, walking past bright-eyed Mayans with gleaming smiles, and watching glistening sunshine catch the tops of mountains and volcanoes, we arrived on site. Good mornings were fired all around, and some good cuddles were exchanged. Everyone always had a job to do. We were all novices of the Earthship build techniques, but the more experienced had faith in us, which allowed them to teach in a very relaxed manner.

There was constant laughing throughout the site, and even when people were stuck in lines hauling buckets of water, cement and stones for eight hours, they were always in good spirits.

I worked on various parts of the build, but I really enjoyed my time with the plumber, Lou. At one point he asked someone to get him a bell end.

I said, 'I beg your pardon?'

'What?'

I said, "If you asked for one of them on-site in England with your head down a toilet and your hand outstretched, you would more than likely end up with a cock in your hand not a cap for a pipe".

Lou was the plumber/drummer from New York and had an amazing way with people. He was always trying to teach you the Earthship plumbing ways, and I fell a little bit in love with him.

I spent the first Saturday of the build lying in the sun having an Om tattooed onto my wrist by a guy called Devon, who I think I manifested in one of my meditations. Since being in India and seeing the symbol everywhere, and spending a lot of time on Om Beach near Gokarna, it really resonated with me. Added to this was the fact it is used all over the world as a mantra, and you chant it in most yoga sessions. It felt fitting, as it can bring an individual to a higher state of consciousness. To a yogi, no symbol is more powerful, and in the words of the Manduka Upanishad:

"OM: this eternal word is all; what was, what is and what shall be."

In Sanskrit the longer lower curve of the letter represents the dream state, the upper curve stands for the waking state and the curve issuing from the centre symbolises deep, dreamless sleep. The crescent shape stands for "Maya," the veil of illusion and the dot for the transcendental state. When the individual spirit in man passes through the veil and rests in the transcendental, he is liberated from the three states and their qualities. It is said in Sanskrit that Om is the original mantra, the root of all sounds and letters, and thus of all language and thought. The "O" is generated deep within the body and slowly brought upward, joining with the "M" which then resonates through the entire head. Repeating OM for 20 minutes is said to relax every atom in your body.

Devon's work was intricate, and when he was finished, we faced each other in lotus position and let out three big Om's. We embraced and thanked one another and went to make some tea.

In Comolapa, I had been very disciplined at practising yoga. I was up at 5:45 every morning for just over an hour's Sivananda practice. It was also giving me a chance to meditate and do breathwork in the morning. Sivananda teaches that we need to become a master of the mind by observing its fluctuations like a still lake having its surface broken by a pebble. We must get a grip of the distractions and negative behaviours, stop living in the past and the future and live in the present. By having some control of the mind we will limit the far-fetched dreaming and self-destructive desires.

This is exactly what I was trying to get under control, not allowing my thoughts to affect my mood so much. I wanted to move away from my sexual obsession, to make room for fully committing to a person and becoming a man who would be a great father, not one disturbed by desire.

It made me think about the way most people's minds work; they go out and buy a new car, and for some time, they feel proud and satisfied, and the mind is at rest. But soon they start hankering after a newer model or a different colour or worrying about it getting stolen or hit. What began as pleasure becomes yet another source of discontent; in stilling one desire, many others are made. This is pretty much the way I had been with women my whole life.

What appealed to me about yoga was the possibility of what it could instil in me, that knowledge that we possess a source of joy and wisdom already inside us, a fund of tranquillity that we can perceive and draw nourishment from when the movement of the mind is still. If we can channel this desire for contentment inward, instead of attaching it to external objects that are by nature transient, we can discover how to live in peace.

I wanted to live in the present more; I could see how much movement existed in the minds of both myself and most people, and could see how little we lived in the present. I wanted to stop associating with my thoughts, emotions and actions and simply step back and assume the role of witness as if I was watching someone else.

Applying this was a massive task.

However, Swami Vishnu-Devananda's foreword to the Sivananda yoga book really helped a lot. He describes how you are not the physical body or the thoughts going on in your mind. You are something more that is a mere passenger inside this body and mind, and which ultimately knows what is best for your soul. I wanted to tap into that and really develop an understanding of it. How do I fully understand this part of me that is beyond the body and mind?

The Earthship people were really inspiring me. Many people had left their jobs, disheartened and discontent with what convention had to offer. Many seemed to have blind faith that everything would work out for the best. There were many people like me, who in a sense were homeless, with many places they could be, but no apparent fixed abode. They were travelling, exploring themselves and waiting to see what materialised.

There was a couple from Quebec who lived in a van, hoping to save enough money to build an Earthship and lots of people had the end goal of living off-grid.

There was this vast coming together of consciousness from all parts of the world; people wanting to make a difference, people wanting change in a peaceful manner and the laughter and joy we were all bringing to each other's lives was intense. It felt like we were all on a quest to do something different, for some sort of betterment.

As Rumi says: "*the most important thing about this quest, is that surely it will come to a reality, it will happen. For example, if you have parched lips from thirst, you are very thirsty, definitely you will reach your water because that parching of your lips is put there into that place by the water, the water that is waiting for you*".

So the thing to be manifested is waiting for you to take control and make it yours. Our work is nothing but two sentences, as Rumi says:

"*Sharpen your pencil and scratch your paper, keep doing what you're doing, sustain, that will ultimately get you to your goal.*"

A line of 40 people were passing heavy buckets of gravel up the hill all day. To keep everyone entertained as the buckets flew from one person to the next, shouts of 'bucket', 'hup' and 'pumice' would alert you of the imminent arrival of a full bucket flying past your head to be caught. I changed the shouts of 'bucket' to 'bouquet' in a posh accent, and one person actually comprehended this reference to the early '90s English TV show called Keeping Up Appearances. It was the big, grey haired-dreadlocked ex-Navy man, Salty (AKA Navy Mike). At six foot four inches, he looked like he could eat puppies. I discovered he had been based in Scotland for a while, thus had experienced some quintessentially English TV humour.

I also amused people by passing notes along the line; personal messages for people 30 people away such as 'you look nice today', 'what time is it?', 'You have a nice face' and 'I love you.' The responses usually came back within a minute, and we soon realised that this form of communication was safer and less dangerous than texting whilst buckets full of cement were flying past your face.

At one point, a dog called Jauncho appeared at my feet. I picked him up and passed him along the line, he made it all the way to the top. My laugh was becoming a joy and amusement to most, and I was considering charging people to hear it. Implementing this would be a challenge; maybe I could ask Monsanto?

It's a hereditary laugh; me mum's laugh was mint and me nana would have people coming looking for her when she worked at the Arndale Market in Manchester, trying to find its source. I would take mates round to see her just so they could laugh at her laugh.

Whilst I was in Comolapa, Lilly from the pilgrimage agreed to connect with one of my spirit guides. She told me the spirit guide was called Agnes and said she brought me much, much love.

Instantly my mind flashed back to my Nana Agnes, to a special lady from my childhood who was not my real nana, but my grandad's second wife. She treated me like her grandson. I knew her as 'Nana Agnes' from birth. Guilt and sadness filled me as I hadn't thought of her for so many years. I thought of all the time I'd spent with her, obsessed with playing with their old fashioned phone, where you had to pull your finger around and wait for it to click back in before you could dial the next number.

She would always be in the kitchen in her pinny, with her purple rinse, cooking with the food the smackheads would rob from Kwik Save and sell to me grandad in the pub. She'd pop her head into the living room to catch the horse racing as she would create 1980s council estate culinary bliss. I would get myself tangled in these multi-coloured beads hanging from the back door, I would hide when I heard Grandad get home from the pub, and for years there would be this rehearsed event of me pissed Grandad pretending he couldn't find me, saying he had given up, me thinking I had managed to elude his detection and then him surprising me and tickling me till I almost pissed myself, and then pouring himself a whisky. Nana Agnes was an amazing soul, and I was so happy to have these memories return.

During the next few weeks, I had some darkness around me and some internal wrangling during what was such a special last few days of wrapping up the build. I managed to keep my outward persona bubbly, but internally I was engulfed in darkness, doubt and despair.

Thankfully I was given the task of putting up the can wall inside the house, so I was having little contact with people. I would sit on this plank raised seven foot off the floor and meticulously build this wall on autopilot.

Inside, I felt like I was dying.

I was questioning everything again. What I was doing here? Why wasn't I at home accruing money to be able to buy a house and provide for the only thing in life I truly wanted; a family? I was beating myself up for what I had done with my life so far, believing I had wasted it and never taken it seriously. I could see nothing good in my future, and I wondered what all this building work I was doing would lead to. Would it lead to my happiness? Would I find my soul mate? Would I have my family, or would I always be in this angst and torture?

The depression hadn't been this bad for a while. I knew it was always there beneath the surface, bubbling away, ready to explode when given the chance. Now it had exploded, and my whole body and being felt intoxicated with dread and anxiety.

I sat there building, not wanting to be there, not wanting to be in this world, knowing I couldn't handle this pain and sadness within. I was suffering, and every time someone came to speak to me, I had to really muster up the courage and confidence and determination to just get words to leave my mouth.

Had I made a massive mistake? Was Fhian my soul mate? Would we be together again one day? I knew I couldn't have her waiting for me, and I knew our lives and priorities were so different... Then someone threw a ball of wet cement at me, and I snapped out of it.

The tyre walls were all up, the dome roofs were finished, the rainwater catchment cisterns were in place, grey water planters dug and filled, shower fitted, black water septic tanks built and finished, black water planters dug and filled, bottle walls artistically crafted, can walls being built, roofing almost done, green house up, landscaping taking shape, solar panel installed and plasterwork nearly there.

Everyone was helping in every department. We were like ants; that's all I could think of every time I stepped back for a moment's reflection. The amount of work we had done in thirteen days was insane.

When I was building can walls and drifting off into thought, I would contemplate why the world was not building these houses everywhere.

I'd think about the rubbish that is put on the market in the UK;

houses and apartments with paper-thin walls that are only being built to last 25 years, so the economy can keep churning over, polluting and raping the world's resources and allowing people less security. I couldn't see how people could not want these off-grid houses; houses that didn't have bills, houses that heated themselves, houses capable of growing food and providing security— all costing no more to build than a conventional home. Why was that so wacky, so out there, so left field?

Young people now seem to want these boxes; characterless, white-walled, heartless apartments that are being thrown up all over the world. I thought of Huxley's Brave New World again and how, when travelling around cites worldwide, I would see these apartment blocks and be amazed at how the visionary Huxley had predicted this in the 1920s.

All I could see were the materialisation of Huxley's fears everywhere; the consumerism, the materialism, the separateness. I realised, sitting there with a coke can as a brick and my own hand as the trowel, that I had never become part of that trap, that net so that I could hopefully pull some of the masses up from out of those deep waters.

I read 'Atlantis Rising' in the evenings and saw similarities with the Atlantians and the Earthship philosophy, in which solar energy was used to heat their houses and all their waste was recycled within the house or taken to highly advanced recycling centres. When we were more in tune with the land, surely that's what we would do.

I felt like I was learning so much through the books I was reading and the people I was meeting. They were telling me about secret governments and the Illuminati and more about the crystal skulls, about how the mainstream denies things like mind control, telepathic communication, healing and consciousness. But many militaries around the world train high ranking officials in telepathic communication, remote viewing and mind control. Even the Russians were caught sending low-frequency radio waves to the US Embassy, which worked as a disruptive agent being beamed into employees' brains, causing a chemical reaction.

I learnt about the High-Frequency Active Auroral Research Program (HARP), which is based in Alaska and tests all sorts of technology to interfere with the magnetic force of the Earth, sending shockwaves into the planet to deliberately trigger earthquakes, tidal waves and ecological disasters. In their short-sighted vision of wealth, power and control, the governments and businesses have exploded atomic bombs and warheads in our seas and deserts to see if they will work in war, blasted, burned, poisoned, bored and chiselled away at the body of Gaia relentlessly taking, taking, taking, raping, raping, raping.

Governments and businesses can do all this, but we can't experiment with housing, just to provide ourselves with the most basic human need; shelter? Earthship had to go through years of legal wrangling just to build off-grid houses, and the main reason they ended up being given permission was because of hurricane Katrina and people's need for quick, cheap housing that didn't just float away.

That's why Earthship builds so much in what we call the developing world. The land is cheap, they can just get on with it and build and don't constantly have to jump through hoops.

On the last couple of days of the build, people were scurrying about trying to get everything finished. Things were being tidied up. The amazing, life-changing experience was coming to an end. I was planning on a week of relaxation with Ananda before making my way north to the states and the Earthship headquarters in Taos, New Mexico.

The last day was filled with emotions. Romeo was busy working as always. His crew of Mayan Guatemalans were by far the hardest working of anyone on the site, and for the size of them, they could carry more than any westerner there. We had a ceremony to hand over the keys to Romeo and his family. Their beaming smiles lit the darkening sky, and you could see the gratitude of the family pouring out. All the loving energy put into the house would be part of it forever. And the family had seen how hard these crazy gringos, had worked over the past three weeks. They now had a house that they would never have to cool or heat, and a million-pound view over Comolapa, complete with mountains and volcanoes.

We were all given a small homemade traditional gift by the family. I handed over the medal I had been given for running the Liverpool marathon which had raised the money for me and Jack being there and was graciously thanked. The building looked fantastic; the beautiful bottled walls that allowed a kaleidoscope of colours to filter into the rooms, the amazing internal planters in the greenhouse that dealt with the grey water and would provide nutritious food all year round, the black water bed outside that grew more food and plants in the terraced garden and quirky touches, typical of Reynolds' vision, were all over the place.

The next morning, I awaited Ananda's arrival. Crissi and Leah came to my place to say their goodbyes, Lou had hooked up with a Danish girl called Dita, so was at our place and available for goodbye love. I would be seeing him in Taos for the Earthship Academy in a few weeks and chilling at his place for a while. People were heading off on their own little adventures. I was going to miss everyone, especially Hippy Jack. I would miss our morning chats contemplating life on the way to work over the hills, miss his groundedness and witty English humour, seeing him upside down every morning whilst in a headstand. As I looked around my bedroom for the last time, I took in the quotes on the walls:

"Only a fool envies the joy of a child a grown up never loses it".

"Once social change begins, you cannot stop it... you cannot oppress people who are no longer scared".

"Sometimes broken things make the best building supplies, and we'll keep on building"

"Whatever you dream you can do, begin it; boldness has genius, power and magic in it. Begin it now".

I would miss my bond with Leah and Crissi. They both left me a note. Crissi's read:

"Express the beauty and truth of your core self.'

And Leah's note read:

'Liam, my divine love. I have adored you in the greatest capacity since the day I met you. I have been privy to your marvellous life details. I have savoured in your glow after your shared circumstances that you were triumphant of spirit. I will relish in the light of your divine. For all of your years, my years, our years. This experience was magical, truly remarkable. It was perhaps one of our greatest acts of love, Liam choosing to be alive at a time when so many live so deeply in the dark. Your finest hours.
Love Leah.'

I felt love for Leah and Crissi, I felt love for all these people; Lars, Lisa, Marvin, Daniel, Sam, Justin, Jack, Dita, Lou, Rosa, Brie, Ben and the many, many more people I'd connected with.

CHAPTER 13
DEALER WITH IT,
LIFE, 2008

We crossed the border into Belgium. It was 3 am, and we were looking for somewhere to camp and get some sleep for a few hours. The roads were completely deserted, and the only light came from the headlights of the car we were driving. It seemed like thick forest flanked either side of us. In the distance, we saw two red lights coming closer and closer. Finally, we were close enough to realise it was a police car.

I drove tentatively behind, not knowing what the speed limit was on this road, in this country. I travelled at a similar speed to that of the officials in front. The police car seemed to be getting slower and slower. Tired and scared, we were all struggling to make sense of what was happening as the police car slowed to an almost stop.

I decided we should go past them, so moving the car into the opposite lane, I pulled away from them slowly. As we did, I increased my speed little by little, still unaware of the country's speed limit. We got further and further away from them, and their car got smaller and smaller. A gasp of relief emitted from each one of our chests and we careered forward, away from the law.

The next thing we knew, two white lights were getting closer and closer to us. We made out it was the police again and we all panicked.

The police sat behind us for about ten minutes, our anxiety growing. Groans of, 'What are we going to do, Liam?' bombarded my eardrums.

The blue and red lights flashed on, and a doomed sinking feeling flickered through my whole body as the panicky heads of my accomplices darted from me to the police car, from me to the police car.

The flashing lights became my cue to pull over. I told everyone in the car to let me do the talking and that if worst came to worst, to say they knew nothing about it.

The officer slowly approached the car as I wound down the window in the fashion my mind had been trained to do from all the American movies I'd seen. His torch flashed into the back seat, copying all the American movies he had seen, and then it was on me.

He asked me where we were from. I said, "England".

He asked me where we were going. I said, 'Spain'.

He asks me what we were doing in Belgium.

I said, 'We are meeting a friend tomorrow in Bruges, and we want to find a campsite to sleep in tonight.'

He told us they would all be shut

I said, 'We just need somewhere to put up a tent then.'

He then asked to see my driving licence and the insurance and registration details for the car.

I was not insured, and I didn't own the car. I passed him my driver's licence, and Little Blonde, who was sitting next to me reached into the glovebox for the paperwork. She was, thankfully, on the insurance, but the car was registered to a Mohammed Chowdery.

I said as little as possible and gave the police officer the papers. He went to the back of our car and talked to his colleague. We could hear him talking on his radio in a foreign language, so we had no idea of what was being said. Panicked whispers bounced around the car, and I told everyone it was going to be fine.

As one officer was on the radio, the other asked me to pop the boot. My heart sank. Everyone's hearts sank. We were fucked, or more to the point, I was fucked, and getting to the music festival in Spain now seemed unimaginable.

The officer looked in the boot, and I inquisitively looked through the rear-view mirror, trying to see what he was up to and whether he was taking anything out. I could see looks of horror saturated across the faces of my three friends in the back.

Guilt squeezed my heart.

I tried to remain calm, but the chances of coming out of this unscathed seemed as remote as the woodland surrounding us.

The other officer had a driving licence in my name and the registration details of the car in the name of an Asian man who was nowhere to be seen. In my head, this in itself justified further investigation and was a definite breaking of the law. I was not insured to drive this car, I didn't own it, and I was driving illegally in a foreign country. I knew in England I would immediately have been arrested.

He stopped talking on the radio and started a discussion with his colleague, then he turned and walked back towards my unwound window. Each step added another hundred beats per minute to my heart rate. I was ready to be taken to the station for further investigations, for the boot of the car to be searched and for my friends in the car to be answering questions their relatively protected lives may not be able to deal with.

All kinds of scenarios were going through my mind. Would I have to serve my time in a Belgium prison, or would I be sent back to England to serve my time, and what would give me the best chances of not being bummed?

The officer took his last step. His hand goes on the window trim of the door, he turned to face me as his other hand passed me back the paperwork.

He said: 'This is fine'.

I felt like I had misheard him.

In my mind, I was shaking my head in disbelief
a little, quickly replaying his words again and again in my head. *He said 'this is fine'???*

Baffled, I took the papers handed them to Little Blonde next to me and looked back at the officer. He told us the speed limits of the road and then pointed us in the direction of a campsite and wished us a safe trip.

We all thanked him profusely.

Adrenaline pushed and pushed up my body until we drove off. A huge sigh of relief exploded from within me. It felt as if my body weight had halved by releasing all the tension that had built up.

Giddily, with an air of trepidation, we said things like, 'Oh my God', 'I can't believe that' and, 'Shit, wow! *Oh my God, oh my God* was repeatedly spat into hands that were clasped around our mouths as if some other entity was saying them and we were trying to keep the words from spilling out, as law-abiding atheists.

We arrived in the most picturesque of villages which, in a way, soothed the plethora of emotions we had just been through.

We found the campsite the kind police officer had pointed us towards. It wasn't open, and the chain had been put across the entrance. We decided to break in and set up camp. We only put up two tents; Little Blonde and Rena take one, and I'm left to share with Mr Japan and The Communist. The Communist is my ex-girlfriend, and Mr Japan is a friend I met at the festival in Spain the previous year. They'd had sex with each other the previous night in the same room as my dad, and now I was sharing a tent with them, and it felt a bit weird.

The next day we awoke to hear families and foreign chatter all around us. We took in our surroundings in the daylight, tried to escape without paying, but some people looked at us weird, so we did.

We arrived in Bruges where we were supposed to be meeting Mohammed, taking in the beautiful historic city and finding ourselves having lunch in one of its many squares. Little Blonde was our Mohammed connection, and we found out he wasn't having much luck getting into the country on a Bangladeshi passport.

We reflected on the intensity of the previous evening and how lucky we'd been. We were repeatedly replaying the events, trying to figure out why they hadn't seized us and the car. We came to the conclusion it must have just been too confusing or too much work for them, and we had given them a good vibe, so they let us go.

As we approached France, we ended up in a huge traffic jam.

We moved slowly towards a border control. Europe didn't have border controls between member countries anymore, and I was in shock at what I was seeing.

As we got closer and closer, we could see that cars on the other side were being searched and completely emptied. Terror filled me; it was less than twenty-four hours ago, this same terror had filled me, but now it seemed amplified. Bags and cases were being taken from the cars in front of us. They were thoroughly emptied and scrutinised. We were all in a complete panic, again I told everyone to stay calm. Inside I was far from calm. Every muscle in my body was fully tensed, knowing again that if what was happening to the cars just in front happened to us we were in a chasm of trouble. Potentially I would be spending time in a French prison.

My mind drifted as I wondered if I would be able to achieve one of my life goals of speaking that beautiful language. After a few years of being surrounded by beautiful linguistic-emitting convicts, surely I would pick it up.

Back in the room, the cars between us and the border guards were gradually disappearing. Seven, six, five, four, three, two... All the cars were let through to continue their journey. The tension was too much. We were all on the edge of our seats, sweat was dripping down my forehead, and thankfully it was a very hot day, so this could disguise my panic. Seven, six, five, four, three, two, one. The car in front stopped and its occupants handed over their passports. We watched intently. Little Blonde had our passports ready and was waiting to hand them in. The guards looked suspiciously into the car in front, which had four Asian males inside. They were asked to pull over, and we watched as the four men were taken aside to have their car searched.

We approached, awaiting our destiny.

The guard glanced at our passports...

ANANDA'S 2, THE JOURNEY, FEBRUARY 2013

This was the strangest headspace I had been in for a long time. I was hoping beyond hope that being back at Ananda's would allow me to find some solace. It all began after the relationship meditation I'd done in Comolapa. I was unsure exactly why I was feeling so low. Was I missing home? Was I missing someone, something? Was I lost? I had no idea, but I wanted to feel all right again.

I felt like I had the world on my shoulders and wanted to shake it off. I was trying to look inside and get answers, but the only thing I was coming up with was that I was missing home. Not in the sense of home as in Manchester, but in the sense of having somewhere to call home. Since my mum had died, I hadn't had a place to call home. Home had always been wherever she was.

Every day I felt as if I was getting closer and closer to insanity, but something kept telling me, 'Be patient, ride it. This will end in a beautiful way, you have to endure this torment for a short time only'. The only thing that seemed to make sense at the time was what I read in 'Kundalini for The New Age' by Gopi Krishna where prana (breath) can get poisoned, and when it hits the brain, it can spin us out in a very negative way. This is why some people suffering from depression commit suicide, they can no longer handle the toxicity of what is going on in their head.

I wasn't feeling bad enough to end it all, but the thought had crossed my mind.

My heart was skipping beats and aching all the time and my mind was like this washing machine of thoughts going around and around of past, present and future sadness. There was no light. I was beating myself up constantly and could see no way out of this pain.

I wanted to fight it. It was the first time I had really considered my soul. It was like it was disconnecting from my body, trying its best to pull away from me. This pain pulled at my very being.

Darkness, but without the dark, there is no light, and I had to go through that to be where I am now. These were dark, dark times, but I wouldn't change them for the world, as they helped me grow.

I was trying to see this episode as something I just had to

process.

My days with the Prince of Panajachel consisted of lavish food, health supplements, yoga, meditation, and trying to cure my predicament. We decided to hit the beach for a couple of days.

We went to Livingston on the Caribbean side. I wasn't feeling it. I needed to be alone. I could have been anywhere in the world and not appreciated it.

Ananda heard that one of his friends in the city had been murdered, which was obviously very upsetting for him. It was so enlightening to see how a spiritual person dealt with death. This was another big lesson for me. He accepted, after some crying, that she had just left this body, her spirit was still about and always would be. What had happened was always going to happen, and we have a choice of how to react when we lose someone close. His friend could have changed her own destiny if she had wanted to, but that was her path. She would have to learn lessons in her next life about the importance of our choices.

We sat and chatted about it for a while, and this pulled me away from my internal wrangling momentarily. Soon I was back thinking of my trivial life dilemmas. Their insignificance in comparison made me even angrier with myself. I had all this energy, so I ran up and down the beach a few times doing as many press-ups and sit-ups as I could, insistent on a better mood.

It was in vain.

We only stayed in Livingston for two nights as I couldn't function.

I was feeling emotional every day and close to tears all the time. I tried to focus on my yoga but found it hard to concentrate.

After one session, I went down to the Krishna kitchen where Ananda was preparing food, full of emotion that I was trying to keep at bay. As I helped a little, I gave Ananda a hug and just erupted into tears. It was this massive deep cry that rose up inside me and poured out water, snot, and painful sobs. I was releasing a lot. It came in waves, one bout would end, and I would just hang there on Ananda's shoulder, waiting for the next. The pain and anguish were intense, and I just wanted it all out. It died down a bit, so I sat down on the floor with my back to the wall, but still it was coming and going. I wasn't trying to suppress it as I wanted it all gone. Ananda sat and just held space for me.

It was so beautiful that I could do this with him that I could cry and it was okay. He wasn't trying to make me stop, and he wasn't uncomfortable in any way. I had only been able to cry like this in front of me mum and girlfriends in the past, and I couldn't really imagine being comfortable enough to cry like this in front of most of my male mates. I was pissing tears all over the place with a bloke I'd only met a month ago.

Ananda went upstairs and came back with some incense and sacred paste called Tilak, that Vaishnavas (Krishna devotees like Ananda) use to mark their bodies. He started wiping it on me and chanting prayers.

After an hour of crying, I came back to the real world, just about able to string a few words together and I realised I looked like one of those holy men in India with brown stuff all over me.

That evening we watched this a documentary called, *Thrive* about the way the world works. If you can watch this and not be moved, there must be something switched off inside you. If you can watch it and not change your life in some way for the better, you are either already perfect or you are truly asleep and very disconnected from your heart and soul. To watch this and not have the fabric of your being changed is beyond me. When I hear what is going on in the world, I make changes accordingly. Sometimes they seem a pain, but it makes my soul happier.

I remembered watching a film called *The Corporation* for the first time. It was the first time I became aware of the fabric of evil that is at play in the material, capitalist and economically-obsessed world we live in. It compares companies to psychopaths, and the similarities are just flabbergasting. It's a must-see movie that I watched just after me mum died and it made me angry at the world for all the cancer-causing toxins that are floating about in the air and in most of the things we use.

A couple of strange things happened just after I got into bed at Ananda's. No, not bumming! The first one was when I was lying face down in bed with my door open. I was shaken by my shoulders from behind. I assumed it was Ananda, but as no further shakes took place and no words were spoken, I looked around, and nobody was there. I went into Ananda's room, and he was just reading in bed. I asked him what he thought it must have been and he said it was something to do with Krishna. I assumed he was right and just got back into bed.

The next evening, I was in bed, falling asleep when this huge roar startled me. I looked, but I saw nothing. I felt the presence of something in the room with me, but I wasn't scared, just startled. I lay there for a while thinking of an incarnation of Krishna's Ananda had told me about. It was called Lord Narsimha and had the face of a lion. It was very weird, and I wish I knew what its significance was.

The next day I felt more angst. I was moping about, fretting, wanting my life to be sorted, wanting a home, wanting a base to launch my world adventures from. More than anything else in the world, I wanted my own family; a family of joy, one without the complications and drama of my own, one of pure love, understanding and compassion. I wanted my financial woes to be sorted, and that worry of 'where is my next cash going to come from?' gone. I needed stability to be able to provide for my family.

All the social pressures of what I should have by the age of thirty crippled me. I thought of my friends with jobs and houses and money, and began to think, 'When will I have that?' But I knew I was unable to conform to a materialist world and the toxic mortgage situation I never wanted to be part of. Paying an evil banker an extra three hundred thousand for a one hundred thousand loan to have the privilege of every human's basic need; shelter. No, thank you.

I was reading Huxley's *'Heaven and Hell, and The Doors of Perception'* and again I was stunned at the extent of this man's genius. After his trip to India, he travelled to the US observing that what was happening there was a revolution of values where all established standards were being altered in a very negative and cumbersome way.

He saw this in the early twenties and thirties when Americanisation had been around in Europe for seventy-odd years, and he was calling it 'a travesty'. *'Brave New World'* and George Orwell's *'1984'* both made pretty good predictions of how the crest of that wave would break. They are cited as the twin pillars for all that is most repulsive and spine-chilling in today's world. Even Huxley's *Island* has become a reality; beautiful places of paradise commercialised, and indigenous people made to suffer in a world of increased greed, mass communication, oil guzzling transport and skyrocketing population, where co-operative communities have little chance of survival.

The Doors of Perception is about Huxley's observations regarding the use of mescaline, a synthetic version of the plant medicine Peyote, used in Mexico and by indigenous North American tribes as a way to connect and be guided by spirit. Peyote was something I really wanted to try. Huxley discusses how what is seen under the influence of mescaline is what the artist is equipped to see all the time. Parts of the brain are opened which are usually locked. The right side of the brain becomes more active. Under normal circumstances, only geniuses have the key. With mescaline, everybody gets a glimpse.

Hypnosis, meditation and drugs can also change our consciousness, allowing us to see what visionaries, mediums even mystics see.

Huxley wonders how normal people can ever know how it feels to be a nutcase?

I guess we would have to get into that frame of mind in order to understand. But then maybe we would discover we were mad all along?

People who take mescaline seem to open their imaginations and become visionaries which seemed very appealing to me. When I researched mescaline, I discovered it didn't seem to have that many negative side-effects, though it was not advised for people suffering from depression or anxiety and was seen to provide the heavenly part of schizophrenia.

People taking it know it will only last for about eight hours and leaves no hangover or craving for more. To say that humans can let go of vices such as alcohol, drugs and sex seem far-fetched. People's lives are so full of suffering, with the depressive repetition of work in an unhealthy world, they will always find short-term fixes.

Chemical intoxicants have always been our main escape, along with religion, dancing and music. It's interesting that all the natural hallucinogens that grow in the forest, that have been used by humans since the start of time, are deemed illegal by the west, while alcohol and tobacco are permitted. All other chemicals are labelled dope and their takers addicts or fiends. It's crazy how we spend more on drink and smoking than on education because of the urge to escape. Most parents are only interested in education for a few years their own children are at school. Huxley's observations then are so spot-on for what is happening now. At the same time, it's scary to realise that nothing has changed, even though we have been warned over and over again.

We know smoking gives you cancer and alcohol provides us

with deaths from drunk drivers, an array of fights and murders, and sends millions into misery as practising alcoholics. For a rationalist, this may seem odd, but to historians not so much. Huxley calls it, the material reality of Hell. He has an argument for adults using better drugs than alcohol and tobacco that are killing so many.

It's crazy that these wars against terror kill a fraction of the number that these legal stimulants do. Imagine if someone whose child was killed by a car went out and started blowing up cars. We would think they were mad. The way we react to things and the fears we have truly need to be put in perspective. People wear helmets on a bike but not for walking across roads.

Huxley asks people to change their habits for new and less harmful ones; less toxic than opium and cocaine and less likely to produce undesirable social consequences than alcohol: These better drugs or plant medicines that can give us direction and understanding of our purpose in life seem preferable to escapism from monotony and a temporary release of all inhibitions.

People could just start following their hearts and get out of what is actually leading them to continually want to escape. Huxley feels that mescaline is almost innocuous; the taker quietly minds his own business, and the business he minds is of the most enlightened kind, which doesn't have to be paid for by a compulsory hangover.

J.R.R Tolkien wrote about Peyote, saying:

"It does not seem to produce any increased tolerance or dependence. I have known people who have been Peyoteists for 40-50 years and the typical period between rites is around a month without feeling any cravings for it".

All over the world, people use different forms of escapism to transcend from the outward reality we live in. People go to church and endure boredom for the duration of the service, whilst at Peyote gatherings, people experience a direct spiritual experience, not one provided by a priest, vicar or pastor. They see visions, hear the voice of Great Spirit, become aware of God and see their own personal shortcomings which must be corrected if they are to do His will.

I have never come out of church with direction. In my society, when do we ever go to church? Only for funerals, christenings and weddings, and most of us who gather there are atheists. We don't consider God anymore. It's like God is Father Christmas or something, forgotten and ridiculed from a certain age. People look at you funny if you say God and you're under sixty years old. We are never given an opportunity to consider it and are laughed at if we do so. The pub and social hangouts have become our churches, and TV has become God. Peyote can show us death, so we don't fear it, but embrace it and find our soul's purpose and the most beautiful expression of ourselves.

I was researching these drugs, wanting to use them as the next step on my spiritual journey to open up creative avenues of thought. I'd had this vision that Ayahuasca would take me there and I was eager to experience it, especially in my current headspace.

I wanted answers and direction fast.

My plan had always been to do Ayahuasca in Peru for the first time. But I felt like I needed it now to ease my mental suffering. I also thought that Peyote may become an option in Mexico. I was open to the experience before Peru through sheer desperation.

That evening, I did yoga on the roof as the sun was going down. I watched the moon appear, and the stars come out, The Pleiades, my favourite constellation like a little angel smiling down on me. I finished yoga, and I was in complete darkness on the roof terrace. I sat in half lotus and meditated. After ten minutes I could feel waves of emotion rising up my spine and into my belly. I sat there with a sheet over me, flooded in tears. It was as strong as the previous day, but I was doing it alone. I didn't need someone to cry on; I could do it by myself.

The waves came and went, and it felt like forgiveness again for all the wrong I had done and all those I'd hurt. More than anything, it felt like I was forgiving myself and moving on.

Twenty minutes later, Ananda found me. He held me again, saying his mantras over and over. Soon the crying stopped, and part of me felt a little normal.

I'd been reading that yoga could help get rid of blockages and release emotions once you were fully connected and had been practising for a while. I was also considering whether it was the Kundalini rising in the spinal column. There is this amazing psychic energy in all of us. Kundalini provides a channel for the exploration of the mind, and I was hoping this was one of the steps to figuring mine out and finding happiness within.

I'd read that having the Kundalini fully awake (which can be a very long process and can be obtained through years of meditation and yoga) sees amazing activity commence in the whole nervous system, from the crown of the head to the toes. The body becomes a miniature laboratory working at high speed.

I had felt different parts of this going on in the last year. At times my whole body would tingle, and my feet would feel like there were vibrating at a hundred miles per hour. It's said that when the Kundalini awakens, parts of the brain and body start to function differently, and consciousness is forced into a new activity. This was exactly what I wanted, to be open, to be able to pick up on some of the amazing ideas floating through the ethereal world and to share them.

Gopi himself cannot explain where his writing comes from. He had no education or formal training but just sat and meditated for many years and eventually, thousands of poems and books just came to him, so he wrote them down, and then they started getting published, and he became a prophet and a sage.

He thinks it is insane that advanced nations are frantically engaged in a life or death race to be the first to develop the supercomputer and artificial intelligence, but nothing is being done to create the super brain. He sees the super brain developing through the study of Kundalini. I could see similarities in my recent writing behaviour.

I wrote my first poem when I was 25. My mum had been diagnosed with cancer, and I felt compelled to write something down. I'd never written anything before, and this fully formed poem came into my mind. I hadn't even read a book until I was 21. Luckily, I found *Harry Potter*, which I couldn't put down, and my love for literature began.

Falling in love with Fhian had a massive influence on my ability to write. Constant love songs and poems flashed across my mind. It was like meeting this girl and having this love allowed my creative side to blossom.

Many poets and scientists have described their inspiration as whole passages or stanzas — finished products — flashing across their minds.

I wondered where it came from. Why was I writing so much?
Nietzsche said that his ideas just dropped into his lap.
Child prodigies: how does that work?
Mozart, people like Joan of Arc, a peasant girl.
Where does it all come from? How do they tap into it? Why them and not us? Or are we all capable of amazing feats, but have to search for what our special gift is?

It's said that the current depression and dismay individuals in the west are experiencing is the fruit of civilisation and leisure, and can only be eased by an awakened Kundalini. Nothing was making me better when I was depressed. The doctor could do nothing, the tablets made me weird, and no one wanted to talk about it. The only person I could talk to was a counsellor who kept telling me to meditate. No one else really wanted to know unless they'd been through something similar.

In 2011 I meditated, prayed, read and went to Buddhist retreats which made my thoughts easier to deal with. I started to realise so many people I knew were in the same position. They wanted to get better but had no desire to change their lives. I was willing to try anything. Willing to change any part of myself and my life to find inner peace. Willing to do whatever it took. I wanted to know how to become a better person and serve the planet and humanity.

To quote Woodrow Wilson: *"You are not here merely to make a living. You are here in order to enable the world to live more amply, with greater vision, with a finer spirit of hope and achievement. You are here to enrich the world and you impoverish yourself if you forget your errand".*

I wanted to die, knowing I had done my bit.

One night at Ananda's, I did myself an angel card reading. One of my cards was New Love, which excited me. It was placed in the future, but it did say that old love could be healed and renewed. I then did a reading for Fhian, and the strangest thing happened. I pulled out three cards. I always pick the card on the left first, which is the past card. But for some reason, I went to the right first, something I have never done before. I pulled out New Love, and this tingling sensation erupted through my body. It was beautiful.

I couldn't believe that out of all those cards I had chosen the same card for us both. I spent the rest of that evening looking at pictures of the girl that, in my heart, still seemed like mine. It was hard in more than one way to look at the women I had such an attraction to. My soul wanted her, every part of me wanted her, but I knew it would be in the future. For now, I had to follow this path and see if it led me to some sort of peace.

I could feel her energy on me. In a way, I was glad she wasn't there because the six months "without sex vow" would have been broken! The no-masturbation vow almost fell, but I reined it in. Maybe cutting my hands off would be my only chance!

It was time to leave Ananda's. I felt bad about how down I'd been, sad I couldn't have been my usual funny self. I was hoping the low feeling would pass soon. It was sad to be leaving the comforts of Ananda's place to go back into the unknown. I was hoping to get my happiness back before my arrival in Taos. When you're feeling so down, you miss the beauty of life; the things other people show you and tell you and the things nature gives you. You only see the negative. Ananda had been an amazing host, above and beyond anything I could have imagined. Maybe I was playing the character of the spoilt little prince?

CHAPTER 14
DEALER WITH IT 2,
LIFE, 2008

...he glanced at us and waved us through. Relief poured over me like a golden shower. We slowly made our way to freedom, passing the car in front that had been taken to be searched. The men got out, and the police started to pull the car apart. Bags and cases were scattered all over these metal tables, being meticulously scrutinised by rubber glove clad border control officers. We then noticed that all the people who had been stopped had brown skin. After quickly taking in so much information in this almost war-like situation we tore off into the French countryside.

The girls told me they couldn't handle that again.

Me and The Communist were stunned by what had taken place as we had driven around eight European countries the previous year and not once had to show our passports. We hadn't once been stopped at a border, nor had the police pulled us over. On this trip, we had achieved all of the above in less than twenty-four hours.

The rest of the trip down to Spain was as eventful, but not as scary. We bathed in the fountain of a town we passed, washing our hair and frolicking in the water as cars passed, beeping their horns. We swam in some beautiful fresh rivers and lakes. We camped outside a campsite, and in the morning, a one-armed man was running towards us shouting angrily in French. I told the others, and they said, "Shut up, Liam," until they popped their heads out of the tents and panicked. We scrambled around packing away our stuff as the furious one-armed French man threw a torrent of abuse at us which, fortunately, none of us could understand. We raced through the winding Pyrenees, breaking the speed limit as often as possible, smoking hash and daydreaming as we lay in fields of hay. We set up camp on a barren hillside in Spain and could hear partying gipsies in the distance as we tripped out on acid-laced Ecstasy.

Fortunately, we arrived to meet our friends in Benicassim unscathed. This was the second time we had all descended on this quaint Spanish town for a week of sun, sea, sex and music. The whole place was flooded with party-hungry Brits wanting to get high and dance all night. I planned to capitalise on this want, as the previous year I had made a small fortune selling pills and this year I was hoping to make even more money.

The first year I decided to go to Benicassim I loaded up my car with a thousand Ecstasy pills, and three friends, and set off on an adventure to drive to Spain. I was really looking forward to the trip and driving through the whole of France. I wasn't scared about having all those drugs on me, I thought it would be fine. I had all these preconceived ideas about France that had been given to me by my peers. I had opinions and prejudices towards the French even though I had never even been there or met any French people. I was under the impression they were all massively arrogant and unhelpful and that, although they were the closest country to us, they were actually the most different. I realised I sounded like my step-dad.

After the Germans, the French were the people I was supposed to hate the most. As I was growing up, I gathered all these prejudices from the people around me and misinformed opinions mainly created by the media and history. I was supposed to dislike anyone who was different from us in the area we lived. There was always a reason to hate a certain group of people, and even at school we would have fights with other schools and with people from other areas.

The attitude of my step-father provided me with most of my extreme opinions. Anything that was different or from another place was deemed as awful and meaningless unless maybe it was American. Then it was okay because they'd helped us in the war. To him, England was the centre of the universe and the greatest country in the world, and I firmly thought this whilst growing up.

Every time there was football on the TV, there was always a reason I should hate the country England was playing. Germany: the war, and even if we lost to them, well at least we won the war. When we played France, we hated them because they were deserting bastards, Holland was just a joke of a country for having lax rules on drugs and sex, being full of prostitutes and how could you take a completely flat country seriously? The Spanish were dirty spicks and again were on one side then the other in the war, the Italians were greasy hired puffs and stunk of garlic like the French. The Argentinians were disgusting because of the Falklands, the Scandinavian countries were a joke because they were insignificant in the world, the USA should stick to basketball and Brazil, well they were just too good at football and should be hated because we invented the game and we own it.

These slightly racist, xenophobic, homophobic, sexist views attached themselves to me, until I went off into the world alone as a fully-rounded, open-minded individual. I began to be amazed by the beauty I saw in everything; other countries, people of different colours and nationalities, and the vibes I got from each place I went and each person I met.

The more I viewed the world through a different lens, the more I would get annoyed with myself for the way I had been. I'd been so impressionable and taken on the thoughts, feelings and attitudes of the people around me as I was growing up. I was angry at them for misinforming me, I was angry with my step-dad for his conservative, fascist views and for exposing them to me. I was even angry at me mum for exposing me to stuff I should have been protected from. I was angry with my dad for the fact that his only interests were tits, karaoke and painting and decorating. I wondered how different my world view would have been if I'd had educated, open-minded parents.

I quickly realised the wool had been completely pulled over my eyes, and that all these countries and people I had been brought up to fanatically hate were all beautiful in their own individual way. It was as if a veil had been pulled from my eyes, heart and soul.

I fell in love with France. The vibe I got there was so different than at home; all the places we passed were really quiet and chilled, people were always helpful, and the food was out of this world.

As we drove further into Spain, we could see in the distance that a huge storm was brewing. We looked at it and thought that we needed to set up camp soon. A golf course appeared on our left, and we all looked at each other and said, "Yes, that's it, let's check it out". It was the first grass we had seen during the four hours we had been in Spain, and it had appeared right on cue. The golf course looked like it was shut, but the gate was open. We drove up a hill to the holes that were less visible to any prying eyes below.

I was driving a Renault Clio Oasis, and my mechanic had told me the best place to hide my drugs was the front dash, which came off completely with a special star screwdriver. The Renault had become a drugs mule, and the drugs mule was now on a golf course on a very steep and narrow dirt track with nowhere to turn around. The only way back down was to turn the car in what can only be described as a fifty-six-point turn. The car almost fell off the edge every time I reversed. I sat petrified, turning the wheel with all my might against the unassisted steering.

We set up camp on the eleventh hole. We watched the electrical storm pass over the Pyrenees and got high in our tent, setting an early alarm to avoid being hit by golf balls.

The festival was so amazing that first year. All my friends in one place and I was with a girl I was in love with. The music was amazing, the drugs were amazing, and love filled me every evening as we all danced to electronic music hugging, cuddling, laughing and smiling all night.

After the festival, we headed for Barcelona. I hadn't slept for the last two days, and a crazy guy from Leeds had given us all a big line of coke as we were leaving. I was driving exhausted, and at one point I fell asleep. My friends managed to pull the car into a petrol station as I fell out of the door and slept on a hard surface that was full of spiky plants. They tore into my skin, but for a couple of hours I just lay there and slept, oblivious to the pain that would become prevalent later.

When we got to Barcelona, my girlfriend booked us into a hotel, and I threw all the money I had made from selling pills onto the bed, and we made love on top of it. We then travelled around Europe spending the money and camping in some beautiful places—at the lakes in Italy, by beautiful rivers in France and in the Alps of Switzerland, before heading to her parents' in East Germany. It was one of the first times I had felt real freedom, and it was something I never wanted to let go of.

The second time I arrived in Benicassim was after the treacherous dive in which I was convinced I was going to prison for a very long time, twice. I unpacked the drugs and saw that they had all crumbled up from the heat and being packed tightly into the car. Maybe they had felt the pressure from the prying eyes of the police and panicked.

It seemed like I would be making less money. Some of them were salvageable, but most were just powder. I decided to buy smoking papers and make little packets from them. I spent tedious hours repackaging the powder, and when it came to selling them, people were very dubious.

I'd become really interested in Ecstasy when I was living in Manchester. At the time, I was a big drinker as was expected of people who grew up where I did. Cocaine and drink were the themes of most nights out. I loved the feeling and confidence Cocaine gave me, but there was something false about it; something that didn't feel like me. I didn't like myself on it, and I didn't like myself as a drinker. Then I found Ecstasy.

It allowed me to feel this immense love, and it changed something in me. The fabric of who I was changed, and it helped me connect to another side of me; a side I liked.

When I moved to London, I was thrown into a world of party drugs without the necessity of drink and lad culture. I made a conscious effort to not become involved in it again and made friends who were more alternative. I decided not to play for the university football team and stepped away from boozy, sexist male-dominated circles.

Clubbing, parties, Ecstasy and any drug I could get my hand on became the thing. Everyone was paying so much for drugs I could get for a tenth of the price back home. There seemed to be a gap in the market, so I started buying for a few friends, and then it just escalated. This income supported me through university as I had no support from my family. I played up to being from Manchester, being very working-class and having a thick northern accent. I pretended to be hard, something I was not. I didn't mind having a fight now and then, but I was never a hard man. I just gave the southern softies the impression I was, and this helped in my new drug dealer persona.

At university, I became the crazy, moody Manc that made people dance, that made people have amazing sex and that made people connect to a side of themselves that facilitated stronger, less inhibited friendship bonds. People would come to my house all the time to get stuff. It was like a conveyor belt of guests and customers; beautiful girls would enter my room where I stood half-dressed, and they would giddily ask for what they wanted.

At parties I would be the guy everyone would come to score, and it became something I really enjoyed doing. For the first time in my life I wasn't worried about money. The kid from the council estate had his pockets full.

The amount of drugs I was taking started to take its toll. I became a shadow of the young man who had arrived in London and started modelling, I looked tired and ill, and for a year, I wouldn't even look at myself in the mirror, scared of what I would see. My skin was red and itchy, and my scalp was infested with sores. Every time I went out it was drugs, Coke, MDMA, pills and Ketamine. We were out four or five nights a week.

After I went to Benicassim for the second time, I flew into Manchester from Bordeaux, after spending some time at my uni housemate's parents' place in Cap Ferret. Myself, The Communist and my friends Tie and Justin had travelled by train from Benicassim to Bordeaux. We had become separated in Barcelona where I had left the rest of the unsold pills in a train seat pocket.

This was becoming an extremely traumatic time for me. I was not only coming down off a week of taking drugs, but I was also facing the reality that I might lose my mum, who was battling lung cancer back home. The Communist seemed like the only person I was truly close to, even though we were no longer together.

I was constantly crying as we rode trains without paying, slept in stations and adventurously made our way to the beautiful beach house of the amazing Red and Laurence in Cap Ferret.

I formed a special bond with Laurence just at the right time, because not long after I returned to England, my mum died, and for the first time in my life, I felt completely alone. My world had fallen apart, my everything had been taken away and, as The Communist put it, 'Liam has no one else, his mum was all he had'.

My whole world changed. For the first time in my life, I felt like Mum was watching me, that she could see my every move. Back when she was in Manchester, and I was in London, I had felt as though I could do anything. I was invincible as I had my mum to fall back on. She couldn't see all the bad things I was up to when she was alive, but now I felt she could see my every move. I really needed to get my shit together and make her proud.

RAINBOW, THE JOURNEY, FEBRUARY 2013

I had a lot of land to cover if I was going to arrive in Taos in ten days' time.

The week spent with Ananda had been massively healing. I knew not everything I had been going through had passed, but I knew some important work had taken place, as more layers of past hurt and emotion had been unearthed.

I didn't have much of a plan other than to head north and make my way through Mexico to the US. Ananda dropped me off in a bustling town called Escuintla. I jumped on a bus and squashed myself into the conductor's seat with bags piled on top of me. Six hours later, after breaking down twice, crashing three times and somehow not killing anyone, we arrived at the border.

I transferred to a smaller bus, hoping to be taken to the right place, despite understanding absolutely nothing that is going on. As I got on, a family started spraying aftershave on themselves, after the sweaty bus ride. I was thrown into the middle of them and almost killed by the fumes. Gasping for air, I prayed for the smell of sweat or shit or anything but this.

When I arrived close to the border, I walked across and bid goodbye to Guatemala. It had been epic on the grandest of scales, but now I was stepping into Mexico for the first time. I looked down the river and could see people making their way across on foot and boat. Even bikes were frantically rushing through the shallow waters. The building at the Mexican border was intimidating, with big gates and designated routes with coloured lines to follow. I instantly felt like I was in a first world country again.

I needed to find a cash machine and get a bus to Tapachula. The border town was pretty sketchy. Some boys offered me passage into Guatemala, where I had seen the people crossing, then a car slowly cruised up to me asking where I was going.

'Tapachula,' I said.

'So am I,' he said. 'Get in.' I jumped in, pulling the front seat down and throwing my backpack into the back seat. As the weight released and the straps slipped from my fingers, all these horror stories of people being taken at borders flashed through my mind. The guide books all said not to take lifts at the border. Then I thought of this news report about a couple who had been taken at a border, robbed, killed and left in the middle of nowhere. But I had gone past the point of no return as the straps had left my fingers and my bag was floating through the air onto the back seat. I pulled the seat back, got in, looked at the guy and nervously settled, making sure the signs we were passing had the name Tapachula on them.

They did, but horror story after horror story came into my head. I couldn't relax. We were driving down what looked like dirt tracks to my death. Maybe he had people waiting for me in some deserted place to rob and rape me. I wondered if it was just going to be him attacking me? Would I be able to take him? I thought about what I would do if he had a gun. Would I have time to take it off him? Would I react in time and save my life, and would saving my life only be possible by shooting him? Would I be able to do it? Would the non-violence practising me be able to kill another man?

I started asking him questions and, seeing a scar across his face, my theories started to gather momentum. Slowly, however, I began to realise he was a mechanic from Guatemala City off to get car parts. Or was this a made-up story to make me feel safe? He said he was called Carlos, he was Guatemalan with a wife and son. He was obsessed with Volkswagens and had a collection. I was starting to feel at ease; he was a car geek.

We arrived in Tapachula safely. I was alive without being robbed, raped and murdered. Carlos took me to get cash, showed me the station and became the person I had asked for in meditation that morning.

When we arrived at the station, I booked my first class night coach, however, after getting some food, I lost track of time, and when I got back, the coach was pulling away. I ran through the terminal to the bus doors, slapped on them, but the driver just ignored me. I waved my ticket, he waved me away, and I watched the coach that had cost more than all my previous bus journeys in the last three months put together drive off into the night. I went back to Carlos, disheartened but never angry, as I quickly discovered the lady at the computer desk could only get the computer to say 'no' and was being as unhelpful, unsympathetic and as rude as possible.

It was like being back home, hitting a brick wall of rules. I decided then I would always travel second class where computers don't make decisions and compassion and heart can come into play. Carlos managed to sweet-talk her, and she let me buy a child's ticket for the next bus which departed in thirty minutes. I would arrive in Oaxaca at 6am, contact Brie from the Earthship build and go and meet her. I wished Carlos all the best, thanked him for everything and jumped on my bus.

I arrived in Oaxaca feeling tired, still in this headspace of 'What am I doing?' 'I feel so alone', 'What am I missing?' 'What is this whole trip about?' 'What am I escaping?' 'What am I scared of?'

Find Brie quick before my mind destroys me.

I contacted Brie, but her plans had changed, and she was heading south to Nicaragua.

Nooooooooooooooooooooooooooooooooooo!!!

I was alone, but deep down, that was what I had been wanting: time alone, writing time, thinking time, me time, no people, just peace and space. I had the fear again, it was encompassing me, and I wanted it gone.

I pulled myself together, decided I would find a hostel and stay in the city and work out what I was doing here.

Breathe! I figured the universe had brought me here for something, obviously not Brie. But something else must have been lying in wait for me. I knew I was putting far too much emphasis on every part of my trip having meaning, but I was impatient — and that's another thing I needed to work on.

Oaxaca was similar to Antigua in a few ways but grander, with more open space. The streets were busy, but what made it really cool were all the Volkswagen Beetles and campervans everywhere. It felt like a really classy place with a bohemian feel.

The Spanish got town planning so right in all the countries they colonised; so many open plazas adorned by locals, always with this vibrant buzz of people of all ages, with little places for people to sit, relax and chat and the surrounding buildings were painted in orange, yellows and purples.

I sauntered past the botanical gardens and then decided to go to the main church which was magical and beautifully decorated. Mother Mary adorned the alters and I found a good place to meditate, asking for my mood to change and for happiness, laughter and myself to return soon. I bumped into some nuns, had a 'smile and nod', and headed out.

I caught a girl's eye. Seventy per cent of me wanted to ignore her and have the day to myself, but I didn't. We chatted, and I discovered she was looking for a hostel, so I took her to mine.

Then I decided it was 'me time.' I went for the most amazing walk to another church, The Church of the Mary of Solitude, the Patron Saint of Oaxaca. I sat in silence and asked for divine guidance. I walked back down the stunning stair path with pretty coloured houses on both sides, trees overhanging to give them shade. The sun was starting to go to sleep and darkness was drawing close.

That evening I met a few others from the hostel, and we went for street food; big tacos filled with cheese, guacamole and black beans. I met Hacobo, an American fisherman who travelled when he was not fishing and did six months of each. His Spanish was spot-on, and he was like a Ray Mears, Bear Grylls, Crocodile Dundee sort of character. His name was actually Jacob, but the Spanish couldn't say that so, it became Haa Co Boo, which I couldn't say. I almost choked every time I attempted it.

He was off to a Rainbow gathering on the coast with his friend who was due to arrive the next day.

I woke the next morning and started with yoga practice on the roof terrace to prepare me for my day ahead; Monte Alban ruins then to Mazunte on the night bus. An hour later, as I was about to leave, Hacobo came back with his friend Sandy. Her bag had been lost at the airport, and she had to get it before they could leave.

Me and Hacobo got some food and made our way to the bus station so I could head off. On the way, we bumped into Sandy in the main plaza, and they tried to convince me to go to the Rainbow gathering.

It worked.

Hacobo and I visited the ruins of Mont Alban, climbed temples we shouldn't and got whistled down by guards like you would for bombing in the swimming baths. We meditated under a tree, away from the blistering midday sun.

The journey to the Rainbow gathering was a six-hour bus ride, followed by a thirty-minute bus, followed by a one hour and thirty-minute bus, followed by picking up some supplies and a twenty-minute taxi.

We arrived at a private beach. The beach was seven kilometres from the nearest road, and a dirt track led us to some half-naked people greeting us with a group chorus of, 'Welcome home'. A few people were covered in grey mud from head to toe and looked like something from *Avatar*.

We were greeted and hugged by naked people, saying, 'Welcome home'. I wonder if this is the place I've been looking for.

We made our way down to the beach, which as our view expanded, opened up to reveal paradise. My jaw dropped, bliss and perfection stunned my vision. Mile after mile of untouched white beach, the crushing Pacific roaring and crashing down on the delicately crushed shells. Palm trees and mountains offered the backdrop and as my mouth subsided from being dropped, we saw the Rainbow flag and a little covered area in the bushes, indicating the Welcome Centre.

We were greeted by a tanned fair-haired naked man from Argentina called Nando, who said, 'Welcome home' and hugged each of us in turn. He sat us down and gave us some coconut meat and a drink, and proceeded to tell us the rules of the Rainbow gathering.

'It's a healing rainbow, so no psychedelics, no alcohol, no drugs, no smoking, no sugar, no coffee and no sex.'

We were shown via a map drawn on a piece of cardboard in crayon the amenities on offer, the main fire, the shit pits, the well for drinking water and the waste disposal rules. Organic waste was scattered in the thick natural surroundings, and inorganic waste had to be taken away with you. Nando told us the first crew we passed were rebels and that they go down there to smoke and drink coffee. The whole time he just lay there, his penis pointing at me, not in an erect fashion, but pointing nonetheless, in more of a curled finger fashion. It was the best briefing I've ever had; thorough, very thorough.

One of the *Avatar* girls came in and told us more about the rebels. She was naked, and because she was standing, her bits were at eye level. It was the only place my eyes wanted to be. She was stunningly beautiful with the body of a supermodel and completely covered in mud from head to toe.

I needed a swim. It was hot.

I dived in and looked up at the cloudless sky, out to sea. I turned, looked to land and got a flurry of exaltation running up my body.

This is paradise man, I'm in heaven!

Surely this was how Utopia would be. I wanted to thank Hacobo from the bottom of my heart for bringing me here. I felt rewarded for my faith and my questioning. Emotionally I turned to Hacobo and said, "This is a great opportunity to get me white bits brown, full-body tan man."

Further down the beach naked people swam, sauntered and lay in the sun. We found somewhere to camp. All I had was a very, very thin towel.

It was like a Utopian dream. Beautiful people everywhere, people playing instruments, people deep in meditation, others doing yoga and some splashing in the sea. We decided to take the plunge; take all our clothes off, dive in the sea and then collapse with exhaustion in the sand.

That evening, there was a sound healing in a little tipi at the far end of the beach. Everyone lay with their heads in the tent and bodies outside. The instruments, singing bowls, flutes, hang drum and other tappy things lay waiting to be played in the centre.

We meditated, and I found my focus shifting from instrument to instrument. At one point my face and shoulders started to be touched by one of the *Avatar* people. It felt amazing. My head and consciousness started to expand, and it was like I was in Heaven. I felt all warm and tingly and overjoyed. A group Om ended the session as I reluctantly opened my eyes and sat crossed-legged.

As that finished, dinner was called. We picked up Hacobo, who like a magician, had turned our little space in the bushes into a little pocket of bliss, and was standing there sweaty and naked. We all went for a bath in the sea then made our way for dinner.

The central fire was situated in a deeper part of the beach, which expanded back towards the lake where everyone had gotten the mud from. We all held hands, as the moon and the stars perfectly covered us. People kissed your hand, and you passed it on. We had covered ourselves as it was chilly. I didn't want people thinking I had a micro penis.

The food was then served by some of my new now-called brothers and sisters. I ate from a pan Hacobo allowed me and Sandy to share. I felt unprepared to be living wild.

The next morning, I woke and meditated on the beach before the sun got too hot. My friends soon joined me, and we body surfed for a while before yoga on the sand. It was time to get the white bits brown for possibly the first time in twenty-five years. It was time for breakfast and to see how everything worked in daylight. Naked bodies of all shapes and sizes held hands in a huge circle, songs were sung, announcements were made, and hand and face kisses were passed around. I was completely naked, self-consciousness and ego were showing their evil head. I decide to ignore what was going on with me downstairs bits (does it look really small?) and have conversations with people, trying not to focus on their bits for too long.

Hacobo then told me I should be careful as it looked like me arse was gonna burn. I wondered why Hacobo was checking me arse out, and I said, 'It'll be fine'.

Breakfast went round, and announcements were made for workshops taking place that day, followed by a day of silence. After eating everyone descended into the sea. A hundred naked people were surfing the waves and playing. When I glanced back to shore all I saw were beautiful naked bodies, chatting and playing and kids running about on the beach. I thought, what could be more normal than birthday suit frolics? Had I just been privy to a very un-normal societal upbringing?

Myself, Hacobo and Sandy decided to do a chocolate ceremony later that day and were joined by a stunning German girl called Elaine and a dreadlocked German boy, both covered from head to toe in mud. I'd burnt my arse to bits and was having difficulty sitting.

I knelt while everyone else sat around chatting about life, awareness and consciousness. Elaine talked about the dissatisfaction she'd felt in her marketing job, and her dissatisfaction with normal life which had made her decide to leave it all behind and go on a journey of self-discovery, living and finding happiness outside of the consumerist, materialistic society she was part of.

The chocolate took us deep, and the conversation was vastly stimulating. It was fascinating self-observation to be next to one of the most beautiful women I have ever seen on so many levels and not be constantly distracted. I was behaving normally and not having constant sexual thoughts going through my head. Aesthetically, this girl was perfect to me; the figure, the dark features, the high cheekbones and the delicate limbs, added to this the amazingly stimulating conversation. However, I was trying to learn something bigger, so sexual thoughts seemed not to be present.

The Germans left, and I decided to do a healing meditation with Sandy and Hacobo. I had never led something like this before. I went with my instinct and tried to switch off my mind and let my intuition guide me. When I did it became really easy. Under the influence of the chocolate, my focus was completely concentrated. I took them softly into meditation and after a while started working on Hacobo. I was being directed to different parts of his body, spending time on each. Then I had this big draw to his kidney area and back. My left hand was getting masses of energy and tingles like pins and needles, and then this kind of big explosion happened, and it felt like my hand was going to catch fire. I shook it off, trying to rid it of any bad energy I may have picked up.

Then I moved on to Sandy, who was lying down on her back. I worked on her body, spent a lot of time on her head and neck and was then drawn to her solar plexus, which felt unbalanced. Whilst I was doing this, Hacobo started playing his flute, and this amazing air of peace blew over our camp. We all sat around, chatting and then headed for the sea.

That evening, me and Sandy headed to a Thai massage workshop. I decided it was time for some shorts as my arse looked like a beetroot and I couldn't sit down.

We sat with our knees to our partner's shoulders so we could work on their head and neck. Some people were still naked. I learned how to slowly work all the different areas, then we had to move over to get our hands under the back. As I looked across the tipi, I saw this one guy leaning over his male friend, and his cock just grazed across his whole face. He coughed and spluttered a bit. I internally pissed myself and spluttered a few guttural laughs, and I really struggled to concentrate for the next few minutes. It was hysterical, and these hysterics had to stay inside, as everyone was concentrating on what they were doing. I wanted all my friends back home to have seen what had just happened and for us all to just roll about on the floor laughing.

I was unsure if it was inappropriate to laugh in these surroundings. I have certainly laughed a lot telling that story since. It reminded me of a time I started laughing hard in a sweet shop in Sweden when a kid knocked down a massive display of sweets. I had my eyes shut and was crying with laughter. When I opened my eyes, I looked around and realised no one else was laughing and the whole shop was staring at me.

That evening we ate food around the huge fire circle. I wanted to stay in this place for longer, I didn't want to leave. It was paradise, like a dream or a fantasy of how the world should and could be.

The next evening was the full moon, and there was to be a party, with special food, music and drumming. I woke to watch the sun come up (which was spectacular), I meditated for a while, then saw Hacobo, and we went to the far end of the beach where I led an Ashtanga Yoga session for an hour. Then, led by Hacobo, we did some manly press-ups and sit-ups.

It was then time to cover our whole naked bodies with mud for the first time. It felt like a special day. A beautiful Indian girl's angelic voice floated through the air as she delicately strummed the guitar sat on the sand outside her tent.

I was relaxing in the camp when Hacobo arrived and said, 'You have to go in the sea, man.'

I said, 'Why? I'm chillin'.

He said, 'You just have to'.

I sauntered into the ocean. 'What do I have to go in for?'

He said, 'Go in the sea, man, and put your head under the water. I promise you it's worth it'.

I went in and put my head under, thinking it was gonna be some sort of practical joke. As my ears became submerged, I could hear this whale that was like nothing I had ever heard before. I got past the break and lay on my back with my ears submerged. It felt like the whales were next to me, and at first I was a little scared I was about to bump into them, they felt so close.

The whale calling and the sounds of the cubs reverberated through me. It was like the most beautiful and elegant piece of other worldly classical music was serenading my soul. It didn't feel like the sound was coming in through my ears, but rather through my mind and my heart. It was this perfect frequency, filled with love and caring. It was like I was being healed as I listened.

People lay to my left and my right like lily-pads in the water, listening to these graceful beings chatting to one another. It was truly magical. I felt so grateful to be experiencing this, and I welled up with emotion. It was stunning, sublime, a feeling I struggle to explain, but one I felt changed the fabric of me and created a connection with these elegantly mesmerising spiritual creatures.

On the way out of the sea, we saw that a game of beach football had begun, so we joined in. It was skins against clothed people, and when I say that it was actually naked men against naked men with a scarf, hat or small bit of material.

It was another amazing experience. It gave the phrase, 'tackle' a whole new meaning. Sixteen naked, tanned, beautiful men running around after a ball, goalkeepers diving along the sand and naked men chasing down naked men to jump tackle them.

It was insane. The game was taken really seriously, and other than getting tangled up a few times, it was a good match. I couldn't help chuckling to myself at times at what I was currently a part of. Thinking, I'm going to have to arrange a charity game when I'm back home based on this. It was such good fun, but I had to throw the towel in— well, the scarf I borrowed— as I managed to wind myself running too fast, turning and getting my actual balls tangled up. I typically wear very tight cycling shorts to keep them controlled whilst participating in sporting activities.

That evening there were festivities around the central fire. Special food had been made, of which we had been part of by going on the long hike to the well to fetch water. We ate raw chocolate balls for dessert and lots of people were in party spirits. After food, everyone gathered close around the fire. I wasn't feeling it; I felt a bit funny. I wanted to get away, even though what was happening was amazing.

I realised I had left my t-shirt at the end of the beach that morning, so I went to look for it. I'd left it at the far end near the rocks, and as I walked down this stunning beach looking at all the stars and the vast ocean, a calmness filled me. I walked a few more steps and could see this big black rock moving slowly. I realised it was a sea turtle. I was completely on my own with it. As it saw me, it turned around and slowly made its way back into the sea. I couldn't believe what I was seeing. It was so graceful, so melodic and slow in its actions.

I kept my distance and stood back as it disappeared into the water. I stood alone and savoured the moment. I found my t-shirt, meditated by the rocks and made my way back to camp, not feeling too well and still missing something.

I didn't sleep to well and woke the next day feeling awful. My whole body felt completely weak, and my stomach was funny. It was a day of silence, so I couldn't even let Sandy and Hacobo know. We had to go and fetch water for the kitchen again, and I could hardly carry the empty can. It was an ordeal hiking to the well, filling up the drum and then hiking back and taking it in turns to carry the big drum.

We dropped the water off at the kitchen. I hugged Elaine and didn't think about making love to her, and went back to our camp. I didn't move from the hammock the whole day, except to go to the toilet (which was quite often considering the state my stomach was in). I didn't go to breakfast or dinner and, as Sandy and Hacobo seemed fine, the only thing I could think of that could have made me ill was the healing I'd done. That energy I'd taken out of Hacobo was pretty powerful, and it reminded me of the feeling I had had back in San Marcos when I'd healed Connor. I wondered what I was doing wrong. Why was I picking other people's stuff up? And what did I need to do to protect myself more?

I was only supposed to be staying for two days and ended up staying for four. I wanted to stay and be there for my birthday, but I had to get moving. I was feeling a bit better and told the guys how ill I'd felt. They hadn't realised; they'd just thought I was fasting and withdrawing for the day of silence. I wished Hacobo goodbye and me and Sandy headed off on a seven kilometre walk to the main road to hitchhike.

We grabbed some water, Sandy stuck her thumb out, and van stopped. I jumped in the back and found out he was going exactly where I wanted to go, so there would be no waiting for buses.

Sandy jumped out at the shops, and I continued my two-hour ride with the very kind Ferdo. We chatted for a while with my very basic Spanish. 'Where he was from', 'Where I was from', 'Kids', was about all I could muster.

He told me his daughter lived in Miami with his granddaughter. I told him in Spanish my best mate lived in Miami with his little daughter. I kept repeating it over and over again in Spanish, and he was looking at me funny. The rest of the journey was difficult as I had nothing I could say. Since I'd told him about my friend, the whole atmosphere had changed, and I couldn't figure out why. Had I offended him? I occasionally said 'muchas gracias', and he smiled.

He dropped me at the town, and I made my way to the bus for the six-hour ride back to Oaxaca. As I was looking out the window at the rolling green hills and mountains, it suddenly dawned on me what I had actually said to Ferdo.

Noooooooooooooooooooooooooooooooooooooo
oooooooooooooooooooooooooooooooooooooooo
oooooooooooooooooooooooooooooooooooooooo
oooooooooooooooooooooooooooooooooooooooo
oooooooooooooooooooooooooooooooooooooooo
oooooooooooooooooooooooooooooooooooooooo
oooooooooooooooooooooooooooooooooooooooo
oooooooooooooooooooooooooooooooooooooooo
oooooooooooooooooooooooooooooooooooooooo
oooooooooooooooooooooooooooooooooooooooo
ooooooooooooooooooooooooooooooooooooooooo!

I had told him that my man lived in Miami, with our daughter, and I was going back there soon to spend time with them and that she was two. I just kept repeating mi hombre, mi hombre, over and over again. Meaning my man, my man, my man. It was no wonder he looked at me funny. I had been trying to say 'my mate.'

It had been a truly magical time on that beach; something more than special. There had been something otherworldly about the events that had brought me there and how much better it had made me feel. I didn't want to leave, I wanted to stay and become a part of it. It really had been a healing Rainbow gathering for me. I couldn't have picked a better one. It was amazing to see what is possible when people work together, with the love everyone gives one another just pouring all over the place. The energy was so pure and to be able to source such a spectacular setting and location for free, showed me the frequency of love these people were vibrating at.

The instruments that were constantly being played made me feel so in love with everything. Waking up to classical violin every morning was divine. The conversations about borders, freedom, food, work, peace and human rights were inspiring, and Huxley came into my head again and how to be enlightened is to be fully conscious and fully aware of the totality of all realities and possibilities, but to remain centred and non-reactive and able to survive as a human being. It is to see things from all angles with a system of diplomacy to give powerful guidance. It is knowing we are always exactly where we should be

This made me think that my experience on the beach— the whales, the turtle, the healing and the naked football— it had already been written. I just had to follow the signs.

CHAPTER 15
ROCK BOTTOM,
LIFE, 2011

I am in the garden of a multi-millionaire banker's house whom I've never met. His wife is so uptight that over the last few months whilst I've been tending to their massive garden which backs onto Richmond Park I've often said to my boss that the only thing that would loosen her up is a good fucking, preferably in the arse.

Today I am alone in the garden. My boss is on another job, and Mrs I-need-a-good-cock-in-my-arse is out. I sit crying on one of the garden chairs contemplating whether to end it all by sticking the garden fork into my chest.

I've reached rock bottom.

I was told I might end up here.

I have never felt so low.

I don't want to be here anymore.

I don't want to exist in this world.

I don't want to be inside in this toxic body.

Stuck in a downward spiral of depressive thoughts, a washing machine of negativity continually circles my mind. My chest feels heavy, anxiety makes breathing difficult, and my ability to speak to people has become a challenge. I stutter my words and don't want to be around anyone, but at the same time I'm crying out to be held and to be saved.

Something I can't explain feels disconnected.

I've woken after three or four hours sleep every night for the past four months with pains in my chest and stomach as thoughts spiral and spiral. I can't stop beating myself up for all the pain I have caused in the past and all the people I've hurt. I can't see any positivity in my past, present or future. I can't see a future, so my brain asks me, 'What's the point? End it. Get out of here.'

This can't go on much longer. Something has to give. I have to start feeling better soon, or I am going to kill myself. I realise I must be in a deep depression and I'm beginning to realise why people kill themselves in these situations. It's like you are being psychologically abused by yourself, continual abuse is cycled around and around in your head. It must be worse than any abuse anyone else could throw at you because with this form of abuse there is no escape. How does one escape one's self?

I toss and turn in my bed every night, wanting this pain gone, wanting it out. A detached feeling is all around me in every aspect of my life. I feel alone, very alone, even with so many people around.

I lie in bed suffering, abusing myself, feeling as if I am losing the plot, going mental, wondering how long I can survive this torment.

For the first time in my life, I consider my soul. It feels like it's detached that it's hovering somewhere outside my body, and it won't return to this poisoned chalice. This is the only thing that makes any sense; something is so clearly missing from inside me. My heart is in so much pain, my stomach churns, I grab my chest and writhe around in agony as my heart feels empty.

I continually fight emotions, floods of tears run down my face, and I want this all to stop, but I don't know how.

Every night I torture myself in bed. I get up for work or if I have no work, a day of uncertainty. I can't even smile; it feels too foreign. My flat-mate has noticed, and while we eat breakfast, only negativity emits from my lips.

I have completely lost myself. Who is this person residing inside my body? What has happened to the happy-go-lucky, cocky, slightly arrogant, good-looking boy I have always been? In his place is a heavy-shouldered misery who I am trying not to become acquainted with.

I had always considered depression to be made up, a thing for weak people. Just smile and be happy was my answer. Don't take all those pills, go and see counsellors and psychologists, just start doing things that make you happy. Surround yourself with good people and have fun. I thought depression and misery were just for weak people, and I had always considered myself strong.

My northern working-class roots had ingrained in me that showing emotion or being down or depressed were not illnesses, they were just for weak people, of which I was now one.

I can't look in the mirror any more. I'm tired, and it shows, the stress is splashed across my face, and the tension all over my body gives me a red, panicked glow. What is happening to me? I need out of this. I want it to go away. I want to be saved or spared of this torment.

Will it ever end?

What does it mean?

Who can help me?

The tears stream down my face. I am crying for my mother, *please Mum help me, help me, I miss you so much, please help.* The fork is pressing against my heart with more and more pressure. I can't take this feeling anymore. I want it gone, it has to be gone, it needs to be gone now. The only way is to pierce my chest and rip out my heart to stop the pain and anguish that pushes itself around my body every time it beats.

I press the fork harder and harder.

I know I will have to exert a lot of pressure to pierce the skin, then get through my rib cage and to my heart. I realise the possibility of me being able to rip my heart out is pretty far-fetched but piercing it and stopping it beating seems more realistic.

I can't take this pain anymore. I see nothing positive in my past, present or future, just an array of destruction, failure and pain. All I feel is anguish.

I press harder. Any physical pain I feel I could endure, but what I have felt since this depression kicked in outweighs anything else. The only escape I can rationally see is jabbing this fork into my heart and stopping the pain here and now, on the paved patio of 'I desperately need a cock in my arse' lady's house. I don't think about who will find me or who will be upset or anything. It is purely about stopping the abuse, the internal torment, the torture.

I sit slumped the fork still pressed viciously against my chest, trapped between the paving slab below. My whole body feels empty, there is nothing left. Turn off the life support please, my spirit has gone, I am just flesh and bones and madness. Insanity fills me, madness, severe discomfort, my skin crawls. I want to scratch off my face, rip out my heart and dance on it, I want all my skin to be peeled off, for wolves, and pigs and vultures to feed on my flesh, for any evidence of my physical existence to be eradicated.

I take a deep breath, I am ready. This is it. No one is coming to save me. I hope the up-tight fuck-me-hard-in-the-arse woman will not return to scupper my endeavour. I contemplate nothing but getting out of here. This journey has taken me here, sweeping up leaves in rich people's gardens, 'loser'.

Go, just go, do it, flips and flips through my head like a doctor's receptionist flicking through files to find your name. I take another deep breath hoping it will be my last, then plunge. I dig deep, rummage around, crack through the obstacles, moving things aside determined to get it out, for it to end, to receive the help I need, to be rescued from this life.

After a battle, it squeezes out, pulling all sorts out with it. I can't believe what I'm doing; a cry for help, a final plea, a momentous gesture? I have no idea. I hold it in my hand and press at it with my index finger, and after a while, I hold it to my ear and listen.

MEXICO CITY, THE JOURNEY, FEBRUARY 2013

I arrived in Mexico City at 5 am.

I had wanted to sleep on the bus but had chosen to sit next to the only person who could speak English. This young man started asking me some weird questions, like, 'Do you think the bus will crash?' and 'What if there is a bomb?' He didn't seem autistic but considering these questions were asked towards the end of the journey, I was glad to be getting off.

I had to catch a tube to the artistic district of the city. I was thrust into the sardine storage unit and hurtled down the line. Immediately I felt the same angst I had felt in London; the scramble, the rushing, the busyness, all these people squashed next to me so they could get to work to pay their rent. My mind flashed back to when I'd return to London after a weekend away, somewhere semi-normal like Bristol, Buckinghamshire or Norfolk. I would get on the tube or overground and would start crying because I wanted to escape this place and I didn't know how. I would look at other people and wonder how they weren't being affected the way I was.

It was my birthday, and I was longing to be back on that blissful Rainbow gathering beach. I booked into an overpriced hostel with a private room. It wasn't nice, but I wanted to drop my bags, have my first shower for almost a week and go and explore the city.

The area had an upper class, bohemian artistic feel to it. It seemed there was a lot of wealth, and soon I was flung into a mezze of swish little coffee shops, restaurants, gyms, yoga studios and spiritual centres. I found a Buddhist centre and decided my birthday evening would be well spent there.

As I entered the building, an air of calm filled me, the gentle light wood and soft furnishings accompanied by the glow and helpfulness of the people made me feel peaceful. The radiant smiles of the monks and Buddhists gave me that kind of stoned feeling I get after yoga or meditation; their smile soaking into my soul. It was as if all the compassion, understanding, love and peace they had practised hit me square in the jaw for a perfect moment.

I bounded around Mexico City, massive parts of me imagining being back at the rainbow beach with Sandy and Hacobo, with family and friends at home, sitting on a rock looking over my favourite lake, lying on the beach in Cap Ferret, in bed enjoying the company of a lover, or anywhere but a huge city like this.

I decided to just be and enjoy. I headed for a museum and soon realised museums made me feel weird and flustered, a bit like smoking weed. Maybe I felt the death inflicted on the people the artefacts were stolen from. They are displayed with such pride as if there were no victims in their acquisition.

I headed to a quiet park, found a place to meditate under a tree and asked for my head to be clear during my time in Taos and for the coming year to be a happy one. I was feeling a lot better than I had when I'd left Ananda's, but I still didn't feel fully myself.

Why had I not been warned of the mental challenges you would encounter as an adult when I was a child? Why was I so unprepared for all these issues? Why are we not given a manual for life? Is that something the lucky ones get from their parents? Everything we're taught at school is predominantly verbal, ignorant of nature and the workings of the universe. We're churned out knowing nothing of humanity. Teachers always pushing us; if it's a sport we want faster, longer, harder at any cost, but what about heightened creativity or mind control? Goethe said, *"We should talk less and draw more"*. Educated people find it difficult to pay attention to anything but words and notions. Consciousness is dismissed, and we are taught that pure monetary gain is the only thing that matters.

We need to become more capable of controlling our own automatic nervous system like 'Wim Hoff the Ice Man'. However, when it comes to non-verbal education no respectable university or church will do anything about it. If it doesn't fit into any pigeon holes, it's ridiculed, left with a patronising smile and the people who embrace it are deemed nutters, weirdos, charlatans and unqualified armatures. There is so much suffering in the world now on so many different levels; emotionally, physically and mentally.

My mind drifted to Peyote and Ayahuasca again, wanting this fix, this awakening of vision, this guidance. I didn't want my imagination to run wild. I wanted this veil of dogma that filled my vision to be lifted so that I may see. I wanted light to be thrown onto the unknown regions of my mind, I wanted everything I had done in life to somehow merge to give me an element of stability. I wanted to share all I had learnt with people, to shine light on their fears by filtering out all the rubbish that swills around in our brains making us incapable of concentrating on one thing.

Rhonda Byrne shows in *The Secret,* the extraordinary power of concentration and that belief can get you exactly what you want. When you experience those moments of perfect concentration, it is like you are in another world. Or as the great Ayrton Senna said: *"experiencing this reality in another dimension".*

Gopi Krishna talks about how focused attention and retention is more evolved in people with a high IQ. He believes this to be a form of genius.

They say Peyote is not just a shortcut to the visionary world, but also an instrument for creating loving solidarity among the participants. Tolkien says:

'takers never get out of rhythm or fumble their words as a drunken or stupefied man, they are all quiet, courteous and considerate of one another'.

This doesn't tend to be the case during an alcohol-fuelled evening.

I had spoken to a few people over Skype that day, and again I had connected with Fhian. She had made me the most amazing card, and I wondered why I'd let this goddess go. The card was a drawing of all these beautiful Earthships dotted about with lots of people looking happy. It was the way I imagined my future, living off-grid in a community in the countryside, where everyone helped each other. It was called Browne Town, and the peace sign was dotted about the picture.

I felt this girl was so connected to me that I felt her presence wherever I was. I wanted her here. I was sad to be alone on my birthday, and if I could have had one wish that day it would have been to be held by her for just one moment. I wrote this poem thinking about our situation:

Apart
Being apart, time spent apart
Seems to bring you closer to me
I think about you every day
Every minute of every day
Your picture runs through my mind constantly
I take out my phone and look at you

I can't get away from it all
I see you, I hear you, I feel you near
Every part of your body is with me
I touch you, I stroke you, I hold you so close
My imagination runs wild with you
Looking deeper and deeper into your eyes
Every moment seems spent with you
When I'm sleeping, waking, walking through
My mind is stuck on you
Painful feelings of now what to do
I let you go, I let you down, let you slip away
But now I don't know, I don't know what to do
Should I try and take back your hand
Spend the rest of my life with you
These visions, this image
Feels heavy on heart
Should I stay stronger or listen to you
But I know I can't share this, can't tell you my heart
It wouldn't be fair to you
But this is torture, this longing runs fast through my veins
I want to hold you and tell you I miss you
I can't trust what's my heart, what's in my mind
That's the one thing I would love to know
What is true

    The Teotihuacan Ruins were my destination the next day, situated about forty minutes outside the city. It was the most touristy of all the ruins I had visited. There were fleets of school trips and people. The ruins were spectacular, so vast, and the two main pyramids were massive. The sheer scale of the grounds was phenomenal; a mile from one end to the other. Maybe it was the fact we were in the desert, and there was no jungle gave it the impression of being bigger than the ones in Guatemala.

    I mediated above both pyramids and drifted into wondering what life would be like 2000 years from now. Would the cities we live in now be viewed by our future generations? Would there be as much mystery around what we were up to, and would there be a plethora of archaeologists finding new artefacts and a stream of reconstructions trying to piece together fallen ruins?

    Would people in the future be so advanced that they don't need these places as entertainment centres, as the utopian world they have created meets all the needs of their citizens? Would everyone have these super brains to tap into all that has gone before?

I was thinking about the brain again, as its evolution is so evident even in just the past fifty years. What would happen to it in another fifty, a hundred or a thousand years? Would we become aware of how to use the 85% of our brain that currently lays dormant? Imagining the possibility hurt my head a lot.

The towering pyramids were such a feat of architecture and engineering. How on earth they had done it, was beyond me. As I walked down the main avenue, I imagined the history of the place, the people who lived there when it was thriving, the hustle and the bustle. I imagined the ceremonies, the speeches given from great heights, the colour, the tradition, the clothes and the lack of cameras.

I was expecting to be in Taos in two days, which would be Saturday. I'd planned on a day to travel through Mexico to the border and then a day to Taos. I had ground to make up, so I opted for a twenty-four-hour bus to take me to the border town of Ciudad Juarez.

Hour after hour, the bus drove through the arid desert landscape. It was like what I was seeing was on loop, with the occasional tumbleweed breaking the monotony. Every hour or so we would hit different checkpoints where either army officials or police would jump on the bus to check passports and search the place a little bit. Luckily there were only three of us on this massive bus.

The morning arrived, and we hit a service station, and I thought I was given fifteen minutes to go freshen up. I used the facilities, and as I came back out the door to my horror the bus wasn't in its bay. I rushed up, and down the line, sure I must have come out of another door or something, but no, the bus was gone.

Pure panic rose in me. Everything was on there; my passport, wallet, angel tarot cards and phone. I rushed around trying to get answers from what I thought were officials, but no one could help me. I was screaming inside. Anxiety filled me, as I thought, 'How are you gonna get out of this one, Browne'? How could I just take this in my stride and stay calm when my head was about to explode?

Will I get to Taos?

Where do you get a new passport from in the middle of the desert and actually, where am I?

Where should I head?

I can't head anywhere, I have no money. Will I have to work for one of the drug cartels for a couple of years, make enough money and gain their trust to escape over the border with one of the drug deliveries then ask the US government for exile and compassion and a ticket back to England?

Then a guard tapped me on the shoulder and pointed far across the concrete park to where a bus was being washed. Hallelujah, I'd found my bus, panic over and no need to get into drug trafficking. My whole body relaxed, and an air of calm ran over me. I went and got a hot chocolate and waited for my clean bus to return.

The bus managed to do this to me three times and each time I shit my pants with the same velocity. One of those times, it disappeared for thirty minutes, and I just had to keep the faith. Each time I would go into a fantasy about what I would have to do to get back home from here without a passport and money.

Would I try and continue my trip and illegally enter the US and get to Taos, or would I have to return to Mexico City, find the embassy and get them to send me home?

I remembered how I would daydream about what I would do if people died, and I found them. Who would I call if my housemate died? I didn't know his parents' number, and I didn't know the code on his phone. Would the hospital or the police know how to do this when I took his corpse to them? I would also get worried when people who were picking me up were over ten minutes late. I'd imagined they'd crashed and died. How would I find out and how long should I wait, and if they had died, should I wait longer out of respect? Should I still go to where I was heading? My head started to hurt thinking about what I often perused mentally.

Everyone taking the bus thought they had missed it. I rushed around offices trying to find out what was going on, while other people made phone calls, which made me even more nervous. Eventually, the bus just nonchalantly returned, but why they insisted on putting us through that torture so often was beyond me.

We arrived in Ciudad Juarez just after dark, and I was looking for a way to cross the border into New Mexico. I discovered that I had to head into El Paso in Texas. I tried getting a lift and looked for a local bus, as the Greyhound seemed pricy. I attempted hitchhiking, but I had no idea where I was actually going, so I decided this wasn't the best idea. Finally, I got on the Greyhound.

Later I found out Ciudad Juarez is the most dangerous place in the world, with more murders than anywhere else on Earth.

Nervously, I approached US passport control, hoping to be

allowed into this great nation. I knew that in a legal sense, I should not be attempting to get into this country and that if they knew about my convictions I would be declined entry.

I decided to not tell them the truth. It was in contradiction to the new me that was all about truth, but telling the truth would have meant being thrown back into Mexico and possibly being interrogated for hours and losing my anal virginity to a gloved fist officer. In this case, I thought withholding the truth would have been looked on favourably by the powers greater than myself.

I'd booked a flight out of the US to Peru as I was told you had to have evidence of outbound travel; otherwise you would not be allowed in. They asked me a few questions, never asked to see my outward flight and back on the bus to El Paso I got. I was asked if I was a communist amongst other things, and again I really wanted to show my truth but opted against getting into a seven-hour debate with a border guard about political policy, the predicted demise of democratic capitalism and the positives of a more socialist system.

When I got to the States, I immediately noticed there were no people on the streets. Places felt like ghost towns in comparison to Mexico and Central America. There were cars about but no people. No food vendors on every corner, no music and people chattering in plazas, no one playing music, playing football, juggling and dancing.

It was dead.

People must be in watching TV, I thought.

I immediately noticed the massive cars and massive roads. I planned to try and hitchhike to Albuquerque that evening or get a bus. It was around nine at night. The next bus wasn't until 10am the next morning. I thought about how constant public transport had been in the previous countries I'd visited. The first bus, 10am. Wow I thought, welcome to America.

I tried hitchhiking to no avail. I was a guy with a massive beard on the side of the freeway at night, in the country with the most scared human beings on the planet. Even if they felt like picking me up, they would be asking themselves, 'Am I insured for this'? Where I had come from, I could be squeezed into a trailer with three families as I balanced on one leg while hanging over the side.

I headed back to the Greyhound office, where I had to buy a ticket to be able to sleep in the waiting room for the evening. I snuggled up on the most luxurious of metal benches and drifted in and out of consciousness.

I woke up early. I had been mildly watching the comings and goings of a couple of buses and the meth-heads who frequented the bus station. It was weird to think I had gone from the palace of the Ananda's house to the paradise of the Rainbow beach to this in less than two weeks.

I needed fruit and water. I asked where the nearest place to buy fruit was, which got a strange look. A thirty-minute walk I was told.

Wow, I was in a different world. Fruits had always been less than a stone's throw from every populated place I had been on this trip.

This place was populated, there were buildings everywhere and lots of cars but no fruit. Obesity beckoned.

I settled for some eggs in the station café. The people in the station all looked pretty down and depressed or very angry. It was a weird place; lots of blokes wearing huge baggy jeans and oversized t-shirts and crazy people going mad about their bags being lost. I smiled and nodded to myself as I tried to concentrate on my breathing.

I arrived in Albuquerque at around two. It was strange being there as I'd been watching the series Breaking Bad over the last year, and in a Hollywood sense, it felt like I had been there before and knew loads about it. Well, mainly about its meth problems.

I discovered there was a train called the Rail Runner that ran to Santa Fe, which was on the way to Taos. I was directed to the station, expecting to have to wait twenty minutes or so. But no, this was America. The next train was in two hours and thirty minutes. The longest I had ever waited for a tube in London was three minutes, and in Central America, you never had to wait more than ten minutes, unless your bus was held up at gunpoint.

I headed out to hitchhike.

Two and a half hours later I was on the Rail Runner to Santa Fe. I was told by a lady to get off at the station before as it would be better for hitchhiking to Taos and sometimes there was a free bus.

The train dropped me off in what seemed like the middle of nowhere. There was no sign of a bus or any civilisation as far as the eye could see. I asked some kid, who said nothing and seemed petrified at having been spoken to. Then I saw a couple walking to their car. I approached them saying, 'Excuse me, can you help me?'

They retreated into their SUV, immediately put down the locks and then headed the long way around the carpark to avoid me.

I reiterate, *I AM IN THE WEIRDEST COUNTRY IN THE WORLD!!!* and as they say *PERIOD!!!*

I walked along a road heading for the lights I could see in the distance. I realised the lights were a gas station and when I got there, I asked the clerk who couldn't run away from me for directions.

I started asking people in the carpark for a ride, and an indigenous-looking man was nice enough to take me into Santa Fe and point me in the direction of Taos. Santa Fe seemed enormous. You had to drive from one shop to the next as they were so far apart. Again there were no people walking around, and there were no people to ask questions. It was strange, really strange. It felt scary; people were only in their cars.

After walking for about three miles with my huge backpack, and trying to hitchhike to no avail, I decided to bite the bullet and get a motel for the evening and set off early for Taos. I had a Jacuzzi and arranged to meet Brie at midday outside the Walmart in Taos.

I woke and set my intention for the day.

I did yoga, meditated and prayed for a smooth hitchhiking trip to Taos. I walked out of the motel, stuck out my thumb and a pickup truck stopped immediately. I jumped in, and the old man asked where I was heading. He said he didn't know why he stopped, he never stops for hitchhikers.

I looked up at the sky and said, 'thank you'.

He dropped me a few miles down the road, and I walked for a few miles with my thumb out. In the distance, a car was beeping so I ran towards it as there was no one else around. A young guy told me to jump in and dropped me off in a place called Espanola, thirty miles closer to Taos.

I walked for a while. It was now almost 11:30am, and there was no chance I was going to make it to Brie on time. Would she be wondering if I was dead, and who she would call if I was?

I heard another beep, and an indigenous-looking bloke told me to jump in the back of his pickup and keep my head down.

I did as I was told, and fifteen minutes later, jumped out in the middle of nowhere. I walked and was picked up and dropped off at a gas station.

I started asking people for a ride towards Taos.

I approached one guy on his way in, and he said he could drop me halfway there.

I jumped in and told him what I would be up to in Taos.

He said, 'My twin brother works for Earthships.'

'Rory,' I said.

'Yes,' he said.

I was getting a lift from the twin brother of the guy I'd worked with, which felt crazy.

He was a cleaner, less rough around the edges version of his identical twin. He kindly dropped me off in the middle of nowhere. I could see for miles and miles around, as far as the eye could see, and all there was was barren desert. I thought I'll be screwed if I get stuck here.

It was getting really hot. I was in the searing midday heat with no shade. It was 1 pm, and I wondered how long Brie would wait at the Walmart for me.

I covered up as best I could and got picked up by this big, expensive-looking car. A guy named Buck, who was travelling a further three hundred miles said he could drop me at the Walmart in Taos. I told him about the Earthship project, and he said, 'Those guys would probably hate me. I work in the nuclear industry not far from Santa Fe.'

I thought, 'Yes they would, but I don't hate you, Buck, because I don't hate anyone.'

Finally, I was in Taos; two days later than originally planned, but I'd made it. I was in the land of Earthships and the concept that had fascinated me for so long and changed my way of thinking on so many levels.

Not really expecting Brie to be waiting for me I headed towards the entrance as huge people with huge trolleys of shopping headed towards me.

Brie was sitting on the floor outside, and I shouted 'Brie!' in a drawn-out Aussie accent. A loud 'Liam!' came flying back at me. She greeted me with the biggest, warmest hug, and said, 'Let's get out of here. I have nearly been sick twice looking at the obese Americans going in and out.'

CHAPTER 16
ROCK BOTTOM 2,
LIFE, 2011

I met Ralph for the first time after a guy who was sponsoring me via the CA (Cocaine Anonymous), and AA (Alcoholics Anonymous) meetings introduced me to him.

Ralph was sponsoring him. His name was Dom.

Dom had steamrollered me into letting him be my sponsor, but I knew he was not for me. The pace everything was happening at was too much, and I needed a breath.

Dom's story was mental. He had been a coke addict, which had destroyed almost everything around him. Somehow he still had a big flat and his own business. He had returned to sobriety after being caught by the police driving his BMW erratically, wearing only a dressing gown, with a boot filled with steroids and ten grand in cash. This had all been brought on by a coke binge, which luckily had peaked with him crying on his toilet whilst flushing the coke that was controlling his life down it. His outing in the BMW had been to replace what was now swimming around the Thames Water Treatment Centre.

Ralph was a short, grey-haired bloke with a proper boozer's nose and face. He took a real hardline, not mincing his words at all. He had the kind of attitude I would have thrived off as a kid, but now I was a bit put off, and for some reason I didn't want my already-miserable life being affected too much.

Ninety meetings in ninety days was being drummed into my head. No way, I thought, how do I see people, how do I have a social life? It was as if the people here had allowed this world to become their world. I definitely didn't want that world, but I didn't want mine either.

I sat in Dom's flat where most of his incredible antics had taken place. I was being bombarded with stream after stream of words and text from the twelve-step book.

Like an over-eager actor craving attention, Dom performed in front of me. I had to say prayers and make statements of commitment and admit some of my faults. I thought it was all bullshit, but I needed help, and I was looking everywhere. I didn't want to go to prison, and I didn't want to feel the way I was feeling anymore. I was doing this primarily to try and avoid prison, but something else was stirring.

Where had all this started, how had I ended up here?

I could say every facet of my life had brought me here, but more specifically, it was my impending court case.

After the success of having my first feature film going to festivals around the world, I thought I could just sit and wait and work would flow to me. I spent most of my time on my allotment, growing an array of fruit and vegetables. I was claiming jobseeker's allowance and housing benefit, a far cry from the glitzy New York parties I'd been attending twelve months earlier.

What led me to these meetings and working through these twelve steps was the arrest. I needed to build up a case to avoid going to prison, and I quote the drug worker when I say, 'for a very long time'. With the initial thought that I was going to be charged with possession with intent to supply a class A drug, it was looking like I would be in prison for a minimum of 3 years, with the maximum sentence for my crime 15 years. That scared the shit out of me.

The drug worker I met could smell alcohol on me from a night out two days earlier. I started to tell her about my history of drinking and drug use. I was honest about how much I used to drink and how often I used to blackout.

Regardless of the reasons behind my actions, I definitely needed help. She told me I'd been an addict for a long time.

'Before it was alcohol and now it's drugs,' she said.

She told me I had to start going to the AA, CA and NA meetings and find someone to sponsor me and take me through the twelve steps of recovery so I could get better and show the court I was a reformed character. I thought this was bollocks, but I had to do it for the court case and to save my arse.

Speaking to this lady for the first time did make me look at the way I used to drink, and I could see there had been many issues with it. She gave me a list of all the meetings in my area and arranged for me to see a counsellor for my depression and addiction once a week.

At this time, I was working mainly as a gardener, wondering if it was something I should commit to long-term. It was definitely something I was good at, and the girl I worked for wanted me to work all the time.

I started attending meetings all over south west London,

mainly in the Kingston and Surbiton areas and soon discovered the world of addicts. Some of them had been clean for twenty years but kept coming back to the meetings. They said if they stopped, they would end up in the same place they had been when they had first started the meetings; fucked, alone, depressed, suicidal and unconsciously trying to destroy everything around them. These meetings were their medicine, and if they didn't take their medicine, they would soon become ill again.

There was every walk of life at these meetings; rich people, poor people, people who looked like addicts, ladies who looked like sweet little old grandmas. There were bankers, gangsters, actors, builders, hookers, transvestites, ex-ravers, any type of person you could imagine. They all had the same illness, an illness that was out of their control and needed a cure. That cure was to admit they were powerless to their addiction and to allow the twelve steps to work as a program to aid recovery. A programme that, if stuck to, guaranteed sobriety from whichever substance they were powerless against. In this world, there was no difference between alcohol and drugs, they were seen as the same thing, something that these people couldn't control their use of.

The main theme of the program was to hand over the power of your life to something greater than yourself, be it God, the Universe, a passed loved one, or something else you believed in that was bigger than you.

I couldn't stand the meetings. I felt like they were getting in the way of my life and seeing my friends. Getting in the way of a life that was currently causing me so much pain. It seemed that it had to become your life. You had to fully commit, that's what the program demanded and what the people at the meetings demanded of each other.

I kept going, not as often as was recommended to me, but I gradually became part of the community and started to make friends. I felt like a real fraud, being there just to get evidence of my determination to reform, to back up my case. If the court believed this, it would mean a lot less severe sentence and a good defence against the 'with intent to supply' part of my charge.

When I listened to people speak during the meetings, things really did start to resonate in terms of how I had been feeling and the deep sadness inside of me, the pain and disillusionment I'd always had. I learnt that when I was drinking, I'd had a problem.

Blacking out all the time was not normal, and not being able to stop drinking until I fell asleep was not normal either.

Everyone who was there had this blackness inside of them that they couldn't handle and drink and drugs were the only thing that made them feel better. Maybe when I lived at home with my mum and step-dad, getting off my face every weekend was the only way to escape from the pain I was truly feeling at being separated from my mother and feeling so uncomfortable in the place I called home.

There seemed to be something deeper that was bringing me to these meetings. Something that, looking back now, I realise was making me take notice subconsciously, something that was pushing me to make changes in my life, something that wanted me to let go of the baggage of my past, something that wanted me to stop being angry and feeling like the world owed me something.

My mother used to say, 'You were an angry little boy, and now you're an angry young man, Liam.'

Something wanted me to be a man free of this anger. Something was trying to make me aware that I could change and become a better person.

For the first time in my life, I was saying the word 'God' and thinking about its meaning. All the people in the meetings were putting their faith in something greater than themselves. Typically, that was God, and that was working for them. I would hear so many stories of how people had turned their lives around with this program by handing over the power of their addiction to God.

As part of the twelve steps, you had to wake up each morning and say the serenity prayer and ask God to guide you and help keep you sober. I was told by my sponsor that I had to do this every morning and then ring him to make sure he knew I was okay.

Every morning I battled with getting down on my knees and talking to God. I was a massive atheist. I thought all religion was bollocks and was the reason the world was such a mess. But I was witnessing the way the program and faith of handing power over to God was working for all these people. I thought maybe, maybe I could just do it. I didn't have to believe in God, I could just try and see if it helped. I felt so stupid getting on my knees in the morning and reciting the prayer, but reluctantly I did. I spoke to God, even though I didn't believe.

I didn't tell any of my friends about this, not even my housemate. I did, however, tell Fhian. She thought it was nuts, and that I was becoming part of some cult. When I stayed at her house, I rarely got down and prayed. She also thought it was nuts that I had to go to all these meetings and ring so many people, have a sponsor and do work and all the steps. She kept reminding me that I was not an addict like these people, and I should just do the bare minimum to back up my case. Part of me knew that, but part of me also saw that I had a massive problem. Parts of this program were helping me, so I kept going back.

For my counsellor and drugs worker, it looked like I was staying clean and getting better. But I wasn't getting any better in myself; in-fact I was deteriorating. I was becoming so anxious because I couldn't get away from the barrage of abuse I was giving myself mentally. I felt like life was ending, I had lost myself, I couldn't find where I'd gone. I wanted myself back, or I wanted to die.

Maybe I wanted a new me? Maybe I was sick of the person I had become, the character I played in society? I wanted change and the only change I felt I could make was to end my life. It seemed the only logical answer. I wouldn't be able to endure much more of this feeling.

I wondered if people felt like this for years, and I wondered how they carried on? Did they not have the bottle to kill themselves? Did they imagine death to be worse than this?

I couldn't imagine anything worse than this. How could there be? I felt there was no chance of escape, and that's when I found myself with the fork pressed against my rib cage.

TAOS,
THE JOURNEY,
MARCH 2013

Brie and I started to hitchhike to Lou's place.

That morning during yoga and meditation, I asked to meet some indigenous Americans whilst in Taos. I stuck out my thumb on the main street, and within five minutes we were in a van with a young indigenous couple from the Red Willow People tribe who lived in the Pueblo Reservation on the side of a sacred mountain. Leatrice and Carlo dropped us off outside the town at a place called the Blinking Light, which had no blinking light. Pretty much everything I tried to manifest that morning in my meditation had happened.

As we walked towards Lou's, a rough-looking hitchhiker was standing where we wanted to stand. I suggested we walk a little further to get a ride as we looked a little more presentable than him. Five minutes later a car stopped, a lovely slight red-headed lady jumped out and put our bags in the boot. As we jumped in, we realised the scruffy hitchhiker was already in the front.

Our driver, Patricia, had an Earth-built home out on the Mesa and invited us to come and see her house whilst we were in town. The Mesa is a vast barren desert littered by two-foot-high sage bushes. Lou had this cute little bungalow at the bottom of this dirt track right in the middle. The walls were made of Adobe bricks, and with a tin roof, blue windows and a pink door, it looked exactly like a house a kid would draw.

Our nearest neighbour's house was a good five hundred meters away. There was a swing outside made of pallets and a drop hole toilet with no door, so when you sat on the throne, you had the most breath-taking view of the snow-capped mountains in the distance. It was definitely the most picturesque number two experience of my life.

Taos is a Spanish, Indian, Anglo valley and like most places in the States, seems massively spread out and impossible to navigate without a vehicle. It's seen as a place for hippies, yuppies, and is famed for the number of artists it has living there.

I had been placing a lot of emphasis on Taos for a long time. I think part of me was hoping this would be the place that felt like home and the place I had been searching for. It was somewhere I understood I was engulfed in alternative thinking, different ways of living sustainably and had an active conscious society which was also steeped in spirituality and love. Lots of people I spoke to told me Taos had been a life-changing place for them, catapulting them in the right direction. I'd heard how it had this magical hold over many people, and once they came, they couldn't leave.

It had been made even more famous since the attention of the movie 'The Garbage Warrior' brought one of its residents, Michael Reynolds, who is the founder of the Earthship Movement. He was the reason for me being in this part of the world, but I did feel other unknown things must also have pulled me here.

It was refreshing to be back in Brie's company. She made some amazing food, and it was lovely to feel like I was being mothered. I had missed that so much. She had been travelling for what seemed her whole life, originating from just outside Melbourne, and had a laugh to rival my own. One thing we seemed to do very well together was making each other laugh constantly.

The next day was the start of the Earthship Academy, and we were both deep in anticipation, looking forward to the life-changing six weeks ahead of us. We would be meeting the rest of the thirty-four students, who would include a few from the build in Guatemala. It was also exciting to see where some of the Earthship crew we had met lived and the buildings they had constructed in Taos.

There was an introduction, and then we were off to settle into our homes for the next six weeks. There were three locations: 'Reach', which was forty minutes out of town and on the side of a mountain with spectacular views over the whole of Taos. 'The Castle' which was in the middle of the Mesa and was the party house and the place I wanted to avoid. The people who had been on the Guatemala build were all located in 'Canyon', an area of land on which Michael Reynolds lived in the first-ever Earthship.

Brie and I managed to get our own place called 'The Hobbit House'. It looked exactly like that from outside, with a nice wooden door which seemed underground as the back of the building was buried. It was built in the late 70s, still using cans and tyres, but unlike the evolved Earthship, the tyres were just filled with earth and not rammed. As you stepped inside, you stepped down to one large room that included the kitchen, a dining table, a loft bed and a mattress as a sofa. It was strange as there was no sink in the kitchen, but another door led to a corridor room, and the sink was in there, doubling as a washbasin. There was a shower curtain hanging down, and I soon discovered that the shower was in the standing position above the sink; therefore if necessary I could shower and do the washing up at the same time; important in the modern world for saving precious seconds. Daniel, 'The German' was to be our constant guest.

Our weeks in Taos consisted of classroom days and onsite days. I was looking forward to the onsite days the most as I learn by doing. I wanted to impress Phil and the Earthship Crew with my work ethic. So did Daniel and we kind of teamed up on the first day with our experience and connection from the Guatemala build and got stuck into pounding tyres together.

It was so impressive to see the momentum the Earthship movement had taken. We were the fifth academy, and they were booked up for the next two years. People from all over the world were again coming together to learn a better way to build houses; one that gave the occupant more freedom and more control over their own life, away from greedy monopolies. We were starting the process of making that a reality for whoever would move into this one-bedroom Global model Earthship.

On day two of intensely pounding tyres with Daniel and an Aussie fireman called Ryan, disaster struck. My right wrist had started to gradually get weaker and weaker, and by the end of the day it became almost unusable. I had pounded tyres for days in Guatemala, so it was a shock to be out of action. Frustratingly, the next day, I was on lighter duties, and this really affected me psychologically, sending me into this spiral of depression and self-doubt again.

My heart was broken, broken by myself, feeling there was no one I wanted but Fhian, but not seeing how it was going to work. I wasn't enjoying things the way I wanted to in Taos. My wrist was bust, and I was questioning how I would incorporate these teachings into my life. I was feeling drained and had a couple of episodes of complete meltdown where I had to go back to The Hobbit House and miss out on parties, to sleep and rest and be by myself. It was a weird state and one I didn't really understand as I'd been the life and soul of parties and social events for so long.

What was it in me that couldn't relax? I knew it was a feeling of failure for not having a specific thing that I did, knowing I couldn't just go home and walk into a high paying job, feeling I'd wasted so much time. What was I striving for? I wasn't sure. I always had the acting thing at the back of my mind, feeling I couldn't commit to anything as it would ruin my chances of success. In a way, it felt like it had stopped me doing so much; stopped me having a career, but I was learning that it must have been my path. Having a career would have probably stopped me from doing the amazing things I had done.

I felt like I had the world on my shoulders, and I wanted to feel light and agile.

One thing I was doing lots of was laughing. Myself, Brie and Daniel were in constant tears, especially when it was my small pants day, which happened every fourth day. On that day I would wear small Y-fronts as I'd run out of boxer shorts. I would lunge in them, a big long lunge to the right, then to the left, with a little bounce to stretch the groin area fully in each extension. Brie would break down in hysterics and Daniel would shout, 'oh my God' in his deep thick German accent, whilst almost crying. It never got old, even after six weeks and I pledged to make it common practice and a global law that every man wearing Y-fronts must lunge for a minimum of thirty seconds on each side once they are securely on.

I wanted to experience the spiritual side of Taos, feel its magic qualities and start to discover what was so special about this place. Was I trying to force too much into my stay here? Or was I still striving, searching for my peace, my happiness and my sanity?

After a few days of whizzing about in Lou's car picking up hitchhikers, we realised just how spread out Taos was. It covered an area about the size of London with about 0.001% of its population. It seemed that people liked their space away from each other. I had been expecting to be able to walk or cycle everywhere, fulfilling my sustainable ideal.

On the second weekend, we went to see a band called Balkan Beat Box in Denver. It was a six-hour drive but in American terms that was just down the road. Rob was to be our driver and myself, Lou, Brie and Daniel were road trippers. A storm had hit the mountains that divided New Mexico and Colorado and the further into the mountains we got, the more and more the roads resembled an apocalyptic scene. Cars were turned over all over the place, people stood outside their cars calling for assistance, huge trucks were flipped on their side, and at times we couldn't see a metre in front of us as sheets of snow fell. Rob somehow managed the terrain with the acumen of a professional driver.

We arrived in Denver, sat down for our first drink after what had become an eight-hour drive as Lou delivered the news via his email that the concert had been cancelled. We were gutted; all that driving and danger for nothing. Part of me was saying I should have stayed in Taos and gone to the Reiki share and drumming evening.

Almost every Sunday whilst in Taos, me and Brie would head for the Hanuman Temple for chanting and free food. The atmosphere in the place was amazing. Everyone was so friendly, polite, helpful and kind. One Sunday as Brie and I were exploring on our way back to The Hobbit House, I sang a full rendition of Brian Adams's 'Everything I Do, I Do it for You' and Wet Wet Wet's, 'Love is All Around' at full blast. Passers-by thought she was my carer. We hit the chocolate shop where amazing treats were on display in huge glass cabinets. Everything was made in the shop, and you could watch the chocolatiers at work if you timed it right.

I told Brie I loved her in eight languages which put her into hysterics, I then leaned in to look closer at some treats and misjudged the distance of glass and face-planted straight into it. This sent us both over the edge. We were now crying with laughter in the chocolate shop. I was keeled over hands on knees trying to stay upright, whilst Brie was trying to keep her tonsils from falling out of her mouth.

As we got close to home, we went past some shops that were shut. One was a psychic's, which I now call all 'physic's.' When I wrote my intro to this whole adventure, my friend Mr Wiggins proofread it and said, 'So it was a mathematician who set the ball rolling for this trip?'

I said, 'What?'

He said, 'You went to see a physic.'

'No, a psychic.'

He said, 'Oh, well, you spelt it "physic." I wondered why you would be going to see a physic for answers.'

We pissed ourselves laughing, and I blamed my dyslexia.

We passed the closed physic's and came across a few more galleries. We were hanging about one looking at a cool truck and jumping off walls. Then another truck pulled up, and a guy got out who looked like some sophisticated art dealer. He asked us if Claude was about.

We said, 'Who's Claude?'

He said, 'This is Claude's place.'

'Sorry, we don't know Claude but tell him thanks for letting us jump off his wall.'

We headed for the main road and the final leg of our journey home. Our thumbs were out, and the next thing we know, the art dealer picked us up. Originally from Slovenia, he was called Tomal. He asked where we were going, and we said home next to Mike's and Brie added, 'but we are always up for an adventure.'

He pulled up outside The Hobbit House, tore a strip out of how ugly he thought Earthships were and we pondered life, love and Taos. He then decided he wanted to show us his house, which was just up the road. It was a typical New Mexican terracotta adobe walled house with large wooden vigas protruding from the front of the roof. A beautiful Mediterranean courtyard led us to his front door where we were greeted by his beautiful wife, daughter and granddaughter. Tomal introduced us, and holding the baby, gave us a tour of his spectacular home. It had a very Indian feel about it, infused with traditional New Mexican colours and Native American craft. A huge kitchen led to a huge lounge which looked out to the towering snowcapped mountains. Up a spiral staircase were two huge bedrooms, one with this massive bed almost twice the size of a normal double. It had been imported from India where it had originally been used in a colonial palace in Dharamshala.

Tomal's house felt like a palace. All the decorations were so beautiful, everything had a spiritual subtlety, and you seemed to flow and float as you walked around.

While I was upstairs, Tomal asked if I smoked. I said no.

'Not even weed?'

I said, 'Well yes I—', and before I could get the, 'used to' out, he had filled up an envelope with the finest smelling weed and stuffed it in my pocket.

Three hours later, we were finally home. I thought about the beautiful things that happen when you just let the world flow.

Mike Reynolds's lessons always kept my attention. The way he kept track of time was by which wife he was married to in that period. He would remember it as if his brain was remembering every facet of that relationship. The way Earthship had evolved was fascinating, from building houses for homeless people without permits to using the system to build subsidised government housing for his workers called Volks homes.

Mike wanted to own his own life when he started out and to bring that philosophy to the world, allowing more people becoming self-sufficient, away from the system. The early books he produced were about giving people all over the world, with little skills, the knowledge to build their own home. A lot of Mike's designs incorporate sacred geometry, and as I listened to him speak, his spiritual beliefs and mystical knowledge poured out. It was like listening to a wise old wizard. I could tell some of the class felt a tad uncomfortable with him talking about Atlantis and Lamoria during his lectures. When he got onto Fibonacci's sequence, and the role it had played in his early work, people seemed less weirded out because it was proven science.

His ambition was to create homes that provided Sustainable Autonomy for Everyone (S.A.F.E). His inspiration for his houses are trees and the way they live and survive by adapting to the climate they are in, using solar thermal heating and cooling to regulate the temperature inside. He thinks Atlantian people became trees as they had evolved to harmony. That isn't such an outlandish statement as recently I discovered it is agreed by scientists that the most evolved species have the most chromosomes and trees have thousands more than us. Trees just chill, something we all aspire to!

My next spiritual adventure in Taos was '5 Rhythms' where you danced around un-inebriated to music. It was 11am, and no, these people were not still up from raving. Maybe they were daytime ravers dropping amphetamines just after breakfast.

As we entered, it was like going into that crazy Fat Boy Slim video. Limbs and heads were shaken and jerked in every direction.

I decided to let myself go and allowed my body to do whatever the music told it to do. After some initial embarrassment and nerves. I went crazy. Sweat was dripping from me, and I was in this dreamy, beautifully happy world. Everyone looked so content, as we danced and glided past one another. At the end everyone sat in a circle, and a small meditation took place. People talked about where the moon and stars were situated at the moment as I 'smile and nod'.

I felt like I had gotten rid of all the week's built-up tension without destroying my body with drugs and alcohol. I'd let my hair down just by changing my mind-set, something me mum had done so well. I reminisced about when I was at parties and events, and me mum was there. Friends and would say to me, 'your mum is well pissed' or 'your mum's smashed, mate.' I would say, 'She doesn't drink, she's just nuts.' They would be convinced I was lying so I would march them over and show them her Britvic 55 orange juice and watch their jaws drop, unable to fathom how someone could naturally have so much fun. Me mum was always tripping balls at parties, smashing back the Britvic 55's. She could find that place and confidence most of us can only find through mind-altering substances.

We would finish work at 4:30, be home around five, and have the whole evening to do stuff. Sometimes we would chill, sometimes go to yoga, sometimes hang out at other people's places, but the most magical part of working there was the numerous hot springs dotted about the Rio Grande River. We would go there tired and dirty from a hard day's work in freezing conditions, wearing layer upon layer of clothing, strip off in the snow and dive into the natural hot water. After an hour or so the sky would darken and the stars would start to appear, and under the black, sparkly blanket, we would laugh and frolic in the water. I thought about how polluted London was and how on a very clear night it was still almost impossible to see any stars.

It was naturally spectacular. The river and springs were at the bottom of a huge canyon, like a smaller version of the Grand Canyon, similar to the Dermitor River Valley in Montenegro. The river meandered through the drastically rugged, terracotta terrain, and the hot springs randomly appeared as nature's treat for us.

For some reason, I was irritable and anxious the whole time I was in Taos. I always felt like I had this heavy energy surrounding me, I couldn't relax, I never felt comfortable and my head would never rest. Funnily enough in Mike Reynolds's book 'The Coming of Wizards' he talks about how all humans should find the energy band their energy is compatible with. He discusses how finding this allows us to reach our full potential. If we let this energy into our energy band it sparks greater consciousness. He talks about how stepping into our energy band allows us to transform rather than develop, and not doing that would be like a caterpillar developing into a greater caterpillar instead of transforming into a beautiful butterfly.

It got me thinking that maybe Taos was the wrong energy band for me. Maybe my future wasn't building Earthships and showing the world this amazing building practice. I needed to find the energy that made me feel light and uplifted so I could surrender to my natural energy band. Like Mike says we have to surrender to higher levels of consciousness. Like the caterpillar and the butterfly, leaving everything we were behind to become who we were always supposed to become. We do this by stepping into our energy band and finding the place and the people we should be around. We have to surrender and remember who we truly are. When we find the people and place that resonates with the energy of who we are, we become limitless.

This was exactly what I was on this adventure for, to look inside and to see who I truly was and what I was truly supposed to be doing. Allowing myself to forget all the barriers, fears and expectations I'd picked up in life and become the butterfly I was always supposed to transform into. I didn't want to be a result of my reality, I wanted my reality to be a result of me.

One night, Brie and I were invited to Brian and Swift's place. Brian was Earthship's Carpenter and Swift was his dancer girlfriend. They live out on the Mesa where laws don't really exist. People can build whatever they like, do whatever they like, and within the Mesa lies the erratic, sometimes beautiful and sometimes miserable nature of the human. There is a runaway gang aptly called 'The Runaways', who lawlessly terrorise parts of the area. Guns and far-right ideals meet the conscious inclusiveness of the far left, and somehow they all seem to live in this pocket of freedom together.

Lots of the Earthship crew lived out here and had built their own houses which ranged from the sublime to the ridiculous. Brian and Swift lived in this 3.5 metre by 3.5 metre square straw bale, south-facing glazed house. It was a tiny little space with just one room. There was a raised bed with storage underneath, and this took up most of the room. Across the opposite wall was row of cupboards, a sink and a stove which added up to a kitchen. There was a log burner in the corner, next to which was the dog's bed. There were some small planters to grow veg next to the south-facing glazing. It was the most compact and best use of a small space I'd ever seen. I thought to myself, what a beautiful space for a young couple in love. I was envious of how they lived; I wanted to be a hippy in love with a hippy.

I'd heard that sweat lodge ceremonies could awaken you to

more spiritual knowledge, more creative juice and greater consciousness. So when I heard there was one happening, I really wanted to go. When we arrived, we discovered that it was a Lakota Indian ceremony. Indigenous tribespeople had travelled from North Dakota to lead the ceremony. We brought offerings of tobacco for the elders and then stripped off.

A low bell tent had been erected, and around thirty people stood waiting for the ceremony to commence. Ladies made their way in first, followed by the blokes.

We had to crawl in as the tent only stood a few feet tall at its lowest point. It was a tight squeeze, and half-naked bodies were everywhere. As I sat down, a long-haired bloke in front of me turned around and aggressively said, 'Did you just touch my back? Keep your hands off me.'

I said, 'No, I don't think so', but I had no idea as there were bodies everywhere and very little space.

He said, 'You shouldn't be touching people's backs, it's not proper.'

I said, 'I don't think I did.'

Fury filled my body, and I started to curse this guy, calling him all the names under the sun in my head, thinking, how the fuck can you expect not to be touched in this place, and also I was pretty sure I didn't touch the prick. I was thinking, are we not partaking in spiritual practice? A place where we are accommodating? Number one, how could this guy expect not to be touched, and number two, even if you had been, why would you make a scene? And how could you pinpoint one person in a sea of unbalanced fumbling bodies?

My mind exploded. I wanted to punch the bloke in the kidneys as hard as I could. I wanted to smash his face in, I hadn't felt rage like this for years. What was I angry about? Him or the fact I was embarrassed that he had brought attention to me and maybe people would think I'd touched a man's back in some perverted way?

As my mind raced with vulgarity and violence, the ceremony began, and hot rocks that had been on a fire outside were being brought in on a spade and placed in a pit in the middle of the tent. More and more hot rocks were brought in as the temperature rose. My blood was boiling, and I couldn't get the irritation caused by this man in front of me out of my head. I was imagining kicking him in the back and into the pit of the hot rocks, melting his head and face, so he understood the use of the term, 'not proper'. I thankfully decided against it.

The ceremony began, and prayers were said, blessings made and gratitude given. I was taking very little in, my fury still bubbling away. I tried to centre myself, but little was working. I thought maybe this was my test, to be able to let it go and move on. I seemed to be becoming very good at this in life, with the Buddhist-induced realisation that I always had a choice. I'd always chose a reaction, and often that was anger. Halfway through the ceremony I let it go. In my head I forgave the guy in front of me and assumed he must have some real problems to be behaving that way.

Finally, I was present, and I realised it was unbearably hot. There were numerous rounds of prayers and intentions set, each time focusing on people in your life who needed help. I asked for beautiful souls to be given to friends of mine trying for babies, and for all those I touched to be healed and awakened.

The Lakota leader sang songs and recited poems. There were a number of rounds where each person in the tent would show gratitude to the spirits. On one of the rounds, sacred tobacco was passed. The pipe you smoked it from was about a foot long, with a bowl at the bottom that you lit and puffed away. I tried my hardest not to cough.

After this part of the ceremony, everyone stood outside in the freezing cold, unaffected due to the temperature of our bodies.

The next part of the ceremony took place at another house. All the windows of the room were blacked out. In the centre of the room stood a man and the ritual was part of him gaining 'spiritual credits' I had no idea what this meant. He set out his altar and space where the ceremony would take place. All the other people from the sweat lodge sat against the walls of the room in a large circle. There was a big mat laid out, and his sacred space was meticulously created using candles, rope and ribbons.

Things started to get weird. I hadn't really been feeling the whole thing so far. It didn't seem the warmest, most welcoming of spiritual gatherings I'd been involved in, and then the 'not proper' man, and now this man was being tied up in a sort of ceremonial straitjacket that covered his whole body, including his head. He looked like a cross between a mental patient, David Copperfield and a member of the Ku Klux Klan, albeit wearing black. Prayers and blessings were said, and a rope was tied around his body, binding and locking him in. The lights were turned off, and instruments and singing began.

We were in total darkness. I could feel things moving around the room, but I couldn't see anything. The ceremony ended, the lights went on, and the man stood there unbound, surprise, surprise. We were supposed to believe that spirit did it, but in my typical sceptical fashion I saw the whole thing as a hoax; he either managed to untie himself or one of the elders freed him. I wondered how many people here genuinely believed spirits freed him? I believe in spirits, but I didn't believe they freed him. I wasn't feeling the whole day's events, and my first Indigenous American experience was a bit of a let-down.

I hitchhiked everywhere in Taos and met a lot of colourful characters. One indigenous guy picked me up and was heading for a pool tournament on the other side of town, but decided to go three miles out of his way to drop me off at my door. However, the craziest was one day when I was heading to Lou's place, and a guy picked me up. As I stepped into the car he was pulling piles of paper and pens off the passenger seat, so I could sit down. As I took him in, I noticed this very Jewish-looking face; he was scruffy and erratic, unshaven with a bald head and little wisps of hair flapping about. His glasses sat on the end of his nose, and he lifted his head so he could take me in. He set off and spoke in the thick Jewish New York accent at a hundred miles an hour, like Woody Allen on speed. He was a writer and was currently trying to get a musical produced and make the big time. He was also looking for a barber's shop to clean himself up. We tried a place he had used three years ago, but it wasn't there any longer, and I wondered if this was actually the last time he'd been groomed. He then told me the plot of his musical and started singing an ensemble song from it.

As he sang he would stop to explain the plot and the subtext behind the song like a director's cut. The song was sung in this heavily theatrical musical way. I was blown away by the performance I was getting from this almost sectionable man I had, as of yet, only said a few words to. He finished an eight-minute song and then told me about his six-foot junkie girlfriend who was a musical genius. She had written the score for the production, but would only work if he brought round hard liquor.

We were close to Lou's place, and I got him to drop me at the giant guitar statue so I could walk the last bit and I didn't feel obliged to ask him in for tea which, as an Englishman, is almost a gag reflex.

As a parting shot, he gave me two kids' books he had published. I said goodbye and thanked him for the ride and the books. I started reading them as I walked the mile to Lou's, becoming aware of how crass and innuendo-stricken these almost-pornographic books were. I laughed at the explosion of personality I had just witnessed.

My time in Taos was coming to an end, just as the team ethos was at its peak. We had almost finished a Global Model Earthship. On the build site, we'd had every extremity of weather; lots of hot days when we were bare-chested, we had wind, we had rain, we had extreme cold, and one day we ended up working in a blizzard. The temperature could go from twenty to minus twenty in the space of an hour.

'The Castle' hosted our leaving party. I wasn't drinking, but I danced all night in this little bunker we had set a sound system up in. I was sweating so much and loving being around all these amazing, free-spirited people. Most of my goodbyes were said. It felt like we were all part of a movement and something special for the future of humanity.

The next morning Brie left in a rush, and we had a quick hug. She jumped in a taxi to take her to the airport, and as the taxi pulled away, emotion swept over me. I realised there, and then this was someone with whom I had a deep connection. I cried my eyes out thinking of how amazing our time together had been.

I decided to spend another week in Taos at Lou's
place. I wanted to chill out before I headed to Arizona to catch my flight from Phoenix to Peru for my long-awaited meeting with Lady Ayahuasca. I spent the week writing, surrounded by the mountains.

Daniel was staying with us, and we decided to climb Wheeler Peak, the highest mountain in New Mexico. We set out on a windy day in our waterproofs, warm clothes and hiking boots and hitchhiked to the base of the mountain. We began our ascent, which should take three hours on a good day. Everywhere was still covered in snow and spectacular landscape after spectacular landscape was brought into view. The wind was blowing hard, but fortunately Daniel had climbed it on his first week, so he knew the way. We were completely alone, and the higher we got, the fiercer the wind became. Large open spaces were covered in snow, and we marched across like hobo explorers. We had been walking for a few hours when the summit came into view. The last section of the hike was extremely steep, and the wind was intense. I could lean forward into it, and it would keep me upright.

I became exhausted. I could only take two steps, and then I would have to rest. The altitude, sheer fatigue and the wind were destroying me. I sat halfway up the latest ravine, stuck in this mental battle with my body not wanting to continue, wondering if I could actually make it. How would a rescue helicopter manage in this wind? And how long would it take me to die here? Would Daniel go and get help or could I just close my eyes, evaporate and open them and be back in Lou's front room in front of the open fire?

From somewhere, the energy I wanted came as Daniel energetically pulled me towards him. When I caught up, he told me last time he did it was so much easier as there had been no wind. I wished I'd come last time. The terrain became even more treacherous on the last section, and it felt like I was walking on a tightrope with a thousand-foot drop on both sides. Hundred miles an hour winds were trying to send us both to our death.

We managed to get to the peak, and the view was breath-taking. Three hundred and sixty degrees of divine beauty. I felt like I was on top of the world. I thanked God and my angels for getting me there safely, and we both jumped about, buzzing our tits off. It was like we were in a wind tunnel; you couldn't hear anything because the wind was so noisy.

We headed back along the tightrope, and the wind picked up further. We had to lie flat down on the ground as it would have swept us off our feet to our death. We lay there grasping onto rocks, trying not to be taken away on a suicide skydive. As I lay there, I wondered how long we could hold on for.

It felt like we were there for an eternity. We would occasionally feel a calm break in the wind, begin to stand and then be almost swept away again and have to flatten our bodies to the rocks grasping on for dear life.

We were stuck there for fifteen minutes until finally, there was a drop in the wind. We meandered down in another direction, and when we got to some open space we just lay on our chests and fired ourselves down the slopes at this crazy pace like two skeleton bobsledders' in the winter Olympics. I felt at one with the mountain, and completely vulnerable to its power and majesty as the landscape around me flashed past.

We managed to reduce our speed and stop just in front of a wooded area. We were joined by a Bluejay who decided to follow us through the woodland like a guide or protector. I meditated under a tree with him above me and thanked the Universe and God for this amazing experience. We arrived back at the road, and as I looked to the right I realised the road ended so there would be no chance of us getting a ride. As I thought this, a car came out of an obscured driveway and turned. I turned to Daniel and said, 'There's our ride man!!'.'

We jumped in, he dropped us off in town, and we saw no other cars during the ten-minute drive.

We started to tell people where we had been, they thought we were crazy and making it up. They said people were having to batten down the hatches in town because of the wind and they had no idea how we were still alive if we had been up there. Someone said, 'Crazy fucking Europeans.'

CHAPTER 17
ROCK BOTTOM 3,
LIFE, 2011

I listen and listen, and it beats and beats. Finally, Ralph answers.

'I need you man; I need you, I have reached rock bottom,' just about manages to emit from my trembling lips and anxiety-stricken voice.

"I knew you would call when you had," he softly whispers.

Within two minutes of me getting off the phone to Ralph and arranging to meet him, he assured me I would get better if I committed to the twelve-step program. People I had never spoken to before started to ring me telling me they had been there and that this program would save me as it had saved then. They said that hitting rock bottom was the first step and then making the cry for help the next. They said it was an important moment and one I should rejoice in because the only way was up.

So many selfless people were helping me when none of my friends could give me an answer or a solution. These people had all been where I found myself. Phone call after phone call of support started to flood in, all with encouragement and kind words and so many positive things to say about how transformative the twelve steps were.

I started to feel a little bit better. 380

They told me it was hard work, but it would get easier. I didn't want hard work, I just wanted to be better. How could I be ready to commit to this program? I wasn't even an addict. Why was everything they were saying resonating with me so much? Why had I got to the stage where I felt powerless over my own life? Why had Ralph saved me and picked up his phone? Why had he been waiting like a facet of the Matrix, as if they already had a plan in place and when I had reached rock bottom, the plan had been set in motion? It was like I had been resuscitated by Ralph and his team. They had given me hope.

I was still teetering on the edge of insanity and suicide, but I had put the fork down, finished off my work and gone home to get ready to meet Ralph before I went to my first meeting.

For the next few months, the depression continued, but I felt like I was in my body a bit more, and I started to gain some strength. My friends that knew about the court case assured me that when it was over, I would start to feel better. I knew it was something more than that.

I was working for my step-dad's company, labouring on a site in Teddington. After not being capable of speaking to people when I first started, I got to the stage where I could chat without wanting to crawl into a hole. I was in and out of court, and I would tell the boss I had an acting audition. It was like I was living two different lives. The only person who really knew the truth was Fhian.

I was working most days and then heading to as many meetings in the evening as I could. Before the first meeting after almost killing myself, I met Ralph outside a church in Richmond, and he talked me through what I needed to do to get better and 'stay clean'. It didn't appeal to me at all. It seemed like so much work. Again I was made to admit I had a problem and was powerless against alcohol and drugs, and that my life had become unmanageable. I had to believe that a power greater than myself could restore me to sanity. Even though I didn't believe in God, I was hoping someone or something would save me. I then had to turn over my will and my life to the care of God, as I understood him. Again, I didn't believe but thought, 'fuck it, I'm not doing a very good job at life myself, so let's see what you can do, God.'

I then had to make this moral inventory of myself, which was one of the hardest things I have ever done. I had to sit down and analyse my character defects.

Pride and fear were so present. I'd always felt that everything was someone else's fault, and it was so difficult to see fault in myself. But once I started to write down the things wrong with me and some of the bad things I had done, I started to feel lighter. It was as if I was facing myself and seeing parts of myself that I had been showing other people and the world but hadn't seen myself.

I realised I was the main cause of all my problems, that it had been me all along. I had been the cause of my failure in life so far, and unless I was willing to work hard on the things wrong with me, happiness would always be out of reach. I realised I had to tear up my old life and the person I had created over the years to protect myself; that person I had projected onto other people, so they thought I was strong and didn't give a fuck about anything.

The questions I had to ask myself were deep, and one of the first was about sex:

'When and how, and in just what instances did my selfish pursuit of sexual relations damage other people and me? Who was hurt, and how badly?'

It opened a can of worms, and I wrote page after page of how sex and sexual thoughts had controlled my life since its explosion in my mind and genital region at the age of 13.

I then had to look at my finances and their instability. Where was I at financially? Why was I never secure? Why was I leaning on the state to pay my rent and give me money each week to eat? And why was I not paying any tax on the money I was earning?

Then I had to look at symptoms of emotional insecurity such as worry, anger, self-pity and depression and consider all my personal relationships. I had to look at all the problems I had with people and organisations and see where I was at fault and why I lacked the ability to accept conditions I could not change.

It was like my brain was exploding. I saw everything through fresh eyes. I started appraising every situation fairly as if I was an unbiased observer, seeing both sides of the story and taking it all into account.

Did I have unreasonable demands of people?

It was all stuff I'd never considered before, and I was going crazy inside my head.

The Big Book said: *'These are the sort of fundamental enquires that can disclose the source of my discomfort and indicate whether I may be able to alter my own conduct and so adjust myself serenely to self-discipline.'*

That got me thinking about Gandhi and the impact learning about him had had on me. He had shown great self-discipline to set an example to other people and show that we can change any part of ourself for the greater good.

The Big Book says:

'It is from our twisted relations with family, friends and society at large that many of us have suffered the most.'

As I flashed through my life, I could see so much discontent and angst. My problems with sex, my problems with my dad, my problems with me step-dad, my problems with those around me, my problems with people damaging the planet, with the government, with America, with war, with capitalism, inequality, materialism –

everything started to come up and be jotted down. There was so much anger and so much hate in me, so much pain inside me, so much frustration at how the world was. I wished I could just turn my back on things, and I wondered how people could get on with their lives when there was so much suffering and injustice in the world. I was angry with everyone, frustrated by everyone and felt like I could explode at any point.

The Book said that some people would object to the questions posed in this step and think their own character defects have not been so glaring. It suggested that conscientious examination of one's self was likely to reveal the very defects that one first objects to. People bury their own defects deep down and cover them with layer after layer of self-justification. By burying these defects and not confronting them, dealing with them and ridding one's self of them, we ultimately are led to some sort of addiction and misery.

Ralph told me to be as thorough as possible with this step to get it all out.

After I got past the pride and the fear elements, I started to tear into myself and finally see the error of my ways. These ways had led me to exactly where I was, depressed, angry, bitter, frustrated, disillusioned and suicidal. It was only me who could help 'me', and this was becoming more and more evident. I wrote page after page of cutting self-evaluation and handed it over to Ralph.

The next step was to admit to God, myself and another human being (Ralph) the exact nature of my wrongs. Then I had to be ready to have God remove these defects of character.

Again I had to get down on one knee in front of Ralph and asked God to remove all my short-comings. I then had to make a list of all the people I had harmed or had a problem with. I had to write down all the problems, why I didn't like them and list the wrongs I felt they had done to me. I then had to look at it from their side and write how I felt they would perceive me and my actions and how what I had done made them feel.

As I wrote, I started to see the difficulties I had caused, started to see how my actions had played a massive part in all the problems I'd had with people and with all the people I felt had done me wrong. It started to become clear that it was me who was causing the issues, me who was always surrounded with drama. It was me who had always been in trouble and left others to pick up the pieces. It was me who always strayed from loving partners and brought misery to people's lives so I could satisfy my desires. It was me, it was me, it was me. It. Was. Me.

This realisation made me feel awful. I felt worse than when I had the fork stuck in my chest, but at last, I was starting to see the truth and remove the veil that had hidden me from any fault for all these years.

The next step was the most difficult of them all. I had to make direct amends, wherever possible, to the people that I had wronged. Primarily these people were my dad, step-dad and some ex-partners. Ralph said it was best to make the amends face-to-face, to confront the matter, take full responsibility and apologise for the misery you brought and let them know you are truly sorry. Ralph said it was best to talk to ex-lovers over the phone, just in case seeing them stirred up old emotions that needed to be let go of.

I rang up some of my ex-partners and said how sorry I was for the way I had been in the relationship. The main person I apologised to was Renie, The Greek. After looking at all the problems we'd had, I saw they had all came from me, every one of them. She had given me everything and had been the angel I needed, and I'd thrown it back in her face by being dishonest and unfaithful from the moment we met. I was truly sorry to her and to her family for all the pain I had caused them. She was very understanding, and she knew I was going through a lot. She said she didn't hold anything against me.

The next person was me dad. This was tricky because he doesn't listen very well and is pretty terrible dealing with emotion. I remember once I went to his flat and told him I wanted to kill myself. He turned and went in the kitchen and asked if I wanted a cup of tea, brushing it under the carpet and singing 'Love on the Rocks' in his Irish accent. I apologised to my dad for holding the fact he used to beat my mother as my trump card in any argument. I also forgave him for being a terrible dad and told him he had done his best in the situation. I forgave him for everything and told him I would try and respect him more in the future.

The hardest of all these was making amends with my step-dad. Whilst I was writing everything down and trying to look at it from his side, I started to see some sort of truth and remorse for how difficult the relationship had always been. I still blamed him for it all, saying to Ralph that he was the adult in the relationship when we had first met and how could I be to blame for the way he had treated me?

Ralph would have none of it and started to pick holes in my defence.

Soon his rhetoric hit home. I saw it from my step-dad's perspective; suddenly having this very naughty, overactive, cheeky ten-year-old in his life which, up until that point had been the life of a bachelor with freedom and no responsibilities. I feel guilty about how difficult it must have been for him to have my mum and I move in and the extra pressure of having two more people to feed, keep warm and house. I was seeing it from his side, and I was seeing it from a third side that was independent of us both, and it was giving me this kind of overview of the situation, allowing me to become aware that the years of difficulty weren't just my step-dad's fault.

I started to see that years of him and my mother being called into school about my behaviour must have been grating, as I wasn't even his child. Then there was the fighting between me and my mum about him and him getting ear ache from her. There was the aggression and anger I had towards my sister, there was my general anger and hate towards most things and there were the tears I would bring to my mum's eyes so often with my behaviour and temper. There were the many times the police came knocking for one thing or another, and there was the girl I had gotten pregnant when I was 14. For the first time, I started to see how disrupting this must have been to his once quiet, easy and stress-free life.

I made my way to Manchester, sat down in the living room of my mum's house and said, 'can we talk? I have been having Cognitive Behavioural Therapy, and I have some exercise I have to do to help me get better and stop being depressed. I want to apologise for the way I was growing up.'

He said, 'You don't have to apologise. You were just a kid, and you were growing up.'

I said, 'Yes I do, because I hated you so much my whole life and I want to apologise and let you know that I hope we can have a better relationship in the future.'

He said, 'Okay, but there is no need.'

I felt like he was trying to sweep it under the carpet, so I pursued. I started to talk about how I felt as a kid and how I can now see all the difficulties I brought to him and his home, and for that, I was sorry. We then started to talk about me mum and how we both felt about her death. It was the first time either of us had approached the subject of feelings the whole time we'd known each other. I asked him if she was happy with me at the end and he said yes. I asked him if she was upset that I had gone to the music festival when she was ill and he said, 'No, not at all. She wanted you to keep doing your thing.'

This was a massive relief because it had always been playing on my mind and I'd been unsure if I would ever be able to ask my step-dad about it. Finally, I had this huge weight released, knowing that my mother hadn't felt abandoned by me.

We both ended up in tears. It was the first time I had ever seen my step-dad cry. A lot of things that had been unsaid for so many years came out, and I had the 'Steps' to thank.

We had an emotional hug and went for a pint in the pub (well I had a lime soda). After this, it was like a huge boulder I had been carrying around on my shoulders had been dropped into the ocean. I felt lighter and happy, I felt like years of anger and baggage, and hatred towards him had been let go of. Regardless of how scary it had been to actually sit down and bring it up, I felt so much better for doing so.

From that point, I started to see so many things in my life change. I felt like I was on this mission to become a better person. I wanted to be good, and I wanted to create someone I liked to live inside, considering death was my only escape. It was like my soul was carving me into who I truly was and who I had the capability of becoming, after ridding myself of all the garbage I had collected over the years. It was becoming evident that I didn't have to be this loud-mouthed, arrogant, cocky, aggressive, sexually possessed young man anymore. I could actually move into something new; like Madonna, I could recreate myself. I wanted to recreate myself into someone and something my kids would be proud of.

The next step was to continue to make a 'Personal Inventory' so that when I was wrong, I had to admit it promptly. This really was a game-changer.

I had to start being a good person.
I had to change my ways.
I couldn't lie anymore.
I had to start being honest.

I started to see the changes in every facet of my life. I couldn't steal anymore; I had always stolen stuff. Always from large corporations that didn't need my money and were doing awful things around the world (this had always been my justification) but I realised by doing what I was doing I was being just as bad. I was starting to believe in karma, so I stopped. Just like that.

It was hard because I was so used to not paying for stuff. I would get to the self-service checkout and have to fight this instinct to pay for only a few items. I'd stolen from the supermarkets for so long. It was what I had always done since I left home and had started paying for my own stuff.

I remember when I got a phone call from my friend once, and he said, 'Marks and Spencer's have got the self-service checkouts.'

I said, 'I'm on my way,' and I started to eat better quality food. These new tills that were replacing people and reducing jobs were my meal ticket and stealing from these corporate companies was my personal revenge.

I began paying my way for the first time. I wasn't sneaking through ticket barriers or getting a child's ticket on the train. I was bringing gifts when I went round to friends' houses for food, and I was getting their girlfriends flowers. I was spoiling Fhian more, taking her out for meals, not being as tight with my money, I was pampering her. I was taking the blame for most of our problems. I came off benefits and stopped getting free money.

When I moved out of my flat, I could have carried on getting a huge amount of money put in my bank for rent by not letting them know I was moving, but I was honest and told them I was leaving and no longer needed the money. Every time my natural reaction to cheating and to be dishonest bubbled up, I would put a lid on it.

I started to let go of my anger. I stopped allowing situations that I could not control frustrate me and ruin my day, and the days of the people I was around. It was like they were on a tightrope with me all the time. It was like I was on a tightrope with myself, ready to lose balance and explode in anger. I was changing. I was seeing people do things that would have typically sent me into a rage like throwing litter or cutting me off in the car, and I wasn't reacting. I started to realised that when I reacted badly, I was only affecting myself and my friends. The person I was aiming my anger at could have had a really bad day, they could be really tired or stressed, or someone close to them may have died that morning, so I decided I should always try and be compassionate.

I then started to try and cut out swearing from my vocabulary. I was starting to see that any character defect could potentially be changed. This was big for me as I swore a lot and always had. I would start sentences with swear words and throw a few in mid-sentence. I would say "fuck", "fucked", and "fucking" so much.

Once I became aware of it, I started to see how uncouth it was and how cringe worthy it must be for people around me. I had no filter on it, and I had always done it in front of my mates' parents, older people and younger people and, often, accidentally in front of kids. It was like swearing was part of the Mancunian persona, the cocky northern lad that I lived up to so much when I moved down south.

I made a conscious decision to stop it, and I did. It took a few weeks of me stopping myself or picking myself up when I did. Soon, I no longer swore at all.

As I was working through the steps, I appeared in court a few times before they realised I had to be tried at the Crown Court. At the Crown Court, I had to await my trial, which ended up being eight months after I was initially arrested. This meant that I couldn't commit to anything because there was a good chance I would be going to prison, but I always seemed have an excuse for not committing to anything, so what was the difference?

I was building up my case of being a drug addict. I was seeing Ralph outside of the meetings and working through the steps, I would cycle all over southwest London, meet him and be drilled into admitting my faults and becoming a better person for myself and society, and primarily for God.

I was doing gardening work for people who went to the meetings, and I was socialising with them from time to time. I was not drinking at all. I was following the line required by the meetings, so I wasn't a complete fraud. With all this new truth, I was feeling guilty that I was lying at the meetings, pretending I had an addiction when I did not. I got through it by realising that although I didn't have an addiction to drink or drugs, I had always had a problem with them. They had always been part of my life. More importantly, I saw that I was sick in a very similar way to a lot of the people at the meetings. I was depressed and in need of help. My life had become unmanageable, and I wanted it to change. I carried on going to the meetings, and as I worked through the steps, I started to look and feel a lot better.

I started to speak to God every day. I had begun to realise that speaking to God was a very powerful thing that was helping me immensely. I still didn't fully understand what it meant or know if I believed in it, but when I didn't speak to God, I felt depressed again and would feel myself spiralling out of control.

When I would go away with Fhian for a weekend and not be able to get down on my knees and pray for two or three days, I would just cry when I got home, feeling so black and heavy inside. I saw that what they were telling me in the meetings was true. I had tested it out, I had believed and gone with what they said, I had done a series of experiments and discovered that when I got down on my knees and admitted my flaws to God and asked for help, I felt so much better. I came to the conclusion that it was a good idea to carry this on. This medicine was making me better.

My court case was approaching, and I had my backstory. I had evidence of attending AA, CA, NA and any sort of meeting with an A as the second part of its acronym. I had a testimony from Ralph telling the court how much effort I had put into the program and that I had gotten through the ten most important steps, that I had been clean and become a reformed character since my arrest. I had shown remorse and become a changed person, no longer posing a risk to myself or society. I also got a character reference from some beautiful friends who were teachers, social workers, artists, chartered surveyors and all-round good, upstanding members of society.

Reading what they wrote about me brought me to tears. I started to see that I wasn't all bad, the letters really helped with my depression. They all told the court I was a good friend and person who really cared about important stuff. I had been so down on myself and been so focused on eradicating my flaws, that I had forgotten about the good things I had done, the charity work, the teaching, the sponsored marathons. Being there for my friends, trying to be ethical and moral in lots of things that I did. Working for Oxfam and teaching for them in schools, having been in a really successful film, doing lots of climate change teaching. It was all there in the letters and reminded me of my good points.

As I read, I started to see that I had these two parts of me that were so far apart. I wanted to get rid of the bad one and just be the good one. To be less of a contradiction. I realised I had some amazing friends who had gone to such lengths to help me avoid prison.

After the miracle that was me not going to prison, I stopped going to the meetings. I felt like I no longer needed them. I felt that

I could have my old life back. I felt that I didn't need a sponsor. I could come back to my truth.

Leading up to the court case, I was also seeing a counsellor. I saw her once a week, typically turning up sweating like a pig after riding my bike as fast as I could to get there on time. The sessions really helped me, she saw me at some of my worst lows and at times saw me the way I wanted to be seen; happy, confident and flowing in speech. She experienced me meeting Fhian and my turmoil of having Renie in my every thought, and we talked about philosophy, literature, ethics, the environment, love and life and the future. She suggested books for me to read to help the depression. I told her how I wanted yoga to be a part of my life, and I didn't know why. I told her that I wouldn't do yoga until I was in India. She thought this was weird as it was available all over London. She kept bringing up the fact that I should meditate, praising its benefits and giving me literature about it, telling me she thought it would help me deal with my stress, anxiety and depression. I kept putting it off and putting it off until finally I went to a Buddhist centre in Bethnal Green.

The eleventh step states: *'Sought through prayer and meditation to improve our conscious contact with God as we understand Him, praying only for knowledge of His will for us and the power to carry that out"*.

I never got around to this step and its only now that I realise I have actually completed it. I started meditating and praying. I was starting to have a connection with God, and I was asking to be guided to happiness and purpose.

Although I found meditation very hard and really struggled to not have thoughts, I found the process very calming and felt better in myself after the meditations. I found the Buddhist Centre to be this otherworldly, serene place that made you slow down, become more conscious and lower your voice. It was a place that had a profound effect on me for the better. I started to consider all these concepts of life, death, rebirth, afterlife, levels of evolution, animal welfare, and consciousness, topics I hadn't even really been aware of before.

I remembered when this Christian band would come to our school and do songs about God and me, and my mates would take the piss out of them and say they were all ex-drug addicts and that this shit saved them from carrying on as druggies. However, in the back of my head, I remembered how certain messages, words and concepts they spoke of stoked a little fire within me. I wondered if I would end up joining something like that where people were generally nice to each other.

With the meditation, I completed step eleven without even knowing it. Completion of Step Twelve would lead to a spiritual awakening, but I didn't feel that I was going to have one or even wanted to. I just wanted to be happy and have my life back.

I was unsure of what was going to happen next. I didn't know where to turn. I felt like I had no part of my life sorted and no stability and I felt pressure from everyone I spoke to, asking me what I was going to do now. I didn't know, I had no idea, I didn't know why I was alive, I didn't know what I was supposed to be doing. I wanted someone to tell me what to do, I wanted someone to guide me, guide me to happiness and fulfilment. I wanted it soon because I couldn't handle this uncertainty much longer. As the pressure started to mount, I began to wish that the judge had sent me to prison. I felt that if I was in there, my brain would have time to relax and not press against my skull so fiercely. Maybe I could even write that book I'd always dreamed about writing.

Step Twelve says: *"Having had a spiritual awakening as a result of these steps, we tried to carry this message to alcoholics and to practice these principles in all our affairs".*

I definitely hadn't had a spiritual awakening, so I hadn't completed step twelve. I didn't want to become some sort of God freak. I still struggled to say the word 'God' or bring the topic up without feeling uneasy and embarrassed and, although I'd been using the word 'God' in my new circles and asking God for help, I still didn't know what it meant. I would probably still have labelled myself an atheist. So from that standpoint, once again I had managed to do most of something, but not quite complete it.

I felt that I had used the steps as a form of therapy. It was like a cognitive process to help me feel better and change myself into this new person who could shake off his past. It didn't matter what I used to be, it was about what I was now and what I was going to become. I certainly didn't feel that I'd had a spiritual awakening and at the time I didn't know what that meant. I hadn't really taken any notice of step twelve. I was championing the Steps program to people, and I really thought that, regardless of whether you were an addict or not, it was a program that would benefit everyone and make society a much better place. By doing it people would see that everything they blamed on others was more likely than not their fault.

    I felt like a new person. I felt lighter with less tension. I felt that getting arrested had really made me look at myself and I really had not liked what I'd seen. I was brave enough and prepared enough to look at my demons and start to get rid of them. I was a new man, but I wasn't into any of this, 'God shit'. I wasn't into any of this spiritual stuff and wasn't going to be awakened. I was ready to find my happiness somewhere and to get myself better with this latest obstacle out of my way.

ARIZONA, THE JOURNEY, MAY 2013

Lou, the plumber, was the man who had come closest to changing my sexuality. He was beautiful with striking blue eyes and big, masculine hands. He cared about stuff, was a vegetarian and valued the life of all beings and was also a drummer and a plumber. There was a connection between us. It was like we both found each other very attractive, but we were both heterosexual and loved women, so it was never gonna happen. But it's as close as I've ever come. He dropped me off at the bus stop, and we had an emotional farewell.

I hit Flagstaff just after dark. I had no reservations and, as usual, was assuming somewhere would have a bed for me.

I got to the train station and asked the lady behind the counter for directions to a hostel. She pointed at two girls and said, 'Follow them'.

The girls were here to see the Grand Canyon. I followed them, and within minutes, we were in a hostel which did have a bed for me, in your face Rdhian. It was so strange, the dread that had been following me for the last few weeks seemed to have evaporated. I instantly had this warm feeling about Flagstaff, even though I couldn't see much in the dark. It was the first place I'd been in the States where things looked within walking distance, and it didn't feel so weird and full of monster trucks. There was even a chap walking down a street and a person riding a bicycle. This now felt weird.

I dropped my bags off and went for a walk around the downtown area. The place was cool, I liked it, I was happy again. Maybe the energy of Taos had been too much for me, maybe I was really affected by the energy of a place, maybe now I could look forward to lighter moods and not as much heaviness around me.

I woke the next day at 6am, feeling energised, fresh, and eager. I meditated in bed, jumped up and made the most of the beautiful sunshine outside, running around town to get my bearings.

I was really impressed by the place. It looked like somewhere I could live. Everything was walkable, unlike most of America which felt like a disjointed retail park with buildings dumped miles from one another with no choice other than to get in the car. People I bumped into were happy, smiling, and everyone said hello, which was shocking; people were actually out of their cars and communicating. It was like I had been thrown into some utopian American parallel universe.

Flagstaff was similar to Taos in a few ways; high altitude, 7,500ft above sea level and has a mountain overlooking it at 12,500ft. It was much smaller, with higher density buildings. The parks I jogged through were beautiful, and the streets felt like liberal middleclass suburbia.

I meditated under a big pine tree in the forest, did a little yoga and then headed back to the hostel. I was so full of energy, I wanted to do everything. I couldn't believe the way the heaviness I had been carrying in Taos had just shifted. When I had stepped off the train in Flagstaff, it was like the suit of armour I had been carrying around in Taos had fallen off me.

I realised how much I was affected by the energy of places and the reason I couldn't stand London started to make sense. It was strange because Taos had so many things I found amazing. The ethos, the buildings, the art scene, the spirituality, the yoga, the meditations, the indigenous people, and the friends I had there. Fundamentally I had always felt off-kilter though, something wasn't right inside me. I had been expecting to fall in love with Taos. I'd heard it had this pull and many of my friends had told me that when they arrived there they couldn't leave. This wasn't the case for me, and considering everyone carries different energy and each place has different energy, it's about finding what works for your energy and your vibration.

I felt Flagstaff was on my wavelength, and I wanted to stay longer, but I was heading to Sedona. My Airbnb host, Juergen, was picking me up at 1 pm, so I went to climb one of the smaller mountains. It was so strange not seeing this mass expanse of place and everything looking sane and not revolving around the car. I walked the Solar System, Galaxy and Universe paths, learning about black holes and stuff at the Lovell Observatory, before heading back to a famous traditional European coffee house called Macy's for a hot chocolate and soup. I felt so good and so light, I was beginning to like the new me.

I was in love with the place.

I had found my sanity again, and I was about to leave after less than twenty-four hours. I was sad to be going and was wondering if I had made a mistake wanting to see Sedona. Would it bring me crashing down? I decided I should just smile and nod and assume the days before I headed for Peru would be full of magic.

Juergen collected me from Flagstaff, and we drove to his house in Cottonwood about twenty miles from Sedona. He'd come all the way to Flagstaff which was fifty-one miles away, to pick me up.

We decided to go on a drive up the 8,000ft mountain. At the top, I stood looking out in awe at the vastness, dryness, redness and sheer brutality of the jagged, frantic almost crumbling landscape. I'd only seen landscapes like that before in cowboy and western films. I was a little unsure of Jurgen, for no reason at all other than I had watched lots of American movies in which a traveller was murdered, raped and held hostage. I was also questioning the kindness he had shown me so far. I always found it hard to accept kindness without thinking there was an ulterior motive. I imagined Juergen throwing me off the side of the mountain. I tried to figure out if he could overpower me. He was a big man, but he was in his late sixties, so I figured I could take him if need be.

I'd heard so much about the spiritual significance of Sedona. I'd planned to see a few of the vortices there and woke early to catch the 7:22 am bus, which flashed by me as I had my hand stuck out, not realising you had to stand at the bus stop.

That was relayed to me by a six-year-old girl.

'What a dick!' she must have thought.

The next bus was in an hour, so I decided to run the four miles into town. Juergen's house was technically in the town but was four miles away from its vast three-mile diameter centre.

I ran in, missed a few more buses and ended up on the 9:47 to Sedona.

The scenery was dramatic. Huge red rocks were breaking the Earth's crust and piercing the cloudless sky in these breath-taking jagged formations. I headed for the Airport Vortex, climbed the main point and sat and meditated at the summit. It was huge, like nothing I had ever seen before and the landscape seemed to go on forever.

I followed a path and decided to scurry up the side of a rock formation through the barren, cactus-ridden ground. Out of breath, I reached the top, shocked to see a huge fence and landing strip. I guess it was called Airport Road, but I wasn't expecting a huge runway on top of one of these beautiful rock formations. Planes were taking off and landing every few minutes.

I then headed for Cathedral Rock, another vortex.

A Canadian couple gave me a ride into the town where I saw a girl sitting on a wall playing the guitar, so I headed to her to ask for directions. She told me about a drumming session there that evening. I said I couldn't go as the last bus back to Cottonwood was at 6:38pm. She said, 'You can crash at my place.'

'Cool,' I said.

She dropped me off in the uptown area, which was full of yoga studios, meditation and spiritual centres. I went into a shop and started chatting to a lady called Astra. She told me they had a healing share that evening and that I should come. She offered me a place to stay, but I already had one, and I thought I'd better let Jurgen know I was staying out. I'd been offered two places to sleep for the night in ten minutes. There was no need to have booked an Airbnb, I thought.

I headed into another psychic shop which was adorned with the biggest crystal collection I'd ever seen. I was allowed to meditate on this chair I'd been weighing up. It was very regal with a fancy purple velvet finish. Above it was a gold pyramid hanging from the ceiling with a huge quartz crystal hanging from its centre. I sat and placed two huge crystals in my hands and placed my now-shoeless feet on the other two huge crystals on the floor. I sat back and drifted off. After battling to free my head of dogma and romantic thoughts, I aligned my chakras and felt my whole body being energised. It was as though spirals were spinning around my body. Reluctantly I came back around and ran in the direction of the Seven Sacred Pools and the Sink Hole.

I raced through trail marks, at times losing them due to distracting myself by singing. I jumped up boulders, scurried across ledges, wondering at times if I fell, when would I be found? I raced around steep edges, dropping dry loose rock 100ft to its new home for the next few years.

The sinkhole was drastic, maybe thirty metres deep with these huge pieces of rock precariously balancing on each other. Some of the rocks were bigger than cars. It made me wonder how it had happened, when it happened and would some more of it sink while I stood here? As I made my way around to the other side, I realised a massive piece of rock had fallen from the ledge I'd just been standing on. Trying to piece the rock formation back together in my head, I chilled for a while, hoping another piece would fall.

It didn't.

I sprinted further along the trail to The Seven Sacred Pools. It was a little terrace of waterholes dropping down like mini waterfalls, but without any water. Apparently, the indigenous people would hold ceremonies there. It felt like a special place, and I meditated for a while, feeling rushes through my body. I got up and ran back to town, stuck out my thumb, jumped in the back of a pick-up and was dropped off before managing to get a further ride to Astra's shop on the other side of town by an old crippled guy called David who offered me marijuana. I remembered the Canadian guy in Belize and said 'no thanks'.

I got to Astra's shop, and she had arranged for someone to drop me off at the drumming after the healing session. The healing was a form of South Korean meditation practice that concentrated on the life particles we all have floating about us. They take their principles from the founder of Dahn Yoga, Ilchi Lee, who has written lots of books on meditation and yoga. I was reading some of his leaflets at the centre which talked about how creativity is not governed by time and space but takes place in a space where everything we have ever wanted can be manifested; a place of expanded consciousness he calls the Mind Screen. He talks about Qi (life energy) and how we all have it inside us and that the cosmos is sprinkling life particles on us all the time. They drench our consciousness with information that expands our consciousness. This gives us the ability to manifest our dreams in a positive way and move obstacles aside to create our own reality.

Through the Mind Screen and the Life Particles, we get closer to self-realisation and a better world in which humans treat each other harmoniously, regardless of race, religion or creed. The session used many of these principles; breathing, dance, massage, meditation, focus and energy movement. It focused on ridding yourself of negative energy and thoughts and replacing them with positive ones, a bit like an oil change.

After this, I was off to Cathedral Rock to meet the guitar girl and listen to the drumming. I got a lift to the other side of town with a lady called Valerie.

We arrived, and the place was empty, no drumming sounds

anywhere, no cars in the car park. It was the wrong night. Jodie, the guitar girl wasn't due for another hour, and I was thinking, I'm not staying here on the off chance a girl I met for five minutes might turn up for a drumming session that actually isn't happening.

It was twenty miles back to Cottonwood, and I'd missed my last bus. I trotted off, wondering what I was going to do.

I sauntered up and down the street. There were a few shops scattered about. I looked for a church to sleep in, looked at Big Rock and thought 'that would be an experience to sleep up there under the bright, almost full moon.' Then I realised I was only wearing a vest and a very thin jacket and had been cold last night in bed under my covers.

I walked aimlessly up the street hoping for divine intervention, ruling hitchhiking out in the dark as no one would pick me up wearing a black coat and ripped pants. I walked towards a light that seemed to be calling me.

Was this the divine?

Was this light I was seeing about to change the course of my evening?

Was I to have a vision of divinity in this sacred place?

The gas station had a few people around. I approached one car and asked a guy how far Cottonwood was, what direction it was, and how much would he charge for a ride there?

He said he lived in Cottonwood, I was thinking bingo. However, he was on his way to his friend's house but would be back in two hours and would get me from the gas station.

Yes, I thought, sorted, I would just chill till then.

Then I thought, what am I going to do for two hours and is it certain he will come back? I decided to hitchhike for two hours before he came back, I had nothing better to do.

Five minutes later, a black Lexus pulled over. I thought it was just stopping.

They asked where I was going.

'Cottonwood,' I said.

'Oh sorry, we just live around the corner.'

'I'll give you ten bucks,' I said.

The driver turned to the passenger and said, 'You wanna go Cottonwood?'

'Why not' he said.

I jumped in and off we sped. Two young brothers called

Miguel, and Carlo were my chaperones.

I had found my saviours.

Thirty minutes later, we arrived at Juergen's door. I thanked them with all my heart, gave them the ten dollars which they flatly refused, saying, 'I won't take your money, man. You're a good guy, Liam, thank you for your words.'

Shocked by the beauty of Miguel and gobsmacked at how amazing my day had been, I stumbled into the house, feeling high, happy, so grateful for the day's events and so gracefully aware of how beautiful the world could be. I told Juergen about my day, and he just sat there with a dropped jaw, unable to fathom such extraordinary events. It was a day to remember and a day that confirmed to me to just trust. Trust and everything you need will be provided for you.

I needed to be in Phoenix in two days for my flight to Peru. It was 150 miles away, and I couldn't find a way to get there. There were no buses, only expensive shuttles, so I would probably end up hitching again.

I headed back to Sedona the next day, wanting to climb the vortices I hadn't seen. I was still feeling so light, so pure, so clean, full of love and happiness. Where had this come from? A few days ago I was waking up in angst, now I felt fresh and ready to take on anything.

Jurgen drove me into town to catch the bus back to Sedona for my second attempt at Cathedral Rock. I arrived by running a few miles from the bus stop feeling great and started to head around the base of the rock away from the tourist trail. It was so steep, and I was struggling to keep my footing. I was aiming for a corner where two huge rocks met, hoping I could use them both to get up. When I got to the top I realised there was a huge drop at the summit, so I had to head back down sliding on my bum, almost rolling over a few times before getting back onto the main trail. I wondered what would happen if I died? Who would be called? At least my mum would know straight away, and I'd be with her again.

I got to the top of the massive arms of rock pointing up to the sky. One represented the feminine and one the masculine. I sat and meditated, before running up the backside to what is called The Church, which had the most breath-taking views of the vast landscape.

I heard there was a creek a few miles away, so I sprinted down

Cathedral Rock around these huge bends. It reminded me of driving around the hills in the south of France, tight bends meandering further and further down. The terrain was becoming greener and more fertile, I was intoxicated by life and beauty.

Hot and sweaty, I wanted to swim, and as I cut around the bends. I saw hundreds of little statues of rock stacked on each other, randomly placed on the pebbly shore. I asked two ladies where was best to swim, they said half a mile down or just here. I looked out, and it was deep enough, so in my boxer shorts I dived in and had the most refreshing dip. It was so cold, but I had run about six miles, so my body could take it.

I got out, and the ladies started talking to me. They said there were leaving for Phoenix tomorrow.

I said, 'Oh, I'm going to Phoenix tomorrow.'

'How you getting there?'

'I don't know, hitchhiking I think.'

'Well, we could take you if you like. We are leaving early though.'

'Perfect,' I said.

We arranged to meet the next day, and again it had perfectly fallen into place. I had trusted it would be cool and work out and it had. I was buzzing, even more, trying to show gratitude as I sat there eating my food. I lay back in the sun, giving thanks and letting the overriding beauty of the world flow over me. I was in heaven, (not Devon where my mum lives in a caravan). I got up, jumped back in the water, got out and started running, heading for my final vortex of Bell Rock four miles away.

I made it to the main road, ran another mile with my thumb out. Eventually, a car stopped. I jumped in, and they dropped me off at Bell Rock to start my final ascent of the day.

It was an almost symmetrical formation and the place that apparently opened up the heart chakra. Many locals hiked the site daily as a meditative ritual. I hiked up, and the view was astounding. It was like you could tell the earth was round, and then these piercing red rocks with green pines and cacti growing out of them were strutting out of the earth everywhere. I was mesmerised. I meditated and brought in the energies of the area. The whole front of my chest started to expand, and I could feel love, lots of love and again a spinning energy around my heart chakra. I sat and enjoyed it until my knee started to hurt. I said goodbye to the rock, thanked it for having me and headed back to town to catch the bus.

I got a lift pretty quickly off a French woman who I kind of bribed by looking into her eyes exhaustedly as she was about to speed off. She took about five minutes to clear the seat which was covered with magazines and papers. She looked like a crazy version of Cruella de Vil and was this nutty astrologer who didn't really like America because everything here was about money. She predicted the downfall of the whole economy within the next three years.

I had an hour to kill, so I went to say hi to Astra and use the internet. She convinced me to stay again that evening for the full moon ceremony they were doing at the centre and offered to take me home if no one else was heading that way. I agreed.

There were offerings, and everyone wrote their special wishes and prayers in a card. They could be for yourself, family and friends and humanity. I stuffed as much on my card as I could, and each one was placed on the altar and blessed individually. I was completely focused on all my wishes and the wishes of everyone in the group, willing them to come true, believing in the life particles and of mind over matter.

After the ceremony, everyone hugged, and a huge buffet came out with an array of food. Again, I felt as if I was in heaven (not Devon). Everyone was so kind and generous and welcoming. I felt a real air of love, peace and contentment. I took a moment and breathed it in.

The lady who was going my way had to leave. I jumped up and left with the lovely Rina who didn't live too far from where I was staying (well six miles, but in America, that meant we were pretty much neighbours). I hooked up with Juergen again, relayed the day's events and the acquisition of a ride to Phoenix. His jaw hit the ground. 'You did all that in a day without a car?' he said.

He agreed to drive me the ten miles the next morning to meet Patti and Jenny from the river so I could get my ride to Phoenix.

I went to bed and replayed the day's events in my mind, wondering why I couldn't live my whole life like this. I'd had an amazing time in Sedona. I'd loved every minute of it, everything had flowed so perfectly, and everything I'd asked for had become a reality. Maybe I should have asked for something bigger than rides, food and good friends? It was like the energy of the place allowed you to instantly manifest anything you wanted, but other than a family, I still had no idea what I wanted on a bigger scale.

I knew that when I understood exactly what it was I wanted, it wouldn't take me long to get it. Maybe I would head back to Sedona then?

Next morning Juergen dropped me off. I met the ladies, thanked him so much for being cool and going above and beyond the call of duty for a host. I jumped in the back of the van for the drive down to Phoenix. Patti, the driver, was from the countryside of California but was now living in the sprawling city of Phoenix. Jenny, her co-pilot, lived in California and worked as a carpenter and marijuana grower.

Phoenix was spread over almost a hundred miles in the middle of the desert. It was hotter than you could imagine and it was only spring. Everyone had air conditioning, and again the whole place looked like a retail park. If only America had developed before the car, then maybe the place would be more people-friendly.

We headed for Patti's place to drop off her stuff. Her apartment block reminded me of a terrible US show I used to watch to perv at Heather Locklear called Melrose Place. It was funny that her neighbour introduced himself as Ronnie Wood and then he went on to tell me about all his pot-smoking days and seeing the Rolling Stones at Woodstock in the sixties.

The ladies dropped me off at the airport, and I thanked them with all my heart. I was eight hours early, but anything would have been better than hitchhiking in that searing heat. I was in a great mood, having had an amazing time in Arizona. It had brought me back to me. I felt alive again, free, vibrant, blessed, and full of gratitude. My shine was back, and I hoped it would hang around forever.

Peru and Ayahuasca here I come.

CHAPTER 18
MUM,
LIFE 2007

Me mum died on the 17th of September 2007. My world, as I knew it was shattered.

I'd just moved into a new house, didn't have a bed and in two weeks' time, I was due to start back at university for my final year. After that I would be thrown into the world and be forced to survive as an adult.

Before the summer holidays, I had split up with 'The Communist' who I'd been with for the last two years and immediately I met Renie, the Greek girl. I'd booked a round-the-world ticket for the summer, paid for by the drug-taking students and residents of Kingston-Upon-Thames. Thank you, well thank you to your rich mums and dads and the student loans company.

A month after meeting Renie, I set off to visit friends in New York, Miami and Auckland with stops in Los Angles, Fiji and finally a month in India, which was what I was looking forward to the most.

I'd always had this vision of being in India. It was definitely not a place anyone from where I was from would have dreamed of visiting, but I had this fixation with it, and I didn't know why. I hadn't ever studied or heard much about it, I just knew I wanted to go. I also had this vision of being a yoga teacher, which also at the time was extraordinary as I was a mildly xenophobic, lager drinking, sexist, racist, football-crazed nutcase.

While I was in New Zealand with one of my best mates, Ben, I called home, and my step-dad told me Mum was in hospital with a problem with her leg. I was due to fly to India in five days. A couple of days later, I woke early in the morning to my step-dad ringing me.

He told me that I needed to come home.

'Why?' I said.

'Because it's worse than we thought and your mum's got lung cancer. She is very ill, and she's got to have chemotherapy.'

SHIT, FUCK, SHIT FUCK, SHIT, I thought.

He said, 'We didn't think it was going to be this bad and we didn't want to tell you unless we had to. We didn't want to ruin your trip, but she is really ill, and you need to come home now.'

(I break down in floods of tears again seven years later as I write this. I end up having to take a 10-minute break to let these still-raw emotions flow through me once more.)

This was the worst moment of my life. It was off the Richter scale, nothing had ever even come close to how powerful the emotions were. It felt like I was going to internally combust. I felt like my heart was being ripped from my chest and I didn't know if I should help rip it out or try to pull it back in. Tears had already started to stream down my face as I tried to hold my emotions together.

(Another 10-minute break to let my tears flow and emotions pass again. Wow, this chapter could take a very long time to write at this rate. It's amazing what emotions the sense memory can instantly trigger when you truly feel something from the past.)

My step-dad kept talking. I couldn't hear anything. Trembling, I said, 'I'll be on the next flight.'

I hung up the phone, and this deep built-up emotion exploded. I sobbed deep sobs that built and built, and I started letting out cries of 'No, please no.' It was like everything that meant anything to me in the world was embodied in that one person, and the realisation that she may not be around in the future dawned on me, and I wept.

I wept for my mother and her illness, I wept for the pain she might have felt, I wept for everything she had ever done for me, I wept for her laugh, for her smile, her eyes and her embrace. I wept, wanting to take away her pain, wishing it was someone else, wishing it was me and not her.

I wept for me and for not having her in my life, for all that she gave me and the possibility of it being taken away. I wept for my first call with exciting news, my first call when I was in trouble or ill, for all I wanted her to see me achieve. I wept for us both and for my children, for not having the greatest grandma in the world. I wept for this woman who was more than just a mother to me.

She was also, my friend, my father, my sister, my brother, my aunty, my uncle, my grandma, my granddad, my step-dad, my home, my beacon of light, my everything. She did the jobs of all those people, who all had their shortcomings. Somehow my mother, in the body of one person, embodied all the qualities you would want from those people. The possibility of losing her was like losing my whole family, like being the only survivor when a bomb took out a family home.

I felt like I had been shot in the chest, and the pain was intense, nothing had come close to this in my life. As I wailed and screamed, Ben opened the door to my room to see what the commotion was. I told him and said, 'I need some time alone.'

An hour later, after the hysterics had subsided somewhat, I left the room and told him, I had to go home.

It was the holidays in New Zealand so every plane was booked up and I couldn't get on a flight for two days. I stayed at Ben's in-laws' in this shell-shocked state, trying to see the positives between intermittent breakdowns of tears, snot and heart palpitations.

The night before I was set to fly home, I managed to speak to me Mum on the phone in the hospital. As soon as I heard her voice, I wanted to break down, but I'd told myself before the call that I had to be strong and not get too upset and scare her. I had to stay light-hearted and positive, so I tried my best as tears rolled down my face.

It was so good to hear her voice. I wanted to hold her and tell her it would be fine like she did for me whenever I was ill. I gave her all the positiveness I could muster and told her I would be there soon. She said she couldn't wait to see... *(another breakdown mid-sentence. I can't hold it together writing this. Okay come on, breathe Liam, breathe)* me and give me a big cuddle. She said she was sorry to cut my trip short and I said, 'Don't be silly,' and that the only place I wanted to be in the world was by her side. As always, there was lots of laughter as we spoke, even though it was the worst of times. She told me how it had all happened, and I told her bits about my trip she hadn't already heard, like missing my flight to LA by two days and whilst sitting in my mate's flat in Miami realising (as I looked at my printed tickets) that my flight left two days ago.

My mum mixed laughter with worry for her son, who often made these kinds of mistakes. The love we had for each other poured down the phone, and I could feel it so intensely. This was the person in the world who meant more to me than all the other people in it combined, it was that simple.

I would have given up everyone else for her on the spot.

I told her I'd see her in two days as it was going to take forty-eight hours to get to London. We told each other how much we loved each other as we always did, but this time it wasn't out of habit, it was deeper, it was meant with conviction, meaning and understanding.

I had kept strong for my mother during that to try and give her strength, to try and give her hope, and to try and give her the positivity she needed whilst she fought this illness.

As soon as the phone cut off, I collapsed on the floor and became a blubbering mess. I'd kept all the emotions locked inside, and it was like all the tears and snot and coughing and sobbing and clearing rushed out of me all at the same time. It all started to drip down off me onto the already-tear-drenched carpet below as tears, snot, spit and eye gunk mixed together, forming an appetising cocktail of excruciating pain on the carpet in front of my knees.

She'd been in my every thought since the moment I'd found out. Our lives together flashed before my eyes; all the things we had been through, the good times and the bad. They all bubbled up to the surface as I contemplated what she truly meant to me.

I saw us sunbathing together in Tenerife. I saw her dropping me off at primary school in her Peugeot 207 and watching me run to the fence and scramble underneath the wire with my bag before turning to watch her drive off. I remembered the happiest times of my life when we lived together in The Battered Wives Institute and in the council house in Wythenshawe. I saw my school clothes hanging on the rack in front of the fire as I came down the stairs in the morning because we had no central heating and the house was like an icebox in the winter. I heard her shouting me to get up in the morning. I saw her trying to get to me in the bathroom to give me a good smack after I had done something naughty. I remembered her sniffle, I remembered her cough, and I remembered her roaring laughter. I remembered our weekend bus or car journeys into the city to go shopping and to see my nana at the Arndale Market. I remember how we got to stand at the front of the bus talking to the bus driver because me mum was dating him and it made me feel more important than all the other passengers.

I remembered all me mum's boyfriends, especially the magician with the fruit machine in his house. I remember getting the aerial of one of my toy cars stuck in my ear and perforating my eardrum just before Mum was about to go on a date. I remember sitting in my house with her on New Year's Eve. She was in floods of tears because we were all alone and I joined in with the crying, wondering why I wasn't enough for her. I remembered everything; all the beautiful times and all the dreadful times of violence, tears and upheaval.

Most of all, I remembered the life with me Mum and that I had shared almost every moment of my life so far with her. She had been my ever-present, the person whose side I would always run to...

(Wow, now more floods of tears. I break down again, this time it's like that missing element of my life is coming to the surface. It's bubbling up through my stomach and bringing floods of emotion to the surface as all the tears and snot come out, and my body coughs and splutters deeply embedded emotion out of me. When it passes I wait for the next wave to come and it fizzles up from the pit of my stomach and builds, then quickly moves through my organs and up my spine, ribs and chest up my throat. It bursts out of all the orifices on my face except my ears. I step out of my room and into the bathroom to grab some toilet roll to wipe my nose and blow this build-up of mucus and snot out of me. I get myself together, go down the stairs, get a big cuddle from my housemate Collette and tell her I'm fine and felt that it was nice she let me process it alone, after obviously hearing my cries. I go to the kitchen to make a brew, and three amazing tunes came on in a row on the radio, climaxing with "Flat Beat" by Mr Wazzo which I rave to like I've come up off a pill in my kitchen. Then I come back to my writing feeling upbeat and clear, wondering if more emotions will come to the surface as I try to finish this piece)

...the person I had always been in pictures with, the person I would always be in those pictures with. She had always protected me, kept me warm, tried to keep me out of trouble, fed me, made me big and strong, loved me, and she was always on my side (at times blinded by love). She always defended me, she could see no fault in me when there were many, she was always so proud, she always worried about me, she always put me first, and she told me I would always be special because I was her first and we had been through so much together. She was always scared to go to my parents' evenings at school, she was always scared when the police rang her, she always held me so tight, and she always held me tighter now as I was away from her most of the time, and she always had a tear in her eye when I was leaving her again.

She was my everything, and I was her... *(again tears, emotions please stop, let me write this, I need to finish this chapter)* ...son who could do no wrong and whom she thought the sun shone from. How could it be possible that this woman might be taken away from me?

How would my world be without her? How would I go on? Who would I have? Where would I go? I had no idea. I just knew that she had to get better. Otherwise I would have nothing. With all these thoughts and emotions racing around my mind I wrote my first ever piece of poetry, sitting on the floor of a house in New Zealand, looking out to sea.

Mum
Trying to get from the other side of the world to see you mum
Trying to get on a flight so I can be near you mum
The pain I felt today really brought meaning to you mum
When I sit back and think of all the times I needed you mum
Bring tears to my eyes every time I see you mum
A heart wrenching almost drowning sensation fills me mum
Don't know what to do just got to get near you mum

Finally, I got a seat home. I had to fly from Auckland to Sydney, wait for eight hours then fly to Bangkok. By this time I had been travelling for over thirty hours and hadn't gotten a wink of sleep. I was looking for valium everywhere. The few I'd gotten off the doctor for flights had long gone. Everywhere I went you needed a prescription, except in good old British high street chemist, Boots, which had a branch in Bangkok airport and was willing to sell to anyone who enquired.

I got on my final plane completely exhausted and desperately in need of sleep. I popped a few valiums as a passenger in front of me was sick. A cleaner had to come on the plane to clean it up, delaying the flight by a good hour. The stench was fully ingrained in my nostrils for the rest of the flight. I drifted off to sleep shortly after take-off. I then woke up feeling refreshed, thinking, 'Wow we must almost be almost home, that felt like a really deep valium sleep.'

I looked at the flight details on the screen in front of me and, to my horror, I had only been asleep for two hours and had eight left. I only had one valium left. I took that, but I just wouldn't drift off again. I became more and more agitated, I couldn't get comfortable, and the vomit smell was making me feel sick. I tried putting my legs up against the seat in front, I tried stretching my leg out under the chair, I tried everything, but I could not get comfortable. The people beside me must have thought I was a deranged mental patient, with the amount of fidgeting and groaning and moving around I was doing.

I was the most frustrated I had ever been in my life. I was stressed about the situation with my mum, I had this smell of sick under my nose, and I felt like I could taste it in my mouth as well. My skin was crawling, I hadn't had a shower in days, and I wanted out of my body or to get off this plane.

There were no stops between Bangkok and London, and I wanted off the plane so badly. I had never felt like this travelling before, but I was at the end of my tether. I decided I was that uncomfortable in my body that I would be quite happy for the plane to fly into a mountain and for that to be the end of this life. I prayed for that hour after hour, and I was quite happy to come to terms with dying as long as it meant I was no longer in this plane and in this body, both of which were making me feel anxious and trapped.

LIMA, PERU, THE JOURNEY, MAY 2013

Finally, I was heading to Peru. I felt like my destiny was there and that all the answers I was looking for lay in the hands of the sacred Amazonian plant medicine, Ayahuasca. During my wait at Phoenix airport I grabbed a hot chocolate, and the girl behind the counter asked where I was from.

I said, 'England.'
She said, "Oh, my friend, like, lives there.' 'Where?' I said. 'Wales. Do you know it?'
I told her that was like me asking if we were in Canada.
She didn't get it. *Smile and nod...*

Disoriented and not knowing how long it was since I had last slept, I arrived in Lima. I was on the hunt for someone to share a cab with to the Mira Flores district, which was supposed to be safe.

I spotted a couple, but my bag was taking ages, and they had escaped out of the airport. I tried to rush through, but I assumed they'd gone. I got outside, and they were still there.
I asked if they wanted to share a cab. They said yes.

We passed what seemed to be very run down, rather scary looking parts of the city and I spotted a random statue of John Lennon.

When we arrived in Mira Flores, the streets were buzzing like any commercial European city on a Friday night. Scantily clad girls and dressed up boys littered the streets and bars, as we navigated through the flesh.

Joe and Elle were my cab buddies from Australia, and we walked around the city together for the evening. I was surprised at how wealthy, and new everything in the area seemed. There were new Huxley-style apartments everywhere, storing the masses.

The next day I wanted to do a little exploring of the city. The lady in the hostel viscously scribbled out the places we should not venture to on the map, hinting we would meet certain death if we strayed from the safe zones. I jumped off the bus and decided to go and look at one of the spots she scribbled out from a bridge that separated the safe zone from the danger zone.

Lima was a massive city. It had taken an hour to get to the centre from one of the central districts, and that was in flowing traffic late at night. It was a huge sprawl that seemed endless, people were selling things everywhere, there was food everywhere, the hustle and bustle, horns tooting, kids playing, people, so many people.

I ate one of the typical menus that are all over Latin America, offering a two-course meal in a local restaurant for about £1.50.

I bought some weird fruits and nuts and wandered around, taking in a crazy market, Lima's own Chinatown and a huge open park. I wondered why every city in the world has a Chinatown! Is there a central office in each with a big red phone, which when the time is right, lights up and rings and the Chinese government tells its people to invade, they are weak, the time is now. They then take over every city and rule the world in fifteen minutes. I could see no other feasible explanation.

I wanted to explore Mira Flores and Baranco further south, so I decided to stay another night. I went for a walk along the seafront for what seemed like miles. Sophisticated landscaped gardens draped over the cliffs which drastically dropped down to the sea. I walked south, and there was so much wealth that I felt out of place. It was like Fulham or Parsons Green, that West London feel. Ladies were jogging, and people were stretching and picking up the shit from their tiny dogs. It had an ambient, safe, calm and clean feel; a far cry from the madness of central Lima.

I decided to meditate on a bench to test my resolve against the distraction of passing people. I wanted to connect with the energies of Peru for the first time, of the Incas, the Nazcas and all the ancient people of these lands. I wanted to introduce myself, ask for a pleasant stay and for all my needs to be met.

I sat for around half an hour, concentrating, not being distracted by thoughts and passers-by. I felt as if my body was being pulled slightly to my left. It was saying just ride this, be open to whatever is happening, have no fear, be open. I felt like I was going to leave my body, float up and look down on myself. The spinning intensified, and it felt like I was in one of those rides they strap you into at a fair in a star jump position, and you go in every direction imaginable and start to feel sick. I was starting to feel sick, and I was thinking, hold on, try and keep a clear mind. I tried to straighten my body as it felt like my whole left side had collapsed. I couldn't take it anymore. I was fighting it but couldn't come out of the meditation, it was so strong. Then unable to take any more, I flung my body forward, my head jilting into my lap. Panting, I sat there out of breath, unable to fathom what had just happened. I kept my head down and started to feel the real world again. I recovered my senses, wiped my moistened brow and wiggled my hands and feet.

What had just happened?
What did it mean?
Where had I been?
What should I do now?

Well actually, handstands. I found a patch of grass and practised. All my money obviously fell out of my pocket as I flung myself upside down and I unsuccessfully clambered around looking for it in the dark.

That evening I was staying in a six-bed dormitory in the hostel. I was on the top bunk, and everyone else was asleep when I retired. I climbed up and fell straight to sleep. The next thing I knew, the alarm on my phone was going off. I pushed my legs off the wall, pushed my bottom into the bed and flipped off the bunk to land on the ground. As I did this, the slats from my bed came loose and landed on the guy sleeping below.

I clambered away, not knowing whether to take the slats off the guy or turn off the phone. Why was my alarm even set? I went to the phone, realised it was 6:30 am, apologised in a very low voice to the bloke covered in slats, placed them against the wall and promptly left the room with my tail between my legs.

I sat in the lounge wanting to go back in and get my running shorts and head out but feeling too embarrassed to do so. Then the guy I had just removed the wooden slats from came out of the room. He has a neck brace on and his arm in a cast. I didn't know whether to laugh or cry. I decided to laugh internally and cry externally, again apologising and thinking, Wow, this guy must have some bad Karma attached to him.

A micro taxi whizzed me towards the notorious La Victoria part of town where I would get a ten-hour bus to Nazca. Some locals had told me not to get the bus from that area as it was too dangerous. I doubt they'd known Wythenshawe or Manchester city centre in the early 90s. If you tripped over in them days, there was a good chance you would stand up with some sort of needle sticking out of you, and your wallet would probably have been taken by someone pretending to help you up. I could possibly have been robbed in La Victoria according to rumours, but what damage is really done if you have all your possessions stolen? We are so rich we can just work hard for a week and buy some new ones.

The Nazca lines intrigued me as they are somewhat of an enigma, and various theories about their purpose and origin are batted about. There is a series of animal figures and geometric shapes, some of which are two hundred metres long and spread across five hundred square kilometres of desert. Each one is a sophisticated motif such as a spider, hummingbird or monkey, made by one continuous line. Theories about them vary from landing strips for alien spacecraft to some kind of agricultural calendar, aligned with the constellations above.

When I arrived at 6am, very few people were around, and all the hostels in my guidebook seem to have disappeared. I eventually managed to find a room and fell asleep for a while before planning my flight over the lines.

The town had many unfinished buildings and many that looked like they were about to fall down. Malnourished dogs shuffled around the street as well as all kinds of rubbish that I have to navigate to get into the centre of town.

I was flung into a van and hurtled to the micro airport, which was packed with tourists. I was told it would be an hour's wait. Two hours later, the people I'd arrived with got in another van, so I assumed this was my next move.

I got in, and I asked if they had flown, and they said yes.

I said, 'I haven't,' so I got out and tried to make headway in the office.

Forty-five minutes of anxious waiting later, I was crammed into this tiny plane. There was a pilot and co-pilot and five passengers.

I sat next to a Dutch lady whose English accent and grasp of the language was far superior to mine, I thought she was from Surrey at first.

We headed over the lines and, although my eyes were enjoying the sights, my mind wasn't connecting as I was trying my best not to vomit. The sudden turn to get a view of each line from both sides made my insides twist and turn.

It was fascinating afterwards to think about why the lines had been built and how we don't know the truth of why is there a six-thousand-year-old landing strip for an aircraft in the middle of the desert. These people were either highly advanced or something else had been at play.

I'd been chatting a lot to Fhian on Skype. We both seemed to be very much in love with each other again, and without the title, it felt like we were a couple. She was eager for me to do Ayahuasca and saw it as a pivotal part in deciding our future. I wanted to wait to see what the Ayahuasca told me in regards to Fhian before we committed to each other. It is said to give you the truth and to show you your heart, and I wanted that more than anything. Was she was the girl I would spend my life with? We'd both found the break impossible and had pined for each other every day. I felt like I was in love again and intoxicated poetry was flowing from me.

We were both looking forward to seeing what secrets Ayahuasca would reveal, but inside we were in love and couldn't wait to see each other again. We wanted to be together forever, to become this amazing unit, to watch each other grow and become these super cool hippies! She worried that I wouldn't be able to adapt to life back home and the fact she was in London, but I felt that love this strong would conquer all.

CHAPTER 19
MUM 2,
LIFE, 2007

I made it to London without my wish coming true and the plane crashing into a mountain. Renie picked me up from the airport, and I went back to her house to shower, make love, sleep for a couple of hours and eat before making my way up north to Manchester.

Me step-dad picked me up from the train station and took me to the cancer unit. The car journey was typically uncomfortable as every journey with my step-dad throughout my life had been. It was like I couldn't breathe, and I was suffocated when I was in a confined space with him.

I don't think I could have been any further away from me Mum on the planet than I had been when I found out. Finally, I was home. She was my home, and I was her homing pigeon, and I'd found my way back to her with the help of some planes, trains and automobiles. It was a joy and a relief to be there, to give her my love and feel her love. We cried and cried and embraced, which made me feel uncomfortable in front of my step-dad. But still it seemed like we melted into each other, no one's embrace can beat that of a mother – her only son back in her arms.

She was having tests, and the seriousness of what was happening to her seemed daunting. Me step-dad left, and this was our cue for making each other laugh as we always did. Crazy laughter boomed around the cancer unit until we got told to keep it down. It was always so beautiful to have my beacon of light to myself, to be able to bring laughter to her in this time of darkness.

For the next couple of weeks, I felt like I was in limbo. All I wanted to do was be around my mum and look after her, spend every minute I could with her. I'd planned to sell drugs at the festival in Spain again (unbeknown to me Mum) with lots of my friends, but I wanted to stay here. Me mum told me I should go and, in some ways, this was a bit of a relief, as staying in the house with me step-dad, sister and the dog was driving me insane.

Me Mum actually seemed to be doing well, and I spent as much time as I was allowed with her. I remember us getting in trouble and being told to keep the noise down by one of the nurses as we laughed hysterically, our two unique and distinctive laughs mixing and reverberating through the wards. We were laughing so hard because I had told me Mum a story about me Japanese friend, 'Mr Japan' who I was going to the festival with. He was a very skinny Japanese guy, and he had told me he was trying to put some weight and muscle on so he would look bigger and fit into his wok head. Me Mum laughed straight away, which made me laugh too. During the laughter I told her that I'd asked him, 'What have you been doing to fit into your wok head?' and he said, 'Squats and lunges.'

As I told me Mum this, still with the image of a Japanese boy trying to fit into his wok head, we tipped over the edge and couldn't stop laughing. We were almost crying with laughter as people were almost dying around us. Then we were asked to keep it down by the nurse, which made us look at each other in a mischievous way and internally laugh even harder.

This became a theme of most of my visits to Mum's bedside; no doom and gloom, just masses of laughter and piss-taking and me squatting and lunging away to set her off again.

I left for Spain with a few thousand pills. Me mum was due to have more tests and start the chemotherapy. I kept in regular contact and enjoyed the working festival as much as I could.

After making enough money to pay for my final year at uni, I flew back to Manchester from Bordeaux. Me Mum was back at home after her first round of chemotherapy. She said it was the worst feeling ever and told me how dark and horrible your body gets.

At some points in the coming weeks, she was really ill, and at other points she was as I'd always known her.

We looked at this wig brochure together, as she was trying to decide what style she wanted. I wanted her to get something wild, but she took the sensible option. Her hair wasn't actually falling out too much, so there wasn't much need for it when it arrived, but she did wear it now and again as part of some sort of funny performance.

Me sister would be out playing with her friends, and me step-dad would be at work, so I got me Mum all to myself most of the day. I would spend my days sorting things out around the house that she hadn't had time for and keeping it clean and tidy as she liked it. I would sit cuddling her, watching TV and laughing. At the time I was big into my cooking so I would make the evening meal for the family. It had always been me Mum's job, but she was too ill to do anything too strenuous.

All I wanted was for me mum to get better and for the house and her time in it to be as stress-free and comfortable as possible. She hated the dog, so I kept it out of her way. Every night when my step-dad got home from work he would let it into the living room and instantly destroy the calm environment I had created in the main part of the house. This made me livid, and I wanted to stamp on his head, but as with most things with me step-dad, it was his way only and no compromise.

In his eyes, he went to work all day to provide for us, so when he got home, everything was his way (even though I no longer lived there). It was his blind love for the dog that destroyed a lot of things in his relationship with my mother. A year earlier she had given him the ultimatum of 'me or the dog,' to which he'd replied, 'Don't be stupid.'

She said, 'No, I'm serious.'

And he said, 'Well, the dog then.'

She never had the bottle to leave him as she felt she was too old to start again and wasn't strong enough to take that leap. I remember her crying to my nanna who said, 'You've done it once before when you left Bernie (me Dad), so you can do it again.'

She never did.

One night we were all having our evening meal (which all through my life had made me uncomfortable). Sitting with my step-dad for a sustained period of time, unable to escape until I'd finished eating, unable to be myself. I had this feeling that when I was with him he was trying to change the very fabric of who I was.

Talk of holidays was brought up by me sister. I hadn't been part of any holidays with them since I was twelve, so it didn't involve me. Me mum and step-dad told her it wasn't possible because 'Mum was too ill and needed to get better'.

Like the spoilt brat, my sister was at the time, she got upset saying all her friends were going on holiday and it wasn't fair that she couldn't go away. She was upsetting me Mum, and they were apologising to her as if it was even an option.

I couldn't take it. I was either going to explode and shout at my sister and punch her in the face, or explode and kick the shit out of my step-dad for not putting his daughter into check as he'd done with me my whole childhood. He'd endlessly told me that if I was his son, I'd behave this way and that way.

Instead, I just went and sat in the garden and cried my eyes out.

How could I make this time better for me mum? Why were my sister and step-dad not doing all they could to help her get better and make her recovery as peaceful and stress-free as possible? I felt like I was going nuts. Was I in some other world in my head where it was instinctive to make a seriously sick person's life as relaxing and cared-for as humanly possible?

I went for a walk with tears streaming down my face, wishing I had a beautiful place. I could take my mum and wait on her hand and foot whilst she got better.

(As I write this my housemate returns home and I tell her I have been writing about my step-dad.

She says, 'You look white and pale. It's really affecting you, are you okay?'

I say, 'Shit, my childhood was traumatic.'

Thinking about it and actually recounting it as its all flooding back into my head, I realise I had forgotten how hard every day had been.

As I sit, the memories resurface. Why hadn't I left home at sixteen? I know the answer to this: ME MUM. I wanted to be near her; I had to endure the trauma for that privilege.

The amount of time I spent feeling uncomfortable and in fear of doing something wrong and not ever wanting to be in the same space as my step-dad was vast. When I was in the same space as him, I felt suffocated and unable to relax. This was at its worst when we went on a caravan holiday in Cornwall, and it rained the whole time, and we were stuck inside. After that I decided I never wanted to go on holiday with them ever again as my impression that my step-dad was a horrible man and an arsehole had been confirmed.

I would often go to the football in his car and struggle for conversation the whole journey, feeling tense and agitated. When we got there, I would jump out of the car before the ignition was turned off.

When my step-dad got home from work, it was my cue to go upstairs or get out of the house. Before he got home, I felt like I could relax in the house and chat with me mum and be comfortable, as you should be in your own home and around your family. But as soon as he got home, it changed. It was like I was no longer part of the family. I no longer felt at home other than when I was in my room, but even then, I was made to feel like I was in someone else's house.

I remember when we first moved in with him, and I would sit and watch the TV after school, Neighbours, Home and Away and The Simpsons. He would march into the living room, passing me without any acknowledgement and either turn the TV off or change the channel to the news, stating in an arrogant and dismissive, dictator-ish way that he wasn't having this crap on his TV.

After this happened a few times, I learnt to go to my room when he got home. Maybe this was his aim. I would come back down when I was called for me tea to endure thirty minutes of being in his presence, being torn to pieces for my character or what I was wearing and thinking the sun shone out of my dad's arse. Then I would return to my room and spend the rest of the evening there until it was time to go to sleep, tucked away from the rest of the family.

Even looking back at family pictures, it looks like I'm some random kid who's been superimposed onto a nice picture of a mother and father with their perfect daughter. I never wanted to be in those pictures — my soul seemed to pull me away.

I remember when my mum and step-dad got married. I think I was about fifteen, and for a week leading up to the wedding, I had been so sick with the worst diarrhoea imaginable. Anything I ate came straight back out. I lost about a stone in weight and looked like someone who had just stepped out of a concentration camp. In all the wedding pictures I looked awful, like an intruder and an outcast.

I was ill for another week after the wedding and lost so much weight. Maybe my body was reacting to the pain that I felt about my mum marrying this man I couldn't stand to be in the same house as and had no way of communicating with at all.

I felt like I was losing myself. I had been this funny, outgoing kid, and it was like he was trying to wipe any sense of humour out of me and reduce me to what he thought a boy my age should be like.

When they first met, I was at a primary school where there was no school uniform. Not long after, we moved in with my step-dad, for some reason, he insisted on me wearing trousers and a shirt, stating that 'A kid should wear smart clothes to school.' (Yeah maybe a kid going to a school that has a uniform...) I felt like a complete knobhead and bowed my head as I walked into class. My bounce and confidence were being gradually eradicated. I was in clothes I had never worn before, and all my mates took the piss out of me, saying I was some posh kid now I'd moved to Gatley. I felt so uncomfortable. Unbeknown to me, this feeling would endure for the next twelve years of my life.

I would cry to my mum that I didn't want to wear it. Even then, I was really conscious of my clothes and was fussy about what I wore. Sometimes I would get dressed into what he wanted me to wear whilst he was still in the house, and then when he left for work my mum would let me get changed into my normal clothes, and I would go off to school happy. It was like my whole life had changed, and I was being dictated to. This man was a mini Hitler, incapable of love and laughter and passionate about rules, being in charge and reducing people to tears.

He never praised me, ever. If I was amazing in a football match, he would say to me mum that I'd done all right. It was like if I knew I was good at something he would stop me getting better, or it was like he had no capacity for being nice, or maybe he had a bitterness inside him that didn't want me to be good at anything. It didn't take me long to never actually seek his approval. If anything, I think I sought his disapproval.

I remember how often he would say, 'If you were my kid, you would have to eat your veg, or you'd be straight to your room,' or 'If you were my kid, you wouldn't be able to play video games,' or 'If you were my kid, you would always have to wash the pots.' If you were my kid this and if you were my kid that.

I would think, 'Yeah but I'm not your fucking kid you stupid fucking prick.' (I would honestly think this; you start swearing early on a council estate). He would also forever be slagging off my dad and call him all sorts of names. Now I knew my dad was a bad man and that he had done lots of terrible things to my mum. But he was still me dad, and I still wanted to see him, even if sometimes it was just so I could get away from Hitler. But that's all I would ever hear growing up; my dad being put down by my step-dad. I was so sick of it, and I would advise any step-parent to never put the child's real parents down in front of the kids. It's completely unacceptable, and it made me hate him even more.

I despised him. His every word made me cringe, and I prayed he would go away, but because we were more financially secure, I was always told (by him mainly and sometimes by others) that I should be grateful. All I wanted was to be loved and be in a loving environment, I wasn't fucking starving before my mum met him. We'd always had food, so it wasn't like he had rescued us off the street, cold, starving and hungry.

From an early age, I would say to people that I didn't care that we lived in a nice area. (It wasn't like we were rich anyway, we just weren't on a council estate.) All I wanted was someone nice who loved me, and I could love back and that there could be some emotional attachment to. Even someone who would just play with me now and then and possibly acknowledge me. I never understood why my mum was with him. She was amazing, funny, loving, beautiful, the life and soul of parties and social events and the linchpin of her family. His only interests seemed to be football, work and his dog. Mum would say she always felt like fourth or fifth on his list of priorities and I would wonder why she was with this man, even at the age of twelve. Why would this amazing woman settle for that?

I was also supposed to be grateful to him for lying for me in court when I was being prosecuted for criminal damage. My girlfriend at the time (aged 16) had taken an overdose because her mother was an alcoholic and her step-dad a pervert.

Her mother and step-dad picked us up from the hospital where she had been recovering. They were dropping me off at home, and I was already not happy about being in the car with them as they had caused this situation. Then her parents started telling her off and shouting at her for being stupid, saying they wouldn't let her stay at my house and wanted to take her home which was somewhere she never wanted to go back to ever again.

When we got to my house, I got out of the car and prised her away from her mother, who was trying to keep her there. Me mum and me step-dad came to the door and helped her into the house. I turned around once she was safe and started to kick the car whilst her parents tried to drive off.

The next day the police came and arrested me, and I said, yes, I had done it. When I got to the station, my stepdad turned up and said, 'Deny it all. Say you didn't do it'.

Anyway, I ended up in court instead of getting a caution, which would have been the case if I'd just told the truth. My step-dad gave evidence in court supporting the lies we were telling. After that, any time I had an altercation with him, he'd tell my mum he lied for me in court. I would think, actually it was because of you I ended up in court, you prick.

I look back and see how my life was just drama, drama, drama.

No wonder Mum used to say I was an angry little boy and now I'm an angry young man. I only have to look at my life and see the reasons why. I think what made me lose the most respect for my stepdad as I was growing up was his lack of consistency and the way he contradicted himself. As soon as my sister was at an age where she was wanting certain things and showing various types of behaviour, I noticed how she wasn't made to do the things he had made me do. She didn't have to eat her veg, she didn't have to go to bed early, she didn't have to do housework before she was allowed out, she wasn't continually dictated to and made to feel bad about herself.

When I became an adult and me sister was still at home, I witnessed the disparity and thought, actually if I'd have been your fucking kid growing up all that stuff you said wouldn't have happened to me and I would have had an easier life. Because if I was your kid, you wouldn't have been horrible all the time, you would have been a complete walkover. Still you would have been incapable of emotional love and support and been completely unapproachable, but I would have felt less shit and unwanted most of the time. Consistency is all I asked for, then some remnants of respect would have been achieved.)

The next night I cooked a meal again and after we finished I asked my sister to tidy up and put some food aside for her dad. Not anything too challenging for a fifteen-year-old, I thought. She said yes.

When me step-dad got home, immediately the dog was let into the living space, which made me want to smash his head against a wall for disrupting my mother's tranquillity. Then he started shouting, asking what all the mess in the kitchen was. He shouted up to me, and I said me sister was going to sort it out. Me sister said she wouldn't do it and she wasn't my slave. He started huffing and puffing, exploding in anger as I heard pots being banged and cupboards being smashed shut as me sister sat in her room watching TV, undisturbed by her father. I heard me step-dad shouting at me mum and heard her in tears, and I felt awful. Then everything cooled off for a while. I couldn't hear any more commotion, just an air of tension around the house, which was nothing unusual when I was there.

I decided to go out and see a friend. I kissed me Mum goodbye.

When I returned, I walked up the stairs, and I could hear me mum crying. Sniffles and weeps were coming from her bedroom, and I could hear my step-dad moaning at her about me being in the house, about me making a mess in the kitchen and not tidying it up, about my heavy breathing when I did press-ups on the upstairs landing. I just stood there and thought - I'm not your bitch, I'm not gonna spend hours cooking a meal for you and the family and then clean it up whilst two-able bodied people ungratefully eat what I've made. **I'm not your bitch, I'm not your bitch,** I don't care if you have been at work all day, I've been cleaning your shit hole of a house and looking after my dying mother.

But as usual, my step-dad was working in an office all day, and unless I was doing what he classed as work I was a 'lazy cunt' and needed to be doing more around the house. I was often told I was a student bum and needed to get a job and that all universities were just a joke. That's all I heard growing up; 'Get a job, get a job.' never 'What do you want to do?' or 'What's your passion?' just, 'Get a job.'

FUCK OFF, I would think. FUCK OFF, FUCK OFF, FUCK OFF, FUCK OFF, FUCK OFF, FUCK OFF, FUCK OFF, FUCK OFF, FUCK OFF!!!

(When I go back there in my head I can feel the pain, frustration and anger I would feel at the time. It makes my skin crawl and my body tense. The desire to destroy something or beat something to death would be trying to explode from my body, and I would have to try so hard to keep it at bay.)

As I listened to my mother's cries, I decided I had to leave.

It broke my heart, but I thought it was best for me not to be there. All I wanted to do was look after me mum, but I felt my presence in the house was actually making it worse for her. I was scared that if my step-dad pushed me any further, I might snap and kick the shit out of him. Doing that would make the situation even worse, and I wanted me Mum to be in as calm and peaceful environment as possible. Heart-wrenchingly, I decided this was without me there, and I broke inside. I felt disabled, confined, restricted, debilitated and so, so, so frustrated. Then next day I left for London to buy myself a bed and try and find somewhere to call home.

MACHU PICCHU, THE JOURNEY, MAY 2013

When I arrived in Cusco, I was internally wrangling with myself. I was so eager to do Ayahuasca. I wanted to know which direction I should take my life. I wanted to be able to make decisions without going crazy. I was hoping beyond hope that the sacred vine would show me a path. I was hoping for some cognitive process which would allow the penny to drop and for all the things I had done in life to come together and make sense. I wanted to become whatever I was put on this planet to become.

I'd heard that a place just outside Cusco called Pisac had ceremonies. I didn't know what to do. I was walking into Cusco centre carrying my huge bags after my long bus ride from Nazca. The bag made me feel bogged down, heavy and sluggish. I'd heard Cusco was the most beautiful city in Peru, so far all I could see was mess and dirt.

I was heading to find Joe and Elle the Australians, who had booked me on the Machu Picchu Trek. All of a sudden, I saw a bus with 'Pisac' written on it. Decision made, I jumped on and was once again thrust into the crazy would of Latin American bus journeys. The drive was breath-taking; green lush jagged mountains similar to the pictures you see of Machu Picchu were all around me.

The hills changed shape with every vicious bend we took. I sat hoping my bag was ok on the roof as all sorts of things were going on around me to stimulate my senses. There were people selling ice treats and food, all being shoved through the windows at you, chickens were getting on, there were people with no shoes and ragged clothes, traditionally dressed folk and then a few people with Armani or Abercrombie and Fitch plastered all over their attire. People chatted, some carried traditional tools, ladies carried baskets on their heads, and a young school girl sat in front of me watching music videos on her laptop as myself and everyone close by looked on with transfixed stares at the moving screen as if possessed.

I arrived in the sacred valley town of Pisac with a name of a person and a place that I'd got off a girl I'd met back in San Marcos. I stumbled into a couple who told me about some Ayahuasca ceremonies coming up. I was closing in on my kill. My head was going to be clear again soon. Then I bumped into a group of lads who 'welcomed home'd' me up like they had done at the Rainbow gathering in Mexico. They told me they had an ashram with yoga and meditation down the road and I could stay there if I wanted.

'Maybe,' I said, as I was focused on Ayahuasca.

I was directed to Ayahuasca Wasi, who were the main source of information and had ceremonies on their premises. They had one ceremony coming up in a couple of days. I thought I'd think it over, so I headed for the ashram. No one was there, but the door was open, so I poked my head in like Little Red Riding Hood and discovered a beautiful house.

I called out for people, but no one was home.

There was an altar in the middle of the room where most people would have their TV. It was showered with crystals, mandalas and candles. It was too inviting, and the energy of the place was so pure in comparison to what I had witnessed over the last few days.

I stayed in the ashram for a couple of days. A Canadian called Dennis, and a guy from Bristol called Kyle were its permanent residents. Pisac was a lot bigger than I thought and had quite a large population of alternative, spiritually-minded westerners, plus lots and lots of locals.

That day I climbed the citadel which took a few hours of scraping through loads of sharp prickly bushes. I took the locals' path and saved myself some money. It was so steep, but the views got more and more spectacular the further I went.

At the top, magnificent panoramic views flooded my eyes. Picturesque stone terraced patterned fields were everywhere, and each had been built with floating stairs to travel up. The piece de resistance was the Temple of the Sun towards the top of the mountain. Its intricate buildings were spread out over a small, flat area.

I sat and meditated, trying not to think about home and Fhian. She was never out of my mind. Poems and songs about her constantly raced through the ether as I meditated and tried to reduce the internal noise.

I sped back down the mountain to make some guacamole for a party I had been invited to that evening. Right at the bottom of the hill, I slipped, catching my right arm on a really spiky bush. Three weeks later, I was still picking out blackthorns that had porcupined my hand, arm and wrist.

On the way down, I was thinking about Fhian and wanting to be near her again. It got me thinking about this invisible cord we have that can stretch any length, to any planet, any solar system or galaxy, even to other dimensions and realms of awareness. It's that connection you have to someone you love when you are far away from them. You can feel it, and you can feel when they are thinking about you, and you know they can feel you when you think of them. It's like they are with you. I was pining for my girl, and I wrote a little poem about my thoughts:

One Pulse
Our hearts beat as one
My heart vibrating, pulsating
Sending you messages
Like texting would
The frequencies we send
Emitted all over the universe
But it's a private channel
Only we can tune in
We feel the beating, vibrating, pulsating sensation
Its message sent
Like two radio antennas
We wait for beta rays that penetrate
Signal sent message received
Our knowing love will never leave
From across the globe
We feel each other's hearts bleed
The anguish and torment, there is no need
Like salt and pepper
We need to be back together
Message sent
Message received

I decided to delay the Ayahuasca until I was in the jungle so I would experience the most authentic journey for my first time. It was a tough call as my whole trip was geared towards my meeting with this great teacher. I was disciplined and decided that another week or so would not cause me too much further pain and insanity.

The party that night was for a girl from New York who was leaving town. I ate some amazing food in a really cool little ornate wooden house which had cushioned beds in an L-shape pushed against the wall downstairs. Within half an hour of getting there, I was fully engulfed in this massive cuddle puddle. Everyone was cuddled up to everyone else. People arrived late to the party, and at first they were shocked by the lack of action, but straight away they jumped in and became part of the L-shaped cuddle puddle. It was like a motionless spooning conga line. I was kind of sad to be leaving the newest group of beautifulness I'd met, but I was booked on the trek with Elle and Joe so needed to leave the next morning for Cusco.

I left the party early with a beautiful American girl who I'd been spooning in the cuddle puddle. I was very attracted to her; she and was totally my type. She was stunningly beautiful and had the perfect slender figure and skin that I would usually just want to devour. Her scent was like the intoxicating smell of femininity floating through a mountain top covered in rose petals. It was interesting that I was just appreciating her for being beautiful and not thinking, how do I get to devour her and what's my next move to get in her pants? She wanted to leave early to go and meditate together and have an early night. The signs were there, but not only was I on my sex ban; my heart was firmly with Fhian again, and it would have felt like cheating, which was something I was trying to eradicate from my life.

I took the beautiful lady through a guided meditation, and although my thoughts did occasionally wander to the side of sexual fantasy, I managed to focus on the meditation. Afterwards we had a huge hug and went to our separate rooms. I wasn't kicking myself for not taking what was on offer, I was actually kind of proud of myself for not breaking my vow when temptation dangled its ever-so-tempting, succulently scented fruit.

The next morning started with meditation for an hour and then yoga. I got to Cusco, traipsed across the city with my baggage, wishing I could travel light like a proper yogi and found the hostel currently housing the Aussies. We went for a walk to this crazy market looking for San Pedro, which is natural mescaline I had been reading about in Aldous Huxley's *Heaven and Hell and The Doors of Perception.*

The market was selling everything you could imagine. The meat section made me heave from the smell, and if there was anything I needed to confirm my commitment to vegetarianism, that was it.

Then there was witches' lane which sold all the natural medicines, including San Pedro. You could even buy Ayahuasca. It felt like the seedy part of the market, and an air of magic filled you as you lingered.

We bought our supplies for the trek and headed for the Plaza De Arams, the central point of the city. I was starting to see some of its beauty; the cobbled streets, the little bridges and tunnels and beautiful fountains. We approached a tunnel, and suddenly my hair was full of crumbs, a woman barged into me. What was a calm setting was now a hustle as two women were around me and my hands were in my hair. I felt someone go for my back pocket. As my hand arrived, I realised my phone was still there. I reached for my other back pocket, and my wallet had gone. Frantically I knew something weird was going on; the ladies' hands were all over me, my hair was full of stuff, and I was trying to regain some level of control. The next thing I know, the ladies had disappeared into the crowd, the crumb droppers from above were nowhere to be seen, and I realised I had put my wallet in my bag three minutes earlier.

Elle, Joe and myself were stunned. They had no idea they'd attempted to rob me. Good trick though, I thought, get the tall guy to put his hands in his hair by dropping bread crumbs from a bridge and get short little fat ladies to go for his pockets. Bad luck Peruvian thieves — Manchester boys aren't that easy to rob!

Having eluded the complete pain in the arse that would have been having my wallet and phone stolen, I decided to find solace in Jesus. There was a statue not unlike the one in Rio, and Jesus towered over the city. I climbed the steep cobbled streets passing beautifully dressed Inca ladies and flamboyantly decorated llamas.

I got to Jesus, lay underneath him and drifted off. I was meditating with the big man, layers of energy were passing over my body. I had no idea what was going on or what it meant, but the deeper I went, the more beautiful it felt. The next thing I knew, a huge crucifix was being lowered down towards me by a group of locals. I thought maybe this was my time, my time to become the son of God to replicate and experience Jesus's pain and give the people salvation.

Would the people carrying the cross be kind enough to nail my hands and feet to the wood?

I scurried underneath, getting out of the way of the huge cross that was being placed on the ground for some kind of ceremony. As my hair fell towards my shoulders, many of the cross-bearers did a double-take and started chatting in Spanish, and all laughed. Maybe it was something like 'We have just resurrected Jesus by presenting him with the option of the cross again?'

I spoke to Fhain that evening via Skype as it would be the last time we would be able to talk for five or six days. She wanted to know when I was doing the Ayahuasca and was a bit disappointed I hadn't already taken part in a ceremony.

I wanted it to confirm the feelings that I had for her, not trusting my own mind, to confirm she was the girl I was going to adventure through life with.

It was 3 am, and Elle and Joe and myself made our way to meet our group. It was dark, and the bus ride would take three hours to get to our starting point. We arrived in this little village just after sunrise and started to mingle with the rest of the group. They were a mix of western people from Australia, the US, Finland, Yorkshire, Sweden and Germany.

The next five days consisted of at least ten hours of walking a day. At times I felt like I was in the Lake District in England as the scenery was so similar, with beautiful streams flowing crystal clear drinkable water past the glittering rocks below. The group dynamic worked, and everyone was getting on great. The guides were funny and every time we would sit down to eat Fran would say, 'Now you are eating,' and when we would sit down after four hours walking he would say, 'Now you are relaxing,' and when we had finished our food he would say, 'Now you are enjoying, enjoying.'

I really liked another Aussie couple, Liam and Carly. Liam was a carpenter and built houses back home from a lot of reclaimed materials. He'd lived in warehouses that he and his friends had converted. He had also built lots of sustainable and eco-buildings and was fascinated with the work I had been doing with Earthships. They had flown into Chile, bought an old camper van and converted it into a mobile home and coffee shop. They had been giving away free coffee on their travels through Chile, Argentina and Bolivia and into Peru. I was a little bit in love with this couple, and again my thoughts drifted off to my love and the things we could do with our lives together. We slept in tents, and I was given a wife to sleep with who was a lesbian from Austria.

It was a constant incline for the first two days, walking through post-glacial ravines. There were drastic changes in scenery going from the almost-tropics where we had begun to the random rock-laden plateaus a few miles up. Ragged summits of different mountains fenced the perimeter of the plateaus and seemed to be leaning over to peer at the human ants making their way to the sacred Machu Picchu, the way pilgrims had done for thousands of years.

On the third day, we reached our highest point, the summit of Salkantay. We were at an altitude of four thousand, six hundred metres, and it was cold. Towering above us were even bigger mountains, one of which had never been conquered. The year before, two very experienced Japanese climbers had died trying, their bodies never recovered.

Fran explained some aspects of Inca history and its spirituality. He told us about the symbols used and the connection to earth, sky, wind, sun, moon and spirit. They seemed similar to Pagan symbols, ceremonies and the worship of Mother Earth. Lots of the patterns he drew had a very Ancient Egyptian feel about them. Fran took the information he was giving us very seriously, and you could see that he was moved very deeply.

After our lecture, we were all told to collect a small rock, and together we said a sacred prayer whilst holding it. Then we placed each other's stones on top of one another to build our own little towers, just like I had seen in Sedona.

It was now time for the descent and the final push for Machu Picchu. We again hit tropical rain forest, and wild strawberries, bananas, avocados and papaya grew everywhere. Little tuck shops would sell us refreshments in the middle of nowhere, and I remember whilst we were in one of the most desolate spots of the whole trek, a family of mother, father and child sold fabric, pashminas, gloves and jewellery. They were draped in layer upon layer of traditional clothing to keep them warm. They were all so small, the father barely reached five foot.

We arrived at the tourist town at the foot of Machu Picchu completely exhausted. Most people had varying injuries, and my Achilles tendon had actually started to squeak. The next morning, we were up at 4 am as the gates to Machu Picchu opened at five. In the pitch-black we stood waiting so we could ascend the steep 1900 steps to the ancient ruins whilst the sun was rising.

Around fifty people were queuing to be one of the first to reach the summit and earn the right to enter Machu Picchu. This was the final push for the reward of the spectacular famous views and energy of these famous ruins.

It is said that pilgrims had to earn permission to seek the special powers of Machu Picchu and trekking for five days was the only way the gods would respect and permit your entrance. After an hour of gruelling step after step after step up the steeper and steeper steps, I finally reached the entrance to the ruins. My Achilles was making this almost robotic sound as the tendons and ligaments scurried around trying to fix themselves and hang on for dear life as they were stretched to their limits.

The fifty step-climbers lingered around the entrance. Other tourists started to arrive via the coaches and buses that lined the streets of the town below. As we all stood there tired and sweaty, the fresh-faced and limbed bus riders couldn't comprehend the lack of an organised queue system, so pushed their way to the front with disgusted and disgruntled faces as if they had just earned the right to be the first into the ruins by taking a train from Cusco and a coach up the tiresome winding road. I smiled and nodded and actually laughed at the absurdity of these trigger-happy camera-holding professional tourists.

Machu Picchu had this air of magnificence about it. The clouds passed by slowly as if they were respecting this sacred place on tiptoe. Everything seemed to slow down. Even a guy who was dressed as superman seemed less funny than it typically would have been.

The Aussies said, 'He's definitely Australian.'

Visual perfection splattered into my mind, and the stone buildings atop this huge mountain hidden from the world below made me wonder of times gone by. Other mountains surrounded us, and it felt like we were enclosed in a high-altitude world that made its own sense. A haze filled my mind, and I tried and connect with the energies of the mountain and the ancient civilisation.

It was difficult with this mass of tourists, and my confidence wasn't as strong, given that I was with regular people and not my typically awakened souls. I stood and pondered how this place would have worked. How it would have been as the bustling capital of the Inca Empire and what secrets had they had about the world and the universe? I looked out at the famous image, which actually isn't the peak of Machu Picchu but is, in fact, the peak of Wayna Picchu.

We arrived back in Cusco after a train journey that is said to be the most spectacular and breath-taking in the world. I couldn't agree or disagree with this as we were travelling late at night. I assumed it couldn't be as breath-taking as the five-day trek we had just done.

I was very excited!!! My next port of call was to be Iquitos in the jungle and finding the Ayahuasca lady, Otilia, my French friends Grieg and Marie had recommended to me all those months ago in Belize. I spent a couple of days in Cusco with the guys from the trek, and we all hung out drinking coffee in Liam and Carly's van.

After realising you couldn't fly directly to Iquitos from Cusco, I got a twenty-four-hour coach to Lima. There were options to get boats along the Amazon from different places, and they took around five to ten days. I was in a hurry to arrive, so I decided I would take the boat back. Rule, Livika and Tank from the trek were all also going to Iquitos, so we jumped on the bus together.

I had received a message via Facebook whilst I was in Nazca from a girl called Anaze Izquierdo, and it read:

'Hi Liam, I know you don't know me but I think I took the movie The Orgasm Diary ('brilliantlove') too far. It is one of my favourite movies (I still believe in teenage love), well I realise that you are in Peru now, probably Lima, a thing that is so surreal for me. I would love to meet you (I hate sounding like a groupie) So... hope to have an answer! Hugs!'

I'd assumed that I wouldn't be going back to Lima as I thought I could go straight to Iquitos so I'd had to say, 'Glad you liked the movie, but I won't be coming back that way.'

Still, it felt amazing that a Peruvian girl had seen the movie and seen that I was in Peru via Facebook and contacted me. However, I was now heading back to Lima as this was the only route to Iquitos. I arrived there with Rule, Livika and Tank after sitting for twenty-four hours at the back of a coach that stank of piss.

We had no idea where we were, so we wandered the streets looking for a place with internet so we could book flights for that day. We walked aimlessly for about an hour until we finally found an internet cafe.

I decided to contact Anaze and try to meet up for a while and say hello. She got straight back to me, and when we told her where we were, she said, 'You need to get out of that area, it is so dangerous. Get the guy in the shop to order you a taxi and don't walk the streets.'

We had no idea the place was dangerous. It seemed fine when we were walking, and we pretty much had a sign that said 'rich westerners' on our backs in the form of our large rucksacks and pasty white faces.

Anaze directed us to meet her, and we jumped in a cab.

We waited outside a KFC in what seemed a quite commercial part of the city. Rule and I practised handstands as we waited. She arrived on the back of a huge Harley Davidson being driven by an equally large, huge moustached biker, who could have easily passed for a member of Hells Angels. I hugged Anaze and shook the biker guy's hand that dwarfed mine into insignificance.

She was like a giddy school girl and kept saying, 'this is so weird.'

It was my first encounter with a fan, and her reaction was as if she knew me but couldn't quite believe I was real.

She wasn't a silly young bimbo fan, but a highly intelligent woman who had a massive passion for independent cinema. She was a proper hipster with nice tattoos and piercings, with really dark short hair and striking brown eyes. She was an artist and specialised in performance art and was born and bred in Lima. We walked the American block style streets looking for somewhere to eat. It was Mother's Day and a national holiday, so everywhere was shut. Rule and Livika decided to get to the airport early and wanted to leave me alone with my new friend.

We walked and talked and as everywhere was shut we headed back to her place to drink some tea. As we walked, we saw Anaze's boyfriend across the street, who she told me was also a massive fan. She said that 'brilliantlove' was their favourite film and that they'd fallen in love while watching it. This was one of the most beautiful things I'd ever heard, and it made me feel so grateful to all the amazing people I'd made the film with.

I thought it would be funny to approach her boyfriend from behind and say hello. Surprised and shocked, he was kind of lost for words and eventually in his American accent said, 'Wow man I can't believe you're here.'

They both did the giddy thing again and kind of looked at me with excited eyes as if I was some kind of animal in a zoo. Their excited energy was contagious, and I was buzzing off the spectacle of the situation.

Her boyfriend, Parker, was an American studying photography in Lima. He had this huge black beard and short hair on top and these dark sunken eyes, again his look was complete hipster. They had been together for eighteen months, and after more 'Wow man, this is amazing,' they both started to become normal again. I could kind of see how me being there had triggered thoughts of that wild love they'd had at the start of their relationship. Parker then said, 'I have a tattoo of you on my leg dude.'

I laughed and said, 'Yeah, right.'

He said, 'No, seriously, I do.'

I unbelievingly nodded, thinking it was just a wind-up, but they were both adamant (not the 80s pop star).

He said, 'Anaze tattooed it, it's the first things she's done, it's pretty awesome.'

I still thought it was bullshit and said 'You can show me when we get to your place.'

Their place was a tiny flat with two rooms and a bathroom, no kitchen and the room they shared only had a single bed. It was like a trippy version of the room my character Manchester shared with his girlfriend Noon in 'brilliantlove'. These guys, however, lived as part of society in an apartment block and not in the secluded Northumberland countryside Manchester and Noon sauntered through in the film.

They made me tea, and I sat on this small stool in their room as they fussed about, half trying to tidy the place for their guest.

They sat on the bed, and I imagined what they got up to with each other in this place, watching my naked body and a film made with so much love.

I considered whether they wanted some kind of kinky threesome with me. In a way, I'd been present in the consecration of their early love. In my non-sabbatical state of yesteryear, I may have considered it, but my heart was fully attached to my girl. Although my mind still considered these things, I knew even if it was offered, I would refuse.

We talked film and how they came to hear about 'brilliantlove'.

It had been given to them by a friend who said 'You guys have to watch this', and they did, again and again, and again. They asked about all aspects of the movie, and they couldn't believe it hadn't been more popular.

Memories were returning of making the film, the amazingly loving people and the environment in which it had been made and the way that had been infused into the finished product. They loved the stories of how things were done on set and their enthusiasm for the film made me really proud. It made all the dark times of being an actor seem worthwhile.

'So when do I get to see the tattoo?'

'Now, if you want.' Parker pulled down his jeans.

I was hoping this was real and not a ploy for him to be able to remove his pants and instigate the threesome. He didn't, and as he seductively lowered his jeans, he revealed a huge tattoo of the 'brilliantlove' poster on his left thigh. It was crazy to see my face on someone's leg. I couldn't believe what I was seeing, and I had a kind of giddy glee tingling through my body. There was an artist's impression of me holding a love heart with my co-star, Nancy, who was riding a bike with a cat for a head.

It was a perfect copy of the picture and a crazy situation, one I could never even have dreamed of or imagined. It was surreal to be sitting in a flat with an American and a Peruvian I'd just met in Lima via Facebook and him having his pants around his ankles and me kneeling down close to his crotch, pointing, having my picture taken with a tattoo of me on his leg.

Surreal, but nice. After the excitement had died down, they took me to the bus stop and off I went in search of what I was really in this part of the world for.

CHAPTER 20
MUM 3,
LIFE, 2007

I was in Kingston with Renie buying stuff for me new house when I got a phone call from me step-dad. '

You need to come home. She has gotten a lot worse.'

It sounded final! The day before she had sounded okay. I'd spoken to her, there was no panic, she was just going through the treatment. Now I was getting the feeling that this was it. I leaned against the Argos window and broke down. I felt like someone had just blasted my kneecaps with a shotgun as I tried to keep myself upright, tears streamed down my face. Passers-by looked at me awkwardly.

Renie held me, and I fell to pieces.

That afternoon, I walked into the specialist lung cancer centre at Wythenshawe Hospital. Me mum had been in the main ward previously. I was taken into a private room. When I entered it was full of people, and I thought, fuck, fuck, fuck, this is it, FUCK!

I didn't really take anyone in. I went to me mum and hugged her. Emotion raced through my whole body, from the depths of my gut, pain raced up my stomach, into my chest, up my throat, and I had to stop myself from being sick.

I held her, and she just about managed to say, 'Hiya, luv.'

As I came out of the hug, I noticed her stomach was really inflated, and she looked like she had been pumped up like a balloon. I looked into her eyes and could see that she wasn't really there. She was drifting in and out of consciousness, and when she was conscious, she was really confused and struggling to make sense of the world around her.

As I looked at the faces in the room, I saw me nanna, me two aunties, me uncles, me sister, me step-dad, me cousins and me nanna's sister. The only time the family was together like this was for a fleeting twenty minutes at me nanna's on Christmas morning. Their presence made me feel this was big, that this could be the end and why everyone wanted to be near her.

Drained and gloomy tear-filled hugs greeted me from my

relatives as I made my way around the room saying hello. I then realised some of these people didn't even speak to each other and that they were putting their differences aside to be here and be civil in me Mum's hour of need. I also thought about how much me step-dad disliked most of me mum's family and how he'd always had something negative to say about them whilst I was growing up. I'd thought it was normal to slag people off and put them down. Being in this room must have made him uncomfortable.

Then I looked around and realised in the midst of all these people with their childish grudges towards one another, that I was actually on good terms with them all. I didn't have a problem with any of them, and neither did me Mum. She was the linchpin of her family. She brought them all together.

I took the seat to my mother's left, and my step-dad sat to her right. My mother was in the middle of us again, battling to stay alive and keeping us from clawing out each other's eyes. Even then I felt uncomfortable, trying to give me Mum the love I wanted to give her. Feeling conscious of him looking at me and judging my level of emotion and making me aware of my behaviour, so I was unable to fully feel the moment.

Me step-dad told me she had taken a real turn for the worse yesterday and had started to deteriorate. He still seemed to think she would be okay and that she needed some time for the drugs to take effect. This gave me some hope. I couldn't stand seeing her there like this, it shattered me.

They told me she was being pumped full of morphine to take away the pain, and that's why she seemed like she was in another world. My inquisitive drug-mind wanted to be in this world with her, away from the misery of the people in the room. Maybe they put us on morphine whilst we are dying so that we can't tell the people around us how the transition to death feels and how the other realm looks so beautiful.

The severity of the situation hit home when my step-dad's brother and wife came into the room. Me Mum had managed to gain some form of consciousness and noticed them as they came in. She looked around and saw the room full of people and said, 'What's happening?' She started to cry, moan and scream a little.

'Why is everyone here? It's really scaring me,' she sobbed. I went to her and told her it would be okay and that there was nothing to be scared of. I stroked her head and her arm as she relaxed back into a drug-induced sleep. I then became aware of this peculiar smell that was in the room. The only time I had smelt anything similar was when our Rottweiler, Lucy had died slowly on our couch ten years ago.

This smell has not left my mind since.

All I can really remember from this point on was all the family being around and conversations and debates being had about second-hand information that had been given by my step-dad about what the doctors had said. He told us they needed to do more tests, but she should be okay for now and that she would get stronger soon.

Everyone thought it seemed more serious.

The next day, the close family members were called into a room with the doctor. All I remember is that the doctor said the cancer had gotten a lot more aggressive and she wasn't responding to the treatment. He said that there was nothing else they could do for her.

My world shattered.

Everyone in the room gasped. My heart jumped into my mouth, and I managed to splutter out, 'How long does she have left?' *(I break down again as I write recalling this for the first time in a very long time).* He said it could be any time in the next couple of days, but they expect her lungs to shut down in the next few hours.

At this point, my sister got up and ran out of the room. *(Shit this is hard.)* I got up and followed her. She was inconsolable. I had to bury what I was feeling to be strong for my sister. I hold her, tears and snot covering my T-shirt as she sobs deep loud painful sobs. My tears fall onto the top of her head, soaking her hair and I rock her the way me Mum rocked us both when we were upset.

Finally, my aunty and step-dad came out of the room and took my sister off me. I turned and ran, scurrying out of the hospital as fast as I could, as if I was going to shit myself or be sick. I felt like was going to disintegrate, something needed to come out of me and had no idea what it was. I needed an exit so that something could exit me.

I see the exit door and race towards it hoping the sensor on the automatic doors recognises me before I run straight into them and knock myself out.

Fortunately, they did.

I got outside and ran onto the grass, collapsing on my knees as I let out a shriek, unlike any sound I have ever made before. I started beating the grass and mud in front of me as all this pain and sadness inside flooded out of me in convulsions. I didn't know what to do with my body or my face or my limbs, it was like I was not in control. I beat and shook and cried and wept and sobbed and spluttered and blubbered and coughed and snotted and hated and pleaded. Wave after wave of emotion flooded up my spine, making my whole torso shake and vibrate as my bodily fluids mixed with the grass and mud below me. I then realised it was raining hard and I had slid on my knees in the most dramatic of fashions onto Manchester's typically piss-wet-through earth.

I took shelter under a tree while I came to terms with the severity of what I had just been told.

Everything was fucked.

I had no idea what I was going to do without her. It was only in the three years since I had left home that we had started to build up our relationship again and now its fucked, over, gone, finished, ca-fucking-put. I didn't want to be here anymore. I wanted to go with her to wherever she was going. I didn't want her to leave me alone. I'd always been with her, she couldn't leave me, she had to take me too.

My future life flashed before my eyes, and it seemed pointless without me Mum. Everything I had ever wanted in life was to make her proud and to be able to eventually support her financially so I could get her away from me step-dad and all the running around she did for everyone. She'd never put herself first, it was always me or me sister. Then me nanna and me step-dad, her sisters and brothers, her friends...

Some would say this is selfless. I say it's selfish, because you can't truly love anyone or anything until you can love yourself, and my mother did not love herself.

I thought about her life and the two abusive marriages she'd had. Abusive in very different ways, but still very unhappy and difficult. I wondered why she had gone into these relationships, I wondered why someone as wonderful as my mother had married my father, and I wondered why she had married someone like my step-dad. He was an alcoholic like me grandad. Not to the extent of always being in the pub and not providing for his family like me Grandad, but to the extent of getting drunk seven nights a week. Starting with beer, then wine, then spirits and then one of us would find him asleep on the couch with a whiskey in his hand in the early hours of the morning, the TV still on flickering light to the outside world.

All this flashed through my head. Why, why, why had she not looked after herself? Why, why, why all this abuse? Why, why, why was she about to die? I looked at her life, and it made me think she'd just had enough. She was unwilling to let go of all the things that upset her, so by not letting go she'd killed herself. By not being strong and looking after the most important person in her life (her) she had gotten ill and was about to die.

I started to get a bit angry towards her for leaving me for not having looked after herself.

I sat under my tree and just pondered and pondered. I pondered all of our life together and how on Earth I would get through this. I found some light in the fact that this was the easiest way for it to happen. A mother should die before her children. I would be robbed of this amazing woman, but I felt relieved that I hadn't died before her, as I don't think she would have been able to cope.

I was sad that my mother was scared of death, and I wished she could have embraced it. More than anything in the world I wanted her back just for a minute so I could tell her I loved her and so that I could say goodbye, looking into her knowing it was her I was talking to and not the drugs. I wanted that split second of connection with my everything, with my one and only Mum.

I sat there under that tree for hours until someone came to get me and bring me inside because they thought she might be about to die. I got back into the room, and everyone was standing around. I assumed my place to her left and watched as her breathing struggled more and more. This went on and on, and I put my head against hers, trying to block out the disapproving looks from my step-dad. I told her it was okay to go, that we all loved her and that she just let go. I kept saying this over and over, even though it was making some people uncomfortable. I was telling her to not fight it and that we knew she was strong. The room was filled with people all anticipating her last breath. I kept saying over and over. 'It's okay, Mum, we love you, just let go, don't fight it, just let go.'

That last breath didn't come and scares like this came every few hours as we waited for the now-inevitable end.

It ended up taking four days. Every now and then I would get fetched from outside to say they thought she was going. At times when I was at her bedside, I would send for the family scattered around the building because the erratic breathing would start again.

We were all at the hospital twenty-four hours a day. There was nothing any of us could do. We were just waiting for that last breath, for that passing, for the functioning body to no longer function at all and start to disintegrate.

People talk about not being able to eat at these deeply emotional times. I was eating loads, and I'd sweet-talked all the catering staff into giving me and my family nice warm meals three times a day for free. I would sit with different family members and reminisce about times we'd had with me Mum. We would laugh so much, and it brought light to this very dark situation.

I discovered that when we were told by the doctor me Mum was going to die, after me and a few others ran out, me nanna turned to one of me aunties and said, 'What did he say? I didn't have my hearing aid turned on?' and my auntie had to break the news for a second time. This made us laugh a lot.

She was deeply sedated, and there was no communication since that first 'Hiya, luv,' when I arrived back from London. Other patients on the ward would chat to me outside, and I would tell them me mum was dying. They would stand there smoking and say there was no point stopping now as they were going to die soon and it was the only thing that kept them going. I was angry at this illness, and because it was lung cancer, I knew people would assume she was a smoker, which she wasn't. These other people had killed themselves with tobacco. My mum didn't smoke, but maybe she did kill herself by not changing her life.

The more time we all spent together at the hospital, the more frustrated we started to get. We were basically waiting for her to die. There was no way of her pulling it round. The doctors had said that was it, there was no chance it was over, she was going to die, so we were just waiting.

I wanted to put her out of her misery.

She looked like she was in so much discomfort, filled with morphine, bloated with fluid, breathing with difficulty and having no control over her bodily functions. Any other animal would be put out of its misery, but we keep ours alive so they can suffer. The pain is still there but drowned in morphine.

Why are we not allowed to feel pain in this society? Why must it always be sedated, not dealt with and covered up?

Please, God, let me feel my pain, let me process it. Please let me feel my pain when I die. Please put me out of my misery if it gets too much.

It crossed my mind a lot as I sat there and waited for her to die, breathing in that smell of imminent death and listening to the horrific sound her breath was making.

I was sitting there with my Aunty Brenda, and we were looking at me Mum. We were talking, and she seemed in so much discomfort that it didn't seem fair, it was like nothing of her worked, and this stench of death was unbearable. The sound of pain in the form of breath, the life force was being cut. It cut me each time she breathed. I could feel this sadness and her need to be released from this no-longer functioning chalice she'd called home for the last fifty-four years.

As I watched, I was urged to take the pillow and cover her face with it until the pain was no more. To cry and weep as I put my mother out of her misery and allowed her to pass over with some level of dignity by the morals of her only son and not the morals and rules of a western system of medicine which is primarily a business and a way of eradicating symptoms, rather than curing or preventing illness in the first place. I realised that for this system to start preventing certain illnesses, there had to be a financial benefit. Things in the capitalist world had to be driven by financial gain, and it was no different in the health industry.

I sat there, and I knew it was the best thing to do, I knew it was what my intuition wanted me to do, I knew my mother would have wanted to be put out of her misery, I hoped my family would understand. I wondered who here should have been making decisions for me Mum, I wondered who was most important to her. I knew my step-dad had been the point of reference for the doctors, but I wondered if this was for the best.

I started to think about what he had kept from us about the severity of the illness. I knew he was a man incapable of talking about feelings and was in denial about many things. He would only hear what he wanted to hear and instantly delete what didn't fit into his opinion or perception of the world.

When our dog, Lucy was dying of cancer, she had this massive tumour on her face that was getting bigger and bigger. It would weep pus, and the smell was horrendous. The whole house would stink, and the smell made you heave when you were in the same room as her. People would come into the house and almost vomit.

When we brought it up with him, he would say he couldn't

smell anything and we would start to think it was us being oversensitive.

It wasn't.

He would just pretend it wasn't there, pretend he couldn't smell it.

People would come to the house and say, 'Oh my God, what's that smell?' and want to leave. We asked them if it was as bad as we thought and they would say, 'Yes it's the worst smell I've ever smelt.'

He wouldn't have it. Everyone thought it was cruel keeping her alive as it was evident she was in so much pain. We were all being affected by the smell and the cries of anguish that she made if she knocked the lump. But he held onto this blinded view that she wasn't suffering, he denied there was any bad smell, he denied she needed to be put out of her misery, and he ignored people's opinions that it wasn't fair. Like in all situations, he was unapproachable for a discussion and just dismissed people if they brought it up.

I started to wonder what he had kept from us about my mother's plight. Had he known for a while that she was going to die? Had he been told and, like with Lucy, been so much in denial that he had convinced himself of another story? Should someone else have been closest to the doctors, so the rest of the family had been more prepared for that terrible and shocking news? The day I'd arrived he'd said she was just in a bad place with treatment and that she would get better. This must have been completely wrong, as hours later the doctor told us that was it, she had days, if not hours.

I fought with my instinct and intuition to put that pillow over her face. Social rules and ramifications were the only things holding me back, knowing my mother wouldn't want me going to prison for her. I looked at my Aunty Brenda, and something in me thought she was thinking the same thing. Years after when I brought it up she said yes she was, she said it was killing her inside to see my mother like that, and she had fought such a battle inside to not place that pillow over her face when I'd left the room.

I felt useless, I felt controlled, I felt restricted, I felt like I was failing her. I felt anger at the system, I felt anger at everyone accepting this was the way things should be. How had society gotten to the stage where this is the way we sent people off, in a world of drugs and altered states? Society looks down on those who take these drugs recreationally, but as we are dying, it's fine? It made no sense to me. I wanted to shake everyone; my whole family, this whole society, shake them into seeing how inhumane, unjust, unethical and ridiculous the way we let people die was. I didn't want this for myself. I wanted to die in an accident or peacefully in my bed. I wanted to feel death, to embrace it and experience it as I had experienced all the other parts of my life. Me Mum didn't like drugs, she wasn't a drug user, surely these states would be scary for her. Was her brain still functioning? Was she still having her own thoughts?

I pondered and pondered as I sat there, hour after hour, day after day, waiting for this powerful force in my life to leave me and to be gone. To be more at peace, dead.

Being gone and being dead, in my eyes meant that there was no longer physical pain, there was no longer misery and suffering, and she would no longer be part of this messed up world with its messed up people and messed up beliefs. I'd had enough of waiting for the inevitable. It was no longer my mother who lay there, it was something that was just about surviving, managing to cling on to life because of the uncertainty of what was to come next.

I wanted to get back to London and not be in this place anymore and try and get on with my life without her, away from this place where I found it so hard to breathe and away from this smell that somehow felt like it was draining the life out of me.

We had all become regular occupants of the Lung Cancer Unit. Most of us would spend the nights there, sleeping across chairs or falling asleep at my mother's bedside. We would take turns to go home and freshen up. On the fourth night, myself, my sister, stepdad, Aunty Brenda and Nanna were asleep in various parts of the hospital. I was lying across four chairs in the day room as I was shaken out of my sleep and told, 'She's gone, Liam, come and say goodbye.'

I jumped up and briskly walked into the room where my stepdad was at her side with my sister and my nanna. Something in the room had changed, a different feeling and atmosphere I couldn't put my finger on it.

My mother's body had started to turn grey; she was starting to get cold. The smell was still there, and I kissed her head and told her how much I loved her, more than all the world combined, she was my everything. Take all the rest away you are all I need, and now you are gone, and I have no one.

Tears streamed, not the dramatic tears and emotions that had exploded four days ago, but contented sobs of emotion slowly being released. They ran down my face and onto the floor. I held my sister, and I held my nanna and my Aunty Brenda. I didn't know what to do with my step-dad. I looked at my mother as parts of her turned blue and wondered how this could be, how could this be taken away from me? What would I do now?

We soon realised that this evening had been the first time that we had all been asleep. Before, one or more of us had been by her side twenty-four hours a day. That night we had all settled down and drifted off at various places around the hospital. It was the first time she had been left without someone looking over her and that had been the moment she had decided to pass, that had been her chance. She hadn't wanted to leave when we were awake around her, she wanted to be with the family and found it hard to tear herself away and let go. This had been her window, her opportunity, the moment that the least amount of drama would take place.

This was my Mum; she didn't like a fuss, she liked to fuss over everyone else. My hero, my warrior mum had been given hours to live by the doctors and had blasted it out for four days straight. She wanted to be there with her family who meant everything to her and whom she was the heartbeat of. I realised then that, without her, this would all fall apart. No one would make time for my nanna, and her house wouldn't be full with a passing trade of relatives. Me mum had held this together through all its turmoil. It was to take its true course now.

As her body got colder and colder and parts of her started to discolour, we decided to leave the hospital and head home, never to return to this room again. I kissed her forehead and left the body of the person who had been the only constant in my life to slowly rot and deteriorate.

We arrived back at the house with a deep gloom over us, and I wondered what my mother would want now. What would she want us to do? What would she want me to do? I started to think this all the time from that moment on.

As I lay down in my bed, I felt sorry for myself. The one thing in this world I could rely on, the one thing that would jump in front of a bus to save me was gone. I was alone in this world, and I was dreading everything I would do without her from that moment on.

IQUITOS, THE JOURNEY, MAY 2013

I had been told about a fantastic lady called Otillia, who lived at Kilometre 51, between Iquitos and Nakula. I found out about her from a French couple I'd met in Belize at the start of my trip. I told them of my desire to experience Ayahuasca, and they said that Otillia was one of the best. They'd drunk Ayahuasca with her and had had the most beautiful experience. They gave me the contact details of a friend called Bruno who lived in Iquitos and was something of an Ayahuasca connoisseur. They all firmly believed that Otillia was one of the most authentic in the whole of Peru. I had thought I was going to have to do a lot research and digging around to find a good shaman, so I felt completely blessed that within the first two weeks of my trip I had resolved that little dilemma.

After a few messages to Greg and Marie, I made contact with Bruno and headed to Iquitos with Rule, Livika and Tank. We arrived late after almost a day and a half of travelling from Cusco. We booked into a floating hostel and saw a monkey riding a dog. That evening we ate at a place called The Yellow Rose of Texas, apparently owned by an American guy — not from Texas — who didn't speak a word of Spanish after living here for twenty years. The Yellow Rose offered an Ayahuasca menu, which stated at the top of the page, NO SALT, NO SUGAR, NO OIL and NO SEX. My internal child chuckled away at the fact that the dish I'd ordered categorically contained no sex. I didn't want to break the sabbatical I had been on for the last five months.

Yes, no sex and no masturbation for that long.

Where does that unused fluid go?

Those who know me wouldn't believe it or fathom how I could do it as it was the longest I had gone without since I'd started twenty years ago. It actually wasn't much of a challenge, and I was surprised by how I seemed to be able to concentrate a lot better and not be constantly distracted by the people around me.

Iquitos seemed like a pretty big city, and it was crazy to think we were days from anywhere. After my dull, bland, dry meal I went to bed, excited to see what the Amazon looked like the next morning in the light of day.

I awoke to see the splendour of the jungle; it's still, lush waters, serenely supporting an array of floating plant life, the constant croaking of frogs and the small splashes as its rich content of fish sprang to the surface. It was something stunning and beautiful, something I'd always dreamt of seeing. It was like I was in in a trippy dream, mesmerised by the extreme mass of flowing water and the richness it carried. I sat and watched as next to me, a monkey chased a dog.

Puerto Belen is classed as the poorest of the barrios (slums/shanty towns), and we had been told by a lot of people not to head there without a guide, and even then to not carry any valuables. If anyone grabs your stuff just push them away and scream. I had everything valuable I owned on me, and we were getting deeper and deeper into the Puerto Belen's Market District. It seemed sketchy, but as usual I assumed the stories were exaggerated and if anything, the victims would have been middle-class westerners unable to carry themselves in such an area. They would not have grown up in the roulette wheel of smack and crack heads I had been accustomed to at Wythenshawe Market and Civic Centre, and the brutish nightlife that accompanied most drinking holes back home. This place seemed more accommodating and friendly but was it a thousand times dirtier.

The smell was intense. I was barefoot, trying to avoid the sludge that poured all over what remained of the road. A beautiful schoolboy with silky, jet black hair followed us and began to talk. He was about nine or ten and looked concerned. When we spoke, it came across that he was worried about our safety, telling us not to go any further. We did, as we were looking for the port and a boat to ride around the stilted slum houses of the Amazon, but he insisted we go back.

An old man with a walking stick pointed out the right direction, acting how to shrug off the thieves grabbing at your every possession. Reassured we thought, we've got this far let's just go for it.

We turned a corner, and there were vultures everywhere. The stench was stomach-churning, and the atmosphere became even eerier. There were people everywhere and kids playing in what could only be described as filth. The road and wooden benches were filled with blood, guts and entrails. The vultures would sweep down to feed on the animal offal that had been left all over the street, pouring out of black bin bags. Hundreds of vultures sat aloft buildings in lines, bringing an even darker and more sinister view to an already petrifying scene. We had resisted so far but what we were witnessing was so unlike anything our eyes had ever viewed before, so we instinctively pulled out our cameras and started to snap away, capturing this possibly once-in-a-lifetime moment. We knew this could lead to us being prey for the thieving human vultures that loomed, but first-world kids act in strange ways in dangerous places.

We passed this section, and it was like we'd completed a level on some mental computer game. Next, we were thrust into stalls crammed together and covered in canvas, overlapping each other to create a dark, dank, damp setting. The air tasted thick and stagnant. Meat in all its many varieties adorned wooden tables as far as the eye could see. People looked enquiringly at us, ladies laughed, revealing missing teeth and the occasional gold stud. Children looked like they were having so much fun in these somewhat desolate surroundings. Monkeys on leashes tiptoed around squeaking, rancid mangy dogs were everywhere (Livika kept saying 'minge dogs' which tickled me massively) and cats, rodents, and birds flitted about.

Then something I never wanted to see appeared in front of me.

It was a turtle without the shell, being sold as meat. It was a sorry sight; its pink, scrawny body with the feet and the head that we are used to seeing on display, but not its distinctive shell. It made my heart feel heavy.

Kids were all over the place. Babies lay flat fast asleep on wooden tables, as their mothers breastfed their siblings whilst serving a customer amid what a first worlder could only describe as 18th-century squalor.

We saw an opening to the river houses and escaped the madness. As we ran off, a guy grabbed us and told us not to go that way.

'It's dangerous.'

More dangerous than what we had just endured? Wow!

We then met a bloke called Marlon who sold us a boat tour of the floating barrios. We followed him through more madness to his awaiting brother, part of me thinking we were being taken to a place to become tomorrow's meat.

Everything was so dirty and chaotic, the people were all covered in filth, the streets the, stalls, everything was just rancid, and the people looked at us as if we were aliens.

We jumped onto Marlon's brother's boat.

It was our first time on the majestic Amazon, and once away from the market, a more serene setting encapsulated us. The calm water undulating around the stilted houses made an air of serenity surround us. The way the houses were positioned made it feel like the river was the street. They were simple wooden structures, and many of them had collapsed into the water. The whole place seemed to be full of life. Kids played everywhere, jumping from houses and boats into the water. We passed floating schools, a floating gas station and even a floating 24-hour club. As we passed, what looked like transvestites tried to encourage us to come in. They looked really high, so we declined. After a few hours out on the water and seeing Marlon and his brother's shared house, we headed back to the hostel.

I was starting to worry; I hadn't contacted Bruno. I wanted to get to Otillia as fast as I could. That was the only reason I was here; inner work, inner work I kept telling myself.

I emailed him that evening, and the next day I had a reply with a place and time to meet. Rule had been interested in trying Ayahuasca as a drug tourist rather than for a specific reason. He had told me about the cocaine bar he had been to in Bolivia where you get a table and can order as much cocaine as you want. This would have really appealed to me a few years ago. At the height of my drug use, I often dreamt of going to South America and taking proper un-cut cocaine. However, he and Livika had booked to go on an Amazon boat tour for a few days, and it was now Tank who was interested in joining me for the ceremony.

I'd read so much about the preparation for Ayahuasca ceremonies; the diet, the intention, and being ready mentally. To me, Rule and Tank were neither of those things, they just wanted an experience. For me, it was more than that, it was a spiritual experience, one that I'd prepared for and put so much emphasis on for so long. I felt like I'd earnt it. I believed you had to respect Ayahuasca, getting out what you put in. If you didn't, it would just be like another recreational drug experience. Ayahuasca isn't a drug and, from what I'd read, is not something you can just do at the weekend as an escape. It was never done alone, always in groups and always with a doctor or shaman with the right training.

Tank wanted to be free of his ten-year prescription drug reliance but seemed unwilling to make any effort or changes to make this a reality. I don't feel like there is an easy fix to change, you have to get rid of other stuff. It's a really difficult thing as we see it as part of our identity. They say that Ayahuasca can achieve in a few hours what thirty years of therapy could possibly resolve with slow integration; becoming aware of the actual problem and then slowly finding a way to get past it.

This got my creative juices flowing, and when thinking about my process of not going down the prescription drug route, I came up with this poem that summarised a realisation I had when coming to terms with depression and getting over my anger issues:

Change
Until we realise we are the problem
Our lives will remain in limbo
Full of anger, fear and darkness
Until we realise that the situations
And people we think hurt us
Are exactly what we have chosen
We will remain trapped in sadness
Change your world, Change your life

We couldn't meet Otillia until the next morning.

Tank was still interested, and I was actually thinking it may do him some good, considering the amount of time he had been on those pills. He was worried about the side effects of mixing the Ayahuasca. He was over-intellectualising the situation and was full of questions for Otillia and Bruno. I just smile and nod. Tank sought advice from all quarters; his neurologist, counsellor and doctor, all of course, warning against this unknown entity which actually pre-dates any form of western medicine, is completely natural and known to have astonishingly high success rates in so many areas.

I assumed none of these professionals had had any experience with such practices, so how on earth could they warn someone against it? It's like me warning someone against anal sex when I've never had it myself.

Ayahuasca is supposed to induce enhanced states of awareness, perception and cognation, areas that can help many illnesses, especially in terms of mental health. Ayahuasca gives drinkers their own tools to overcome problems and a heightened consciousness; a consciousness that could, in some ways, threaten the materialistic western society. Surely if these scientists and sceptics actually participated in these practices or studied the effects on the consciousness of other participants, they would be deemed more credible when vilifying such traditions. Their current method of analysis seems more like asking an elderly person to describe raving in a night club.

Western science only figured out the complex chemistry of Ayahuasca a few decades ago and as J.C. Callaway states: *"it is without doubt one of the most sophisticated and complex drug delivery systems in existence."*

Staying in the hostel with us was a very stereotypical American ex-pat. He had quite a square shape to him, a little bit stocky, with a deep gravelly voice. His hair seemed military issue, and due to his age, which I suspected to be around fifty, there was a lot of grey. His combat shorts and plain double-pocketed shirt finished off his look.

I think his name was Rod, but it could have been Chad, Brad, Ron or Chuck. He'd travelled a lot, and had horror stories from everywhere he had been. He warned us against this place and that told us about a French bloke who got robbed by the police in Panama. He thought I was crazy for going into Puerto Belen without a guide.

I said, 'That stuff don't happen to me, man.'

He said, 'So what, you're not a fucking gringo? Your white skin ain't saying "rob me I have money"?' I said, 'No, I don't think it does, mate. I've been in lots of situations on my travels where I was in the worst places and around people who could have robbed me, but it never happened".

He just laughed and said, 'Well you're living in a fucking dream world, man.'

I thought, yes I am, and my dream world doesn't
include your bullshit. Why would I include that in my world?

'I'm always looking out and being careful, knowing some motherfucker is lurking around the corner to rob me,' he said.

Of course, you are because you are looking for it, you usually find what you're looking for if you look hard enough, I thought. How frightfully miserable and on edge your life must be I thought, constantly manifesting bad situations.

Obviously, he was warning Tank off the Ayahuasca as much as possible. I really wanted to be out of this man's space. The negativity, the fear and aggression he carried, were very unattractive to the new me, but he was a character, so I observed him a while longer, thinking I could possibly use some of his traits if I was ever asked to play someone like this in a movie. I tried not to add much to the conversation and keep the guy's negative energy from having any effect on me.

We were due to leave for Otillia's place that morning, but there were riots and demonstrations all over Iquitos, so Otillia said she would be back at 4pm to take us to the Jungle. Apparently, the president had taken some backhanders, so the streets were all blocked. It looked like a war zone outside. Gone was the madness of traffic and people selling stuff. The roads were now empty but for rubble and garbage scattered everywhere with groups of thugs going around smashing things up.

We were told we would leave that evening when the trouble died down.

We were hostel-bound; we couldn't go out. Apparently, this was the first time this had ever happened, so in a way I felt privileged to be privy to such excitement. We were told we would leave at four, but four came and went, so did six, then Otillia called, saying she would collect us the next morning.

By this time Tank had opted out, saying too much weird stuff had been happening. We had been held hostage in the hostel all day. The hostel owner was Brazilian and seemed to love drama. He said Otillia would not return for us.

I knew she would.

In this part of the world, it was nothing to be ten days late. Some places take weeks to get to, so a few days here and there is probably the equivalent of a few seconds in the west.

With Tank being from the epitome of westernisation, where nothing is waited for, this minor delay threw his customer complaint ridden mind into overdrive.

CHAPTER 21
INDIA AT LAST, LIFE, NOVEMBER 2011

My trip to India was first planned for 2007. I had three months off university and really wanted to experience India, the colours, the culture, the mix of religions, music, meditation, history and scenery. It appealed to me more than any other place on earth.

My friend Sadie had told me so many fascinating stories about the place and how, in the summer months, many of the travellers would escape the heat by moving up to the hill stations at the foot of the Himalayas, a practice apparently started by the Raja. She would tell me about all the cool hippy-natured travellers there and how the food, sights and ganja were the best in the world.

I'd seen the change India had had on Sadie's brother. When I'd first met him, he was a typical south London nineteen-year-old rude boy who loved to party, had short hair, took a lot of class A drugs and needed constant entertainment. On his return from India he was a long-haired bohemian yoga teacher. He would tell me about the different teachers he'd trained within the north and how he moved to the south in winter. There were all these varied types of yoga, and each one required discipline, calmness, relaxation and a flexible body. This was all so new to me and all so enchanting. These were all things I wanted and felt I really needed to try and regain some sanity.

India was constantly in my thoughts. With Renie, there was the discussion of getting there on the Trans-Siberian Railway to Tajikistan, through Uzbekistan into China, through Nepal and the Himalayas and into India. The other option was getting to Istanbul and going through Iran and Pakistan. This seemed a lot more fraught with danger. I then got the part in *'brilliantlove'* and the itching to get to India subdued.

When I got with Fhian, she would tell me stories about India and other places she had been. India was the place I wanted to hear about, and it seemed the most magical and different. She said that if I didn't end up going to prison then we should book a flight to India for a holiday a few weeks after. She'd booked the time off work just in case a miracle happened.

I didn't get sent to prison, so the next thing I knew I was heading to Goa, to India, to the place I hadn't been destined to experience almost five years ago. Fhian knew I had this deep desire to visit and insisted we should go. I was grateful as I thought it might have otherwise become another one of those things I just procrastinated with my whole life.

Although I was feeling better, I was still suffering. I knew that having the court case out of the way wouldn't solve all my problems. I still was so unsure of my purpose. There were so many questions going around in my head all the time. It was just turmoil and angst in every facet of my life. I wanted it to stop, and I needed help. I couldn't stand being around myself, and I couldn't escape.

I was finding it hard to get as excited as I wanted to be because of this constant uncertainty, this wondering about what I should do and what would be waiting for me when I got home. It would be another period of time when I'd be earning no money, and Fhian would be getting paid whilst we were away. These were the sort of thoughts society had drilled into me.

Booking my flight and making a decision on how long I should go for was torture. Fhian could only be there for 10 days, and I wanted to stay longer. I thought I would stay two months as a compromise of being in a relationship that was still in its infancy. I really didn't want to lose her, even though I so often had Renie going through my mind.

I was thinking that maybe I could travel around before she arrived and possibly stay a little longer when she left. I wanted to experience India fully, not just dip my toe in.

I was working in Manchester for most of October and November, and Fhian really wanted me to be with her for Christmas on the Isle Of Wight. She had already booked her flights and was heading off on the 1st of December and returning on the 11th.

I arrived back from The Berlin Porn Film Festival where *'brilliantlove'* had been screened, and I was deliberating on whether to just book a flight and go in the next couple of days now that she wanted me back for Christmas. After days of deliberation, anxiety, worry, stress and my inability to make a decision, I sat in my sister's bedroom in Manchester on the internet with my credit card details filled in for two options. One, Air India booking that would mean I'd miss Christmas with Fhian and one with Monarch. The Monarch option meant that I would still have a girlfriend when I got back. I couldn't make up my mind, so I tossed for it, best of three. Monarch won 2-0, best of 5, 3-0 Monarch. It ended up 5-1 Monarch, a clear sign. I booked the flights.

I didn't want to live in London any more. I wanted Fhian, and I wanted us to move away, but I didn't know where. Part of me wanted to go back to Manchester which seemed crazy as a few years back I'd said I would never live there again. Now it seemed a possibility, I needed something to make me feel better, somewhere I felt like I fitted in.

I worked as much as I could before the India trip to save money. I'd stopped going to the meetings, and I had stopped seeing the counsellor, but I hadn't gone back to my old ways. I was now hitting the Buddhist Centre in Bethnal Green as often as I could, and it felt like one of the only things keeping me sane. Everyone I knew wanted me to go on nights out, to let my hair down, but I had no interest. It was like I had done that for the last fifteen years and was bored with it. I could only imagine doing it now if I really wanted to dance or if I was single and wanted to pick up a girl.

My flights were booked, which meant three weeks in India for me and then Christmas on the Isle of Wight with Fhian. I'd been in Manchester working in a charity shop as part of my community service and had managed to get some nice clothes for India. I'd also been earning money, painting and decorating and working as a window fitter.

We arrived at Gatwick, and I was already flustered after being on the busy tube. We checked in and apparently rucksacks had to go through a separate area. We arrived, and that area was closed. I went back to the lady, and she didn't know what to do with us. She sent for assistance and the old Liam, the Manchester Liam, was cursing inside my head saying, 'You stupid fucking cow, why can't a rucksack go through the same place as a suitcase?' Probably the same reason a 100ml liquid becomes immediately safe when it's put into a see-through food bag.

Luckily I managed to not say any of it out loud, and finally we end up getting sent on a ten-minute walk through the airport, to find the correct oversized bag check-in and relieve ourselves of our rucksacks.

We passed through Duty-free, consumed a few shots of free spirits that we had no intention of buying and both ended up smelling like tarts' handbags. Then we got hit with anti-ageing cream which we were told takes 10 years off you. I got the cream in my eye, so I quickly escaped the superficial world of armed perfume bottle firing squads with my now-15-year-old girlfriend.

On the plane, we end up in two of the middle three seats, next to a rough-looking bloke with a ponytail. Fhian said he looked like one of those new-age hippies, which are apparently hippies that are still smelly and dirty but they don't have the moral and ethical commitment of the full-blown hippies. I was learning new things all the time.

Fhian decides she is going to hate this bloke before the end of the flight. True to form, he pissed her off with his constant loud swearing and rude comments, projected at a volume that everyone around could hear. It was as if he was showing off his lack of tolerance as if it was something that would impress people. All the bloke did was moan about the price of everything, the state of the food, what was on the onboard entertainment and the attitude of the staff. The highlight being him calling one of the stewardesses a 'sour face cow'.

Food and coffee arrived, and our friend got his coffee spilt down his crotch. I started pissing myself in his face, and he started jumping up and down swearing, telling me he had no boxer shorts on. I pissed myself harder, which was accepted by him as we had already had a bit of banter and my working-class roots and thick Mancunian accent had provided me with the right to laugh in his face. I'd also laughed in the right places a few times at things he'd said, or agreed (to his delight) when he was derogatory towards something.

Keep your enemies close and all that shite.

He danced about and was being given tissues by the staff which he stuffed down his pants. I looked to my side, and Fhian had a very smug, regal expression on her face that only she can do justice to. He proceeded to upset everyone on the plane because he spilt his coffee on his trousers which burnt his cock and balls and everyone had to know about it and suffer. He made a stewardess cry, and a few others were also close to tears.

On our way to spiritual India, Karma of all things kicked in before we had even arrived. He had his elbow knocked three times and three more times coffee was spilt into his lap, each time to my hysterical pleasure. He then put the icing on the cake, by getting up after the plane had landed, looking around and announcing that there were a lot of hippyish people on the planet and that India will be full of pussy hippies. But he says, "I'm a new age hippy because I can fight".

DICKHEAD.

I then turned to Fhian and thought, 'you are mint, I love you, you summed him up within a minute of meeting him'.

Her look says, 'Yep, I knew that guy was a dick,' and mine says, 'Yes you did, babe'.

AYAHUASCA, THE JOURNEY, MAY 2013

Sitting in my tin roof hut in the middle of the Amazon rainforest, my feet felt like they were on fire from itchiness. It's almost pitch black, I was writing sitting on a small wooden chair by candlelight. I'd delicately placed a candle on a small stool beside me, strategically manoeuvred, ensuring minimum shadow from hand and pen onto page. I was somewhere between Iquitos and Nakula in the north of Peru in the north-west part of the Amazon. I was about to embark on a spiritual journey I had been looking forward to for over eighteen months.

Ayahuasca is seen as the world's most powerful psychedelic, enabling those thirsty enough to experience other dimensions of reality, past lives and a realisation of what comes after death. It is only administered by experienced shamans who have studied the plants and the places they take you for many years. Iquitos has the reputation of being the World HQ for such practices and was beyond doubt the main reason for my visit to Peru and the focus of my journey.

I was now in the care of the Ayahuasca Doctor Otillia in her jungle retreat a thirty-minute walk through thick vegetation up a dirt track bang in the middle of the Amazon.

Otillia turned up at the hostel at 8 am, not at 11 am as the dramatic Brazilian had relayed. I had an idea he may have been lying to add drama to the situation.

I was whisked off with Otillia.

After forty minutes we were dropped at a bench, and Otillia pointed me towards a clearing in the jungle. I had no idea what she was saying, just that she wanted me to walk into the jungle for about thirty minutes. It was a small cleared path, and I had no idea where I was going. I wondered why she wasn't coming with me. Was this some kind of test, did I have to win her trust by walking for thirty minutes and realising there was nothing and returning? I had faith I was doing the right thing, and after thirty minutes I come to a clearing where I was greeted by a small man in a boiler suit who pointed me towards a wooden cabin.

The large opening in the jungle had bright-coloured flowers growing everywhere. The grounds were lush, and a main large wooden house was situated in the middle and several cabins were dotted around the grounds. I was shown to my room which was a small wooden hut with a beautiful mosquito net covered bed in a nice room with a hammock and a toilet. It was basic but what else would I need? I was taken to the Commodore which was a large long table where you eat meals and was covered with mosquito netting with a natural palm roof. I was given breakfast and my first plant medicine which tasted like garlic. I had no idea what I was drinking, my trust and health were now fully in the hands of Otillia and her team.

I lazily lay in the hammock hour after hour until I was called for dinner. It was so interesting, to be so relaxed and so at peace with doing nothing. My mind was completely blank, which already felt like a massive breakthrough. I stared at my foot and the surrounding jungle canopy with very little else going on in my mind.

The next day I would be fully emerged and participating in an age-old ancient tradition, one that I felt would change my life forever. I was very, very excited but at the same time, the unknown and something new brought an element of fear.

I'd opted for a seven-day Dieta (diet) (Ayahuasca Retreat) under the care of Otillia, which consisted of a plant-based diet and two or three Ayahuasca ceremonies. They can last for seven, ten, or fifteen days or between one and three months and you can work with one or many plants. I would be working with one plant called Ajo Sacha, which would work with specific problems I had with knees and other joints as well as depression and an array of mental problems and past trauma.

The diet you partake in is used to cleanse the system and should be started at least a week before your retreat. It includes abstaining from red meat and pork and cutting back on chicken and fish. You have to eliminate salt, pepper and most other spices (especially hot spices like chilli), sugar including most deserts and pastries, fat and oils are banned. You're not allowed any prescription medicines, especially those that act as MAO inhibitors (Monoamine oxidase inhibitors) or are tranquillisers or anti-depressants. They also don't want you having yeast products, fermented foods such as soya or tofu, pickled foods, acidic foods, citrus and dairy products. Alcohol and coffee are prohibited, as are tea and other caffeine-rich drinks. One must abstain from sex and masturbation, and no iced or cold drinks are allowed. Everything you put on or in your body must be natural, including toothpastes and soaps.

The diet is essential so that the plants can have the best possible chance of doing what they are supposed to do. Because the diet contains no flavour, your sense of smell is said to become more sensitive, your body and its smell changes, your sight gets better, and your piss becomes clear. It has the same results as a fast in many ways, creating the perfect vessel for the plants to do what they are supposed to do, finding the space prepared for them to work. You are ingesting the spirit of the plant, and that is the medicine that works with you. Ayahuasca is the glamour plant, the best known, its name attracts like Tiger Woods at a golf tournament or The Beatles in their day at an airport.

Healers in Peru always use Ayahuasca in conjunction with other plants and the special diet is just as important as the Ayahuasca ceremony itself. However, Ayahuasca's spirit is seen as the top of the hierarchy, it being the mother of all plants.

After my food and plant medicine, I lay in Otillia's living room, reading of all things, a book from her bookshelf about British stylist Gok Wan and his upbringing in Nottingham. As I was doing this, Otillia was sewing. She was quite short with what looked like a mix of Inca and Spanish blood, she must have been in her fifties or sixties, but could actually have been older. She did have a few grandchildren flying about so who knows? She looked like any other grandmother catching up with some craftwork, but tomorrow I thought, this grandma will be administering me one of the most powerful hallucinogenics on the planet.

After I returned to my cabin for a few hours, I was summoned to follow one of Otillia's assistants towards a little blue conventional bath buried in the ground, its contents filled with the most beautiful collection of flower buds and petals. I undressed and readied myself to plunge into my first ever flower bath. A piece of tarp was attached to sticks to block out the sun and the rain. I submerged myself, feeling pampered like never before.

The aroma sent my nostrils into overdrive, as they frantically tried to label and savour these divine scents. As I took in the jungle canopy around me, I listened to the constant sound of crickets, frogs, birds, chickens and insects. A warm, loving feeling soaked through my whole body, and I felt the cleansing effects manifest immediately.

I retired for the evening and sat down to write. I had no idea of the date, time or day of the week; actually I was pretty unsure of the last time I'd had any recollection of these things. A little while later two white men came into my hut. They introduced themselves as Dave and Ferdinand and told me Otillia would like to know if I'd like to join them in ceremony that evening?

"Of course", I said, and Dave said he would collect me when it was time.

It seemed out of the blue.

I felt unprepared.

I thought that my first ceremony would be the next evening, but I had no second thoughts. This was what I was here for. I was excited to experience this age-old tradition and started to think about what would be in store for me. In Joan Parisi Wilcox's book, *AYAHUASCA-The Visionary and Healing Powers of the Vine of the Soul*, she states that *"one must be prepared for the terror and to have enough practice in maintaining ones centre before embarking on such a journey. One thing is certain about the vine, there is no telling what you will get, but it will definitely be what you need"*.

I was hoping all the meditation, yoga, and personal development I'd done over the last year would stand me in good stead, and I would be able to stay centred.

Dave arrived, and we made our way to Otillia's wooden hut which doubled up as the ceremonial space. One candle sat on a bookshelf just about illuminating the space. It felt like somewhere completely different to the room I had been reading in earlier. Otillia sat in the same chair she was sewing in but was now dressed in a full-length ceremonial robe, colourful flowered patterns adorning the crisp white material flowing down to the floor. In front of her was a small knee-high table with various bits of paraphernalia on it, which I couldn't really make out due to the dim light. Otillia sat in her chair and waved at me to be seated. Spaces had been prepared, folded mattresses were placed against the wooden walls awaiting our arrival. Each mattress had its own bowl which I assumed was for when the purging began.

I took the space to Otillia's left, close to the door in case I needed to escape to the bathroom, as I had heard you could be violently sick from both holes.

Dave sat facing Otillia, and Ferdinand sat to Otillia's left but slightly behind. Ferdinand seemed very experienced and was talking us through the process. He said that once you have drunk, you should try to keep the brew down for as long as possible and stay as upright as you can with a straight spine throughout the whole experience. He said that when you drink Ayahuasca, you should keep your heart open, and try and be led by your heart, not your head. He then told us that just as you are about to drink, you should make an intention for the ceremony. What is it you want to be shown? What areas do you feel you need guidance with and what needs to be healed?

We all sat cross-legged in our spaces. I had few butterflies in my stomach, a giddy excitement filled me. Otillia pulled a plastic bottle from a bag that contained a dark coloured liquid which I assumed was the brew. She said some words or prayers as she lit some tobacco. She then opened the top of the bottle and blew smoke inside it three times. She then blew smoke around the bottle three times. Next, she stood and went around to each of us, blowing tobacco smoke around our heads and bodies. She asked for our hands and blew smoke into our palms three times. She sat down and performed a few more rituals and poured the first cup of Ayahuasca, blowing smoke three times into the brew and then beckoning Dave with a stern call of, "Señor". I watched him approach and kneel before Otillia, accept the cup, internally setting his intentions and knocking back the brew.

I studiously watched so I wouldn't mess up my turn. Otillia gave him some tissue to wipe his mouth, and he returned to his mat. She filled the bowl again, and nervous energy engulfed me as I knew I was next. She blew tobacco around it three times and called "Señor," beckoning me forward. I knew what I wanted to ask now. I looked at Otillia as she handed me the bowl and a radiant glow now surrounded her face. I knew what I wanted to ask, "show me my heart and give me direction".

I had written a list a few days earlier of things I wanted to ask, but it just ended up huge. They were: direction, Mum, life purpose, spiritual direction/growth, focus, knowing my own mind, remembering, home/family/life, knee pain, work, place, diet, body pain, friendship, Fhian, what am I here for, where to find happiness, Mum, commitment, family, destiny, stability, home, life's calling, find my place, work, lessons I have to learn, Fhian, headspace, shoulder pain, calf pain, ability to relax, knees, connecting to higher self, connecting to guides, divinity, destiny, spiritual life path, healing, happiness/direction, home/happiness, soul plan, higher purpose, higher self, abundance in everything, creativity, guitar playing, priorities, focus, language of light, yoga direction, building practices, and clear direction.

Just a couple of things I wanted help with, but I stuck with being shown my heart.

I knelt down before Otillia. She poured the brew and handed me the small wooden bowl that seemed to be a carved and polished coconut shell. The smell immediately hit me; a thick earthy foul pong swirled up my nostrils connecting with my brain. I was trying to process what this unusual smell was. I looked at the brew, at my first experience with Ayahuasca, set my intention for the ceremony, asking to be shown what my heart wanted, to be led by my heart and be given direction. I glugged back the dark brown thick liquid in one gulp. I was given a tissue and then headed back to what would be my station for the next five or so hours. The Ayahuasca tasted foul, worse than anything I'd ever tasted before. It was so thick, not gloopy but an even consistency and the taste was like a swamp or rotting vegetation. I was actually expecting worse from the stories I'd been told, but still, it was foul.

I crossed my legs. I didn't feel sick, which was what I was expecting, and the liquid seemed to go down quite well. I sat in my lotus pose and watched Ferdinand take his brew.

Otillia took hers and then blew out the candle.
In the darkness, I was able to see the outline of people's bodies. Illuminated by the faint moonlight, I waited for the effects.

Fifteen minutes in, Dave began to purge. For some reason, my ego was glad I wasn't the first to go. I was feeling fine. Dave retched for a few minutes, and I thought 'has he had the Ayahuasca in his system long enough for it to take effect?' Another ten minutes passed, and Ferdinand vomited, and my ego was gleaming. For some reason in this situation my competitive side was shining through, I felt happy and strong that I had held it down for so long. But what did that actually mean? I knew it didn't matter. Visualisations were starting to form. With my eyes shut, geometric shapes were creating a black and white kaleidoscope in my mind; beautiful triangular patterns were morphing into other patterns, circles, hexagons, squares all bursting into each other with flawless grace.

All of a sudden, I reached for my bucket and was sick a few times from the bottom of my guts. It brought me to my knees over the bowl as it all came out. I wiped my mouth and sat back down to regain my composure. As I closed my eyes, I discovered that colour had erupted into my elegant, stylised visuals. I got comfortable again, ready to enjoy the show. Reds, greens and blues added texture and vividness to the shape show. Sequences evolved into patterns and patterns into vast shapes and landscapes made up of triangles. It felt like the trippy hallucinogenic scene in the Disney film Dumbo, but a million times more beautiful.

I was expecting harder visions, I was expecting people, spirits objects to come to me, I was expecting to be catapulted into another dimension. I was seeing these patterns I had never seen before. It's very hard to explain what I was seeing, to remember, to have the vocabulary to fully describe what was going on in my head. It was stunning, dazzling, beautiful and sublime, and part of me wanted to experience it forever.

As the visions became more and more complex, Otillia started to sing and shake her rattle, her Icaro's (songs) providing another layer of beauty to this already dreamy world I was in. The Icaro's took you on a little journey, and when she shook the rattle, the visions would splatter and dissipate like she was shaking the delicate kaleidoscope in my mind each time the rattle moved. I opened my eyes, and the patterns in my mind were now all over the room. I could see the outline of the two guys and could see the figure of Otillia in front of me. She was rocking back and forth on her rocking chair as she'd done whilst sewing.

The way Joan Parisi Wilcox describes her visions was very similar to what I was seeing; *"I was assaulted by geometry, looming before me were huge spheres, dense and darkly hued, they formed complex patterns, spinning in ways so intricate I could barely fathom their movements, the immensity was overwhelming even terrifying."*

Nail on the head. I actually felt good in myself, calm, happy, serene, blissful. The images of my life started to show a future life of love and happiness. It was showing me simplicity and simplicity was the focus. It was showing me love, confirming what I had felt for the last four months. It showed me Fhian, it showed me I needed nothing more, everything was with her. It showed the two of us together forever, it showed me that all we needed was love, love is all you need. We were holding a baby, I was the happiest man alive, and the radiance that shone from Fhian's being was the most beautiful I'd ever seen in my life. There was a baby and us. That was all we needed. Family close by, a few good friends, but more than anything each other, that was all that mattered.

Lady Ayahuasca kept me focused on simplicity and showing people how to live free by doing it myself. I was building a house for me and Fhian in Chorlton, Manchester. I was converting a garage in someone's garden into a one-room starter home for us to start a family in, a cosy love nest, with a loft bed incorporating the sustainable principles I'd learnt and making it our own. Enticing her with the blissful setting I'd created. I was shown this was my dream. This was the most important thing, no more travelling after this until I'd created a home for us both. I was shown all the construction methods to use, how to maximise space.

The building was full of love, full of Fhian and Liam, everything else took a back seat. There was a small garden with a white picket fence, the garage door had been replaced with glazing facing south to maximise solar gain, and a beautiful free-standing Victorian bath sat in the garden with a shower curtain around it, looking both decorative and functional. We also had a drop toilet around the side using a septic tank, and blissfully we sat with friends around a fire pit made from glass bottles. I sat there with my head resting on my knee in pure bliss. I wanted Fhian to see the smile on my face, the contentedness, the love we had, the love we had brought each other and the love the baby had brought. I sat holding our baby and her, knowing this was all life was about, making this happen, everything else just seemed like meaningless rubbish.

I wanted to show her, tell her, let her experience this feeling, know her opinion. We were so in love, it would have made some people a little sick. The feeling was intense, it was like she was with me, holding me, sharing this feeling with me. We then started this business and a community of people turning garages into small homes. I got a message that said, "Why do people have buildings to house their cars when there are people without homes?"

I thought about this couple I had met in Taos who had lived in this tiny hut for two years. They were both over six foot six, he was an ex-international volleyball player and her, an ex-international basketball player. They'd had their first child in this tiny space, and it had spent the first eighteen months of its life there. Now they had this huge three-bed Earthship, and the hut was used as storage space.

In the vision, it was my mission to turn as many garages into homes, showing people an alternative way to live, to own your own life. The Ayahuasca said do this, and your love will come to you, create a home for you both. I then had a vision of us both writing our names on each other's feet and ankles, it felt so romantic. In our own space consumed by love and each other.

There was this artistic aspect to the whole experience, of us both exploring our creativity. Learning instruments, writing songs, painting, doing yoga, Qi Gong, Tai Chi, and studying Tantra. It was just a massive explosion of love and exploration of our minds and hearts and each other. We were both pushing the other to grow.

There was so much more I struggle to remember and bring back from the world I was in. There were business ideas, designs, all kinds of stuff. There was a knowing that this was the lifestyle for me: simple. Simple, simplicity and simplify were the words being reverberated around my head; being near family, being near my dad in his final years, looking after him regardless and then doing the same for Fhian's parents, putting our families before all our social commitments.

Of all the places Ayahuasca could have taken me, I was back in Manchester. All the tropical places I've visited over the years, amazing lakes, mountains, coastal towns. It was telling me, 'Chorlton — go there, and friends will follow.' It's got such a rich culture and is close to the city centre so our friends might make the move. Fhian would be happy with what we had; eventually, I just needed to show her.

Other things about past relationships came up, people with attachments to me, things I needed to work on breaking, some unresolved issues. I had been expecting more craziness and visions and journeying into other dimensions. However, I had gotten exactly what I had asked for; clarity of heart and direction.

I sat there in the Buddha position with my head resting on my knee. I was so, so, so happy and smiling. The happiest and most contented smile that had ever graced my face. My whole body was pure love, the pure love of Fhian and Liam, it was intense, and exactly what I'd been waiting for.

Otillia was drawing the ceremony to an end. I had no idea how long it had lasted, time and space had evaporated. She went around each one of us singing her Icaro's which she had continued throughout the ceremony. They had provided a beautiful overtone to my sublime visions. Now Otillia was tapping me with this instrument made of dry leaves and singing. A feeling of pure healing ran over my body, tingles passing through every fibre of my being.

It was magical.

The ceremony ended, and I rose to a huge head rush that made me dizzy. I put on my shoes and ventured outside with Dave. I wanted to sit, and process but Dave wanted to talk, so we sat and chatted about our experience in my cabin for about an hour. His had been a lot weaker than his previous experience with a different Ayahuasquero, but still it had given him a lot of answers to many questions and many ideas.

He worked as a herbalist and had a fascination with the healing powers of tropical plants with an aim to introduce them into mainstream medicine. He was so interesting to talk to and intellectually in another dimension to me, so I just told him about my balls.

I'd remembered another part of my vision was of a house I lived in with me mum and me step-dad. The vision showed me my room in that house on Lorna Grove in Gatley and how I used to sit in bed all the time watching TV, playing with my balls like they were stress balls. I relayed this to Dave. I'd spent a good part of the ceremony rekindling my passion for this old trait, obviously with the others unable to see. I wondered why I'd stopped and why I would ever buy stress balls when I had my own impossible-to-lose set constantly at my disposal.

I also got this inclination to send my step-dad an email saying:

Thanks for helping me grow!
Love
Liam

I don't think it meant thanks for letting me grow my passion for playing with my balls as a young lad, but thanks for providing me with the security and discipline I probably needed at the time.

When Dave left, I went outside to look at the stars. Fhian was firmly on my mind, it was like the stars were talking to me. The sky seemed so vast, and millions of stars exploded into my vision, but one star drew my attention. I felt it was trying to tell me something, flashing at me, I focused on it and tried to soak up whatever it was transmitting. Then still feeling pretty high, I crept into my mosquito net covered bed with a picture of Fhain. My heart and mind had spent the whole evening fully entwined with her. I said her name over and over and over and over and over again until I drifted off to the astral plane.

It was my first evening sleeping in the jungle. I felt like I'd been there for so long already as so much had happened. Sleep was difficult, the sound of the jungle was intense, amplified threefold by the cover of darkness. It seemed to bring everything to life, a choir of animal and insect sounds blasting into my dream world. The constant drumming of the cricket, the swamp and river frogs providing the base, birds and amphibians providing a riff, and the monkeys and large animals kicking off the chorus from time to time. Very occasionally, there was a bird that would create this special effect sound that was something like a cross between a foghorn, a kazoo and an ambulance. There were strange rhythmic and often haunting howls, clicks, swishes, buzzes, twitters, swooshes, whirls and whistles.

Wilcox again points out that *"the jungle of what one hears is not only the canopy of living things of the jungle but is also the echo of all that humans have been, and we will be. The jungle at night is the sound of memory".*

I lay in wonderment at the sounds I was hearing, the experience I'd just had, the reality of where I was in the world with all the growth and direction I was feeling. I felt clear and very, very happy, something I hadn't felt for a long time.

I lay wanting daylight. I had no idea of the time, but it seemed like the night was endless. I was looking forward to the morning.

I lay and dreamt about Fhian and our life together.

The ceremony had shown me how we both had to tap into our creative sides more, how we had to paint, learn music, write, study Tantra, yoga, meditation, all things we would do together. I wanted us to lie in bed together and write each other's names on each other's bodies.

When I woke, Fhian was there still ever-present in my mind. When daylight came, I got in my hammock and started to write her name on my foot, lots of little Fhian prints starting to form a love heart. I wanted her to see it.

Dave and Ferdinand were both plant medicine doctors. They were working together, searching the jungle for a tree that could cure cancer. I could have done with you two a few years back, I thought. We ate breakfast together and discussed our various travels and work. We all felt the evening's events had been quite mild, but we all seemed to have gotten what we needed from the Ayahuasca and exactly what we'd asked for. It was only Dave's second time, and he said how his first had blown his socks off, shown him all the power of the plants and given him a vast array of visions. I wondered why last night had been so tame in comparison?

I asked many questions about the Ayahuasca plant, and about the diet I was on. I had no way of communicating with Otillia and her staff, so it was time for the guys to translate for me. They told me that the two main plants put together to make the brew have various legends and myths as to how they came about. Ayahuasca is said to contain 'The Power and Chacuna', the other main plant is said to contain, 'The Light'.

Anthropologists and scholars have for decades been unable to understand how indigenous tribes could have arrived at their extensive knowledge of plant chemistry and healing through trial and error as the complexity of some combinations were equal to anything seen in the west. The people say the plants themselves were the teachers. They say that the preparations for undertaking the journey were given to them by the spirit of the plant. When you have experienced what I had over the last twelve months, I instinctively knew this to be true. The reality that the plants have spirits like we do and that these spirits can communicate with humans who are switched on to such a frequency makes perfect sense. It seems foreign to the western mind, but who are we to think we know better?

Ayahuasca is fast becoming the psychedelic of choice, and even the FDA (The Food and Drug Administration) in the States approved a study of synthetic DMT (Dimethyltryptamine) which is the main component found in Ayahuasca.

Scientists call it, 'The Spirit Molecule'.

It seems that more and more people are rejecting the biology and genetics evolutionary path. They have frustration and disgust with the environmentally destructive, soul-deadening effects of our consumer-driven materialism, which is intense in my own country and impossible to escape in the US. The popular emergence of psychedelics during the 1960s and 70s resulted in a political backlash and the prohibition of LSD and other mind-expanding chemicals. In conjunction with this, I often sat and wondered what the world would be like now if this hard-line hadn't been taken? If hippies hadn't been persecuted? If a balance could have been formed? What would the world be like? I imagine it would be a world that I would have a lot more ease in understanding and being part of.

We all sat around in Otillia's living room for a while, they were all talking Spanish, so I smiled and nodded. I asked what I was to do with my days. Otillia said, "you rest, Señor". We then got talking about the different plants found in the jungle and their healing powers and the specific things they were used for. I started to compile a list, and this is the amazing stuff I was being told:

Guayusa - An aromatic plant whose leaves are commonly used for medical baths. Ayahuasqueros frequently require their patients to bathe with this before a healing session.

Ushpahuasa - A tea made from the plant's roots. Its effect is to open your heart chakra, to stimulate depth of feeling and to help you retrieve memories, especially of childhood. Clears and cleans you, especially with regards to eyesight. Heals emotions. Traditionally called the rejuvenating plant, it won't erase your wrinkles. It works to loosen the emotional parts and memory. It opens the heart.

Chiric Sanang - Helps move energy through the body. 514

Sanango - Helps physically disabled people recover their mobility. Even people who have been unable to walk for five years can be cured. They are treated with teas of plants and baths. After two or three months, they can get up and walk again.

Una de gato - Or Cats Claw, has anti-tumour and anti-inflammatory properties.

Renaco - The rubber tree oozes a white sap that is mixed with alcohol and drunk to cure rheumatism. Healers also apply it directly to joints to ease swelling and pain.

Ochahuaha – The bark is mixed with Ushphausa to make an ointment to treat snakebite.

Yahurapanga – Means "leaf of blood" because it oozes red sap. To treat addiction, especially crack and cocaine addiction. It forces you to vomit, it is very effective. The healer grinds leaves in a food mill and then makes a tea, for prolonged purging only half a cup is needed. After taking Yahurapanga, addicts are invited to eight sessions of Ayahuasca in eight days, followed by days of Ushpahuasa. That usually takes care of addiction.

Trumpetero or Trumpet Wood – Vegitalistas boil the leaves and stems, and then babies who are on the verge of walking are dipped in the cool waters. The bath imparts strength to the babies' legs, helping them walk.

Estoraque – A leaf to make tea, this tonic is made to imprint sexual potency to men who are impotent.

Chamburo – Attracts luscious fat worms that the locals fry and eat. Supposed to be delicious and provides protein and rich oils.

Bobinsana – Does not fall down as its roots are so deep. Ingested, it makes a person more connected to nature, and as the root of the plant opens up, so does the person.

Chuchuhuasi – Is tall with a big trunk. It gives endurance to the body.

Juster Sacha – A relatively rare creeper vine with distinctive heart-shaped leaves that are boiled to make a tea. This must be left overnight to be exposed to dew. Only then is it ready to treat kidney problems.

It was mental to think about the vast plethora of medicines that were at the disposal of those living in the Amazon. What gifts nature has to offer us and our children, but in the west, we know so little about the healing powers of plants. More often than not big businesses exploit them, coming in and destroying land and contaminating the spirit of the plants.

After the amazing revelations of what the Amazon had to offer it was time for the guys to leave, they were off deeper into the jungle in search of their super cancer plant.

I wished them well.

When they left, the realisation dawned on me that I was unable to communicate again. After my next encounter with Ajo Sacha, all I wanted to do was relax in my hammock. Ferdinand had told me that Ajo Sacha was given to relieve body pain and allow my mind to be clear. I thought I'd just been tired when I first arrived and lay in the hammock all day, dozing, listening, thinking, not thinking, watching. After that day's dose, I did the same. I couldn't remember the last time I'd just sat and done nothing, no reading, no writing, no music, no conversation, no yoga, no other people. I was in no way bored, and it was joyful and refreshing to be doing nothing with no pressure to be achieving anything, I actually felt I was achieving so much by just being.

This was what I did the whole day until I went to get water. I was then asked by Otillia if I wanted to do a ceremony again that evening.

"Si bien," I said, basking in the glory of the fluidity of my Spanish.

Again I didn't feel prepared, but soon I was called for another flower bath, in preparation. As I bathed I spotted another guy walking about, a westerner, not one of Otillia's staff. I assumed others would be joining in tonight and without any evening meal I was called to the ceremony space.

CHAPTER 22
INDIA AT LAST 2,
LIFE, NOVEMBER 2011

As we stepped off the plane the first thing that hits us was the heat, then this smell of a mixture of flowers and spices. As we moved through the airport, we started to see how dirty and dated everything was. There were people everywhere, standing, sitting, sleeping, running, it was like everything had been sped up. Not a frantic craziness like in London, but an organised madness with a purpose. We stepped outside and were greeted by a million taxi drivers.

Fhian had been here before, so she took care of the situation as my senses were bombarded. We made our way to Palolem Beach as I took in the most fascinating scenery my eyes, ears and nostrils had ever witnessed. The beeping of the car horn was constant as I tried to figure out what the rules of the road were, and I soon discovered there were none. It was 4 am, the sun was not long off rising, and there were people everywhere. In the middle of nowhere there would be someone carrying huge pieces of luggage or a crate of chickens. There would be cows in the road, school kids playing in the street.

Coconut trees lined every road as far as the eye could see. As we passed small towns, churches and places of worship were packed with people. The towns were vibrant, and already people were selling food, drink, papers and clothes. I was captivated by the colour everywhere, bright and vibrant splashes of purple, baby blue, yellow and reds were sprayed into my eyes. I was seeing faith everywhere, I was seeing smiles everywhere, I was seeing purpose everywhere, and I was seeing and seeing and seeing unsure of whether my mind was processing all that I saw.

We got to the beach, having paid two pounds for an hour-long taxi ride. It was then a case of finding accommodation. It was just about light enough to see, and very few people at the beach were up and ready for the day. We sat and looked at the ocean, exhausted from the flight.

We found a fantastic place to stay at the end of the beach that had these little huts with double beds in them. The hut was circular, and the bed sat in the middle, covered by a mosquito net. Outside there was a hole-in-the-floor toilet and a massive bucket of water for washing. We would throw a bucket of water at each other, then scrub with soap before throwing water at each other again. We had our own little patio with a table and chairs and a couple of loungers. It was perfect and all for the price of a single journey on the tube in London. Next door was a yoga retreat which was about twenty times as expensive as our place to stay, but you could just walk in there and do yoga for a couple of pounds.

The next day I headed there and sat in this space in front of this old yogi man who was wearing all orange. I began to do breathing exercises and then some stretching postures. I loved it. I found some of the postures really tough, and I was losing my balance a lot, with all the sweat that was dripping onto my mat.

I was sliding about everywhere, but I had positioned myself at the back, so I was not as embarrassed and nervous. For the next few days I kept going back. It was all I wanted to do. Fhian wasn't as keen and wanted to explore more. I felt I wanted to explore yoga and explore my body.

At the same retreat centre, they also had Ayurvedic massages which I was told really complements the practice of yoga, so we booked in. We walked into this hut where incense was burning, and we were both taken into a room and placed on these beds, which were huge pieces of wood with grooves in for your body. A small skinny Indian guy started to get stuck in as he poured tons of oil over me and worked on every muscle, including ones I didn't know I had.

Palolem Beach was stunning, beautiful sandy beaches and clear blue sky stretched for miles around. It was busy, and people sauntered up and down the beach wearing sarongs. Hippies with dreadlocks and mystical looking guys with long beards sat cross-legged looking out to sea with their eyes closed meditating for hours. The beach offered everything; there were signs for yoga, meditation, tattooing, massage, enlightenment, Ayurvedic medicine, treatments and healing. There was everything someone who was just opening up to this world would be intrigued by. I was still at my, 'all that shit scares me' stage. These were things that I looked at, read and had no idea about but I knew I wanted to know more.

After a few days of enjoying the beach and all it had to offer, we headed south to a place called Gokarna. We took a train, watching the rich array of people, religions and the beautiful landscapes we passed as the train raced along. We were able to sit at the door and dangle our feet outside like a piece of beautiful freedom. I felt like it was enriching me and making me realise how repressed and scared we are at home. It was like we were a novelty on the train. People would just stare at us for an uncomfortably long time, and when we looked at them they would just keep staring which made us look away. Again this was foreign to us as eye contact and staring is not socially accepted at home and you're deemed a weirdo if you partake in such practices.

When we arrived in the state of Karnataka, we jumped off the train and into another new experience; my first ride on a rickshaw. We raced up steep mountains through rural villages, were chased by a pack of dogs and were dropped off near the steps leading to Om Beach.

As the beach became visible, we started to see how it was shaped like the sign that represented the Om. We found somewhere to stay which was two pounds a night as we opted against the one pound a night place and went for a bit of luxury.

There was no yoga on Om Beach, but the next beach along had some places, so we went to explore. It was an hour's walk over the coastal cliff, and then a beach similar to Palolem came into view. For the next few days I was an ever-present at a place called the Yoga Farm. I would wake up early to run along the sandy Om-shaped beach, up the stairs, across the cliff and down the rocks, then fast along the straight flat beach and up the hill to the yoga farm. There was a hut where the reception was situated, and people would make their way to the open-aired yoga space that looked over the beach. The yoga teacher would descend a wooden ladder from a treehouse above the reception and take us to his class. Immediately I was in awe of this long-haired, yoga-teaching, tree-house-living beautiful German man. I looked at him and felt a bit shit, everything about him in some way oozed what I wanted, and I sat in his classes transfixed by his graceful body movements, calm teaching and his soft, mesmerising German accent.

The place we were staying was amazing. Our little hut was on stilts and had a small veranda that looked out on tranquil gardens, providing us with shade from the searing midday sun. Some real characters were staying there from all over the world. One guy spent most of his time reading books at the front of the restaurant, occasionally glancing up to look out to sea and reflect.

One day he gave me a joint and considering I didn't have anything to do other than sit on the beach and chill, I decided it would be okay. For the next four hours, I was really paranoid and again remembered why I didn't really like smoking weed.

The next day me and Fhian decided it was the day we wanted to have a Bhang Lassi, which is a yoghurt fruit smoothie with cannabis (Bhang) in it. We found the restaurant that did them and because it was illegal and pretty hush, hush, we sort of shuffled to the counter and asked one of the waiters. He told us to wait around the back. We were in this outside space with all these puppies and kittens which we played with until our Bhang Lassi arrived. We drank it, and within thirty minutes we were both completely stoned.

We went for a walk and sat on the rocks. I found conversation really hard, and I thought that we had nothing in common and nothing to talk about. I was thinking, maybe Renie is the girl that I should be with and this is a big mistake. I stewed so many thoughts over and over in my head as we sat there. Unable to really communicate, I looked out from the far side of the beach at the most stunning view of endless ocean, mesmerising me as it delicately caressed the Om-shaped sand. We didn't really say much for the rest of the day, but we did go and have the most beautiful animal-like sex where we were really connected to each other as we sniffed and soaked up the feel and scent of our skin. The way we both smelt and this drug-like feeling that was always present when we made love, seemed overly accentuated whilst high on the Bhang!

Our next move was to Hampi, which is a sacred area with temples and remnants of ancient civilisations. Unlike most sacred places that have been cordoned off and you have to pay to enter, much of Hampi is still lived in and has a bubbling population. The sixteen-hour sleeper coach journey was a first for me, and we got squeezed into this small bed above another couple below us. I was praying I didn't piss the bed. We had bought a load of valium from the chemist, so we slept almost all the way.

When we arrived, we were instantly whisked off by a young guy called David and found a place to stay for the next few nights. We toured around the area on a moped we hired, and we didn't even have to give our passports. We just paid a few pounds and were told we could have the bike for two days. We raced around seeing all the ancient temples, picking up coconut water everywhere and chewing on sugar cane. We lay under delicately balanced rocks bigger than most homes, and I meditated looking out at these stunning panoramas. Kids followed us around, wanting to talk and were obsessed that we gave them pens.

We watched the sacred elephant living in the main temple take a bath in the river in the morning. He was joined by most of the locals who cleaned their teeth, went swimming and washed, ready for the day ahead. The atmosphere at 6 am by the river was electric; so many people talking and having fun in the water. We just sat and took it all in until we became the attraction and what seemed like hundreds of school children wanted to have their picture taken with us and wanted us to take one of them so we could show them on the screen.

As we walked through the wide street that led to the main temple, small mud houses were scattered along the side. I guess it would be what the west would call extreme poverty. Whole families seemed to fill small rooms and congregated outside in the open space that led to the road. Three or four generations must have been squashed into these houses, and although it must have been cramped, they all seemed happy. All their clothing was bright, and all the outside spaces had been decorated with beautiful artwork similar to the Henna patterns, you see on their hands. Dazzling pieces were scrawled exquisitely into the barren earth.

It hit me how everyone seemed creative. There was art everywhere you looked, and to the people, it was normal. Stunning tapestries and clothes were hung over washing lines, and you could spot spinning wheels in most homes. My knowledge of Gandhi's homespun campaign against the British Empire brought an inward smile to my heart. Everywhere you went women were draped in the most stunning fabrics and had these elaborate piercings hanging from their ears to their nostrils.

Everywhere we went, there were groups of men all dressed in the same outfits. There were groups of men in orange, groups of men in blue, groups of men in brown and groups of men solely in white. We were told that they were all making pilgrimages and it seemed that everywhere we went there were dozens of large groups of men on a pilgrimage. My favourites and the outfit I really wanted to wear were these really dark-skinned men who wore black trousers and a shirt. On the sleeves, waistband and the bottom of the trousers were these orange and gold bands which really made them stand out in the crowd in a very subtle, high fashion kind of way. I really wanted to be in their gang!

On our last day, we headed up to the Hanaman mountain which has around three thousand steps to reach the summit. When we arrived at the top we were greeted by an array of tiny monkeys. They scurried around looking for nuts and fighting with each other.

As we walked onto the flat surface that surrounded the temple building at the summit, we became aware of the chanting. Deep-voiced repetitive chants lingered in the air as we took in the views. There was a rich aroma of weed, which we'd read was the mystical drug of choice of the Sadhus who took residence here. There was a mischievous looking boy who started to show us around while he played with the monkeys and seemed in some trance from the cannabis fumes and the ethereal chanting. Sadhus were reading text from these huge books whilst thick clouds of incense smoke wrapped itself around them, and around the microphones they were speaking into that reverberated the sound around the monkey mountain. We then stepped into the room where all the hash was being smoked. Men passed around a chillum as they lay sprawled across thick, brightly coloured cushions that adorned the concrete floor. They looked as comfortable as comfortable can be.

We left Hampi and headed back to Palolem on a twenty-hour sleeper coach. Our compartment was a box at the back of the coach that we bundled our bags into. The coach was packed, and with the door open, we were almost sitting on the laps of four other people. We necked a few Valium and slid our door shut. Now in our private Fhian and Liam world we drifted off to sleep. Thoughts of, 'would it be appropriate to have sex?' flooded my mind, but with people only centimetres away, I reconsidered. I start to get aroused as I pressed against her and the next thing I knew the Valium kicked in and I found myself being kicked off the bus as we arrive in Palolem.

Fhian was leaving in two days, so we hung out with some friends from home who were also staying on Palolem beach. We swam, played Frisbee and went exploring.

The next day she was picked up by a taxi and whisked away. As I was waving goodbye, I got distracted by something on the floor. As I lift my head, the taxi was out of view, and I felt like I hadn't said goodbye to the girl I was supposed to be in love with. I saw this as a bad omen. I didn't particularly feel bad that she was leaving and I didn't feel like I would miss her. My thoughts turned to Renie, and I wondered why I still couldn't get her out of my head.

On the beach, I bumped into a friend from London and decided to spend time with her until I left. In the place she took me to I came across the typical traveller types who just wanted to get drunk, sleep with each other and party hard. It reiterated my point and understanding that I was here to look for something more, something greater than I was used to. Something that would help me out of this internal turmoil that was plaguing me and hung around me like a demon.

I wanted an experience that took me deeper, that taught me wisdom and guided me towards being a better human being. As this realisation hit me, I watched a pack of dogs take down a young calf, as its mother escaped the brutal attack. They dragged the calf into the sea and started to drown it. As this was going on, a woman leapt into the sea with a massive stick and started beating all the dogs. Dogs were flying through the air as this seemingly crazy woman beat and beat at them like Uma Thurman in Kill Bill.

A guy then came along with an even bigger stick. They finally managed to get the dogs off the calf, and the dogs lingered around. The calf was floating in the water. The man and woman and some others who came to the rescue dragged the calf onto the beach. Five or six people stood around the dead calf, the woman wailed, and shrieked as she embraced it. The woman and a few others dramatically ran at the dogs, swinging their huge thick sticks until they disperse. It seems that nobody around the calf knows what to do. By this point the mother was making her way back, and people were in tears knowing that we had just seen a murder take place. I started to well up as the mother was emotionally reunited with her dead calf. She started to sniff around it knowing there was nothing she could have done to protect her baby, but obviously still feeling massive guilt. Tears started to stream down my face and the faces of those around me, it was heart-breaking, and we held hands to console one another.

All of a sudden, out of the blue, the calf stands up, and half in shock and half flabbergasted, everyone starts to cheer in disbelief. After tentatively getting back to its feet, it nuzzles its head between its mother's rear legs, and then they both start to make their way down the beach. You couldn't have written it.

On the sleeper train, I was now alone, and as always when I was first alone, I freaked out a bit. I started having confidence issues, and voices in my head would start telling me I was a loser and had no friends. Shut up, shut up, shut up, shut up I would tell it. Imagine if we all said what was in our heads. Would we all be locked up or is it just me?

I had a bed in this small luggage rack so I popped some valium and drifted off to sleep to be woken in the early mooring to a man shouting at a very quick pace, "chai, chai, chai, chai, chai, chai, chai," fired out of his mouth like a machine gun. This was followed by a man shouting, "coffee, coffee, coffee," in this long drawn out deep tone that was so distinctly different to the chai man that you could be deaf and just pick up on the different vibrations of the words. I grabbed a chai, some coffee and some of the snacks on offer.

We stopped at a huge train terminal and were there for almost an hour as people unpacked and repacked the train. It seemed that so many people in India travelled with huge amounts of belongings. Packages bigger than the people carrying them covered the platforms as people scurried around in circles. After more stops, I discovered that the tone of the chants for chai and coffee were the same everywhere we went. It must be part of the training that if you opt to be the chai guy you are trained in this quick-fire delivery of the word and if you go down the coffee route you given this deep gravely tone to learn.

As the train tore through the Indian countryside, it became evident that the train track was used for so many different things by the people in the towns and villages it passed. I saw women and men using it as a toilet, children being washed and food being cooked inches from the furiously passing piece of metal on wheels.

I was heading to Kerala because Fhian had looked into the place when she was planning our trip and had read lots of amazing things about it. It was supposed to be the most beautiful state in India and the only state where communism was the favoured political system. These both drew me to Kerala but more than anything, it was a lady called Mother Amma. A few months earlier I had read a book called, *Holy Cow* about an Australian woman, Sarah MacDonald who is a complete spiritual sceptic but decides to try different spiritual practices. When she finds herself living with the rich elite in Delhi she heads to Kerala to see Mother Amma who is referred to as the Hugging Mamma by her followers. She gives people healing and gifts them their desires by hugging them and saying a prayer. She has sat for over two days without a break, giving thousands and thousands of people hug after hug. Sarah MacDonald goes to visit Mother Amma thinking these stories about her are a joke. She ends up getting a hug and asking for something nice. Then after a couple more days and feeling like her wish hasn't been granted, she gets another hug from Mother Amma. This time she decides to ask for something silly.

She asks for big tits.

A month later and after various medical advice and observation, she flies home to Australia to get more medical advice to try and discover what these two massive lumps are that have appeared in both her breasts. She states in the book that her tits had become massive. She gets scared that it may be cancer and soon discovers that no doctor in India or Australia can comprehend what the lumps are.

I wasn't after big tits from Mother Amma as I thought I'd get bored of them after a month or so. But I was intrigued to see how it all worked and wanted to find out for myself what the fuss was all about. I was also hoping that maybe she could help me to start feeling better about myself and clear my mind, allowing me to know what I wanted, and what the fuck I was supposed to be doing in the world. I doubted the little Indian lady could do this, but I was willing to try anything.

I arrived at some gates, walked through this massive hall, was then put in a dorm, told when food was served and then left to my own devices. There was a French guy playing some drums in my room, and then a Scottish guy called Dee arrived, and we went for a walk. His full name was Dee Sunshine, and I said, "Wow, you must have had hippy parents," and he said "No I'm the hippy, I changed it myself".

Dee carried this pink ukulele across his back, and I soon discovered he was a poet, writer, painter and traveller from Glasgow who'd been travelling mainly around Asia for the last seven years.

I was being told by everyone I met how lucky I was to turn up at the Ashram when Mother Amma was home, as she was away for so much of the year giving people Darshan (blessings) and doing her global humanitarian work. The Ashram was situated on the famous backwaters of Kerala, which is this huge network of wide natural canals, deep in the jungle. Mother Amma had always lived where the Ashram is. She was born in a small village that used to be here to a very poor family with a very small house and a cowshed. When

Amma was born she was blue, and she would constantly talk about Krishna, and her knowledge of him seemed impossible for a small child to possess. Soon Amma's gifts became apparent, much to the dismay of her family and Indian tradition. In her early teens, she was banished to the cowshed and from there she started to get followers and disciples. Soon it became too small and extra buildings had to be built. Today there are around three thousand permanent residents, which can almost double with passing guests.

The place and facilities were very impressive. There was a huge hall, a large chapel, a big restaurant, several shops, a recycling centre, a yoga studio, a seven-storey block of apartments and various other buildings. Lots of new buildings were also being built. It was like the place was about to double in size, not for the first time.

The next morning, I woke and headed for yoga. My head was not in a good space, and I was feeling mentally abused by myself. *What am I doing here? What is all this about? Is it all bollocks? What the hell is wrong with me that I need all this? Should I not just be enjoying myself on a beach surrounded by beautiful women?*

After yoga, it was time for me to get in the queue in the chapel where Amma was giving out her hugs for most of the day. I got in line and had to wait for a couple of hours. Apparently, people have waited for over twelve hours in the past. I then had to decide my intention for the hug, what I wanted help with, what problems I had or anything specific that needed to be resolved or any ailments I had. I procrastinated and procrastinated over what I wanted and the next thing I knew I was being ushered by the disciples towards Amma, being told which direction to put my head, when to ask for whatever it was I wanted and what language it was I understood. Then, bang, I was thrust into her awaiting arms. She grabbed me tightly, and I melted into her round body and large bosom like a baby, making itself comfortable on its mother's shoulder. I asked, "Please help me, please help me, I don't want to feel like this anymore." Then I was pulled away, given something to eat and drink and made my way outside to discuss the experience with Dee. It all happened a bit quick I thought, and I guess I was expecting more, like some fireworks or maybe seeing God, but it was just a nice rushed hug.

Amma's uncle had died the day before I arrived and was laid to rest one evening. Everyone gathered to watch the passing body being carried by people dressed all in white. I realised I should be dressed in white. Everyone else was. I felt like a dick. The body was carried towards a huge body of water whilst prayers were constantly repeated. The body was laid on a huge pile of wood, and the wood was set alight. Everyone sang and said prayers and I looked at how beautifully bright it was and, although crying, how happy everyone seemed compared to the very sombre affairs I was used to at home. It's like everyone thinks they have to pay respect by being depressive, dejected and quiet. Why can't we just feel whatever it is we are feeling but still with a smile?

Before I left, I crossed the river to explore the locals' village, which seemed like real India with its one-storey shops and people running about. I passed a shop and saw an old white man dressed all in white drinking something, obviously he was from the Ashram. I looked around the open-fronted shop inquisitively, and the man in white said, "You must buy the mixed fruit smoothie."

I did, and we walked back towards the Ashram together. I told him I was leaving later and that I'd had my hug yesterday and he said, "Wow, you are very lucky."

"So I believe," I said.

I then asked him how long he was staying and he said he wasn't sure, maybe he would go home to Denmark and see his children and grandchildren soon. I asked him when he arrived, and he said, "Oh, it must have been about twenty-seven years ago."

I almost spat out my mixed fruit smoothie and asked, "What's kept you here that long?" and he told me that Amma had wanted him to stay and teach engineering at the university she was setting up. He told me Amma has a university that is educating thousands of Indian children each year, and I wondered how this one woman had achieved so much.

He then insisted on buying me some gifts from the shop which were a couple of books about Amma, an Amma picture, an Amma ring and an Amma bookmark, oh and some Amma incense. I was fully Amma'erd up and ready for my trip south. I caught a boat with Dee Sunshine, where we sat and chatted. He told me about his tough times, and I told him about mine. Then we got on to love and women. I discovered he had a daughter in Glasgow that he hadn't seen for many years and I could see the tears in his eyes as he remembered her. He talked about his art, and as he did, he exquisitely sketched the stunning, slow winding waters in front of us with the thick jungle draping over the banks, as if almost wanting to fall into the water.

I then told him about my depression and problems and the fact I felt like I was in love with two girls and it was destroying me every day, but I had made this vow to Fhian that I would be honest and I didn't want to be causing a mess everywhere I went any more. Dee just looked me in the eye and said, "Follow your heart, that's all you can do." Follow your heart even if it causes a shit storm. It's all we can do as people, he said. Instantly my heart seemed to beat Renie. Then I thought it was beating Fhian and then I was unsure which was my heart and which was my mind and then I thought, shit that's what I should have asked Amma. Show me how to follow my heart, please?

Tamil Nadu was my next destination, situated at the southernmost tip of India where three seas meet (Arabian Sea, Bay of Bengal and Indian Ocean). It is also home to Gandhi's temple, someone I wanted to pay my respects to for having had such a positive influence on me. The train ride south was as picturesque as one could imagine, coastal bliss to one side and coconut palm trees bursting the skyline from every available piece of earth. I sat and watched the world go by with my feet dangling out of the train door with an element of contentment of how beautiful the world can be. I felt so free at not being told to be careful about everything and worrying whether or not it was legal. People we passed on roads were piled into cars with not the slightest bit of interest about whether the vehicle was insured. Families of four managed to balance on mopeds, and at one point, I saw ten people on a rickshaw. Kids wheelied their motorbikes and it seemed like everyone was having fun.

I arrived early in the morning, bumped into a German woman and a French lady who was travelling with her daughter, and we all found a place to stay. We spent the day exploring the southernmost tip of India and the temple that sat on a rock just off the mainland. We all went to see Gandhi's temple and were given a tour by the most charismatic ex-military man. He had this moustache that seemed to twizzle across his face and almost beyond his shoulders. In the most theatrical and humorous way, he showed us around. I wanted to be still in this place. I wanted to sit and think about this amazing man Gandhi who I felt would one day be seen as some sort of god, prophet or Jesus-like figure.

The next morning, I was up early, trying not to wake my sleeping French friends and made my way north again towards the

Shivananda Yoga Ashram. Yoga was another thing that swamped my mind when I thought about it. There were so many types, and I knew that I wanted to be a yoga teacher one day, but what was the right one for me? It all seemed too much to take when I thought about it, and with the washing machine of other thoughts that were on a constant spin cycle in my mind, I tried my best not to procrastinate about it too much. I took a train ride to this big city called Trivandrum and then found a bus that took me off into the mountains.

When I arrived, I was having an internal war. I wasn't sure if I should go in, I wasn't sure if I was ready for a strict five days of yoga, meditation and limitations. I was battling inside. I wanted to relax, I wanted to chill, I felt internally tired and felt I needed some rest. A huge part of me wanted yoga and wanted these teachings. I thought about my time constraints. I wanted to go back to Om Beach, it was magical. This place didn't do it for me. It was beautiful but not the same vibe as Om beach. I stood there outside the gates, unable to commit. I was almost walking in, and then I was walking away. It was like I had two people inside me pulling in opposite directions. I walked away, and then I walked back, and I thought I was going mad as two voices in my head fought each other.

I walked in and went to the reception. It was the same atmosphere as the Buddhist Centre in Bethnal Green. It was chilled, quiet, and people smiled politely. I was nervous, and I didn't know what to ask. What was I here for? How long did I want to stay? Did I want to stay? I felt like anxiety had taken over me and that if I tried to talk nothing would come out. I was even starting to forget what I was doing there and what this place offered. I tried to cover up my angst by looking at posters on the wall. I then got into a queue for the reception.

I got one space from the front, and I turned and left. I went back out onto the street, and again I fought with the two polar opposites fighting away in my head. I just wanted to smash my head against a wall and be done with it. I was wondering if I was schizophrenic or maybe I was bipolar or something? I definitely didn't feel like Liam Browne.

I walked off and waited for a bus, very disappointed with myself. I decided that I would have a day or two in Fort Kochi and then head back to Om Beach. Decision made.

In Fort Kochi, I was still in my mope, inside I felt like I was dying. I was feeling alone, I missed Fhian, I missed Renie, I missed me Mum. I wanted someone to be here with me, I didn't like being alone; it made me feel tense and that people would look at me and think, look at that weirdo on his own. I wanted to be travelling with a mate, but none of me mates wanted to do the things I was doing, and I felt like I had no mates who were like I was now.

Fort Kochi was unlike anywhere else in India, it seemed very Portuguese as it had been repeatedly run and taken over by different European Powers so had this rich array of culture, architecture and cuisine. Beautiful, landscaped walkways led to the beach, and Chinese fishing nets lined the coast as men worked hard to lower and then pull back up these very elegant devices to unveil the awaiting loot of fresh fish.

The next day I wandered around the place, it was stunning. I sauntered through plazas, across fields where kids were playing football and cricket but I couldn't even bring myself to join in. I was feeling so detached from my body.

The place seemed very middle class, with a slow pace to life and was a stark contrast to the constant hum and drum of every other town I'd seen in India so far.

I found a rock to sit on and watched some fishermen on the Chinese nets. It was majestic how their small delicate bodies swayed from side to side as they pulled at the ropes that lifted the net.

The fisherman called me over.

I thought it was a scam.

They would let me take some pictures then ask for some money for doing so. It was all in the book. I said no, but they insisted, and one of them came and grabbed me and took me on the platform. I felt massive compared to the four fishermen. The guy who could speak the most English and was the most endearing and friendly was the smallest. His name was Prakash. He was tiny, and I felt like an overweight giant compared to them all. The others were called Josey who looked like an Indian version of some 1950s Hollywood film star. Then there was Koya who had a little potbelly.

Finally, there was Joseph who built and owned the net and had this amazing posture and elegance about him. They persuaded me to stay on the net with them and help them for a while. The next thing I knew I was learning the ropes, collecting fish when the guys lifted the net and putting them in plastic boxes that Prakash ran off with towards the market, returning a few minutes later with cash for

Joseph. I helped lower the net and then it was my turn to have a go at lifting it. The net was lowered, and as Joseph hung over the side looking into the water where the net was, he would give the order, and we would pull her up. It was hard. I hardly felt like I was contributing. I was putting all my weight into it, which was at least two stone more than any of the other guys. I looked across, sweat dripping down my face and Josey and Koya weren't even out of breath. I was panting, they were just flowing. I felt too big, too clumsy and out of balance, a bit like my mental state. When I looked at Joseph, who was the closest to my size I saw there wasn't an ounce of fat on him. He looked healthy and strong, and his frame was very similar to mine. It made me want to be stronger, and to not carry any unnecessary weight.

We caught some big snapper and Prakash told me it was time for food which I helped him prepare. He showed me how to kill and then gut and de-scale the fish, then how to add all the spices to the dish and start to cook. It was eye-opening how easy it was to make great fresh food. He that told me that the sardines would be here at 3 pm. We ate, and I mulled on how he had predicted the sardines would arrive at 3 pm, Had he arranged a meeting with them or something? I thought maybe it was an Indian saying and had a different meaning than the one it suggested. I started getting more competent at pulling the huge ropes to get the net up. The guys still laughed at me as I tugged as hard as I could at the rope, dripping with sweat.

I found out that the men were all married with children except Prakash. I asked him why and he said he didn't know, and that he was now too old. He looked a little sad as he told me and my heart nearly broke.

All the guys wore these long sarongs that looked super masculine, and when they were getting in position, they folded them in half, so they looked like they were wearing some kind of mini skirt. I guess it would have been mildly erotic for someone attracted to men. They all smoked a lot and laughed a lot, and as I worked, I thought what a beautiful job these guys had. It paid them, provided for their families, kept them fit and healthy, they had a laugh with their mates all day outside in the beautiful sunshine and got to jump in the water at their will in the most stunning surroundings. It seemed perfect. Again I drifted off into jealousy of what these men had and in so many ways how it was so beautifully simple.

3 pm came, and the net was lowered.

Low and behold, thousands of Sardines. They were going nuts. Prakash and I packed them into the boxes, the net was lowered again and another full haul. This continued for about forty minutes, and then the frantic sound stopped, and Prakash went to market, and the sardines were no more. It seemed crazy that they turned up every day at 3 pm. My brain couldn't really process it like it can't process how planes work, so I let it slide. We then ate our evening meal which was mixed fish curry, and I got us a bottle of rum to share. I realised that I had been in the sun all day with no protection and looked like a lobster and wondered if I threw myself in the net whether or not Prakash would bundle me into a basket and take me to market. We ate, drank and got merry and laughed a lot after the rum started to flow. I ended up pretty drunk and started thinking that if I hadn't been alone today none of this would have happened and that so far this had been the best day I'd had in India. Whilst I had been on the net, I'd forgotten most of my problems. I had been busy; I'd had a purpose. This was what I needed. I needed a purpose.

I headed back to Om Beach. My plan was to chill, race to the other beach each morning for yoga and admiration for the massive German and try and get good at Frisbee. I returned to the same accommodation. Some of the same faces were there, and some new ones had arrived. I then spotted a guy on the beach who was the best person I'd ever seen at Frisbee. I approached him and said, "Hey man, I'm only here for three days, can you please make me good at Frisbee?"

He said, "Certainly," and Jordan from Canada became my new best friend.

He showed me the basics, and soon we were launching the Frisbee to one another with about fifty meters between us. We made extravagant dives and caught stray throws, running into the sea. It was amazing, I felt so free and focused. Running around all day sweating, laughing, feeling fit and healthy. Jordan was addicted. He was so good, and he played for a team in Canada. I didn't even know Frisbee was a team sport. He told me he played for the third-best team in the whole country.

Jordan was also a traveller, photographer and writer. He was in India to finish a book he was writing about when he walked from the west coast of Canada south through the States to the Mexican border as a photography project. He was a pretty amazing guy, and again I was a bit in awe.

One day we got stoned whist I was sitting in a hammock looking through his massive collection of prints, trying to choose one I wanted. It took me ages because I was so stoned and I really wanted the right one for me. It was as if I had to make the right decision, and if I got it wrong I would regret it and beat myself up forever. This was how I felt with most decisions as if the whole course of my life would be defined by it. I ended up picking this picture of an old man, and a lady sat down on the floor with their legs crossed. They are both looking into the camera, she is leaning towards camera with a slight smile on her face thrusting a picture of a white cat forward. The cat is in the centre of the picture, sat facing the camera. The cat casts a sinister black shadow behind it. As I looked at it, a million reasons why flew through my mind. Was the cat dead and had she loved it very much? Was it a famous sacred cat? How did they afford to have the picture to be taken and have it framed when they look like they have very little? Was the cat evil and keeping away more evil spirits? All of these I pondered. The bloke next to her, possibly her husband, is leaning back with his head tilted slightly to the left looking a little agitated as if to say, "Oh we are having our picture taken, and she has to get the fucking cat picture out again. When will you let go, woman?"

That's why I chose that picture. Jordan said no one had ever deliberated like that before. I thought, What is wrong with me? Why can't I make any decisions easily?

I then got lost, making my way to the beach which was only ten metres from Jordan's room.

I eventually got to there, and Jordan had the Frisbee in hand and asked me where I'd been because I'd taken so long. Embarrassed by my stoned behaviour I said, "the toilet" and we started to throw the disc again. Again I confirmed with myself that I was not a very good stoner and should never do it.

Gokarna was the town closest to Om Beach and was extremely sacred. As I walked around, the spirituality of the place seemed to ooze out and drip onto me. Mystical old Indian men would pass, and sacred artwork and patterns were everywhere. There were little temples, churches and places of worship and incense covered up any nasty smells as I walked through its smokey, chilled haze. The focal point of the town was a huge sacred pool of water. Flowers were scattered around the steps that lined the sides which led into the water. As I looked around, sacred ceremonies were taking place everywhere. Men were chanting as they passed beads through their fingers, women washed their children, and people bowed and prayed whilst flicking water over themselves.

Every morning I raced over to the Yoga Farm. Sprinting along the beach, up the steps, along the cliff top with the vast views, down the boulders onto the beach and through the lapping shoreline, then up the hill to the farm. It was refreshing, and my body was starting to feel good. Yoga was tough, and I couldn't get into any of the positions. I was usually good at sports straight away, but with this I was most definitely bottom of the class. By the reception an old grey-haired hippy guy was looking up at the German teacher's treehouse, admiring the craftsmanship. He then said to the teacher, "I love that you have tied each piece of wood together and not used nails". The German teacher said, "Why hurt the tree man? It's done nothing to me."

Again, I just melted at his words. This man was on another plane to anyone I'd ever met, and as we spoke, a beautiful woman started to ascend the tree-house. I discovered that this was his lady and I was in total admiration for this man and his life. It seemed like a dream, a dream I wanted to be a part of and after fully falling in love with Om Beach, India, Jordan, the food, yoga, The German yoga teacher and Frisbee, it was time for me to head back to the unknown and my unknown home. I was so uncertain of where home was, but I was so sure it wasn't London.

AYAHUASCA 2, THE JOURNEY, MAY 2013

The setting was exactly the same; three rolled mattresses laid out against the wooden plank walls. A tall, slender gentleman sat in the spot Dave had occupied the previous evening.

Being typically English, I went for the same seat I'd had last night.

The new guy and Otillia were chatting in Spanish. I smiled and nodded, feeling a bit nervous and useless. The guy came over to introduce himself. He was called Ollie.

"Mucho gusto," I replied, hoping I wouldn't tell him I had a man in Miami and we had a daughter together.

I felt like I'd had a little more time to prepare for the ceremony. I knew I wanted a stronger journey, to see more visuals, and visions and to be taken far, far away. A lady then joined the room, and again the tradition began. This time a darker looking liquid was produced from a bag in a two-litre plastic bottle. The prayers and blessings were said, and we were all blown with smoke. Ollie was first to drink, and I remember thinking my stomach didn't feel as strong as it had the previous night.

Was this due to it being emptier due to the fasting or was it a bit dodgy?

I was then called up and given my brew. It seemed thicker and darker and more pungent than the previous evening. I held up the cup, blew on it three times, setting my intentions, "to be able to see" and, "for my mind to be cleared". I knocked back the liquid, it tasted so much worse. Was it the same brew, I thought? Or was it because I was feeling different? Instantly on returning to my mat, I was finding it hard to keep down. Was this punishment for my uncontrollable ego last night? I sat trying to get comfortable, hoping beyond hope to keep the liquid down. It seemed to be bubbling in the top of my throat, and I battled to keep it at bay. The lady then drank her brew, then Otillia and the candle was blown out.

I was starting to sweat, praying it would stay down, my mouth constantly filling up with liquid bile, which as soon as I'd swallowed it, it was back in my mouth which led to several minutes of discomfort and frustration.

I was really fighting the sensation to not be sick.

In any other situation, I would have already been sick.

I looked around, determined not to be the first to spew. Everyone else seemed to be comfortable, it was going to be me, I knew it. I was really struggling, but all of a sudden, an air of calm engulfed me, my body settled, and I felt normal again. Visuals began and again they were in black and white but more multi-dimensional, then the battle began again, and my mouth was full of liquid. I was determined not to let it out, frightful that I would not get its full effects with it being in my body for such a short period. I had thoughts of a story I'd heard about a guy going clubbing, who would take a pill and be sick when it started to take effect. He would then root around in the sick to find the pill and take it again. There was no way I was eating my sick!

'Hold it down, Browne,' I kept telling myself. 'If it comes out, you're not eating your sick.' The liquid came, and I swallowed, and after another few minutes I felt I had control again and sat back and relaxed. Then I felt the depth of my stomach explode, and everything came racing up. I reached for my bucket and spewed, my guts hitting the bowl just as my arms brought it into the line of fire.

I felt defeated, first to blow. Was this punishment for my ego? Would I now see nothing? Was the ceremony going to be pointless for me? Had I lost my latest opportunity to travel with Lady Ayahuasca? I had no idea that what was about to unfold would change me forever.

The purging was violent. Four times the depths of my stomach were emptied. Then as I wiped my mouth of the disgusting residue, I closed my eyes to be welcomed into another world. Fluttering geometric patterns, morphing into figures, jungle sounds which I can only describe as the alien sounds from movies like *Predator* and *District 9* fluttered into my ears. I saw beautiful otherworldly creatures similar to those from *Avatar*, but with Egyptian-style longer heads and headdresses that were not headdresses but their actual heads. They looked a bit like the Williams sisters when they'd first hit the news with their beaded hair, but an alien version. I was shown visual perfection only to be replaced by a greater visual perfection, which would make the previous seem trivial, old and unimaginative. I opened my eyes and visions from within were imprinting on the world.

I decided to lie down and enjoy, a decision I have now discovered is never advised. It is said it can invoke the darker side of Ayahuasca. Lady Ayahuasca demands respect for you to remain upright and focused. I read this a day or two later, so there and then I just sank into my mattress in pure bliss, unaware of the danger that lay ahead. My knees were up and my back completely flat on the floor, placing each vertebra individually on to the wood, my hands crossed onto my chest. My eyes were closed, and I was in Heaven. It was Paradise, but a million times better than I could have ever imagined. There were shapes I had never seen before, vibrating and pulsating colours, fluttering figures flickering into view. This was more like what I'd been expecting.

I was fully submerged in another world.

These complex beings with their braided head-dresses, were less human than the aliens in *Avatar*, more elaborate, with huge eyes and elegantly sculpted faces. It was as if they were sophisticated robots, one you could imagine existing in a few hundred years.

My inner world was illuminated.

I was shocked by its vastness, the infinity of shapes and colours that had erupted in my mind. Time and space seemed to stand still. The present didn't exist, and neither did the future and the past, but at the same time, they all existed simultaneously in each different realm. I started to stretch out and loosen my body, moving the sick bowl with my foot to one side and the blissful feeling of my limbs fully extended and stretching erupted up my body and into my head, this electric current fizzing all around my scalp. I stretched out my arms moving the drinking water to the side, my body reaching as far as it could and my mind starting to do the same. I was seeing, this was it, this is what I'd asked for. I was yawning a lot, big deep yawns that brought me bliss and satisfaction, my body feeling like it was reaching its full potential, half on the mattress half on the wooden floor, I was parallel with the wall now.

Bliss and love filled me. Fhian and my baby were back, and I held them so close, so tight, knowing this was all that mattered. I could feel the presence of my mum, of her approval and her deep love. It literally blew away any love I had ever felt before. More intense, meaningful and beautiful than any love that had ever existed. That was my family right there, the security and stability I'd been looking for, I'd created it, I held on and held on. Bliss engulfed me, and I felt like I would explode with pure abundant love all over everybody's faces.

I was now upside down, my legs were up the wooden wall, I wanted to be upside down to turn the world on its head. My head and shoulders stayed on the ground, but my feet insisted on being the highest part of my body. They were stretching and tapping, flinging themselves about. I really wanted to be upside down, maybe it was because I was in the Southern Hemisphere and at home that would mean I was the right way up?

It was the first time in a while I felt like I could stretch unbridled, my body had been so tense, and sore and I hadn't known why. The plant diet had made me so tired the last two days that hammock time was all that had mattered.

I went into a shoulder stand.

I couldn't help it, my body just did it. I hoped it didn't seem like I was showing off.

I hadn't moved for five hours the previous night, and here I was all over the place. I then went into a wheelbarrow and a crab. I utterly had no control, this was all just happening, and in my body it felt so good. I felt free with it, but the real me would have been petrified at the spectacle I was making of myself. My upright limbs crashed down with a thud, then I clasped my feet and stretched my leg out fully. All the while visual after visual cascaded my inner eye and I watched as my head whirled around in blissful glee. I was tapping and banging and making sounds with my mouth, like an institutionalised loon.

Otillia's beautiful *Icaro's* began, and this transported me to another level further, it was like the music was a spaceship, and she was the driver, and we went off into the Universe. My body reacted further to the music, tapping, banging, smashing and crashing. My floating arms would crash around from side to side like a monkey.

When the music stopped, I became instantly still, frozen. I would become aware of my body, and it was always stuck in the weirdest positions. I observed myself with my limbs piled on top of me but finding it so, so comfortable.

I then started to play with gravity, holding my limbs up high and then, as if gravity had been turned up really high, I would release the limb, and it would hurtle towards the Earth and crash down onto my chest or face, and I would make a crash sound with my mouth to add effect. I briefly turned my head to the other drinkers, they were sat completely still like sedated chimps in a zoo. I gazed in amazement while my tongue whirled around my mouth frantically. I had no control at all, then the music stopped, and I stayed completely still for what seemed like an eternity. It was as if the whole atmosphere of the world was collapsing on me. Pinned to the floor by a large imaginary piece of glass, I lay holding it like some horizontal French mime artist. I was so still, worried if I would ever be released.

Gravity had been turned up so high, and I was being pinned down to the wooden floor. The next thing I know I was tucked around my mattress, holding it tight, resting my head on it mumbling, "Mamma, Mamma," wanting her near. My eyes were enquiring, and I could see the moon through a gap in the wooden walls. Wow, it's so bright and beautiful, I thought, with perfect ribbons of clouds drifting by it, giving it a real cinematic feel. I studiously lined it up, so it was perfectly in the middle of the gap between the wooden slats. I gawped at its beauty as if right now the moon and the sky were only for me.

People and their jobs went through my mind, the way society was festering in me, our continual race to meet expectations, the jobs we do, their meaning, their greater good. I wanted to drag Fhian away, take us away, take us home. Away from the swarm of society that wouldn't let go of its perceptions, illusions and patterns of behaviour that it holds onto so tightly in fear of anything different, being brainwashed enough to die for what it thinks it believes in.

Nothing seemed real.

The number of pointless jobs, people building, destroying, suffering, hating, shitting and dying! Just to occupy people, to ensure they don't look within. I started to laugh, laugh so hard at what so many people did with their time, how serious they took their roles, how little fun they had and most of the time at the detriment of the environment, Mother Earth and their own personal health. I couldn't stop laughing, it wasn't at people, it was at the madness of the system. Deep, guttural laughs echoed around the room. Then I snapped myself out of it.

Otillia's *Icaro's* began, and I meandered back through space and time. I was being taken on a magical mystery tour. Gravity was occasionally turned up, and I was starting to feel stuck, starting to have difficulty with reality and how gravity actually worked. Confusion engulfed me, my limbs would tap, noises would spill from my mouth, and I had no control and no idea what was real. The music stopped, and I froze, every muscle in my body tensed and then I let everything crash down to the floor, and I lay silently for a moment, manoeuvring beautifully with my limbs as the music ended in my mind.

I was then flung back into confusion. What was my hand? What were my ideas? What was life? Is this my leg? Who are you? Does anything matter? Why was I born there? Why has life been hard? Is this a room? I sat there curled up and confused, shaking a little. I felt abused, it was like I was being poked at, my skin being pulled. I was being raped, jabbed, my eyes were torn out, fingered, my penis torn off, abused. It was this confirmation that we were moving into the age of the feminine, and it was time for me to pay for the male condition. It's your turn, it's your turn to suffer now was going through my head and I felt disgusted by the way women had always been treated. I could feel their pain, all their misery, all their despair. I was taking it all on, I was suffering for all the times I had taken women for granted, seeing them as objects for so long.

I lay there in my own mess, shit, piss, sick, sweat and vomit all covered me, I had no idea if it was real. I felt stuck, trapped, unable to move my body. None of my limbs felt like mine. I was realising that I am not my body, whatever happens to it is irrelevant, it's the soul that counts, your soul can endure any physical damage to the body.

I was being told that abuse of any sort can be healed, repaired, fixed, and my body became a worthless piece of flesh.

I sprang up, grabbed my sick bucket and on all fours forcefully erupted once again.

From deep down it rose up through me, splattering into the bowl. Every time I wretched it was as if part of me was disappearing, all the dogma from parents, society, government, marketing, religion and consumerism. All the pain that had been inflicted on me as a child was coming out. Everything I had no choice about was being stripped away from my soul.

My soul wanted me clean, wanted me healed, wanted me to see the light, to see the truth, to follow my truth. It wanted me to rid myself of this baggage, these wounds, the anger, the pain and the suffering, so as not to pass it on to my children.

I had to learn from my parents' mistakes, not repeat them. I was being cleansed, ridded of this anguish, putting myself through this for the greater good. I was going back to where I was when I entered this world as a child, an empty vessel, without illusions, beliefs, opinions and prejudices. We become infected as we grow, and I no longer had to carry around this baggage I didn't want and did not choose. I crashed back down, feeling light, feeling like nothing mattered any more. Sweat was dripping from every one of my pores. I was drenched, so hot, grabbing at my clothes to allow some air in.

I took in the moon again and found some comfort as if it was home.

Then I started to feel more and more trapped, my concept of time redundant, occasionally hearing or seeing Otillia captaining the spacecraft. I was here in this room, and I became a monkey fascinated again with my hands and feet, climbing the wall, shitting and pissing freely from trees, primordial instincts filled me. I started to feel more and more empty and more and more lost, only very occasionally getting a thought. I felt stuck in this animal's body, rocking from side the side, forward and backward on my back, as my fingers hooked themselves around my toes and I experimented with the flexibility of my body parts.

Next, I was slithering around the floor, I was a snake now pinned to the ground on my back and belly, making hissing noises as opposed to monkey ones. I think it was at this point Ollie approached me and asked if I could stop the noises and the banging. Spaced out and looking at him upside down, I said, "I can't help it, man, I have no control," and went happily back to being a snake. The sound of everything amplified. I could hear the jungle with superhero hearing, and every time a fly or mosquito came near me, I flicked out my tongue to capture it. My eyes flicked from side to side, focusing intently on my prey. Again I found myself trapped against the floor, my head, shoulders and arms pinned by this huge invisible object that was on top of me.

I became some creature that lived under the water's surface. I would snatch my hands up when insects passed so I could feed. It was damp and soggy, I was sure I had been trapped in this amphibian's body for many years, life after life. Then past lives were flashing through my mind, not mine exactly but the concept. It felt like this was another life, my soul, the 'I' that I knew my consciousness was in this amphibian's body. I was living this life in the body of a small amphibian but with my awareness and consciousness still intact. I was enduring this hellish nightmare as punishment for a lesson I hadn't learnt and the bad lives I'd previously lived. Little snippets of information seemed to prick my brain, life was being assessed in a scary way, its point, its meaning on the bigger scale. It seemed inconsequential and meaningless. But then when I looked at it on the scale of the world, our solar system, the galaxies and the universe and the other universes, it was so very, very insignificant. Less significant than us on this planet, cutting a piece of sand for a million years and saying that final grain we had, had any significance. It has no significance, but at the same time is as significant as everything else, because it is everything else. Still, you would never get to a more insignificant piece on the larger scale of our individual lives in comparison to all that is, but still, we are part of all that is.

I then started to doubt my life. Was it real? Was this my life right here on the floor in this hut or under the water as the amphibian?

Had I imagined the life I had lived?

I started to firmly believe that everyone I'd ever met, every experience I'd ever had, was conceived in my imagination from where I now lay. I was so unsure, so many moments of my life flashed before my eyes. Were they real? Had I imagined them? Were all the people actors, was I in some kind of Truman Show? I felt like I may have created my own life in my own mind. I'd made it all up, everything that had taken place, every event, every person. It had all been a fragment of my imagination. I was saddened by the reality I'd created and the fact it had only existed in my head. I began to accept that all of the people close to me had never existed, I'd imagined them and created them out of boredom whilst waiting for a bug to feed on as I lay under the water's surface. My core knew that everything was an illusion, an illusion within an illusion, within a dream. I had no idea of what was real and what was not and what exactly those two things meant. I seemed to be trapped in a paradox that my brain could not fathom and all I could do was drool. I could make no sense of reality, I was here, I was stuck. I felt like Brad Pitt in *12 Monkeys* or Jack Nicholson at the end of *One Flew Over the Cuckoo's Nest*. I had completely lost it. I drooled and without any control watched my limbs, urging them to move, but they would not. I drifted from my old reality to my new, shame-filled me. I had been trapped in the Ayahuasca institution for either 16, 1000 or an infinite number of years. There were no other numbers.

It was definitely one of these amounts of time.

That was so clear to me.

I'd let my family down with my life and my actions.

I imagined my mum's sorrow for her only son wallowing away in his own madness, unable to control any of his bodily functions. I was hearing all my friends and acquaintances gossiping on how they knew I would lose the plot a long time ago. "If anyone would lose it, you could put money on it being Liam," I heard.

Internally I screamed, 'nooooooooooooooooooo,' ripping at my own body, annoyed with what had become of me. I was never going to fulfil any of my dreams, my own family, watching my babies grow, my only want in life had now disappeared forever, never to be fulfilled, lost, redundant and I was stuck here for the rest of time. Like Bill Murray in *Groundhog Day*, I was stuck, I was on a loop, and I was unable to escape. But I knew I had to figure it out, I was so scared, petrified even, that everything was ruined, and I was a failure. I'd gone a step too far in my pursuit of freedom, of wisdom, of enlightenment and now I was just covered in piss and shit.

I looked around the room I'd been stuck in all this time, 16, 1000 or an infinite number of years. The other two people who had started the ceremony were long gone. I was there alone, being abused by my own mind under the watchful eye of Otillia. She had been keeping watch of me all this time since my incident since I became lost from reality since I'd been unable to function in the real world.

Or was this the real world, had everything been made up? Doubts and fears of everything pursued my thoughts. I was wrangling with this fine line of what anything was and what anything had ever been.

It was frightening to be in a position of not believing anything that went through your mind, being unable to summon your body to do anything you wanted it to do. This must be how some disabled and mentally handicapped people feel, and I was truly experiencing it. I firmly believed this was my life from now on; a constant battle, a constant struggle, unable to do anything for myself.

The open door then came into focus. Maybe one day soon I could summon enough energy to get out of that door. Maybe then I could lift myself from this mess and make it outside and then to my hut. I lay contemplating this for another eternity with as much concentration as a prison break. Finally, after more internal wars, battles and disagreements, I mustered the courage and energy to lift myself.

I staggered to the door, the blood instantaneously rushing to my head like a waterfall barraging and churning the depths of the water below. This turned off the lights of my mind, and I thought I'd lost my chance and any second guards would rush in, putting me in a straitjacket and bundling me into an isolation chamber.

As the lights of my eyes re-established the world around them, I focused again on leaving this *Apocalypse Now* style prisoner of war camp for the insane.

As I peered at what had been my surrounding for the last 16, 1000 or an infinite number of years, the moon struck a series of beautiful white lines across the floor of the darkened hut as it broke through the gaps in the wooden wall. The light was now fully returned to my eyes. I balanced at the top of the steps leading down from the room to the jungle floor. With all the energy and concentration, I could muster, I navigated the darkened, wooden steps to freedom.

I was out.

I rushed towards my hut through the gardens like a prisoner to freedom, and like a prisoner I panicked about what awaited me on the outside. This realisation stopped me in my tracks, and I stood frozen, my body stuck, my mind stuck. Was there even a hut?

Was I heading the right way if there was one?

Would I end up walking deep into the jungle and be lost forever, eaten alive by its inhabitants?

Where was I?

Was this a dream?

Finally, I came to the conclusion I was stuck in *Groundhog Day*. I was not Bill Murray, I was Liam Browne, I was trapped in a day for all of time. I knew this exact situation, I had been here before, that much was clear. I felt that safety was back in Otillia's room. But I didn't want that safety, I needed out of that torture, out of that worse-than-Hell situation. I knew I had to go forward, hut or no hut. I walked and started to think I was seeing the same things over and over again, trees, landscapes, over and over I passed the same repeated sequence, over and over as I trod barefoot slugging through shallow pools of snakes which had now become the ground. I could feel them slithering smoothly between my toes and twisting and constricting themselves around my ankles. Every time I lifted my leg, I would have to shake them off.

One tall tree stood out just ahead.

I recognised that tree.

I decided to remember it and make sure I passed it.

I tied a mental piece of string to that tree. But I just kept passing it and passing it. A thousand times, the sequence was on loop, and I started to panic again. I kept being flung back to where I had started. Finally, I got past it, and in the distance my hut appeared. I ran for it, shaking snakes from my feet.

Safety beckoned. I was free, then, as I was running, I questioned whether it was my hut.

Had I ever been there before?

Was there ever a hut?

Who was waiting for me in there?

I decided death was better than the eternity I'd just spent trapped on the floor.

When I was finally got into the hut, nothing seemed real, objects would warp coming towards me and then bend the other way. I felt like I had been lured here, it was a trick. I'd fallen into a trap. I quickly needed safety, and the only place that offered any was my bed protected by the impenetrable force that was my mosquito net. I crawled under the net, tucked it back under the mattress and lay in a foetal position facing the wall. Sweating, damp and dirty, I was unable to understand anything.

How long had I been gone?

Was I safe now?

What was going on?

This is where they had wanted me, I thought. Now in my straitjacket, trapped in this little space I was now stuck here. I screamed in my head, not wanting anyone to hear. I lay petrified, curled up as tight as I could. I felt like a baby, not a man. I thought of Fhian and never seeing her again. Disgust at what I had done filled me. I'd let my mind take over, I'd been tricked, made to look a fool, there was nothing I could do. Dread engulfed my whole pathetic body and self. I lay for hour upon hour, and then someone was in my room.

I heard them enter.

I stayed perfectly still trying not to breathe. Was this it? Was I about to die? Things were crashing around, footsteps slowly stepped on the floorboards which creaked in an eerie fashion. I was too scared to move, to speak, to do anything. I was praying I would be safe, hoping they would not kill me. I wanted them to just take what they wanted and leave. I was listening in that scared way, where your breathing becomes so shallow you can't hear it and you hold your breath for as long as possible for optimum sound intake. I listened and listened. The person moved around and then took a long piss in my toilet. I wondered who it was, why hadn't I shut the door on my way in?

Even if I had, there was no lock, and the walls were made of wood, and the windows had no glass in them.

I was unable to do anything with my body. It was so tense and contorted.

I was trapped, confused, petrified, and I was now having to deal with a madman pissing in my toilet. His footsteps moved around after he finished and shook, my ears following his every move. He turned into my room, he approached my bed. I could feel him just on the other side of my mosquito net. What was he going to do? I could hear and feel his breath. Who was he? What did he want? Please make it fast, I thought.

I wanted to turn and look so badly, just to get a glimpse, but I was frozen. I hadn't moved a muscle for so long now, and my last breath seemed minutes and minutes ago. I was playing dead and remained as still as humanly possible. My inspiration was one of those guys in the city who paints himself metallic grey and stands like a statue for hours. Only I didn't want money, I just wanted this guy gone. It was such male energy, I could still feel and hear his guttural breathing, in and out. He felt so close he must have been staring at me as I could sense no other movement. An eternity passed, and I drifted in and out of consciousness. The breathing had finally stopped.

I lay there, and my next sensory stimulation started to come from straight in front of me, just on the other side of the wooden wall that my nose was almost touching. Still, I hadn't moved, God only knows how long I had been frozen for.

Soft music began to play. I recognised it as an *Icaro*, hearing the flowing sounds accompanied by the rattle of the dried leaves. It was like Otillia was outside my room, healing me, bringing me back to some level of normality, performing this ritual to close off the ceremony, to avoid bad energies entering me, closing me to outside interference.

I felt the glow return to my face, felt the heaviness leave my body. It was beautiful and magical to just listen, but again it messed up my head. What was real here? Was I imagining all this or had Otillia come to sing close to my bed to heal me? I had no idea. I was again still trapped and petrified, unable to grasp the real and unreal. However, with every sound and shake of the leaves, my mood continued to lighten. After some time of happily listening to these soothing beats, some sort of reality started to return. All I could think about was going home, not wanting to be insane anymore or risk insanity further by staying.

I finally got up, used the toilet and on the way back to my bed, grabbed my picture of Fhian. I just lay there looking at my beautiful goddess, deciding I couldn't risk never seeing her again and never having babies with her. Tomorrow, as soon as the sun came up, I would pack and leave and get back to my sweetheart as soon as possible.

It seemed like the morning would never come again. The rooster under my bed gave me the premature expectation of daylight with his, 'cockadoodledo'-ing on three separate occasions. Or was this another thing I was imagining?

Daylight finally arrived.

I was still set on leaving.

I wanted to talk to Otillia first and tell her my decision.

What had happened to me?

Was it normal?

Breakfast was called, and Ollie and Guylene were already in the commodore. I apologised for my noise and constant movement. They said what I was doing was pretty funny and very entertaining but at the same time disturbed them from their own experience. They then told me how I'd left the ceremony early.

I said, "No, you were gone when I left".

They said, "No, you left after only two hours, not even halfway through."

"Noooooooooo that can't be, I was there for so, so long."

"No," they concurred, "you left quickly and didn't return".

I'd only been in the room for two hours? It seemed absurd, but it had to be true. They were both a lot more sound of mind than I was. I wondered how so many lifetimes of events could have taken place in only a couple of hours. I truly thought I'd died and been trapped there for eternity, but eternity was only two hours in this reality? I was astounded and shocked.

I pondered on reality; was that my reality, is this my reality, what is reality, was that my future reality? Reality seemed such a personal thing, two people can see the exact same event, but their reality of it is completely different. It all depends on where they are coming from and where they're going and what else is on their mind at the time. We all see things differently, and we have to accept that everyone else sees it differently to us and not to push our own reality on others too much.

There is a Cesar Calvo quote that sums this up quite nicely, *"Things are not truly real, or only mere illusions. There are many categories in between, where things exist, many categories of the real, simultaneously and in different times".*

Ollie had been travelling for a few months, and this was the fourth time he had done Ayahuasca. He was a tall, fair-haired, spectacled Swedish young man and Guylene was a fifty-something French lady with short grey hair, a tooth filled smile that lit up the room and infected all around her with the happiness her expression created. She was a filmmaker living in Paris, and she interviewed myself and Ollie as I was still engulfed in fear, fascination and frustration.

Ollie's Spanish was excellent, and he agreed to translate what I wanted to ask Otillia and soon we all sat in the ceremonial room discussing the night's events. Ollie's and Guylene's Spanish had reiterated how non-existent my own was. Fear and ever-present self-doubt and disappointment circled my mind. Did I not have an ear for languages, or was I just lazy? Was it another thing I wanted to do but another thing I wouldn't put the hard work into? I pondered...

I asked Otillia if what had happened to me was normal.

She said, "It can happen, part of your true self came out, but you were filled with fear. You need this diet and this time to learn and grow. Last night's brew was strong with the Ayahuasca still in your system from the previous night, but your fear more than anything stepped forward, and that is what you have to overcome. Not being scared of who you truly are, stepping out of the costume of values and ego you've had people dressing you up with all your life. You need to step out of that and claim your power as yours. Step forward as the true you. The plants will help you overcome this and teach you who you are. It is a lesson you have to make sacrifices for. With the diet, the restrictions and allowing your mind and heart to be directed and your body, soul and spirit to be healed."

I told her that I had thought of leaving that day, flying home to my girl and asking her to marry me and that I wanted that commitment to have her as my family and then to have babies. She laughed and said, "You can't go back as you are, you behaved like a child, unable to control your actions, allowing your body and mind to be lost and unable to redeem your power. Who wants to marry that? Fathers have to be strong. We will get you there this week, these plants will take form in you and do this work, you need to see out the week and finish what you have started. Set your intentions in the next ceremony, but until then just take the plants and be still."

She would be trying other plants on me to try and lower my fear, give me strength and be mentally ready for the next ceremony and the next chapter in my life. We laughed about my monkey movements and shortly after regaining my faith in staying for the rest of the week, Guylene and Ollie left, and it was back to my language-less world.

The next four days were very solitary. I spent all my time in my hut, dividing it between the bed and hammock, occasionally reading and writing. It was a paradise for me. I would wake up, get in the hammock, be called for breakfast, drink some tea and my Ajo Sacha, return to the hammock, doze, maybe write, think about Fhian and missing my family and friends.

Some days I would be called for lunch, some days not, and I would wait till tea time. A flower bath could happen at any time. All of my other time was spent in my room. There were too many bugs and insects to sit out on the grass, and it was so damp and humid that the hammock was the perfect escape from everything. I'd had no idea of time since I'd arrived. Otillia did have a clock in the main room, but it always said 10:50 and every day I would forget it didn't work, assuming breakfast had been called late. I now also had no idea of the day or date, but I didn't need to know any of this. Here now, none of it mattered, and I imagined all the billions of people in cities all over the world running around to a tight schedule. Someone would come and tell me if it was time for food or a bath, saying, *"Señor, banyo"* or *"Señor, desyanuno"*.

It was amazing to not have to think about anything, not once was I bored or agitated. I just sat peacefully, swinging in my hammock, hour after hour, taking naps, having very little energy and absolutely no desire to do anything else. This must have been due to the plants and the diet. Usually I would be doing yoga, or press-ups and sit-ups, exploring my surroundings but never once did I feel like any of that. Before I arrived, I'd thought that with all the free time I would get myself super fit, but no, it was just hammock relaxation time for now.

The heavens would open, and torrential rain would fall. I would watch the droplets bounce almost a foot above the ground, and I would listen to the drops opening fire on my tin roof as damp moisture filled the air and the mosquitoes surrounded the net around my bed, waiting for an opening to get to my tasty flesh.

Darkness would arrive, and during the four nights, there were no ceremonies I went to bed shortly after sunset. The sky became completely black, and I could see nothing. I'd ran out of candles on the second night, so the only option was to go to sleep early. I was actually the only person travelling or just living in these parts that did not have a torch. However, it was so magical to be at the mercy of nature and to be living by its true ways.

I lay listening. It was a challenge to try and decipher what it was exactly making each noise. I found the bird noises the most soothing, there was one that sounded like a laser being shot. There was one like a crazy mobile ringtone, one like the ping-pong before an announcement in a public place and lots of sirens and further pongs.

One night I heard monkeys fighting. It was like war had broken out around my hut. I wish I could have seen what was taking place and known what the disagreement was about. The crickets and insects provided a steady backing track to any other action taking place.

One the fifth or sixth morning I was brought my Ajo Sacha. As I downed it I realised it wasn't Ajo Sacha, it was something else. Otillia's assistant said *"plantas"*, which is the word for all plants. I thought, well I can't ask what it is because I don't know how to, so I just waited to see what happened. Without moving from the hammock which swung close to the door, I watched the curvy lady, whose clothes were dirty and wet from the damp heat return towards the main house. I then got back to looking into space and rocking.

Within five minutes, parts of my body started to tingle. It was like a liquid, or energy was making its way through my bloodstream, entering every fibre of me, all my organs, vessels, cells and the hairs all over me stood on end. As it circulated through my veins, each part of my body it passed would start to vibrate and tingle. It was like someone had tipped a full bottle of energising body wash all over me, but more intense and not just on the outside but deep within me. I felt a little dizzy and spun out, but vitalised and present and the feeling lasted for about an hour.

On the day of my final ceremony, I was called to breakfast. I'd noticed how this was the first day I'd felt a little agitated like I had some energy and needed to be active. The heat had intensified and the rain which had been on and off the whole week hadn't stopped since the previous night. It was like someone was dropping swimming pools onto my tin roof. The mosquitoes had gone from a few here and there to an infestation in my damp, hot hut. I couldn't hammock without a constant battle with that evil taunt of the mosquito buzz. For hours I slapped and banged my legs, feet, arms and chest, trying to kill what seemed my only enemy in this world. My only safety seemed to be my bed and net, and now with the sheer numbers I couldn't even get in there without a few stowaways cadging a lift on some part of my body as I wriggled under. They would have to be decimated before I could relax and rest, endless minutes were spent identifying my targets and going in for the kill. If my mission had been successful I would have blood on my hands from this piece of pure evil that had already taken part of me, making revenge feel all the sweeter.

Later that day, I decided to venture to the hut next to mine. It was a good twenty metres away, and I'd never had the desire to go and have a look before, being so very happy with all that I had in my hut. It was identical to my own. I found a full box of candles and thought if I'd taken this arduous journey a few days earlier I could have had light after sunset.

As I made my way back to my hut, exhausted after this new and challenging adventure, a white couple came towards me. As soon as I started to talk, I felt a bit spaced out, the new medicine had been pretty intense. The couple were Lucias and Lisa from Oregon. I was particularly struck by how good-looking they were. He had these intense blue eyes, and the green of her eyes really drew me to them until I discovered her very large breasts. I wasn't sure if it was me or them on another planet? They had this air of higher consciousness about them and seemed to be floating. Everything was melting into everything else, and I was identifying more with the way I was feeling in the presence of other people. I discovered I would be in ceremony with them later that evening.

Lucias had first seen Otillia four years ago, with the rough directions to get off a bus at Kilometre 51 on route from Iquitos to Nakula and walk into the jungle for 30 minutes until you reach a hut. He said his life had changed from that moment on. He felt he'd found his path and had been to see Otillia every year since. They were now both energy healers back in Oregon and spiritual work, including music, dance and travel seemed to be their thing.

I felt a bit jealous, they really impressed me, I wanted part of what they had. Their lives seemed perfect, living in the beautiful countryside, with beautiful each other, so happy, so comfortable in their skin and sure of their path. I told them about the crazy experience I'd had four days before, and they advised me to stay sat upright, make clear my intentions, not leaving them open to interpretation, so they are not taken literally.

Ayahuasca had done exactly what I'd asked for, shown me what it could do and shown me how it would feel to lose my mind. Something I wasn't in a rush to experience again, and so I was considering what I wanted from this ceremony; my soul's path to be shown to me and the way I was to follow it. I wanted to connect to my higher self and figure out what I was on this Earth to do.

What was God's plan for me?

How could I follow that and be shown a path?

What parts of my life should I concentrate on?

I felt I had so many interests, so many things I enjoyed, felt passionate about, but was unable to commit to any of them as I always felt like I had so much going on. I was never settled, never in one place and felt this anxious dissatisfaction continuously. I really wanted to feel rooted, to have family and good friends and a community around me. I wanted to be in one place, create a home, a base, somewhere I could up and leave, go and work on disaster relief project or eco-house building projects, but always know I had that home to come back to.

My main intention for that evening was to be able to control the experience to an extent, not be as lost like last time. I decided to go with "please show me my life's purpose and give me some direction."

With that imprinted, I was really looking forward to the ceremony. I felt blessed to have Lucias there to translate again. I had been really blessed having bilingual people at each ceremony to tell me what Otillia was saying and to be able to pass on my questions the following morning. I had felt blessed, so often on this trip, everything just seemed to fall into place. The less I worried, the more everything I needed and wanted was provided for me. Maybe it was my new faith in that being the best way to live my life, maybe it was all the amazing trinkets and crystals I had been given by people I love back home and the way this energy was looking out for me, or maybe it was all the work I was doing in meditation, yoga and continually looking for growth and ways to improve myself. Whatever it was, I loved it, and it made life a breeze when it happened. Every time I meditated or prayed or intensely focused on something, it was provided, arrived or happened. If I only knew what to ask for, what exactly I wanted, then I could just focus on that and get it.

A deep hunger started to fill me. I hadn't felt hungry for the whole week. I knew I had to fast as it was the day of the ceremony, but with the heat, the humidity, the moisture and the mosquitoes I was massively agitated.

The light of the sun went out. The black blanket covered with stars was pulled over my head and hut. Time was now ticking down until the ceremony. I felt the nervous anticipation I would feel prior to playing in a Cup Final, excitement and fear brewing together. I washed myself, throwing bowls of water over my head, feeling it caress every part of me before hitting the wooden floor and escaping through the cracks on to the jungle bed below. I got dressed, covering as much skin as possible not to allow the continual mosquito biting. I waited to be called, rocking from side to side in the hammock, trying to keep a good speed so no mosquitoes could settle.

The mosquitos got too much, so I stood outside under the stars, waiting. I couldn't handle them, they were on me, so I went to the safety of my bed. Time was passing, it wasn't usually this long after it went dark that I was called for ceremony.

I waited and waited, but no one came.

I tried to relax, but nothing stilled my mind. I thought maybe Otillia wasn't going to have me there due to my behaviour in the last ceremony. I thought I heard music.

Had they started without me?

Would that happen?

I tried to steady my mind and drift off to sleep, convincing myself that whatever happened was exactly what should happen. I tried to clear my mind totally, make it as clear as it had been the previous days. Was it the fact I hadn't had my Ajo Sacha today? My mind leapt off, making conclusions and theories, I wanted out of it and to relax and not to worry.

"*Señor, señor*" was being called from my door just as I'd drifted off.

"*Si, si*", I said and jumped out of me bed and net. I collected my candle, water jug and shoes and headed for what all my travels had been pointing towards. Hoping Ayahuasca would re-cognate my mind, lead me to my heart and soul's desires. I wanted to be free of my own expectations of myself, be free of society's expectations of me, free of the dogma that continually builds up Lemming-like attributes that take us away from our true selves. I wanted to be who I should be, know the inner workings of who I am and know my heart and its convictions, to prepare me for a beautiful life of love, family, friendship, health and happiness. I wanted to explore more of the creative side that had been shown to me in my first session, I wanted more guidance. I felt I'd underachieved in the acting world due to my lack of confidence and inability to fully go for it, which mirrored my inability to fully commit to anything.

I made my way to the ceremony room, plodding along on the same route I had navigated a few nights previous which then had seemed endless and covered in snakes.

Otillia was in her usual spot. Lucias was to her left and Lisa took the seat I'd been in the previous two ceremonies. I took the one directly facing Otillia.

Guylene was there, not to drink this evening, but to record Otillia's *Icaro's* with her night vision camera. The atmosphere in the room was very relaxed. It felt different from the previous session as if each person was fully comfortable in each other company. I took my position, crossed my legs, put some tissue and water within arm's reach and got ready. Otillia mentioned this was my last ceremony. I would be a warrior after this, a man ready for the world. She said that the Ayahuasca diet was a life-changing moment and after tonight I would be ready, tonight was like my graduation, and she said, "it has been a pleasure to see you grow."

Otillia lit the tobacco, taking a drag with more presence than any Don in any Gangster movie, completely devoid of fear and in complete control of her mind, body and spirit. She approached me,

"Coma esta, Señor",
"Bien, Atu," I said, *"Bien bien".*

She said she was happy for my time here and that my fear should be overcome when all the plants and Ayahuasca had fully taken course.

"You have to be strong and ready for this world," she said. She blew smoke around my hair three times, taking quick drags and blowing the sacred plant fumes atmospherically around me, creating a mist of mystical smoke. She then took my hands, pushing them together and blowing smoke into the cup they'd formed. Sitting in half lotus, I shut my eyes and focused on my intentions, repeating them over and over, reinforcing them with direct instructions. Otillia performed the smoke rituals on the others before returning to her rocking chair to prepare the medicine. She removed a two-litre Coke bottle of Ayahuasca from a shopping bag and put it on her small table and blew the smoke around it, twisted the top off and blew smoke and prayers inside.

Anticipation touched me.

I sat, knowing I was first. Again and again, I repeated my intentions.

Many westerners look for metaphysical or mystical insight during their Ayahuasca quest, and I was no different, striving for physiological answers and resolutions to problems, hoping for insights into my future and a connection to the spiritual world. According to people I'd spoken to, indigenous people want the Ayahuasca to work for them to solve problems, restore health, and foster greater social cohesion and are not interested in the constant search we are.

"Señor," was called.

I was up, it felt like the most significant moment of my life. I had no nerves now though, I was so sure I would be lead home, wherever that may be. I knelt before Otillia. She poured the thick, gloopy, dark, earthy-smelling liquid into the coconut bowl. She then handed it to me. I took it in both hands, blew my breath into it three times, putting my energy and intention into the liquid, raised the bowl above my head and began to say my intentions. Life and soul's purpose, higher self, direction and creative ideas, give me what I need to go forward. I added much more detail to this whilst I knelt, ensuring no confusion. I then knocked it back in one hit, not wasting a single drop, ensuring it was all in me. Otillia handed me a tissue, and I wiped the vile-tasting liquid from around my mouth, wincing at the taste. Sitting back down I closed my eyes and concentrated hard. I don't remember the other guys taking their medicine, I was strictly setting my intentions over and over again in my head, keeping my spine upright, paying Lady Ayahuasca the respect I now knew she deserved.

The candle was blown out by Otillia, and the waiting game began. I kept repeating my intention, focusing on staying in lotus, keeping the medicine down. It felt more settled than last time but not as settled as the first time. I sat and waited with the most beautiful expectation. Waiting to be enlightened, waiting for explanations and direction, excited by the prospect of knowing myself a little better, allowing Ayahuasca to be the gateway not for escape but for eternity, entering those worlds to live at the same time in this and other realities.

My stomach started to pulse, not liking what was inside, I reached for my bowl, but nothing came. The Lady wanted to remain. I was focused, determined to stay sat up, not let my body slip into relaxed lazy mode.

Lisa was sick, retching in a deep painful tone. Get it out, girl, I thought. Shortly after, Lucias was sick. Light visuals began, it was starting, The Lady was near, but when was I to be sick? I wanted the colour, the brilliance, the magic, time after time I prepared myself for the internal explosion that would surface through my mouth.

I held the bowl, but nothing.

I resigned myself to the fact I may not be sick, and this experience would be like my early experience of TV; devoid of colour. I decided to step inside, relax and be taken on my journey.

Like someone had been trying to prise a stop valve on a water pipe, I felt the sick race from my stomach and all of a sudden it gave way, releasing a torrent of built-up pressure. It exploded, rushing like a lightning bolt up my chest and throat. My arms reached out just in time to get the bowl in front of my mouth.

It all came up in one big hit.

I put the bowl down, lent over it and waited for more that did not come. Spitting, coughing and clearing my throat into the bowl, tying my hair back trying to avoid the sick. I drank some water, wiped my mouth, got back into lotus and allowed the most important lesson and healing of my life to begin.

I am an open and receptive vessel, I am an open and receptive vessel, I am an open and receptive vessel, I am an open and receptive vessel, Ayahuasca, teach me.

CHAPTER 23
AWAKENING, LIFE, DECEMBER 2011

I got back from India, and I didn't know what to do. When I was in London, I felt like my head was melting. There was too much going on, and I couldn't feel any life there, it was like everyone was dead. They were stuck in this fast-paced life with no escape and seemingly no purpose other than to make money.

I felt like I was going to die every day I was in that city.

Parts of India were crazy, but it felt like the people had purpose and had faith in something and their lives seemed to have meaning. All anyone seemed to have faith in London was that they would get smashed at the weekend. Yawn!!

Part of me already knew I was going to leave London and move back to Manchester. Maybe it was my higher self-knowing what was best for me, I was sure something internal was telling me to go home. I didn't know which voice to listen to because it was like there were ten talking inside my head. I didn't know which one to trust. I couldn't understand why I wanted to move back to Manchester. I'd moved to London to be with more open-minded people (where being hard and super masculine was not a prerequisite). I felt that the aggressive, violent, tense and small-minded mentality of where I'd been brought up would never call me back. But now these new ways of thinking and being I'd acquired since leaving home were boring me. I was seeking truth, I was seeking meaning, and I was seeking my path.

Something in me knew I was going to move home.

I'd told a few people, and Fhian had gotten wind of it. I wondered why I had a desire to go back. Was it because I felt that I had no home and nowhere that I belonged? Was I running away from my relationship and the chance of making something of myself in London? I wasn't sure, but I knew I couldn't stand this place and its organised madness. It made me feel sick, and it seemed to heighten all the anxiety and nervousness I was feeling.

I didn't really want to be in Manchester either — I wanted to be dead — but I felt that I had nowhere else to go. I told Fhian that I had to do my community service there, I had no intention of being in London anymore.

I headed home and slept on my dad's couch and got on with completing my one hundred and fifty hours of community service as quickly as possible. At first, I was put on general gardening and tidying up of public places. It was amazing that some of the young men I met had only been given thirty hours for their crime but had now managed to incur up to three hundred hours by not completing their thirty hours in the allotted time frame. I was intent on getting mine done as fast as possible, and moving on with my life. Fortunately, I only had to spend a couple of days with these mid twenty-year-olds who couldn't do any of the work and thought it was acceptable to burn plastic chairs and vandalise the van we were transported around in. I thought of India and how the people there had to work, or they would starve. These guys would be forced by sheer instinct to get off their arses and do some work.

After a couple of gardening shifts, I got placed in a charity shop for the rest of my hours as the staff who ran the community service could see I was hard-working and, unlike the rest of the men there, trustworthy. I got a really nice job helping run the clothes and furniture YMCA charity shop in Stretford precinct where I used to queue up for McDonald's as a kid. I was now repaying my debt to society in a nice warm shop with a constant supply of tea.

I'd reconnected with my friend Kathryn who I'd grown up with. She was in a really bad place when I saw her, the boy she had been living with for the past few years had left her for her best friend. Kathryn felt like she had lost everything and she'd lost about four stone. She had these sores and legions all over her face that had been triggered by stress and started talking about all this spiritual stuff. I just ignored her and thought she was going nuts. It was like the shutters came down when she started to talk about it. I wanted to help her, but I thought she was losing the plot, telling me that she could see demons and angels. It was something I'd never given any thought to so I dismissed it as a load of crap. I wanted to see her get better, but the stuff she was talking about was so removed from my reality that I ignored it and told people she was going mad.

Staying on me Dad's couch wasn't a long-term plan. I didn't know what I wanted to do when the community service was done. Part of me wanted to give up acting and get on with my life, maybe get a proper job so I could buy a house and have a family someday.

I had no idea what I wanted to do.

I felt totally alone and lost.

I was constantly beating myself up.

I knew one day I wanted to live in an eco-house and have a beautiful family and be off-grid away from the city and be part of a nice community. It seemed a million miles away, and I couldn't think for the life of me how I could get there.

I pretty much went back to my old ways when the community service was completed. I started working for my mate as a window fitter, helping a friend as a painter and decorator and working with my mate as a tree surgeon. I tried applying for jobs to do with my degree as a town planner and as a surveyor, but nothing seemed to materialise and I couldn't really stand the thought of having to wear a suit and tie every day. I wanted to kill myself when I was filling in the application forms, it was like my soul was trying to rip itself away from getting involved in such work. Part of me wanted to get a proper job in Surrey, so I could be back in the suburbs of London and be near Renie (yes I was still thinking about her as an option) so I could potentially get back together with her and have kids and a simple life surrounded by the support of her family. Part of me wanted Fhian and I to move to the Isle of Wight to be near her family and live a simple life away from the city. I wanted this, and I wanted that, and I wanted to die because I thought I was possibly insane.

What I didn't do was go back to drinking. I was still off the booze, and I didn't enjoy the social side of being in the pub and life revolving around drinking and football. I thought there must be more to experience than talking about football and the hassle you were getting off the wife. I started to find places to do yoga, and I started to find meditation centres, and these seemed to be the only places that brought me elements of calm. I also started playing football again to get rid of this excess energy I seemed to have.

I then moved back in with my step-dad and my sister. I couldn't believe it was happening, but I had nowhere else to go or be. I felt in some way that it was my home and was the only place in the world that I felt like I had a right to be, as it had been my mum's house. I wished so much that she could be there and look after me in it. I felt so low and depleted, I wanted to scratch out my eyes and peel off my skin. I needed my mum so much and was lost without her.

All I got from people I met was, 'What are you going to do with yourself then?' and 'Why have you left that nice girl in London?' I just wanted somewhere I could be alone and scream and scream and scream and shout at the world, everybody and nobody for this pain I was feeling inside.

I told my step-dad I would stay until I figured out what I was going to do. Moving home meant I was over the road from Kathryn again and we started to hang out a lot. I started to listen to all this weird stuff that had been happening to her. I was still sceptical, but the more we hung out, the more it all started to resonate with me. She started telling me about angels and demons and God. I thought she was crazy, but I liked listening. Then she would tell me about what happens to you when you die and how the soul never dies. I thought of me Mum as alive, as a beam of light or a concentration of energy and vibrations. It all seemed to make sense and resonate with me. So many times since me mother's death I'd felt like I could feel her and I felt she was still alive, but in a different form. I felt like she was trying to communicate with me. It was all starting to make sense now as I learnt about all this new spiritual stuff. I was starting to realise that maybe I could communicate with her. That she was still present in some form I didn't really understand.

I was constantly thinking about what I should do to make money. It was all that seemed to matter to people. I had an idea of opening up a mobile coffee shop and selling coffee and tea to the morning commuters. I had all these ideas of how I could make money quick, but they all needed time and knowledge. I wanted to sell snacks and chai tea like I had seen everywhere in India. It seemed to make everywhere I'd visited have more character and seem so much friendlier and alive. I wanted to bring that to the places I lived in.

I started working in a really cool coffee shop, 'Coffee Fix' in Gatley to try and get ready for launching a mobile coffee shop. I was enjoying being back in this little village where I'd spent my teens after me Mum moved in with me step-dad. It was a really pretty village and had so much potential. I could see how amazing it could be with the right people living there. Nice shops were starting to pop up, which was a far cry from the Gatley I had known as a kid. I then discovered that Gatley had a yoga studio, which seemed so out there for a backwards, very conservative typically British village. It seemed Gatley had started in some ways to become a little more open and diverse. It was still very bogged down with old views and was run by people who were of a very much older generation, but it seemed like change was starting to happen, which brought a smile to my face.

I was stuck in my depression at this time and searching for something to make me feel better. I was sad all of the time, and I felt so lost and alone. I didn't know where I belonged or where I wanted to be and I felt like I'd achieved nothing since I had left home seven years ago. Here I was back in me step-dad's spare room looking for work and a purpose, working in the same sort of jobs I was doing when I was 16. I'd not grown at all. Why had my life led me back here?

The only person I felt was helping me was Kathryn. She was giving me books to read about spirituality, the Universe, self-help books and books about the importance of 2012 and all these ancient prophesies that all pointed to 21.12.12 as a pivotal date that would change the world and humanity. I wanted to read them all, and for the first time in my life, I felt like I had found something that I wanted to know more about. Never before had I found a subject that had taken hold of me in such a way. I wanted to read everything, I wanted to know everything. I was starting to learn about Atlantis, Lamoria and Sumeria, and discovering more about Egypt. I was becoming fascinated by these philosophies that were deemed rubbish and fantasy by the mainstream and by the powers that be.

I soon discovered the powers that be are very good at hiding the truth and it was truth I wanted to discover now. I'd been aware of the lies we are fed since I'd become obsessed with the environment and the damage humans were doing to the planet. I'd started to see how big transnational companies were now running the planet and running governments and foreign policy. They would do anything to make more profit year after year and would let nothing get in their way, including human life. It doesn't take much digging to discover this truth, just watch the documentaries The Corporation, Roger and Me, The Shock Doctrine, and realise just how ruthless they are.

These new learnings and this spirituality were really resonating. Something deep inside wanted it to be part of me, for it to become me. This part of me wanted to discover the truth about myself and about the world and life around me. Something was moving inside me, a shift was taking place. I was scared, scared of ridicule from my friends and family, scared of turning my back on what I'd always known and I was scared of letting go of the person I'd created over the years. But the person I was right now was dying, and I needed to let the true me step forward.

I was starting to learn about energy and different ways of healing and medicine. I loved the magic of it all and how it seemed so unrealistic but so true to my heart. The learning was making me realise that there were so many things in the world I'd always been lied to about. I then started to read about Einstein and all he talked about was energy and how powerful the forces we can't see are, and how so much that we see is an illusion. I felt having someone like Einstein with his global credibility backing up what seemed to me at the time as outlandish concepts brought real meaning to them. I realised that there are so many lies and so much deceit from the moment you are born that it's impossible to not be affected by it.

I started to wonder why babies seem like they are seeing more than we can see as adults. I started to wonder if it's because there is more there that we become blind to it as we grow. We know for a fact we can't see infra-red, but it's there, we can't see radio waves, but they are there, and we can't see a text messages fly from one side of the world to the other, but they do. It all started to make sense. We are so heavily affected by our parents and their misguided values that most of them have acquired from the media. It was like my brain was opening up and wanted to suck up this truth, this better way of being and living. I wanted to dispel these lies and discover the truth behind the veil we've all had thrown over us.

At Kathryn's, we would do angel card readings, and I would always be freaked out by how accurate they were. At first I was sceptical, but then it just got weird and trippy, so I had to believe what I felt and not what my perception of what the world wanted me to believe. I started to notice coincidences, and the more I read people like Jung and Castaneda, the more I realised that these were no coincidences and I started to take notice of them. I have learnt that we have to acknowledge the signs. Carl Jung was the master of explaining this, and I know that following the signs will move us on the right trajectory and help us get to the place we need to be. They apparently take us to our life purpose. I really felt my life needed some purpose and I was willing to follow the signs to find it.

I was still massively sceptical and was trying not to believe everything Kathryn told me. However, to see the transformation in her from a party-drug-taking girl who was very materialistic and driven by work, to now this girl whose room was filled with crystals, angels and tons of spiritual books, was miraculous. She hadn't even read a book before all this started and now she was reciting passages from The Prophet, The Secret and all types of books we'd never heard of before. She started to tell me that she had woken up to the truth of what was happening in the world and that we are all spiritual beings, living a spiritual life and that people don't realise it as it has been forgotten.

With my recent dealings with God on the twelve-step program, with my mother passing a few years ago now and with my trip to India where I saw the richness of spirituality and faith, I was certainly changing. Added to this was my disheartened view of our western societies. TV seems to have become our God and pubs, supermarkets and shopping centres have become our churches. I was ready for something better. I wanted richness, I wanted love, and I wanted purpose. This all seemed to make sense to me. Everything I read about ancient civilisations resonated. They were more advanced than us and knew the secrets of the Universe and how to live in harmony with the Earth and the plants and the animals we co-in-habit the planet with.

We're told we are the most advanced civilisation to walk on the planet, but our mainstream history only goes back a few thousand years, and we can't figure out much of what the Egyptians and Mayans left behind. I'd always had this feeling that something had happened on this planet before the history books began. I would wonder, if all humans were wiped out, how long would it take for all traces of our existence to become completely hidden? A thousand years maybe? Well that's is a speck in time if the Earth is 4.5 billion years old. So surely other civilisations could have lived here without our knowledge. I also had this feeling that some of the other planets in our solar system might have had life on them at some point or could have at some point in the future because everything is always changing. All is possible.

I was ready for something new. I didn't know what I wanted. Maybe to be in another country, building eco-houses, working the land, leaving everything that was in England. I was willing to do anything to find happiness. Something was moving me, it was like my soul was guiding me. I was embarrassed to tell people about what I was starting to get into. I was doing as much meditation as I could and reading lots of Buddhist philosophy. I felt like it was feeding me.

However, I was so depressed that I felt like I could die at any moment and was starting to think about how I would actually do it. This poem captures how I was feeling at the time.

Dark/Suicide
One way out, one way out
All these thoughts and all these mussing
Bring me back to you
I want you out I want you out gone
But in me you remain
It all spins around and spins around
A crazy circle in my head
Over and over
Constantly turning and churning Heavy on my head
It always comes back to you
After to-ing and fro-ing
Turning and churning, spinning and spinning, around and around
My final conclusion
Through logic and reason
Brings me back to you
Suicide suicide suicide
Suicide you're my only out
Suicide run away and hide
Suicide, suicide, suicide
Suicide don't find you easy to hide

I wondered if it would affect anyone's life and if I would be missed by anyone. I was so lost that I wanted someone to find me, and I was so confused that my head felt like it might spin-off. Here is another that poured out of me at the time.

Happy Days
If I killed myself would anything become of my words
Would someone find them and make something of them
If I killed myself would the words mean more
Would someone be found to bring my work alive
What would be thought of what I write
Do I only write to seek approval from the masses
Or do I write because I write
Is my work crap and crass, how and when will I know?
And if I killed myself would opinion and critique be kind
Would my notebooks and jotters be impossible to find
If I killed myself would my stuff just be cleared out
My words thrown out into the bin with everything else
If I died today how would my life be viewed by others

Would they say I'd thrown it away
Or would they understand, I felt like there was nothing in my empty hand
Would I be remembered for anything good
If I killed myself tonight who would know what to do with my body
Who would know my wishes
If I killed myself tomorrow, the same day as my mother died
Would that hold any significance, would they assume that was my reason why
What do I do with what I have and exactly what do I have
Am I just a fool to hold on to some dreams
Of a better life of love, no struggle, big hugs
If I killed myself soon, who would carry it around as a wound?
Would I be forgotten, no one's immediate lives consumed
By the day to day missing of me being around, as I flirt in and out, never sit tight
No one ever gets used so no one can ever be right
If I killed myself tomorrow
Will you take all my thoughts, ideas, dreams, love and visions
Give them to a wiser man and make the world better

Buddhism was showing me this beautiful way of life, and I was thinking about maybe leaving western society behind and joining a monastery. Sometimes I wished I wasn't becoming enveloped into this world of truth and spirituality as maybe I was just using it as another distraction from sorting out my life, getting a real job and finding some stability. Some days I didn't want to know the truth, I wanted to be like most people and be oblivious to what was truly happening in the world. Sometimes I wanted to be controlled and in their unknowing happiness. I often wondered why things like truth, justice, ethics and morals affected me so much when other people could just brush them off.

What really helped my progression was the weekend I spent at a Buddhist retreat in the Lake District. It was an introduction to Buddhism and consisted of meditation and teachings and walks around the beautiful grounds. I was trying to take in as much as I could and trying my hardest to clear my head just as the teachers were telling us to do.

The Buddhist centre gave me a chance to be away from the life I was part of at the time. To be in beautiful surroundings, surrounded by very nice, conscious people who were all finding an interest in something more than our society had to offer. One of the biggest teachings I'd ever learnt and the one that changed my life the most happened on the second day of the retreat. The teacher said, "No one has ever made you angry your whole life".

I was thinking, that's bollocks, everyone and everything makes me angry.

Then he said, "You have always chosen to be angry, every time you have got angry in your life you have chosen to react like that, no one has ever made you angry".

Again I was screaming, "Bollocks!" in my head thinking, he hasn't had my life.

Then he said, "You have always had a choice about how to react, there has always been another option."

I started to process his words, and an explosion of realisation hit me like a sledgehammer square between the eyes. It seemed so obvious, why hadn't I ever been told this essential life tool before? It changed my whole world on the spot. I'd always had a short fuse, I was always quick to get angry with people, and I was always looking for confrontation. I was always mad and angry about this or that, always upset with the world and always felt like I was owed something for the traumatic life I'd had.

When me Mum was alive she said, "you were an angry little boy, and now you're an angry young man". I didn't really give it much thought at the time. However, after learning I'd had a choice after a couple of minutes of listening to a monk talk, all my anger evaporated. I realised I didn't have to be angry in any situation, my life changed. I was amazed that I could just be neutral and react to a situation without anger. It was like a massive weight I'd been carrying around my whole life had fallen from my back.

This wasn't how I had been brought up, and it wasn't the way I had witnessed the behaviour of my peers, but it was the way I was going to react from now on. It wasn't that I was about to let people walk all over me, it just meant that I never had to bring anger into any situation I ever encountered again, and if I ever did, I had to know that it was my choice. From now on, I would always have a choice in the way I reacted.

After this life-changing realisation, I wanted to tell everyone about it. They gave me another piece of wisdom, telling me that thoughts were powerful, and we could create anything that we thought about and concentrated on. This was also ingrained into me from that moment on.

As I sat on the train, I received a text message from Renie who

I hadn't heard from for six months. I'd thought about her non-stop for two days, and now she was texting me to see how I was. It made me smile to see the rules of the Universe and the spiritual practices being reinforced. It felt like some crazy synchronicity. Why on Earth couldn't I let this girl go and why she was now contacting me? Was it just a sign to prove that these teachings were correct and that if you get the stuff in your head right then the world you view will be a beautiful place? I didn't know, but I hoped more than anything that soon my mind would be a nice peaceful and tranquil place.

One day I got a phone call from my godmother, telling me that her daughter who had been suffering from cancer for many years was not going to make it, and they were in the hospital waiting for her to die. It was Mother's Day on the Sunday, and I said I would come down and be with them for the day. I felt it would make my mum very happy that I was spending it with her best friend (also called Doreen). As soon as I spoke to her on the phone, I knew for some reason I had to be there. It wasn't like I was a big part of their lives and I saw them often and was close to her daughter. 'No,' something in me said, 'You must go there and talk to her daughter and help her pass over peacefully.' That something that was talking to me had never spoken to me before. It was really strange, but on autopilot and with no resistance, I listened and went with it.

The day before I was set to go, Doreen called and said that the doctors had said Julie could die at any time, so maybe I would prefer to come next week?

I said, "No, I want to be with you guys and see you on Mother's Day."

I remembered how my mother had been in those final few days, struggling to let go of this world. I wanted to try and help Julie pass over peacefully with this new knowledge I had. I made my way to Wales and was picked up at the train station by Tony, Doreen's husband. When we got to the hospital, Julie was in a bad way, and Doreen told me that the doctors had said she would only last a few more days. As I walked into the room, the smell instantly took me back to when me Mum was dying. That smell will always stay with me, and it almost makes me vomit every time I sense it.

I was really nervous to say the things to Julie that I wanted to say and that had been going around my head for the last two days. I felt that I couldn't say them in front of Tony and Doreen and Julie's son Jordy, they would think I was nuts. I spent the whole afternoon there, and we had food, and I talked about death and what would happen to Jordy when his mum passed. Obviously my new spirituality had changed the way I spoke of death. It was now something I saw as beautiful and a transition, rather than the finality I had been brought up to feel it was.

When I was in India, I was having something to eat, and waiter started talking about his brother in a very present way. The girl I was with asked where his brother was, and the waiter said that he had died ten years ago.

She said, "Oh I'm so sorry," and he said,

"Don't be sorry, he is in a beautiful place now, and I will see him again soon when I die." With this he walked off smiling, and I thought, what a beautiful way to be.

However, in this situation, I was still unsure of myself and was scared to ask for some time with Julie alone. I also felt a bit of a fraud because I didn't know Julie really well, and who was I to think I could help anyway? I was there for something, and I had always felt close to Doreen.

Time was running out, and Tony had to take me for my train soon.

I thought I was going to bottle it, that I wouldn't tell Julie what I wanted to tell her but then just before I was about to leave Tony left the room, and myself and Doreen stood either side of Julie. I spent some time telling her in my head that it was okay to leave and that this body was no longer a good place for her to be. I told her that everyone would be okay without her and that she could actually do more to help them from that other realm (like my mother had). She would never leave them. I then told her to pass peacefully, that there was nothing to be scared of and only beauty awaited. I then told her that my mum would be waiting to show her the ropes and look after her best mate's little girl and that they could be together in that other place. I told her to leave and to be free of suffering. I told her to fly high and be all she could be, away from this dying vessel. I then looked up at Doreen after saying all this in my head and smiled as a tear dropped from both of our cheeks.

On the train home I hoped that Doreen, Tony and Jordy wouldn't have to go through the five days of torture we'd had to endure when we were in the same situation waiting for me Mum to die. I went to bed, and again for some reason, I tried to connect to God, to Julie and to my mother. I asked them all to make it peaceful and to help Doreen and her family during this time. I woke up in the morning with a text from Doreen telling me that Julie had passed just after midnight really peacefully. I got a huge tingle down my spine and tears, sadness and happiness filled me. I felt I had done something that was so foreign to me, but something had pushed me to do it, and it felt amazing to have been a part of helping someone pass over, even though I didn't really have much idea of what it was I had actually done.

From that moment, Kathryn saw something new in me. I think she started to feel that I was spiritual as well and that I wasn't just feigning interest in these books so that I could get myself out of this depression. I think she felt that I was actually part of whatever it was that was happening to her. We both felt quite isolated in this new world we had found ourselves in, and although there were tons of books and information on the internet, we wanted to meet people who we could learn from and who were of a similar mindset to the one we were opening up to. I thought maybe we would have to go to India and that we would never find these people around here. Then Kathryn found a healing centre that operated in a small town hall on a Tuesday night, and we went down there together for healing.

When we got there, I read the information leaflet, which talked about how it could actually heal any form of illness just by putting positive healing energy into you from a source above us. I thought, 'bollocks', still conditioned by my limited mind. I was hoping it would maybe give me some direction and stop me wanting to kill myself, but I doubted it very much.

Everyone there seemed to be pretty old apart from me and Kathryn, and I thought, wow this is just a load of mad, crazy old people. I was pretty apprehensive about having the healing, but I thought, well if I'm a sceptic and it doesn't work (which I assumed it wouldn't) then it can't actually do me any harm, can it?

A lady called Sheila came to collect me. She was a very elegant looking older lady, immaculately dressed with a huge bosom, skinny little legs and a pretty grey bob. A warm, welcoming smile, vivid red lips and this captivating glow picked me up and glided me towards the open treatment room. Everyone lay down on treatment beds, and their chosen healer stood by their side as they waited for the lights to be turned down and the soothing music to play. I had been briefed by the guy who was the head healer called Gordon, and he told me it was very soothing, and some of the healers touched you very lightly, and some of them put their hands on you but never in an intrusive way. He told me that the energy came from channels above us and could heal any ailment or condition.

Sheila told me she was just a vessel and that she just allowed the energy to pass down through her from the higher beings and vibrations and into me wherever I needed it. It all sounded ridiculous but intriguing, and I closed my eyes and tried to relax. Still, my washing machine of thoughts and self-deprecation continued to assault me. I couldn't relax and kept thinking this was a load of shit and again I was procrastinating about actually doing something that resembled progress in my life. How was this shit going to get me a decent job, a house and a family? I started to feel a warm glow over me, and the room started to feel very calm and relaxed, my thoughts were still spiralling, and I wasn't sure whether or not I was relaxing, but there was a definite change.

The session lasted for about 45 minutes. I could sense Sheila round certain parts of my body, and different parts of me seemed to get warm and fuzzy. At one point I wasn't sure where she was, and I felt like someone was standing at the top of my head, but I also felt like someone was by my left foot. I didn't look and just thought I would let whatever was happening, happen. It did feel freaky though.

When the session stopped, and Sheila told me to slowly get up and put my shoes on. I realised I was really relaxed because it was really difficult for me to lift my body up. When I sat up, she told me that she could feel a lot of tension and stress in me and she thought I had problems around my right knee. Spot on, I thought.

I then realised I felt really chilled and my body felt loose, and there seemed to be a little bit of space in my head. The barrage of abuse was still there, but it was like 20% of it had disappeared. I was a believer. Something really had happened to me, without the use of physical contact, antibiotics, a doctor or an operation. Something had happened in that room, and I couldn't explain what it was.

The people there were all lovely, and it had a similar vibe and feel to what I had experienced in the Ashrams and at the Buddhist centres. I was won over. I really did feel like it had affected me, something had certainly shifted. How could that be when she hadn't even touched me? My whole reality and sense of truth seem to be shifting again. I seemed aware that there was so much more to life than just the physical. Another penny had dropped, and again Einstein backed me up, so I didn't feel silly and crazy thinking these new thoughts, the big man was in my corner.

The next thing I knew Kathryn told me we were going to a spiritual meditation with a woman she had been told about at the healing centre. The woman running the meditations was called Janet, and she was about to take us on an even bigger journey, opening up my mind to even more possibilities.

When I got to the meditation, Janet gave me a piece of paper with some typed words on it. I had never met her before, and she said she had written this about me by connecting with her guides. I was like, "Your what?"

Fortunately, I didn't offend Janet with my thoughts, and I started to read what she had written. It was a full A4 page and telling me I was starting to awaken and realise there was more than meets the eye. She told me I was very spiritual and had lived many lives on this planet before, but I couldn't remember them. She told me that I was a natural healer and I was on a fast track via the spiritual realm to wake up quickly and discover the truth. She told me things about my mother that no one could have known and she told me that I had never had any positive male role models in my life. All of this stuff resonated with me and actually made me cry. Tingles were shooting all over my spine. The note said that I was always going to move home and come here to meet Janet and allow her to teach me many lessons. The most important thing was that I had found her and the guides were very happy about that.

From that moment, every Thursday, I would go to the spiritual meditation group. I was the youngest by quite a way and usually the only male, typically in a group of around eight. When the mediations started, I never managed to follow the instructions and would get a bit lost in my own thoughts which still seemed uncontrollable. I would try and try, but I would lose where we were going in the meditation and get stuck and clogged up with my life problems.

The group would share their experiences. Many of the women would be getting whisked off through the universe with angels and unicorns and go on these amazing journeys to far off lands. I would not be able to recall anything other than maybe struggling to follow the instructions and being stuck in my own head and maybe wondering about what to eat when I got home.

Something kept me going back. We would work with Tarot

Cards some weeks and do readings on each other, and some weeks we would try and read photographs and amazingly everyone was pretty accurate. Janet was trying to reveal to us that all the powers of the Universe were inside us and we just had to remember them. I was trying and trying, and some weeks I was so low that I would sit in this church hall with six women over 50 thinking, what am I doing? This is not cool, surely I should be with cool people listening to cool music and doing cool stuff? But I realised that was only my ego that required these things to look cool on the outside when internally they were destroying me. I was following my path, and right now this was where my path wanted me to be. I started to get over this and embrace the group and the growth and realisations it was giving me.

During this time, my weeks were so busy. I would be at yoga as often as I could and the other nights I would either be at meditation, spiritual meditation or healing. I was also working as much as I could, but at times there was no work, and I started to panic. Then I read The Secret and started to practice the techniques this talked of. I tried and manifest some work, so I had something to do in the day. One time I got up and meditated on wanting work and the next minute my phone rang, and my mate asked me if I could work that day.

I was claiming a Jobseekers allowance at the time and paying very little rent to my step-dad. But I wanted to work. I wanted to be acting every day and getting better and better, but the work didn't seem to be there. I wanted direction, and every night I would go to bed and ask God for direction and purpose. All my other time was spent with Kathryn, reading, learning and chatting about spirituality and what we should both do with our lives.

I would see Fhian at weekends; she would either come to Manchester or I would go to her in London. I didn't want to be in London, but I had to make the girl I was in love with happy. I had no desire to be there, and it still made me feel mental.

Soon Kathryn and I felt we were ready to do our Level 1 healing module towards becoming energy healers. I was, as usual, a bit freaked out by the title and wording of 'Healer'. I thought it was nuts and ridiculous that Liam Browne from a council estate could be a healer. How could that be? It was so far removed from anything anyone in my family did or the people I had associated with all through my life. Who was I to be a healer, and how did Janet know

I could do it and wasn't this the kind of fantasy that was only found in *Harry Potter*? What if I couldn't do it and it was just a waste of time, would everyone laugh at me?

I was full of trepidation because surely I wouldn't be connected to anything special like that. We had to buy a pendulum for the 2-day course and have a vegetarian diet for a few days leading up to it. When we arrived at Janet's, she told us about all these new powers we would get and how all the activations she would do to us would really open us up to higher forms of energy. I was as usual, very sceptical.

The activation meditations Janet did on us were very powerful, and I felt like I was in a dream whilst she was carrying them out. She then started to talk about the seven chakras of the body and how they operate as energy centres for different emotions. I remembered seeing the pictures of these wherever I went in India and realised that these same energy points were what Chinese medicine worked with. The overall aim is to have these energy centres balanced. Mine were not balanced. Janet worked to rebalance them and get them all working correctly and in sync.

Eventually, we got to do some practice and start using our pendulums. I worked on Kathryn and vice-versa. We had to say a prayer and ask for the energy of the Christ Consciousness grid to come through us and heal the person we were working on. Janet told me that first I would have to repair any holes in the aura, then the inner aura, and then any pains in the body, and finally the chakra system. Inside I laughed heavily thinking, How on earth am 'I' going to do that, is she fucking nuts? Then I held my pendulum like Janet had told me. In my head, I asked it to guide me to any tears in the outer auric field.

I held the pendulum as still as humanly possible, determined to not allow myself to move it and determined to make sure no one else in the room was moving it. It then all of a sudden started moving to the right, and I pulled it back to where it had been. But no, it wanted to go to the right, so I followed it, and it stopped at a spot, and I asked if there was a tear there. It spun anti-clockwise, which as I had earlier learnt meant yes. I asked for the tear to be repaired and it started spinning viscously around in an anti-clockwise motion. I couldn't believe what I was seeing. It took me around the whole body twice, then worked on specific areas and eventually worked on the chakras. I was blown away. I couldn't believe something I couldn't see was moving my pendulum, something was in that room running through me and performing healing on Kathryn. I was doing nothing. Like Sheila said, I was just a vessel for the energy to flow through and I could feel energy all around me as I worked. It felt amazing, and it brought me so much calm.

The week before this, I'd had a reading with the psychic who told me via a message from my dead grandma that I needed to get going and do something with my life. So I went home and booked my place on the Earthship course. After the healing day I stood with Kathryn at the bus stop and said, "Right, I need to manifest £5000 spending money for my trip, plus money for flights." I set the intention and came off Jobseekers and from that moment I didn't have a spare day before I went away. I was working all the time for three months. I managed to get to some Mind and Spirit events which opened me up to more spirituality and different forms of healing, and I did the Level 2 Energy Healing course with Janet, which meant I could take on clients and start charging people for healing.

At a similar time, I met Ladan at a past-life regression day and discovered she led an advanced spiritual meditation group at Gatley Hill house, where I had been drunk as a kid at a few parties. I couldn't believe it; Gatley now had yoga and a spiritual meditation group. This was also when she told me that I had all my chakras open and asked if I would be interested in joining her group on a pilgrimage for the end of the Mayan calendar. My eyes lit up I couldn't believe it. I had just started learning about these special dates in time, and now someone was offering me a place to experience it in Guatemala the home of the Mayans. A synchronicity alarm went off in my head. I knew I needed to be there and with the Earthship course starting in March I knew I would travel in-between. It was all starting to fall into place. I started to meditate with Ladan's group every Friday when I wasn't in London seeing Fhian and Ladan became a big part of my life from that moment on.

Ladan's group were very powerful, and I felt like I was finding a home with these like-minded people. Like Janet, Ladan really took me under her wing and saw something in me that I couldn't see. There were more of a mix of ages at Ladan's meditations, and I wasn't the only boy. It was just like when I began to go to the AA meetings. I became aware of this huge group of people who were putting their faith in something higher. Now I was becoming aware of these spiritual people who were actually everywhere. They weren't connected to any religious group, they were people seeking truth who had an inner knowing that something more existed and that religion was just a doctrine to control people, like the capitalist, consumer, materialism that is engulfing the planet at the moment.

Fhian thought the world I was becoming part of was a bit nuts and it was really hard for me. With me being really open to this consciousness and then being around people who weren't really conscious, I struggled. I knew people were still good people, but with my newly-heightened awareness I was finding it difficult to connect with my old friends and what would be classed as "normal" people. I was still learning about this new world so I wasn't that confident expressing myself, and I didn't feel that I had the knowledge to back up my beliefs. Everyone wanted physical proof, Fhian included.

For Fhian I tried to accommodate and communicate with people, but it was massively frustrating hearing how fucked on drugs people had been at the weekend, and to me this was all anyone seemed to talk about in London. It confirmed to me that I was so glad to be out of that life.

She was actually trying to become part of my new world, but it felt forced. She did take me to a shamanic trance dance night as she tried to accommodate my new found love for anything spiritual. We spent the evening in a cave learning about creating energy and healing and how thoughts fly through the air and connect to the person they are aimed at like texting would. The group leader then took us into a shamanic trance dance where you bounce up and down with your head bowed to the beat of the music. The bouncing up and down allows serotonin to be released from the spinal fluid and you get this amazing natural high. It's pretty similar to the feeling you get coming up off ecstasy, and you just start to let the music flow through you and move you. It doesn't feel like you're dancing, it feels like you are part of the music and it gives you this really heightened buzz, that makes you feel like you're connected to something.

When I was starting to plan my trip away, I really felt that I had a purpose for the first time since I'd left university. For the three months leading up to going away, I felt so happy. I was back to my old self, even though I didn't know exactly where I was going, I felt that this trip was exactly what I wanted to be doing and was the next step in my journey. I had no doubt that my new found spirituality and my heightened awareness to follow the signs had led me to this stage and once I committed to it, everything would just fall perfectly into place. I was excited to discover as much as I could about spirituality and about the indigenous peoples of the world. More than anything, I wanted to find me. I wanted to uncover who I truly was and who I should be in the future.

Now I know people think it's all wanky to go away travelling to find yourself. But thinking about it, I thought what could be better than seeing what actually makes you tick? Moving from Manchester to London changed me so much for the better. Then becoming conscious via the 12 steps and then having a spiritual awakening took me closer to who I truly was.

What is actually wanky is to go away travelling and do pretty much the same things you do when you're at home, like drinking and associating with the same sort of people and then expect to find anything different within yourself. I wanted to be engulfed by new ways of thinking and by the sorts of people I hadn't experienced before. I wanted to be enriched and to get rid of more of my baggage. I wanted to be free of my shackles. I wanted the true me to step forward, and I wanted to make amazing connections along the way.

I was really looking forward to working with shamans and plant medicines and further expanding my mind. Ayahuasca and Peru were calling me and the knowledge and experience I was going to get working on Earthships that lived in harmony with the planet really, really excited me.

I decided I really needed to get my arse in gear and start earning money for my trip. The idea came from the book The Secret that showed you how to manifest what you wanted financially by writing out cheques to the Universe. I wrote one for £5000 spending money and one for £1million in a year's time, so I could build an Earthship village. From this moment I had so much work. I even got a couple of cool acting jobs that paid really well. I had the lead part in two music videos for a band I love called the Stereophonics.

The day I left for Belize I had £5000 spending money in my bank account with all my flights, courses and pilgrimages already booked and paid for. The Universe had given me the exact amount I wanted — well actually it was 93 pence over, but we will let the Universe get away with that won't we?

Again my faith in this new-found philosophy and way of life

was given more weight, and an even brighter glow surrounded me. I looked at my account balance and thanked God and the Universe. I thanked all those who helped me on my path, and I thanked myself for being brave and going with what I first thought was madness. I realised sometimes you have to reach rock bottom before you can grow. Now I was ready to grow, be guided and to follow my path and step out of my own way.

AYAHUASCA 3, THE JOURNEY, MAY 2013

I began to see the coloured patterns again. They were not as vivid and extraordinary as last time. They were softer and felt more psychedelic, slowly melting into each other. Trees shed vivid leaves from thin branches whilst beautiful birds of paradise came in and out of focus, fluttering their spectacular patterned chests. The birds would morph from the geometric patterns that were forming mesmerising image after image. I was amazed at what the human mind could create with a little coaxing. With the left side of the brain shut down, the right side was allowed to take over. It was obvious to see where many artists got their inspiration from. It is like the valve that connects them to artistic creativity is in us all, but our valve is blocked in comparison to theirs. I heard that Gaudi was into LSD and this is evident from his work which shows how the altered state can create wonders that the normal mind rarely sees.

Plants and other mind-altering substances seem to be the cause of so much human growth and development. I'd heard whilst in the Amazon that many things such as language, textiles, patterns, and religions were all handed down by plants that were responsible for altered states.

I must have been on a similar plane to most artists. What a beautiful place, I thought. How lucky people are who can come here at will in a normal state. To be on this vibration, to be able to pick from these creative fruits at will, to pluck ideas and inspiration that float in the ether. Creative minds must be a beautiful place to spend time within. I felt like I was fully submerged in that place.

I wanted to melt into the floor and enjoy the splendour, but I kept saying, "No you must stay upright, don't waste this opportunity, pay respect, nothing comes without hard work. Spine straight, spine straight."

In this psychedelic world of colour, art, creativity and genius, I felt safe, loved and passionate, as if all my desires had been met. However, I knew that if I dropped down into that space two foot above the ground, madness lurked, waiting for my arrival, hungry to try and destroy me again. I battled to hold my body up. Every part of me was so relaxed and sitting upright was the ultimate chore.

The *Icaro's* began again; Otillia took me on a new journey.

Fhain was brought to me, this immense ball of love engulfed us, and we just sat in it. Content with each other's presence, so happy, joyful and in love and this happy contentment filled us both. She lay in my arms, resting her head on my shoulder and chest. Then we were in a hospital, she gave birth, it was so real, I was experiencing every second. This baby brought everything that had been missing in my life for the last twenty years, delivered, solved and resolved the second it entered the world. The pain and anguish of the unconditional love I'd lost six years ago in the physical form was healed. Fhian providing this for me meant that unconditional love was now between us both forever and I would worship her for the rest of my life.

Unconditional love was back in my life, I was drowning in it. The three of us were draped within it. It covered every part of us circling, dancing, jumping, spinning, like an invisible fireworks display around our bodies. The three of us were captured by this enormous love bubble, colours of energy flowing, merging and melting into us. An eternally inseparable connection was made. We were back where we'd started, Fhian on my chest and the baby on my stomach. I sat listening to Otillia's *Icaro's* with everything I'd ever wanted. I was feeling better than I'd felt my whole life. Pure joy spread across my face, the most content and happy smile must have been lighting up my mouth.

So so so so so so so so so so so so so so so so so so so happy, my mother's pride swept through me, I knew in death she could see my children always. A vision of me and Fhian's small house came to me. In the middle of the room, a chair stood with my mother's name, Doreen, embroidered into the headrest. My two daughters were the only ones allowed to use it, unless they granted someone else permission, including me. They would go to it when they wanted a cuddle from their grandma or were feeling sad, and it would give them all the love that massive-hearted women possessed. I thought how blessed I was to have had that love in my heart for so long and how special she must be to be able to do that from the grave. My superhero mum who was capable of being the best grandma in the world, from her little caravan in Devon or was it, Heaven, where she now resides? Well, one of them.

Emotion swept through me. Tears raced down my cheeks. The

beauty of the life I was seeing, the beauty of being shown how to tap into her special energy, my superhero legal secretary mum, who could type two hundred words per minute, was there with me and I could feel her pulsating in my heart.

That house, that wife, those blessed children of ours gave us direction, consciousness and a love that nothing else was capable of providing. I was shown my love, my family, how to reach my happiness, and how to not worry about what the world worries about. 'All will be provided for you, Liam, just trust and have faith,' was the message being sent.

Fhian looked more beautiful than ever before. We looked perfect for each other, and after our child, this new goddess-like glow filled her aura, and she became like an Atlantian priestess. I was the proudest man alive, eternally grateful to have such a great woman be part of me.

I sat in this love, in this house, with this beautiful family for what seemed like forever, I never wanted to let go. My body felt so amazing, soft and loose like I was in a world made of candy floss floating in space.

I wanted to merge with the floor, and as I slipped further and further down the wall, I could see there was a lucid liquid level a foot from the ground. When my head fell and my eyes passed through this lucid liquid level crazy visuals took over; animal, snakes, birds, insects everything you could imagine were there, going nuts in this other realm, enticing me to come and have another adventure. It was all in Technicolor. There were shapes shifting into one another. Part of me wanted to sit and watch, but another part of me thrust myself back up, spine straight back to the disciplined respect for Lady Ayahuasca.

Lucias began to sing. What was happening? Was this allowed? Was he stealing Otillia's show? I don't like this change, I thought. *I wanted to be in Otillia's world, how can this work? The ceremony is going to be ruined. STOP, RELAX, SIT BACK, ENJOY & LOVE... BREATHE, BREATHE, BREATHE.*

Wow, I was taken to a new place. Tingles and energy spread, making its way around my body. Love was being poured over my head like one of those wire head massage devices that look like a huge spider. Electric fluid ran down my spine. Lucias sang so beautifully, like two people were singing like his next word came before the last one had finished and it was delivered in a different voice and tone, overlapping one another. I fell back into my dream world of love. So, so, so, so, much love, so, so many blessings, happiness exploding from my chest like a Catherine wheel. The sparks of love infected everyone they hit, everyone that saw them. I had to spread this love I was being told, like a child with too much energy.

Without an outlet I would go mad, I had to share this love, to cuddle, to hold on to people and pour my love into them, and let its infection be known to the world.

My head threw itself back, the music was pure bliss, utopia, heavenly, perfection, the rattle exploded particles of imagination through my head. The purge rushes came again, I approached my bowl on all fours, my hair down, providing a vial. More dogma and layers of unneeded baggage I had collected through life were being ripped out of me by my higher self, by my soul. It was as if the sick was coming from the bottom of my feet, where every one of these unwanted notions, memories, pains were residing. They were being forced out violently, over the overtones of the most beautiful music imaginable to man. I wretched painfully, forcing out this unwanted plethora of expectation, programming, education, TV, values, monotonous lives that we are made to feel are necessary to fit in, to be respected, wanted, valued and deemed normal by society. It was like I was in the *Matrix*, wanting to take the pill of truth. I wanted to be an open vessel. I wanted the falsity of parts of me to be evaporated, my ego to be destroyed, my confidence to be cemented.

I wretched again. I was eating the tasteless food on the Nebuchadnezza, tasteless slop, but it tasted better than being controlled by programmed tastes, smells and senses. It felt better to evolve than to be chastised by things I'd never had a say in. I was never given a choice to be a meat-eater or not. Never given a choice as to whether I should drink or not. Never given a chance to choose a religion. Never given the chance of a different way of life, nationality, medical options, practices, products I consumed, cancer-giving creams, devices, products, equipment and chemicals that could have been the cause of my mother's death. I wanted to rid myself of all this, to search and be guided to the truth and be able to pass this on to my children. For them to be informed and have choices, for others who read this to think differently about what they put in their bodies and the choices they make.

I knew that telling people how they should live was not the

right way, all I could do was be myself, stick to my beliefs and continue to search for the truth and listen to what feels right, not what sounds right. Our bodies know exactly what we want and exactly what is right for us, we just have difficulty listening to it.

This was in no way me belittling the way others live, it was about me being comfortable living in my body, always doing what is best for it, choosing the right foods, drinks, creams, and products. We don't put less superior liquids and oils in our cars as they will severely damage it. But most of us don't give it a thought when it comes to what we put in our bodies. All this flashed across my mind whilst trying to get my hair away from the passing sick. Still purging on all fours, I could still find beauty in the way my sweaty hair fell before my eyes and flickers of moonlight passed through the gaps in the wall and onto my face.

The music would stop and start. When it stopped, I tried to reposition my body to a respectable posture. When the music played, I could only half control what it did, trying my best to not let it slip below the lucid liquid level into insanity. I was back to tapping, spreading, stretching, slouching. I was so happy, it was the best party ever. Melting and flopping, being fascinated by my limbs, the monkey in me was, here again, it always seemed present, alive.

Otillia, Lisa and Lucias were now all contributing to the musical overtures, and I was overjoyed by their abundant treat. Soon I found myself turning this whole experience into a piece of art. At first, I was given ideas of how to make money back in London. Committing to Fhian would mean London times ahead. I saw myself there. I could take a 5 Rhythm-esque dance class on a Sunday morning, find a room, advertise, get a music playlist. Help people lose their inhibitions, gain confidence, get fitter, loosen up and meet new people, all with their shoes and socks off and without the aid of any narcotics.

I was in East London, with my van. I'd turned it into a cafe. I was serving espressos, emoliente and tostadas. I was learning the guitar, learning to sing my poems, and lyrics were coming thick and fast. I needed a way of delivering them, getting them off my chest.

I was then in a gallery, going through the various stages of the Ayahuasca experience, it was like an interactive performance art piece. It started off with me in a sterile white space, with my bucket and mattress going through the Ayahuasca stages, unable to control my body, but showing its freedom and bliss. The fear and the pain were visible to the audience who had their shoes off. They would ask questions, advice on their own life and be encouraged to participate in acting like a monkey. The idea evolved and evolved, a set was built like the room I was in now. The performance was called 'Ayahuasca Monkey'. I went through each of the ceremonies. I was sick, purging, vegetable soup spluttered out from a bag on my side. I would talk about the old values and expectation, pains and confusion being shed and healed with each wretch. A life-size model of Otillia sat rocking on one side of the room, models of the other participants stayed very still in their places throughout. A spotlight shone through the wooden cladding representing the walls, and a damp atmosphere was re-created. People asked questions in an interactive way, worried by the pain and trauma the actor (me) was going through. The gallery was full. A buzz had begun. It was all so vivid. Nothing could stop me. I was going to do it, this was my direction for now, and where I should focus my efforts, it seemed.

All the artistic stuff seemed to feel right, to flow out of me. It was telling me to focus on this and to let everything else go. To paint, to write, to sing, to act, to create, to build, to talk, to walk. This sense of freedom hit me in the face. This was the only way I would be free.

The next thing I knew, Otillia was asking how we all were. We began to chat, I talked about the love I'd been shown and the simplicity and importance of commitment and discipline, and how I would return home to my girl as soon as I left there.
Otillia said, "You are ready for whatever the next stage of your life maybe". She asked how my visions had been.

I said, "Nice, peaceful, beautiful, important, but I knew the craziness was just below that line."

She said she knew. Again, she reiterated the importance of this night for me, for extra healing and focus. Lucias translated all. Then she started to tell me how my path had to be a creative one, she told me I was an artist, and I had to focus on that. I thought of when I'd read Richard Millward's book *'Ten Story Love Song'* and how the main character Bobby, really appealed to me and made me want to paint. The lifestyle, the freedom, the creative beauty of that life really struck a chord with me. In most books and films, it's the artist or musician who appeals to me the most.

She laughed at my monkey ways again, and the way my feet tapped and moved to the music, my inability to be still, the way I lay down in the living room in the days when everyone else stood or sat. "You are an artist," she said, "a free spirit, explore this more, don't worry about money it will come to you, don't chase it like the rest."

I couldn't believe what she'd said after the visions I'd just had, how did she know? How synchronised was this, it seemed serendipitous. I'd heard that the Ayahuasceros could tap into your experience like a CCTV camera watches people. This felt crazy, it was like a major reinforcement of what I'd seen. It felt magical, beautiful, lovely and right. My direction seemed set. Just be, don't push and what is rightfully yours will come. What you have been put on this earth to do will present itself. I felt safe, warm, found, I felt clear, stress-free and happy.

The happiness I'd been searching for, for so long seemed here. I could touch it, feel it. So much joy was spreading through my veins like an anaesthetic before an operation. It wasn't just my blood and veins, it was every fibre of my being, my cells, my DNA, my organs, muscles, the water in me, every particle of me of my higher self and soul were in total unconditional bliss.

Lucias, Lisa and Otillia all spoke. I had no idea what they were saying, and I just smiled and nodded. They all began to play music together. Otillia fetched a mandolin from her room, and the music they created was divine. I closed my eyes and bounced about in other worlds as they played.

Otillia looked at me and said through the translation of Lucias, "Señor, you are an artist, artists can sing, sing for us"!

"Woah woah woah, oh oh no, I can't sing my voice is awful," I said.

"Everyone can sing, Señor, it's just fear we have created around ourselves and our voice, telling ourselves we cannot or being afraid of judgement and ridicule if we let out our true voice out."

Lucias and Lisa concurred. "I bet you sing when you're alone", they said.

"Yes, all the time, but it's awful."

"You should sing, just sing a song you know," Otillia encouraged.

"But I can't, I couldn't," I was trying to think of any way out of this. "I write some songs," I said. "But I can't sing them."

"Excellent," Otillia said, "you can sing your own song."

I had no way out of this, my supple body was now so tense, fear had enveloped me. There was a lot of peer pressure. On the wider scale of things, I could see they had a point in regards to me conquering my fear and becoming more confident, but I didn't know all the words to any song, and I really didn't want to embarrass myself in this setting. I thought how amazing it would be to have a good voice, I would sing all the time. To be the lead singer in a band would be the best job in the world I'd always imagined. The pressure continued. I wanted a hole to take me away from this situation, but I knew there was no escaping.

"Ok," I said, "I will sing, I have a song called, '21 Souls' that I wrote on my pilgrimage for the end of the Mayan calendar." I closed my eyes, trying to find the words.

"From the heart," Otillia said, "find your voice, it's in there."

The words came into my mind. So much fear was attached to them, and my heart was going crazy. I was scared that my heart was going to beat out of my body, and I felt everyone's eyes on me. I decided to wait until I felt comfortable. With my eyes closed, part of me hoped that if I opened them everyone would have disappeared and this ordeal would be over. Occasionally the words would try and come out, but something was keeping them in, telling me to work through the blockage. I could see myself singing the Liam and Fhian song at my 30th birthday party, the voice I'd used wasn't mine, it was a voice to try and hide the real fear, a poor voice that would get the reaction of 'he can't sing' but at least he'd had a go.

I was fully inside me, searching for these blockages, nothing else in the world existed. I was reminded of the fake voice I'd used in a best man's speech many years ago; again, it was to cover up my fear. I could see all the moments when fear had pushed me from my true self. I hadn't been me, the true me was only for the one I shared a bed with, the one I was in love with. Even my mother, the woman I loved more than all the people in my life put together, rarely saw the true, loving me.

Layers of barriers seemed to be falling from my chest. I was looking in my heart for this true voice, not just for song but for everything my true heart would lead me to. The words wouldn't come, I didn't know them. A voice said, "breathe, forget the world, find that place of comfort and bliss, and when you do just sing, it will all come."

I'd had my eyes shut for a few minutes, I hoped my wish had come true, I wanted them all to have disappeared when I opened them again. More layers and fears began to break off. I thought of how I could become another character when acting and do anything, laugh, cry, be naked, show every human emotion. Because it wasn't me I was safe to speak in that person's voice. But as myself with no mask, I was frightened. I wanted to be brave enough to show this uninhibited true me to myself, to the world, to be full of love and not be ashamed of being so.

All of a sudden, the words just came out of my mouth like purging but less messy. I was confused at first whether I was being sick or singing. Then I lost myself in the song. I had no idea if the words were right or in order, I just sang and sang, lingering on notes, true love and meaning being portrayed towards each person who had been on that trip with me. I was lost in another world, one I'd never been to before, it was a world of speech and beauty, of musical notes floating through the sky.

My heart was connected to it all. I was in pure love, my heartfelt big. '21 Souls lingering in the sky, ascend to the earth, ascend to the sky' reverberating in my head, overlapping with the next lines. I finished, and tingles ran up and down my body. I wanted to cry; instead I laughed. A proud laugh of overcoming a great fear. I hoped beyond hope I could get to this place again to make sounds like I had. I wanted to be confident in auditions, to be able to find my true voice at will and accentuate the poems of love I write with a voice to match their gentile meaning. When I had been fully in the song without worry of forgetting the words or hitting the right note, I'd seemed to be held in space and could find the note and the delivery for each word as I let it out. I felt all warm and fuzzy inside, and all the neurons in my head started to light up. It felt like sprinkles of stars were being dropped onto my head, and they were twinkling around inside. A big 'Ahhhhhh' filled my body. I melted back into my mattress as Lucias said, "Wow beautiful."

Otillia said, "See, you can, you have to keep doing this now, song can free you, can heal others."

I'd never thought of that. Then I realised we have songs for our moods. We fall in love to music, and we lose ourselves after the monotony of a week's work. It has so many uses, it keeps us company in an empty house, introduces us to the sounds we like, it's like food with people liking different types and being moved in different ways by the same taste.

I felt fantastic again, I wanted this confidence never to leave me. We all chatted like we were in our grandma's living room, laughing and joking. I asked about this monkey and baby I'd become in the ceremonies. Did the monkey mean it was my power animal? It was something I had heard quite a bit about in spiritual circles, but I had never actually had one come to me like others talked of.

Otillia said, "This is freedom of movement, your true self, the monkey is in you, it has been in you since your channel allowed it to became open."

"Right then, I'm going to get a monkey tattoo, the one from the Nazca lines."

She said, "Do that, the monkey and the baby go well together, we are more like monkeys when we are children, the child in you is strong. Never lose it. We are conditioned out of that behaviour by society, parenting and a desire to fit in. Monkeys play games and have fun all the time, they are immature and like to mess around, keeping that child within alive. The only time we tend to do it as adults is when we are alone and relaxed, but as soon as someone disrupts solitude, we tense and pretend we were not doing what we were doing. It's the human condition, you are lucky you have not lost this."

I wondered why this was. How had society and consumerism, the materialistic world not managed to enslave me? Why was I still free? Was it so I could experience more, to understand more, to be able to help more people by not being locked into the system? I always knew I never wanted it. I used to always say to friends, "There must be something better than 9-5, man, that's dry." I could never imagine going to the same office for forty years, same drive, same commute every day, hating my job, hating parts of my life. Looking forward to my two-week package holiday, being so disconnected that I had to change the decor in my house every three or so years, so as not to seem cheap and out of fashion with the swarm of society. A mid height border separating two different types of wallpaper, then the next change is a border three-quarters of the way up the wall, then back to one wallpaper, to then be discarded for painted plaster all around, then eventually a feature wall added with paper or paint to give more depth. Living like this would be worse than losing my mind, I thought. Please, please, please never happen to me!

I thought about why I'd always felt like I had never fitted in. Never felt a complete part of any group or team. Was that again my fear of commitment cropping up or had I just never found what I needed? I always felt different from the people I knew, I cared about completely different things. Why my consciousness started to expand I have no idea, but I felt very privileged and blessed it had. Very privileged and blessed to be in this hut with Lucius and Lisa, with Guylene, with Otillia with Lady Ayahuasca.

Lisa and Lucias played and, closing my eyes, I dropped back into the world of Ayahuasca. The singing started, and my body once again felt like pure electricity. Then I felt Otillia's energy on me, I couldn't see her face, but I felt her presence.

I sat listening, feeling Otillia working on me. Some kind of healing was taking place, I could feel it so powerfully. I straightened my spine, trying to focus and be an open vessel for Otillia's energy. I lost concentration and drifted down into the madness. Into the lucid liquid level. My slouching was almost flat to the ground as if all my bones had become mush. I reprimanded myself, "No, Browne, you must sit up, Otillia, is giving you something very special, don't spoil it." As my teachers had said throughout my life, "you have a very short attention span and don't listen". As always there was this constant battle, I could not stay focused, even though it felt like every part of Otillia was focused on me. I found myself drifting off into another thought and again would realise and snap out of it, snap my back straight and try to focus.

Part of me never wanted this ceremony to end, it had been the most powerful, meaningful experience of my life. The emphasis I had put on this moment felt fully justified. I'd always known that this would bring me some clarity, direction trust and love. Fhian knew Ayahuasca was important to me, she was eager for me to experience it. I thought it would give me answers and would be a huge turning point in our relationship. It felt like it was.

As I sat there, what I was going to do flashed before my eyes. I would leave the jungle on day eight, two sleeps from now. Fly to Lima from Iquitos and then straight to Fhian. Surprise her, ask her to marry me, tell her I wanted to spend the rest of my life with her. To have everything with her, to be family, to be the most significant part of each other's lives for the rest of time, to be in love forever, to be sweet, to be soppy and an inspiration to each other. I knew part of my future was at home in Manchester, but I knew more than anything I had to make it work with Fhian. I knew we could, I felt confident that love would conquer all, that nothing could get in the way. The clarity was like nothing I'd ever experienced before. I knew I had to get to her. I wanted her energy bound with mine. I wanted to sit and look into her beautiful brown eyes, to pretend nothing else in the world existed but the two of us and that no one had experienced a love like this before. It seemed set.

I had to wait a day before I set off. Allow the Ayahuasca to settle so I could have the focus for the journey to my girl. I would cut my trip short. I felt excited to want to marry someone, to want to commit, to see the beauty in commitment, to see all the new opportunities it would create, to know that I would always have someone. Someone to look out for and to always look out for me. I was ready. I'd never been so excited in my whole life.

I was snapped out of this love dream by Otillia saying again that my path looked good, looked clear, looked like there would be lots of success in all parts of my life. She told everyone she wanted to end the ceremony soon.

She stood and glided towards me, her wide smile, revealing her white teeth that illuminated my world. With her leaf rattle in one hand, she knelt in front of me. I was determined to try and convey my gratitude energetically. The *Icaro* and singing began; I was lightly beaten on my head, face, shoulders, chest and arms with the leaves. I was transfixed by the feeling of pure love, of the powerful presence of Otillia, her gentle forcefulness, my whole body vibrating, tingling, occasionally a bolt of energy would rush into my head. Pure love, peace, happiness, contentment, bliss and psychedelic joy elegantly glided and danced around my body.

I was in this other world, devoid of anything negative. Powerful healing was taking place. Otillia was doing her thing using her channel and connection to Lady Ayahuasca to pass the good stuff to me and to allow anything negative to leave my body and return to the sky.

I didn't want this moment to end. It lasted for what seemed like an eternity, I was there, my focus was on what I was receiving. Otillia's focused beautiful energy, ambient flowing words and wondrously melodic powerful beat of the rattle reverberated around my whole body. It was like standing in front of a speaker at a drum and bass rave, but more hypnotic and dignified. I felt like I was having a shamanic lesson to trust my own knowledge and capacity, to work with energy and to relax into the uncertainties and strangeness of life.

I was later told it was a special healing as it was my last

ceremony and the end of my Dieta. My gratitude and love for this lady were overwhelming, she had given me the tools to be confident, to see my own beauty and stop beating myself up about what I hadn't done. She'd given me what I had been looking for, had shown me the importance of true love, the fact it's worth everything and that family can change your world. Ayahuasca had fulfilled and surpassed all my expectations. Otillia, as she had said herself, was just chosen by Ayahuasca to learn about the plants and all the wonder and knowledge they hold and to show people the true nature of life. She allowed people to be cured and healed of physical and mental problems and addictions, to see their true selves. To give them direction, to see the oneness of the world and how everything is alive has a soul and meaning. To make people see that Lady Gaia (Mother Earth) is an interconnected system we all play a role in.

Otillia and Ayahuasca seemed like a match made in Heaven. It was astounding the work they had done together, how many lives they'd changed, healing depression, addiction, mental problems, physical problems, showing so many people the light. Otillia has an 80% success rate with getting crack and heroin addicts clean. Boom Otillia, boom!

As Otillia moved on to Guylene, she continued telling me to continue this diet for fourteen days. She said to take it easy and to rest as much as I could, to sit and allow the plants to work. I said that was fine.

"Sex," I said, "can I have sex?"

This was interpreted and smiling, Otillia looked at me and said, *"Si Señor, mucho"*

Everyone laughed, and Otillia said, "This is fine, enjoy."

I couldn't wait for my explosion of love to be cemented with this act, I couldn't wait to hold the most beautiful woman on the planet close to me and caress every part of her body. To look into her huge brown eyes and tell her that I loved her more than anything I'd ever loved. To feel the two magnets that were made in the same mould to reconnect and never part again.

Otillia finished her healing and sat back in her seat and the amazing atmosphere that had permeated the room all evening remained. Otillia asked if I would like to drink another medicine which was a final goodbye and was a plant that would stay in my system for quite a while. It would help me sleep tonight, she said. It was not an uplifting medicine. I thought it must be a natural spiritual version of the after-party drug, Valium.

Otillia said we should take it and everyone agreed. I never even questioned it, my complete faith was in this lady. She told us we must be clean for the medicine and would have to bathe beforehand; I often did this with Valium as well if I had the energy to get in the shower.

Otillia shouted to one of the ladies who worked there and told her to fill the bath outside and make the medicine. It was the early hours of the morning, and the lady Otillia had called had been sleeping — obviously, her contract stipulated being on call during ceremonies, and I wondered if she had a beeper. I never realised there were people sleeping just on the other side of the thin wooden walls. I then thought about all the noise I had been making in that last ceremony and how I must have kept them awake.

Sleepily she prepared the bath. Otillia said after this, I would be able to take on the world. I would be ready to fulfil my potential, nothing would hold me back, and I would have the confidence to be my true self. The bath and buckets were filled with water that I figured had been brought from the small stream close by. Flowers had typically been added, and I quickly bathed, cleansing my body under the spectacular star-studded rooftop of black glitter that ignited my vision every time I looked up. I had no towel, so it was a drip dry and back into my ceremonial attire.

Everyone but Otillia took the bath, and when we were all clean and soaking wet, we were given a small beaker of plant medicine. Otillia said we must all drink together. After a *'Salute'* in unison we all knocked it back. Otillia went into detail of the medicine, but my memory for things like detail always seems to fail me. I am always mesmerised by people who remembered facts, I always remember weird stuff.

The ceremony was officially over. We were told we could stay and chat further and sing. Guylene needed some sleep as she had not taken the Ayahuasca. I was impressed she had managed to stay awake the whole time.

Otillia looked at me and said, "Liam, you are a strong and powerful man, now go forth and take on the world."

A kind of gobsmacked, "Thank you and goodbye" trickled from my lips.

I stayed with the others for a little while listening to them having an Ayahuasca-fuelled jam session. I only lasted a couple of songs, needing some rest and wishing I could contribute. I wanted to go and be with Fhain. I imagined her in my arms, thinking about our lives together, and how I would get home to her as soon as possible. After an un-treacherous walk back to the hut and the gauntlet of getting into the mosquito-netted bed, I felt the plant medicine running through my veins. I lay back and enjoyed the love, happiness and contentedness that was creating this hazy glow around my body.

The next day I woke to this lovely world of love, calmness and manoeuvrability which hazily and fuzzily covered the mosquito net. I had one more night with Otillia. Today was a day to relax, but thoughts and plans circled my mind, it was a vast difference to the blissful emptiness I had felt the previous days. I wanted to ask Fhian to marry me as soon as I saw her. I wrote a beautiful song in my head and dreamed of singing it to her. It went like this:

John & Yoko
Will you be my Yoko
So I can be your John
Lay in bed together
Without the TV on
Sit and laugh forever
Snuggle with my honey bun
Look into your eyes
And tell you you're the one
This will last forever
I'll always be your John
And you will be my Yoko
Nothing much will get done
Laying there in Heaven
Having so much fun
Tickling and laughing
Tell each other you're the one
Planning to get married
Somewhere in the sun
I will never leave you
I won't get shot like John
Oh no I won't get shot like John

I knew love was all we needed. Nothing else mattered to me, nothing else came into my head, no doubts. I lay and wrote for a while, and a creative air filled me. Poems and ideas flashed across my mind at great speed, but I had no pen to capture them. And this story about that circled my mind before I actually got a pen to write it down.

To Piss Myself or Not to Piss Myself
I wake to the incessant sound of the mosquito hum and buzz, I shake in my usual way when the sound suddenly stops to see if the humming, buzzing begin again. If it does, I have company. Fortunately, via in-depth studies, my still-cloudy mind decides I'm safe. This continues for 30 or so minutes and each time I discover again the conclusion of my analysis. My body relaxes and any part of it hovering above the bed crashes back down, melting into the mattress. After another 30 minutes or so I become conscious of how desperately I have to pee, I feel like I'm in heaven though (not Devon where my mum is) The bed and my mosquito net 4 poster esque shaped paradise shelter my need for peace and safety from all the nasties awaiting me outside. I decide to sit it out and forget about it and still feeling sleepy and induced by the plants, I'm in a mellow, marshmallow, rainbow-coloured fellows world, and I want out. I then realise I need to pee sosososososososo bad.That I have to escape, I also need to poo hard, and these two sensations press against the lower part of my stomach. I'm still lay flat in Marshmallow World, wishing the sensations away, discovering I could get past the feeling of my anus exploding but my penis not. I pray and imagine how cool these beds would be with a catheter so I could just piss myself. I consider pissing myself. NO BROWNE, YOU CAN NOT, The monkey would though. DOHH. Miserabled by my latest investigations findings and the poo now moving from category C to A I resign myself to the fact I need to escape under the net and into the scary bug-infested world. My body seems destined for yellow fever, which I seemed to have avoided so far. Just putting my body through the sheer anguish that is crawling under the net, standing upright, walking to the toilet, doing my thing and then getting my notebook and pen, crawling back under my net, slapping the bugs off, hoping none of them get past quarantine and lying back down seems like torture. But I have to, I turn half on my side, which is a quarter of the way towards being on my back again. My hand is holding my bum cheek, fully on the left one and delicately cupping the right. I then think of Fhian, without the hair, and get trapped in the moment for around one minute and forty-six seconds, then pull myself out and escape, going through the previously described ritual; out of bed and net stand, walk in a U shape to the toilet, lean on the wall and squat. DONE. Ahhhhhhhhhh, clean up mess by lifting lid on huge bin of water beside, taking a small bowl dunking to fill, removing and throwing down toilet until toilet is clear. I am being bitten this whole time, constantly slapping my ankles, clapping my hands, searching for justice from the latest culprits to have taken my blood.Crash, bang, slap, smash. It frustrates, I'm bitten, smitten, like a

kitten, but knowing I'm not cos I'm a little monkey. When toilet is clear I take another bowlful, put it on the floor and like an Amsterdamian prostitute, I wash my bits there and then, the recipe for this is twice. Then I get a fresh bowl, wash hands and feel clean to get back in bed and net, with pen and pad and write this. Sleep rest time now, with all my love. Sorry if I disgust in any way but words just flew, flowed and the new true me is an artist, so I have to be led by heart and instinct. Much love and blessings. Liam x x x x

All I wanted to do was get to Fhian, nothing else mattered. I had belongings at Ananda's in Guatemala City and at Tom's in Miami, but that didn't matter. I thought a flight might take me via one of these places, but it wasn't imperative. All that mattered was my love. I knew tomorrow I would wake and head home, regardless of the cost. I was leaving here to spend the rest of my life with her, for us to grow together like one apple tree grafted onto another.

I thought about the things I had planned on doing in the next few months. Surfing in northern Peru, meeting my Aussie mates, building a cob house in Ecuador, more Ayahuasca ceremonies, seeing Bogotá and the pristine beaches and a country everyone raved about. Then Panama and all the Central American countries I had not yet visited. Then heading back to Guatemala City, Ananda's, the Lake, Belize and finally a week in Miami with me best mate. None of that seemed as important now. I was following my heart, all that mattered was capturing that love, catapulting us back together. Skipping through fields, making love in the long grass, chatting for hours, planning our future, supporting each other, saying this is it, you are all that I want. It was a monumental feeling, something so foreign to me, the concept I'd had all my life of how things could be.

I felt creative like an artist. I wanted to be Bobby from Richard Millward's *'Ten Story Love Song'* book, but without the booze, a girlfriend who only ate sweets and living in a high-rise block of flats in Middlesbrough. I wanted not to worry about money, which seemed constantly programmed into me, but to have faith in what was shown. Put on an art piece, keep writing, work on my creativity, to keep striving to strip away my baggage, to unleash my inner child on the world, to laugh loud wherever I went and for my healing laugh and hands to touch as many people as possible.

I wanted to achieve more in the film world, to act, to sing, to dance, to love, to jump and to run fast barefoot on grass. To never listen to people stuck in dogma, to stay close to the true me that I had now found. To push this me to the front, to get what is rightfully mine, to fulfil my potential, to have love, have friends, to teach, to learn, to heal, to help, to support, to fully awaken, to be conscious always, to be the light and let light shine through me.

I felt ecstatic. My heart was huge, and I was so excited to be committing to Fhian. I'd missed her so much, and I estimated that within the next few days I would be breathing the same air as her.

Breakfast was called, and Guylene was already there. She congratulated me on completing the Dieta. We ate, and Lucias and Lisa soon joined us. We chatted about the night's events. They told me how the ceremony was focused on me as it was my last and most important as it was filled with my energy and the healing was for me. Guylene filmed us all, asking how we found Otillia and our experiences. She showed me some of the footage from the ceremony, and the night vision had really captured the mood, and I thought it would really accompany my multimedia performance piece based on the Ayahausca experience.

I was again being bitten to death by mosquitoes as I devoured my food. Guylene was leaving soon. I loved her energy. We sat and chatted with Otillia for a while, I generally smiled and nodded. I said how amazing the evening had been, thanked her for the extra healing and focus she had put on me.

Guylene left, and we had a lovely goodbye embrace. I hoped to see her one day soon, maybe in Paris or England or maybe back here. She was an amazing person, so uplifting, so much energy, such a warm loving nature. I felt like myself with her, she made me laugh, and my own humour poured out. I wished the amazing filmmaker goodbye and watched her disappear into the jungle. I returned to my hut, thinking about making my way to Fhian. How would I get there? I trusted it would all work out perfectly.

I tried to relax in my hammock, and for the first time, I actually had to try. No Ajo Sacha this morning and the heat, humidity and dampness ensured a constant film of sweat covered my whole body. Mosquitoes were everywhere; if I was going to get malaria or yellow fever, surely this was the moment.

I went from bed to hammock several times, unable to find relaxing comfort. The makeshift net I'd put around the hammock seemed to provide little resistance to the army of Mosquitoes vying for my blood. They always found a gap or a hole to get at me from, they could even bite through the material of the hammock.

When I thought I had killed the last one, I would relax into my book and, after a minute or so, I would hear the dreaded buzz again. My concentration would be broken, and I would be back on the hunt, slapping, shaking, rocking the hammock, nothing seemed to work. I was naked and stepping out of the net was like walking in front of a firing squad or throwing a piece of meat towards flies. They were on me straight away, I would spend ten minutes killing, clapping my hands, slapping my calves, shins, thighs, hamstrings, knees, everywhere was being attacked. I would swipe and clench my fist together hoping one would await inside as I opened my hand.

Then suddenly I felt something land on my penis.

Noooooooooooooooooooo! I had to act quick. Did I continue the whacking and slapping with all my might? Did I shake and hope it hadn't already locked in? I opted for a light swipe and wiggle. I inspected myself for damage, and it looked like I was in the clear.

As this had been happening, the mosquitoes had taken the chance and were preying on me from all angles. Had the penis hunt been a decoy, so my full attention was in one place? Did they know a man's major point of weakness? I realised there and then, after thinking there was nothing in the world that I hated, that actually I hated mosquitoes and wanted them to not exist.

I had used the word 'hate' flippantly for many years, and I was taught by Fhian's dad one New Year's Eve that hate was a strong word. He asked if there was anyone I truly hated in the world and wanted to see dead? There was no one I truly wanted dead, so after this important lesson, I started to erase the word from my vocabulary. It was really difficult at first, but when I said the word I would notice it and would make a point of it and say, 'No actually I don't hate them or it, as hate is a strong word'. It took six months for me to fully wean myself off using it and it had not said it since.

Until now. 'I HATE MOSQUITOES'.

Is there anyone in the world that likes them? I really do hate mosquitoes!

I was fidgety, distracted, hot and frustrated, and I couldn't find a place to relax. I started to think about leaving there and then, heading to Iquitos, starting this journey of reconnection a day early. I decided I was going to do it after lunch. I was free to go. I could stay another night, but it was just to rest, something I couldn't do in these conditions.

Lunch was called, and I ate with Lucias and Lisa. We conversed about amazing, beautiful things; life, death, growth and enlightenment. Nowhere in sight was mention of jobs, cars, houses, hair, shoes and the latest trends. I found out Lucias had had the same experience with regards to singing on his first visit to Otillia four years ago. He was put in the same situation, felt the same nervous angst and the firm belief he couldn't sing. I couldn't believe it; he sang so beautifully now. I fantasised about being able to sing like him, words coming straight from the heart. I hoped I could muster a similar sound one day soon. Lucias said he now sang all the time; music was a huge part of the healing work he and Lisa provided.

I wanted to be like this couple and live the way they did. To always be calm, softly-spoken, loving, contented and in the flow of the energy of the Universe. Trusting that all my worldly needs will be met, gaining great satisfaction from knowing that the work I do is not only helping people but pushing them towards a path of love, light, health and happiness and becoming an awakened soul. I told them I was going to leave, to head for my girl, they said how beautiful that was and how Ayahuasca works in ways normal people can only dream of and would have difficulty to fathom.

I let Otillia know and then not in a rush but at a fast pace, frantically trying to avoid getting bitten, I scrambled like John Cleese in a wacky scene from Fawlty Towers, to wash pack, tidy and throw all my stuff on the grass outside to ensure minimum time in the hut and additions to my already savaged feet, ankles, and legs.

I picked up my bag, I was on the move again.

I said goodbye to Lucias and Lisa and then goodbye to Otillia, I couldn't thank her enough. I had no words, but she could see my sheer gratitude and love pulsating from my heart.

"Mucho, mucho, mucho gracias", I said. I thanked all the staff, hugged the ladies and shook hands with the blokes. I hugged Otillia, praying I would see her again, with Fhian I hoped. I really wanted her to see this world. I looked deep into Otillia's eyes, taking in her energy her presence and her stature. I thought of what I was now and what I was when I had arrived. I owed Otillia and Lady Ayahuasca so much and thought if everyone could just experience this once, if they cared about themselves, cared about being a better person, for themselves and for the people around them, how beautiful the world would be. What beauty there would be in this world with everyone pursuing their dreams. A revisioning of who

we are and who we want to become. To know and see the other forces at play in the Universe, at play on Earth, at play between the living, the dead, the future, the past, the spirits, the Angels, the animals, the plants. The plants that give us so, so much knowledge about how to live, breathe, heal and learn and be still. The plants that can help us see, help us be. Ayahuasca for all it does, for the thousands of people it helps every year to see their potential, their destiny, to help them heal, forgive and forget, give clear direction and remember their true self.

Our culture has vilified mystic beliefs and has historically deemed anyone who claims to be able to access other realms of reality a crazy lunatic. Our Judo-Christian heritage has filled us with fear of God and anything spiritual. The conquistadors of South America deemed these practices the work of the Devil and killed anyone with the slightest involvement. I hoped that our society could grow up enough to treat Ayahuasca, as a doorway to the spirit world and our evolution as people and communities. I kissed Otillia on the cheek, adios'ed her up, flipped my rucksack on my back and headed into the jungle, unable to turn back.

I was heading for one thing now, for destiny, to start my life, it was all in front of me. Fear had melted away the chains. The shackles I had wrapped myself in had been broken, my shoulders had lost their heaviness.

The jungle seemed more alive than the last time I had walked through it. Sounds seemed amplified, colours seemed vivid, every step was a step closer to my love. *I'm coming baby, I'm coming,* looped through my mind as I sauntered through the narrow jungle path which would be the first of many journeys I would have to tackle before I got home to my love.

Things, however, wouldn't work out exactly as I expected!

EPILOGUE

After making my way back through the jungle, I could see the road now. To my left was a huge battery farmed chicken factory, a far cry from the free-roaming chickens of Otillia's paradise. There were jetty style bridges going over swamps as I approached the road and I was sure I could hear a crocodile or something in the water. Immediately thoughts of it jumping onto the bridge and dragging me in entered my mind.

As I got to the road, a *collectiveo* was passing. There were other people waiting, everyone was dirty and covered in sweat. I jumped on as bags, and an array of fruits were thrown onto the top of the small people carrier. We collected people every few hundred yards, and it got more and more crowded.

I sat at the back, and this dirty-faced little boy kept turning around to look at me. I pulled some funny faces, and he laughed and smiled. The next thing I knew the van had smoke billowing out of the engine, and we all piled out. They seemed to fix the problem, and we got back in, only to be engulfed by smoke again two hundred metres down the road.

After trying to fix it the driver and the ticket man aborted and all the passengers piled into the next collectiveo heading towards us. The collectiveo's are the cheap way to travel, used by all the locals costing about £1 for a one hour thirty-minute trip. The vans are only the size of a really small people carrier, but they pile in about five times the amount they are designed to carry. The ticket man stands on the step of the sliding door. He tentatively holds a strap to support himself and every time a passenger flags them down, he jumps out and packs their luggage onto the roof and balances himself back in the open doorway.

I could see coconuts, oranges, mangos, papaya, sugar cane and chickens all being passed up to the ticket man as he quickly balanced them on the small roof above us.

People sat on the floor, and some stood in a stooped fashion. At one point a young man, obviously on his way home from a hard day's work, got off. As he does, in the distance I saw this young kid sprinting towards him with sheer excitement oozing from his every cell. His smile was as wide as an obese American's waistline, and as he got to the man, he just stopped, grabbed his hand, and they started to walk home together. My heart opened, and tears started to roll down my cheeks, it was such a beautiful thing to witness. It seemed to sum up how beautiful and free life was here. I was skin-to-skin with three sweaty Peruvians and crying my eyes out. Maybe I would leave this situation with the general consensus that I was a gay man, and my man was in Miami with our daughter? I wanted more than anything what that man had; unconditional love, a joy to come home to and a purpose to go to work for.

We passed many villages where people were just hanging out on porches and in hammocks. As we approached Iquitos, it began to get more and more built up, and the noise started to increase. When we got to the city, the little boy who was fascinated by me and his very scruffy mum got off. As she battled with the luggage being thrown down, the little boy was looking around facing the street. He was eating some sort of sweets on a stick. With his free hand, he tugged his pants down till his little willy popped out and he began to pee. Without holding it, just holding his shorts, he pissed in the direction of the van and onto the road, still looking around and almost oblivious to what he was doing. He continued to chew and then when he was done, flipped it back in and waited to be dragged off by his mother.

I was dropped off in Iquitos and then got a tuk-tuk to the airport, hoping I could get a flight to Lima and then a flight home as soon as possible. I needed Fhian in my arms.

I got to the airport and had to wait an hour for a flight. I hadn't realised it was 7pm. I'd assumed I had left Otilia's around midday, obviously, I hadn't.

I arrived in Lima and was looking at tickets, slowly coming to terms with the fact the ticket I already had was now redundant. Flights were coming in at a minimum of a thousand dollars. I was trying for via Guatemala or Miami, so I could at least get some of my stuff and briefly see the friends I had promised I would return to. Then I saw a flight via Madrid the day after tomorrow for four hundred and fifty dollars, booked it, packed it, fucked off. It meant another day in Lima and a day longer than I had planned on being away from Fhian, but it was the next step taken care of.

I got back in contact with Anaze and Parker, the *'brilliantlove'* super fans to see if they wanted to hang out and show me where I could get my monkey tattoo. We hooked up in Mira Flores, in the artistic quarter with hip bars and shops. We ate lunch, and I saw

Carly the Aussie from the Machu Picchu Trek passing by. It was so random seeing someone you knew in a city of nine million inhabitants. We arranged to meet later that evening, and I headed for a new tattoo of the Nazca Line Monkey. After a few scratches I was done, and with my cling filmed arm, I went off into the city to spend the rest of the Peruvian money on presents.

It was strange to be back in a bustling city after a week of pure bliss, pampering and other-dimensional journeying. I met Carly and Liam, and we went for emoliente which is this beautiful hot ginger and syrup drink. We met their Peruvian friend who was this crazy surfer guy. I was spewing information and stories of my experience in the jungle. All I wanted to do was share and chat and luckily all around me were fascinated. We headed to meet Anaze and Parker before we went to a little party in Baranco.

All I really wanted to do was go to bed before my early flight the next day, but part of me wanted to chill with amazing people I probably wouldn't ever see again. We met them, and Carly wanted to see Parker's tattoo. Shyly, he agreed in the middle of the bustling street to take down his jeans to reveal my face on his leg. Anticipation built and as Parker took down his jeans he soon realised one of his bollocks was hanging out of his boxer shorts, and he frantically pulled them back up whilst turning to a bright shade of red. I hadn't realised Carly and Liam hadn't seen the bollock as only half the group laughed. They thought Parker had just got nervous about pulling down his pants in the busy street and had missed the bollock treat.

To encourage him to reveal the tattoo Carly suggested we all pull down our pants to make him feel more comfortable. So we did, myself, Carly and Liam all stood there with our pants around our ankles, and as we did, Parker readjusted his bollock and pulled his pants down with the bollock safely in his boxer shorts. Everyone was laughing as the four of us had our pants around our ankles. Carly and Liam shuffled to get a better view of the tattoo, and they couldn't believe my face was on his leg and somehow I was standing next to him. As we stood there with our trousers around our ankles in a busy city street, a girl passed and took a photo and as we all tussled with bringing our pants back to their rightful place around our waist, we turned to see a police car ten yards from us with its inhabitants disapprovingly shaking their heads with a sly little grin across their faces. I told Carly and Liam that the bollock had come out on the first attempt. They pissed themselves.

The next thing I knew, I was in this stunning townhouse in the much sought after district of Baranco. I was greeted by this eclectic looking man with a wide smile and escorted into another dreamlike world. Surfboards stood up around the room which had these huge ceilings and an upper balcony peering over this makeshift art gallery. The surfboards were all owned by a pro surfer and my host for the night was an artist who had done these amazing designs, murals and illustrations on the boards and was getting ready for an exhibition. I gawped at their magnificence and felt blessed for not having gone home to sleep, which had been my favoured option.

We all pulled up some mats and pillows and sat in a circle in the middle of the room, a flute, a didgeridoo, some drums and a raga crate drum are brought in, and musical overtones soothed the atmosphere as we all chatted. Was this going to become a theme of my life from now on as Otillia had predicted? A life of singing, music and the special souls who accompany the instruments? Again I was in amazing company in divine surroundings, but I couldn't keep me eyes open, so I headed back to the hostel. I didn't have a room for the night, so I crashed on the couch in the reception. I called Fhian on Skype, disturbing her from meditation and arranged to call her the next day which ensured she would be home when I arrived at her door in around thirty hours. I couldn't get to her quick enough. We talked about how excited we were to see each other in August, and she told me she couldn't wait to get started with us again. Part of me wanted to scream at her, "I'm coming to you, baby, I will see you tomorrow," but I decided the surprise would be more spectacular.

Through the screen, we both felt this crazy energy. It was like we were clawing at each other, so eager to touch each other and be together again

"Speak tomorrow," I said as I hung up. Little did she know I would be outside her door the next day whilst she was sitting in her room waiting for me to call.

I wrote poems and songs on the flights, changing the words to a poem I wrote for my mum the last time I was returning from a trip early. It seemed fitting to change this for Fhian who I now felt was going to be my family forever. This was a return home early again. Again it was because of love, but a different love this time.

Fhian/Home
Trying to get from the other side of the world to see you girl
Trying to get on a flight so I can be near you girl
The joy I felt today really brought meaning to you girl
When I sit back and think about all the times I missed you girl
Brings extra beats to my heart every time I see you girl
An excited expectation tingly sensation fills me girl
Just know I've got to get to you girl

    When I had to return home from my travels early in 2007 it was harrowing, I was frantic I couldn't stop crying, I was scared and just wanted to be home. But it became the catalyst for my writing, poems flew from a broken heart, I sat, and I wrote. I don't know where it came from, it had never happened before, and I hadn't consciously decided to write my mum poems, but her death allowed me to feel, to look inside and realise what she means to me. It bubbled my love to the surface, and I now realise love is the greatest creativity enhancer. When we allow love to surface we all become poets. When we allow love to circle around us, we see meaning in everything. Moments no longer seem ordinary, they seem poignant, we savour them and are sometimes blinded by them. Most of the time when I write in those situations it's as if someone else is writing for me and when I see the results I can't believe it's been written by my hand.

    This time it was different, heading home after a big trip. I seemed clear, I wasn't going over the possible reactions, I just wanted it to flow. What I'd seen during the Ayahuasca ceremonies had confirmed what my heart had felt for such a long time. I was hoping mine and Fhian's relationship could have that level of bond, it felt so strong, it had felt so strong for the last six months, it was like all the barriers she had put up when we were together had been taken down, and now we could be open with each other and get past all our conflict.

    We'd tried and tried to not be in contact after we broke up, but it seemed impossible, there was a cord that could not be cut. I could feel her pulling me back all the time, and I knew she could feel me wanting her every day. She was at the forefront of all my thoughts, she was this ever-presence in my heart, and it skipped beats for her. In every situation I was in, I wanted her to be part of it, to share with me the amazing sights, the amazing people and the simple things like watching the sunset and then waiting for the stars to come and to count the shooters.

Walking one day I saw a lonely hammock swinging from side to side in the garden of a beautiful house, and I imagined the two of us filling the hammock and living happily ever after in the house:

I see
I see a hammock I think of you
I see two birds I think of you
With cute couples I think of you
In a beautiful home I think of you
Eating alone I think of you
You're in the future I'm in the past
Sometimes I want to get to you so fast
Both alone we can't move past
All alone I think of you
With my friends I think of you
In a class I think of you
At work I think of you
I see the stars I think of you
Watch the sun set and think of you
I look into the future you're all I see
All I do is imagine you and me, you and me, you and me.

I was back on British soil. What does that actually mean? Whose is the soil? I don't think it belongs to any of us and, actually, all I could see was concrete. Anyhow, I walked down the now-trendy Chatsworth road in Hackney where it all began eight months ago. I needed to get Fhian out of her house so we could have our reunion on the street and not in her house with all her housemates present.

I asked a couple outside a cafe if I could use their phone as I wanted to get my girlfriend out of her house by pretending I had some flowers to deliver. She didn't answer. I tried again, still no answer. We were supposed to have a Skype date thirty minutes ago, she had to be in. I didn't want to disturb this kind couple any longer and tried to get inspired as to what to do next. I remembered I could press 141 before her number and hide my identity. I did this, and she answered.

"All right is that a Miss Fhian Poucher?" "Yes?" she said.

"Luv, its Keith here from Interflora," I said in a thick cockney accent. "I've just knocked on your house but you ain't there, are ya 165 Glenarm road?"

"No, 178," she replied.

"You don't mind popping out to get these off me do ya? Am just in the street."

"Yes, that's fine," she said. "One minute."

Bingo. Excitement filled me as nervous bliss splattered across my chest. I walked down the street, she came out looked around, then spotted me. I braced myself to be jumped on. She looked at me shocked, clasping her hands over her mouth, saying, "Oh my god, Liam what are you doing?"

"I came back for you, baby."

"Oh my God, oh my God," was being repeated. She stood back from me. Still we hadn't touched, had I read this wrong? Had she not been serious about what she'd been saying for the last few months? Was she not happy to see the man she loved, the man she couldn't wait to be with forever?

"You can't just do this Liam, I need time to process this, you can't just turn up on my door and come back into my life. I was expecting you in nine weeks, I have stuff planned."

Wow, I thought, had I been completely wrong? What was going on here?

Some welcome I thought, there was this tension, the tension she always had when I did something creative or un-ordinary that didn't go along with her predetermined idea of the ways things should be. I was okay with this, obviously it wasn't the romantic sweeping the girl off her feet moment I'd planned, but I was back in the presence of the woman of my dreams, of my soulmate, of the girl who I would marry, spend the rest of my life with and have children with.

I was then told I needed to go away for a couple of days, give her some time to process, "Go and stay with your friends," she told me.

I couldn't believe it. I was shattered into a million pieces.

I hadn't really thought about possible reactions, but if I had, I don't think this one would have even entered my head. I realised then she was worried about the reaction of her friends. I thought she had let go of the limitations others' expectations have on her, but obviously, I was wrong. Maybe she hadn't told them how much we had been talking and how much we were in love and how certain we were that we wanted to be together again. For all the beautiful things she'd said over email, WhatsApp and Skype I couldn't believe what was being said to me now.

"Okay," I said, but inside I was thinking, I came back for you, I want you, why can't you let go of whatever it is that is not allowing you to enjoy this moment? What is it? Where does this barrier come from? Why are we not swinging each other about and screaming? Why are we not looking into each other's eyes and saying it's you, it's you, it was always you, I'm so fucking excited it's you?

No, the ice maiden wanted me to disappear, to not interrupt the plans she'd already made for the weekend and continue to be incapable of spontaneity.

She did say we could hang out for the afternoon. It was like I was being allowed a dog treat and slowly had to build up trust. I was expecting us to go to the anti-Monsanto rally that was taking place in Parliament Square as she'd said she was going, but she was massively in shock and wanted to just chat in the park. I wasn't allowed in the house, she took my bags, and I went to the park and waited for her to come and meet me.

I was wounded. I told myself, 'This is your woman let her get used to it. Be nice and give her what she needs.' *This is the woman, this is the one. She just needs some time.*

We hung out on the park, and after a few hours she started to feel a little bit more comfortable in my presence. It was so nice to sit and chat, to share my experience and tell her what I'd seen for us both during the Ayahuasca journey. I wanted to be in that love right now, but Fhian seemed to have all her defences up. I knew she loved me more than anything, but she was scared of being hurt again and scared of other people's opinions of me and of us being together again. I wasn't, I just wanted to be, it didn't matter what others thought to me, all that truly mattered was how we felt about each other.

All that mattered was that we both had this burning love inside for each other and to deny it had been torture for us both over the last few months.

I was now off to stay with my friend Luke and his wife, Lisa. It was uplifting to be meeting his new daughter Olive for the first time. I made my way to Surbiton, and the many memories the place had for me came flooding back.

Staying with Luke and seeing how much my amazing friend had grown over the last few years was just incredible. A feeling of jealousy entered into me. From a man very down on himself when we had lived together, suffering massively from depression, he had become a man who now seemed to have it all; a wife and his first child and a lot of self-belief. He had started making changes to get the life he wanted and the way he had done it was a credit to himself and an inspiration to anyone who feels like life is passing them by.

That evening when I went to sleep at Luke's place, for the first time in a very long time, I struggled. On and off throughout my life, sleep problems had been a massive drain on my health. I was panicking about whether or not I had done the right thing. I was worrying and panicking, I felt anxious and wondered why this lady couldn't let go? I wanted us to be together and allow the deep love we had for each other to lead us forward.

The next day I headed for Greenwich Park where my mate was having a birthday party and where some of my favourite people would be at the same time. All I really wanted was to be by the side of my lady, but I had to be patient. Patience, Browne!!!!

As I entered the park, Mikey P ran towards me, and we had this massive embrace. It was so nice, and the same thing happened with several of my best mates in the world. It was kind of like the homecoming that would have been nice from Fhian.

The next day was Liam and Fhian day. I had booked us into a hotel, and we were going to spend the whole day and night together, and my chastity belt would be removed. I hoped.

When we met, she looked so perfect, and I didn't want to keep my hands off her. There was a very reserved energy coming my way, one of self-discipline and restraint, one I was very used to and one I had forgotten all about. She had obviously set parameters and rules and possibly been told by her friends to make me work very hard for something we both wanted more than anything.

I had spent many months pining for this goddess, and I had to be polite and not expect the love to be there. It was something I needed to work towards, something I need to take my time with and allow her to be and feel more comfortable. In my head, it made no sense, how could you be so in control of your true emotions to subdue them and restrict your heart and your soul's desire?

We arrived at the hotel, and the fantasies I'd had about not being able to take our hands off each other ended up just that. We were going to find a park and catch up some more, but all I wanted to do was have my girl in my arms. To reconnect on a physical level, to give her what I had been saving all this time and then to lay in each other's arms and talk and talk and talk until we couldn't resist each other again.

When we kissed this rush flew over me, my heart fluttered, and I wanted to be closed away from the world with her, but I was being made to wait. It was a kind of torture as if someone was pulling off my toenails with pliers whilst I was tied up in a rundown council flat and being fed slop once a week with a bar of my favourite chocolate on the windowsill just out of my reach.

I wanted to explore her perfect body, kiss every crevice of her and to be wrapped around her. I thought about how soppy I was and why I could feel my heart so much. I wrote a little rhyme about when Fhian called me Soppy Face. She would call me a big SF if I sent her something, soppy or poetic. I wondered why I was so soppy and connected to my heart, and she was so obviously not?

Soppy Face
I'm an SF I'm just a SF
That's all you call me when I send you poetry
Just your SF your loving SF
That's what you like me for

You are my Goddess
My sexy Goddess
Oh so fine and tall
I like my Goddess
Call her my Goddess
I worship her that's all

She's my bikini girl
I'm her Speedo pearl
We run around and twirl

When we arrived back at the hotel, I was unsure whether or not there was more protocol before we were allowed to enjoy ourselves. Maybe a formal meal and cocktails whilst wearing formal dress, or possibly filling in some tax forms and a disclaimer.

Fortunately, when we got back to the room the fireworks began. I couldn't believe I had denied myself the touch of this lady, denied myself so much for the past year. It had always been this, it had always been her, no one else had ever taken my attention since our split, and that fact said it all. Thoughts of Renie had now fully disappeared. Never before had I had eyes for just one lady, and now my vision was honed and focused. I massaged her for hours using the techniques I had learnt on my travels, touching and relaxing and re-energising every muscle and tendon she had. Her body was perfect, every aspect of it, my hands feeling everything from fingers to toes, not missing one bit. I could have done this for the rest of time, melting the skin, rubbing away the tension, digging into the knots and then fanning away the energy and bringing in new fresh loving vibes. I didn't want to stop, but as I got to certain parts, other thoughts moved in, and both of our minds turned to other things.

As we made love, we looked into each other's eyes, and I told her I loved her, and she said it back. These were words she had avoided saying over the internet throughout the last four months.

All her actions and other words had said 'I love you', but she could not bring herself to say it for fear of being weak. I'd wanted so much for her to let go of that, to be true to her feelings that so evidently said, 'I love you'. I wanted to say it over and over again, shout it from the rooftops. I thought all my actions; abstaining from sex, being unable to not speak to her and now, flying across the world and cutting the trip of a lifetime short said it all. Whilst I lay on top of her she grabbed my arm and said, "my man, my man" over and over. She pierced my soul and said, "MY MAN."

In that moment I knew I had my girl back. I wished she could open up like this when not intoxicated by love, passion and lust, but now I knew I was home. I had my girl back, never to let go, ever, ever again.

ACKNOWLEDGEMENTS AND GRATITUDE

Most importantly, I would like to show my gratitude to me mum who has guided and supported me in both life and death. You went above and beyond as a mother and always provided the best you could. You taught me so many things about being a good person and how to love people deeply. You also taught me infectious laughter, and we laughed so often. Your death allowed me to look deeper and I have always felt your push and guidance. Everything poignant in my life is always dedicated to you as I understand I'd be nothing without you. Your love, warmth, generosity and kindness were so heartfelt, and I am truly blessed to have you in my life every day. I know you see all I do and I hope that I'm making you proud.

My father, Bernard, thank you for always supporting me. Usually having no idea what you are supporting but nonetheless being there and always bringing unwavering mentalness to all situations. I don't understand you and I never will, but there is something beautiful in that as you don't give two shits about what other people think. You are one of a kind. I don't think there is a person in the world who makes me laugh as much as you. You think any problems I have could be cured by me eating meat and for that you are a genius. To my sister Hannah for your love and understanding of my chosen path. To my brothers for thinking I've gone mental but still loving me. To my stepdad Ray for being more open as we both age. To my aunties Brenda and Betty for always reminding me of my mum and always welcoming me into your homes.

Thank you to all the characters I met on my journey; you will always be family. Massive thanks to Kathryn for starting this journey with me, to Janet for taking me under your wing and seeing potential in me. Ladan for all your wisdom, all your teaching and all your love and support. To each person who listened to my stories and said you must write a book. You are the inspiration. To Maia and Marimi for providing me with the most beautiful place to write, looking out to the beach in San Sebastian and becoming my Basque family. To Laurence and Red for getting me through my mother's death. To Renie and her family for doing the same. To Geraldine for coming into my life at the perfect time. To my editor Johanna, I can't believe I finally found you. To my cousin Heather for being so enthusiastic about the book needing to be published. To Chris for your edits and recommendations. To my art designer Matt Crump, your talent always astounds me. Lucy for your photographic skills. Paulo for putting everything together and creating the cover.

To all the kind and beautiful women who have come into my life as friends; Iysha, Charlotte, Joanna, Gemma, Tie, Emma, Jane, Nicole, Lorna and Andrea. Lisa for letting me sit and write day after day in your candle shop in Gatley. Collette and Casper for giving me a home and place to write. To James and Toni for lighting a fire within me so that more words came out. To Keith the Cacao Shaman, Otillia the Ayahuascero and all the spiritual teachers I have met along the way. To Georgia for all her nurturing support and helping with some major edits; I know it was difficult for you to read. To Kayleigh for giving me the kick up the arse to get the final edit done and really focus on getting this thing published. To Wynn for your love. For all the lovers thank you for being part of my story. I have so much gratitude to every person who has been involved and in some way helped with this book. I am eternally grateful and feel so, so blessed.

Finally, to you the readers, more than anything I hope that something in this book can help you find that inner power to make some positive change and to continue to look for growth in all corners and to spread love and healing far and wide. I want to help as many people as humanly possible to step into their power and remove fear from their lives. FULL POWER!!!!!!!

Now sign up to me mailing list immediately! Please!
www.liambrowne.com

CLAIM YOUR FREE BOOK!

As a massive thank you for buying me book I would like to give you a little present. This is only for you, the people who have bought the book and supported it. It's your exclusive free gift. Whoop!!

If you were wondering what happened to me when I got back to the UK, this will give you a peek into the weeks after we left my journey. I wanted to try out hitchhiking after enjoying it's so much on me travels. See how I try and bring this dying art back to life.

Join me on a hitchhiking tour of England and Scotland. See how it all works out when I put myself totally at the mercy of the Universe and put my faith in the kindness of humanity to whisk in me around. You will meet some more than colourful characters along the way and be able to implement my self-designed hitchhiking techniques into your own life.

Thumbs out, I'm looking!

You can download the free book 'Hitchhiking -Feel the good Vibrations' here- www.liambrowne.com/hitchin

Hi

Thank you so much for purchasing me book! I hope you have enjoyed reading it as much as I have enjoyed sharing my life with you. I really truly value you as a reader.

I'd love to hear your feedback on how you feel about the book. If you could take a few minutes to leave a review, I'd be so happy.

To submit your review, simply click below and let me know what you think!

www.amazon.co.uk/dp/B07Z43L1FJ

Thanks in advance for taking the time to leave a review! Feel free to contact me at any time.
liam@liambrowne.com

Cheers,
Liam

BIBLIOGRAPHY

Michael E. Reynolds, *The Coming of Wizards*, High Mesa Press, 1989
Ceri Louise Thomas, Chris Morton, *The Mystery of the Crystal Skulls*, London, HarperCollins, 1998
Kay Cordell Whitaker, *The Reluctant Shaman*, HarperOne: Reprint edition (9 July 1992)
Sylvia Plath, *The Bell Jar*, Faber & Faber, 1966
Mark Twain, Edited by Caroline Thomas Harnsberger, *Mark Twain at Your Fingertips*, Dover Publications, 2012
Carlos Barrios, *The Book of Destiny*, New York, HarperOne, 2010
Peter Joseph (Director), *Zeitgeist*, USA, Gentle Machine Productions, 2007
Gopi Krishna, *Kundalini for the new age*, Toronto, Bantam Books, 1988
Bradley Nelson, *The Emotional Code*, Wellness Unmasked Publishing, 2007
Aldous Huxley, *Brave New World*, Harper Collins, 2014
Patricia Cori, *Atlantis Rising- The Struggle of Darkness & Light*, Penguin Random House or North Atlantic Books, 2008
Oliver Hodge, *The Garbage Warrior*, Open Eye Media, 2007 H.H.
Sri Swami Sivananda, *The Sivananda companion to yoga*, New York, Simon & Schuster, 2000
Rumi, *Poet and Mystic (1207-1273)*, London, 1950
Patricia Cori, *Atlantis Rising- The Struggle of Darkness & Light*, 2008, Berkley: North Atlantic Books, 2008
Steve Gagné, Kimberly Carter Gamble (Directors), *Thrive*, Clear Compass Media, 2011
Mark Achbar, Jennifer Abbott (Directors), *The Corporation*, Big Picture Media Corporation, 2003
Aldous Huxley, *The Doors of Perception and Heaven and Hell*, London, Chatto and Windus, 1972
Robert Tindall, *The Shamanic Odyssey*, Rochester, Park Street Press, 2012
"Woodrow Wilson Quotes." BrainyQuote.com. BrainyMedia Inc, 2019. 20 August 2019.
https://www.brainyquote.com/quotes/woodrow_wilson_121798
Johann Wolfgang von Goethe, A quote by, goodreads.com,
https://www.goodreads.com/quotes/695207-we-talk-far-too-much-we-should-talk-less-and
Bill Wilson and Dr. Bob Smith, *Alcoholics Anonymous- The Big Book*, Dover Publications, 1939
J.C. Callaway quote from, *Ayahuasca: The Visionary and Healing Powers of the Vine of the Soul* by Joan Parisi Wilcox published by Inner Traditions International and Bear & Company, ©2003. All rights

reserved. http://www.Inner-traditions.com Reprinted with permission of publisher.
J. R. R. Tolkien, Questions about Mescaline - The Psychedelic Experience - Shroomery Message Board, shroomery.org, https://www.shroomery.org/forums/showflat.php/Number/4268889
Joan Parisi Wilcox, Ayahuasca: The Visionary and Healing Powers of the Vine of the Soul, Published by Inner Traditions International and Bear & Company, ©2003. All rights reserved. http://www.Innertraditions.com Re-printed with permission of publisher.
César Calvo, The Three Halves of Ino Moxo, Published by Inner Traditions International and Bear & Company, ©1995. All rights reserved. http://www.Innertraditions.com Re-printed with permission of publisher.
Sarah MacDonald, Holy Cow, Melbourne, Read What You Want, 2010 664
Michael Moore, Roger and Me, Dog Eat Dog Films, 1989
The Shock Doctrine, Mat Whitecross, Michael Winterbottom, Renegade Pictures, 2009
Rhonda Byrne, The Secret, London, Simon & Schuster UK, 2006
Richard Millward, Ten Story Love Song, London, Faber & Faber, 2009

ALSO BY LIAM BROWNE

Books
Ayahuasca - Healing Your Soul

Short Stories
Hitchhiking -Feel the good Vibrations

Poetry
Dealer Forget, Healer Remember

LINKS

Everything Liam Browne related and all my social media links can be found via my website below. My Podcast 'Dealer to Healer' can be found where ever you listen to your podcasts and on the 'Dealer to Healer' YouTube channel. Please listen and subscribe. Thank you so much for your support.

Contact Liam: liam@liambrowne.com

www.liambrowne.com

Printed in Great Britain
by Amazon